D0871381

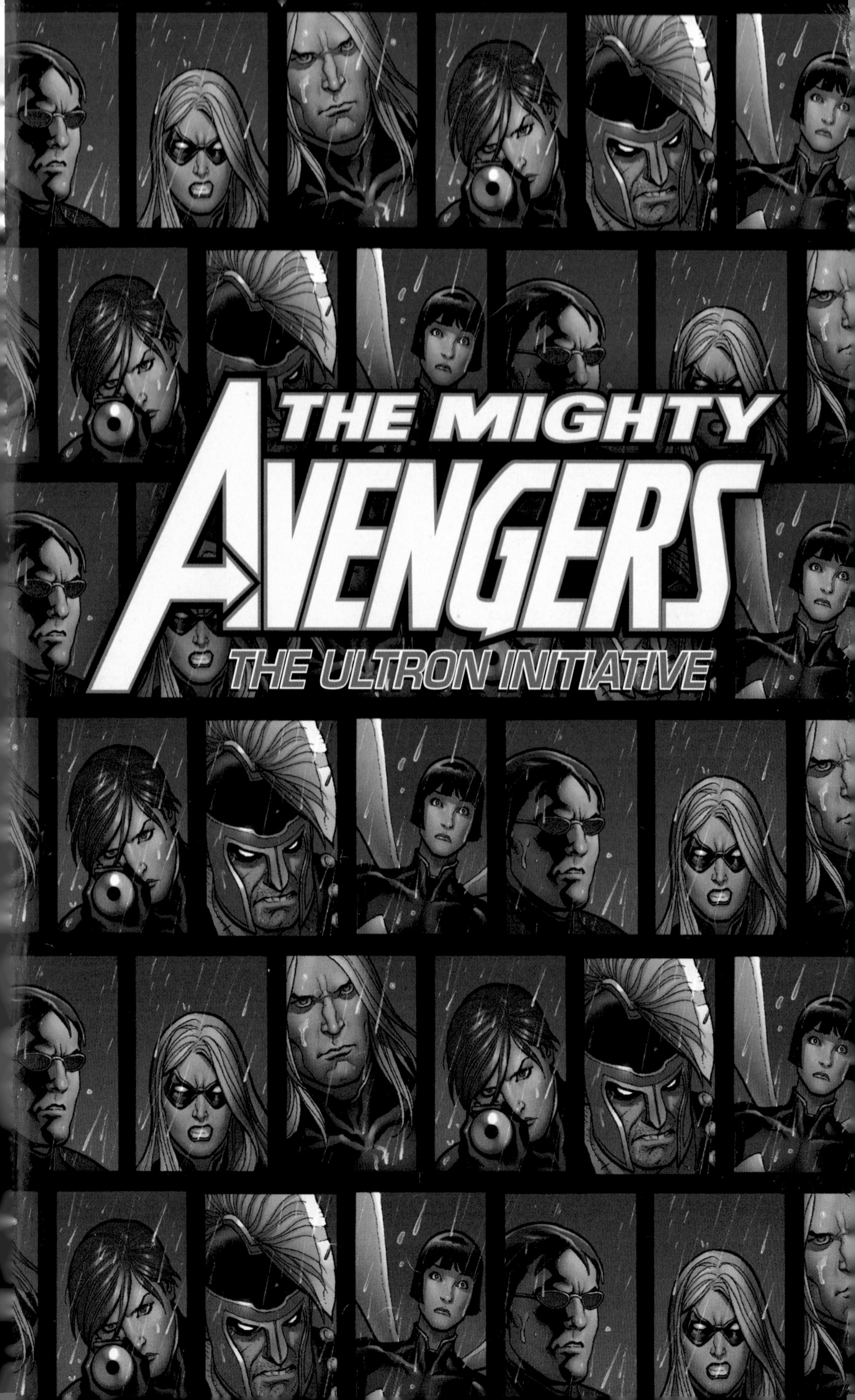
THE MIGHTY
AVENGERS
THE ULTRON INITIATIVE

# THE MIGHTY AVENGERS

## THE ULTRON INITIATIVE

WRITER: **Brian Michael Bendis**

ART: **Frank Cho**

COLORS: **Jason Keith**

LETTERERS: **Artmonkeys' Dave Lanphear
with Natalie Lanphear**

ASSISTANT EDITORS: **Molly Lazer** & **Aubrey Sitterson**

EDITOR: **Tom Brevoort**

**Special thanks to Brandon Peterson**

COLLECTION EDITOR: **Jennifer Grünwald**

ASSISTANT EDITORS: **Cory Levine** & **John Denning**

EDITOR, SPECIAL PROJECTS: **Mark D. Beazley**

SENIOR EDITOR, SPECIAL PROJECTS: **Jeff Youngquist**

SENIOR VICE PRESIDENT OF SALES: **David Gabriel**

PRODUCTION: **Jerry Kalinowski**

BOOK DESIGNER: **Carrie Beadle**

EDITOR IN CHIEF: **Joe Quesada**

PUBLISHER: **Dan Buckley**

**MIGHTY AVENGERS VOL. 1: THE ULTRON INITIATIVE.** Contains material originally published in magazine form as MIGHTY AVENGERS #1-6. First printing 2007. Hardcover ISBN# 978-0-7851-2370-5. Softcover ISBN# 978-0-7851-2368-2. Published by MARVEL PUBLISHING, INC., a subsidiary of MARVEL ENTERTAINMENT, INC. OFFICE OF PUBLICATION: 417 5th Avenue, New York, NY 10016. Copyright © 2007 Marvel Characters, Inc. All rights reserved. Hardcover: $19.99 per copy in the U.S. and $32.00 in Canada (GST #R127032852). Softcover: $14.99 per copy in the U.S. and $15.75 in Canada (GST #R127032852). Canadian Agreement #40668537. All characters featured in this issue and the distinctive names and likenesses thereof, and all related indicia are trademarks of Marvel Characters, Inc. No similarity between any of the names, characters, persons, and/or institutions in this magazine with those of any living or dead person or institution is intended, and any such similarity which may exist is purely coincidental. **Printed in the U.S.A.** ALAN FINE, CEO Marvel Toys & Publishing Divisions and CMO Marvel Entertainment, Inc.; DAVID GABRIEL, SVP of Publishing Sales & Circulation; DAVID BOGART, SVP of Business Affairs & Talent Management; MICHAEL PASCIULLO, VP of Merchandising & Communications; JIM O'KEEFE, VP of Operations & Logistics; DAN CARR, Executive Director of Publishing Technology; JUSTIN F. GABRIE, Director of Editorial Operations; SUSAN CRESPI, Production Manager; STAN LEE, Chairman Emeritus. For information regarding advertising in Marvel Comics or on Marvel.com, please contact Mitch Dane, Advertising Director, at mdane@marvel.com. For Marvel subscription inquiries, please call 800-217-9158.

10 9 8 7 6 5 4 3 2 1

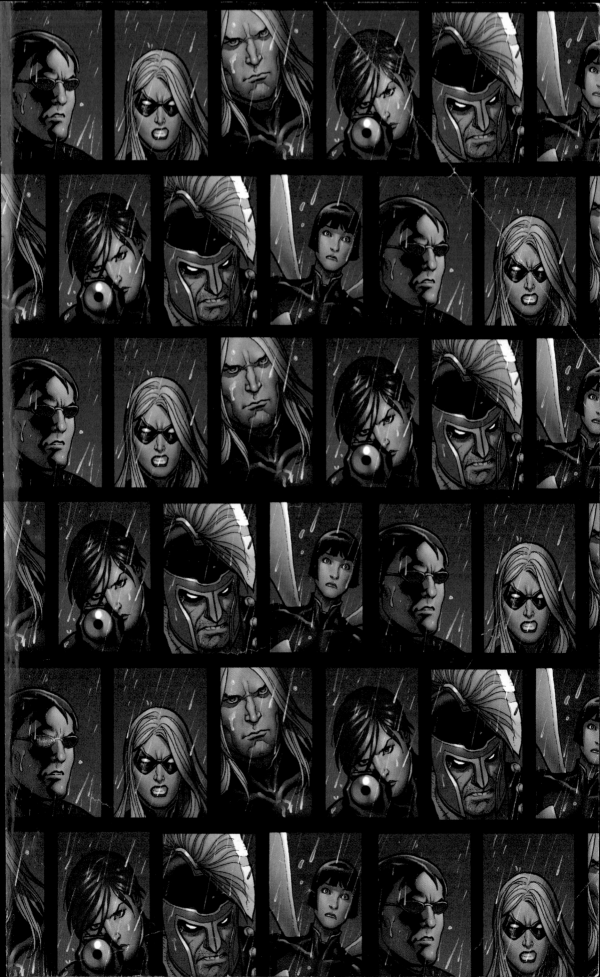

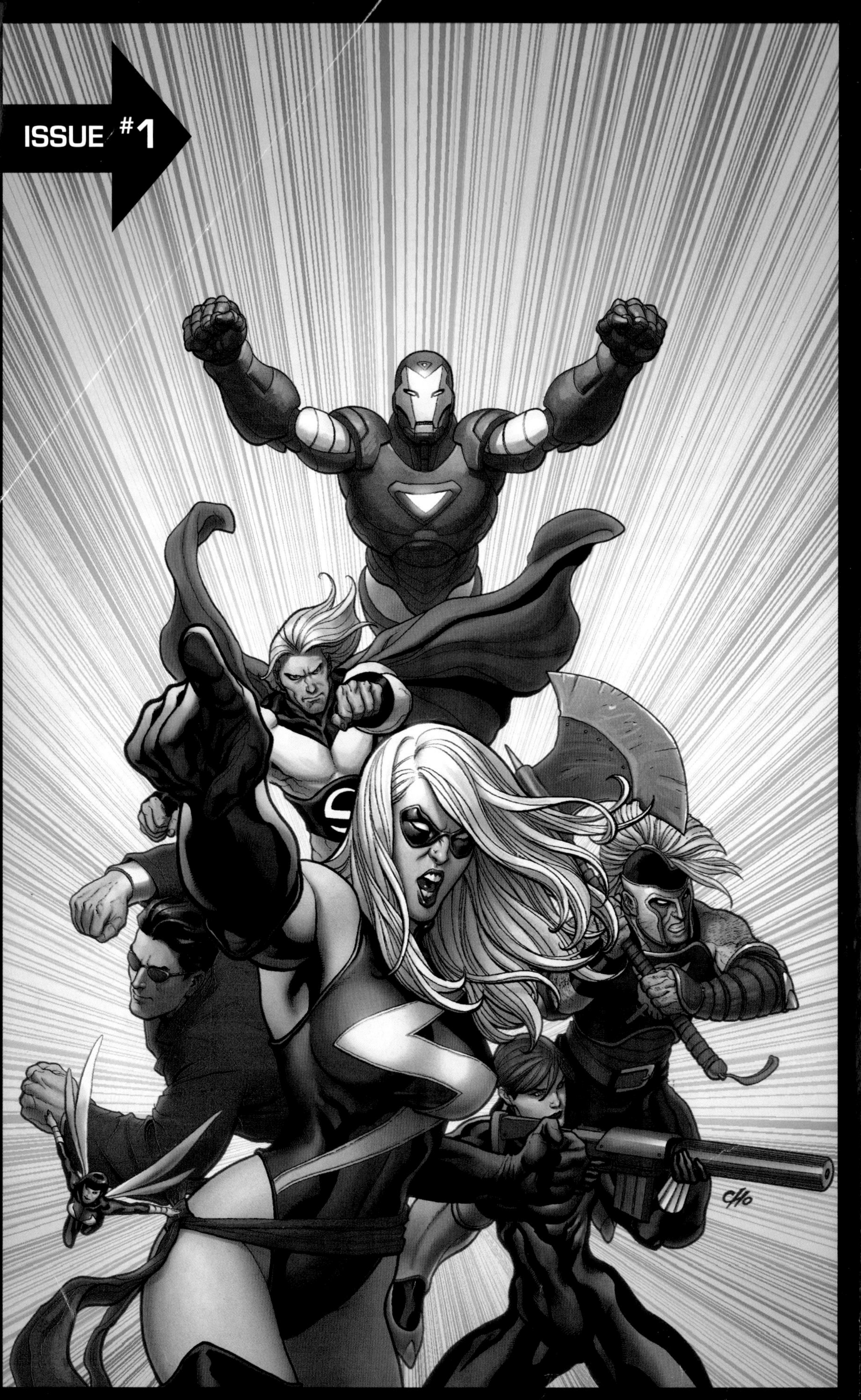
ISSUE #1
CHO

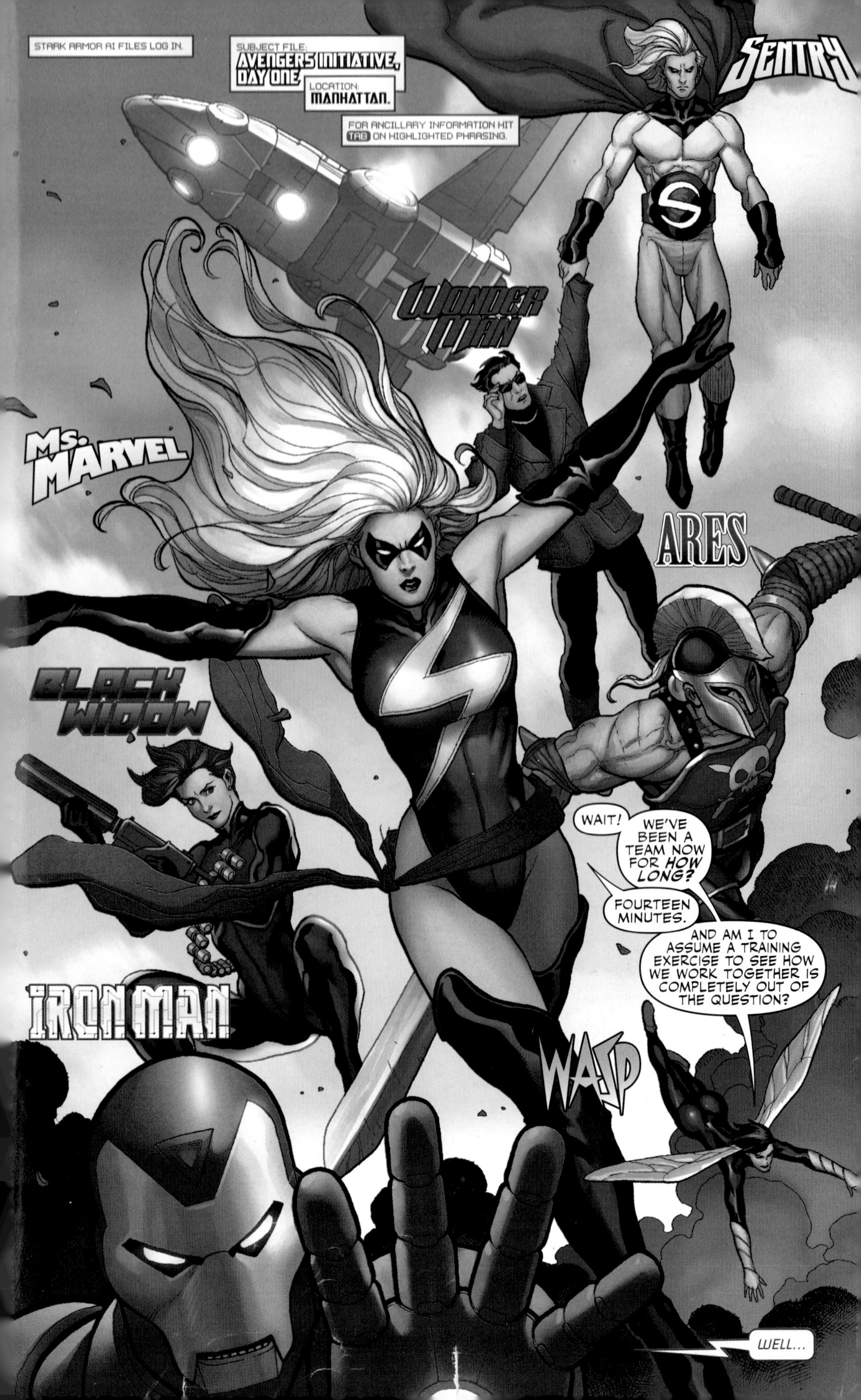
STARK ARMOR AI FILES LOG IN.
SUBJECT FILE: AVENGERS INITIATIVE, DAY ONE
LOCATION: MANHATTAN.
FOR ANCILLARY INFORMATION HIT TRB ON HIGHLIGHTED PHRASING.
SENTRY
WONDER MAN
MS. MARVEL
ARES
BLACK WIDOW
IRON MAN
WASP
WAIT!
WE'VE BEEN A TEAM NOW FOR HOW LONG?
FOURTEEN MINUTES.
AND AM I TO ASSUME A TRAINING EXERCISE TO SEE HOW WE WORK TOGETHER IS COMPLETELY OUT OF THE QUESTION?
WELL...

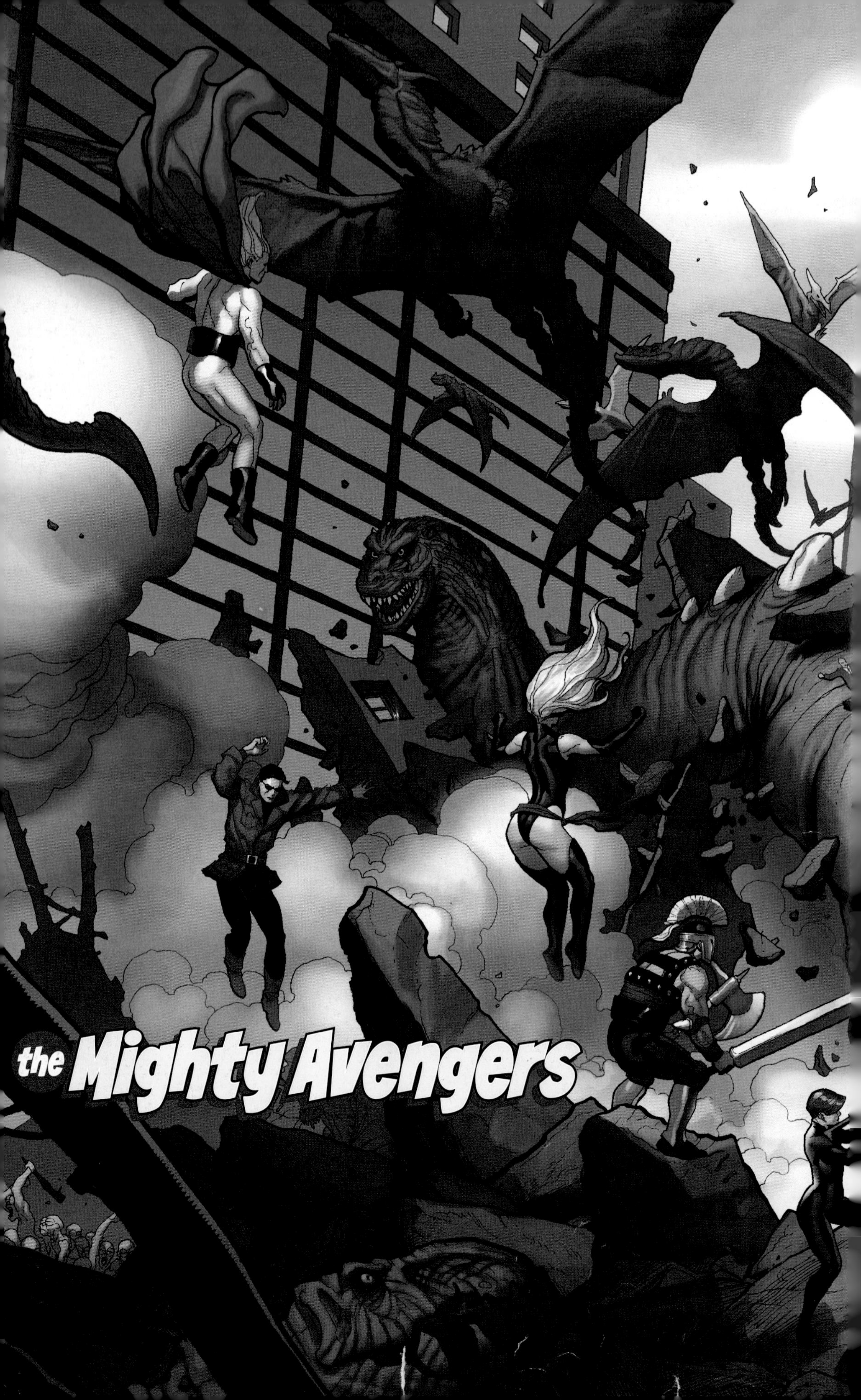
the Mighty Avengers

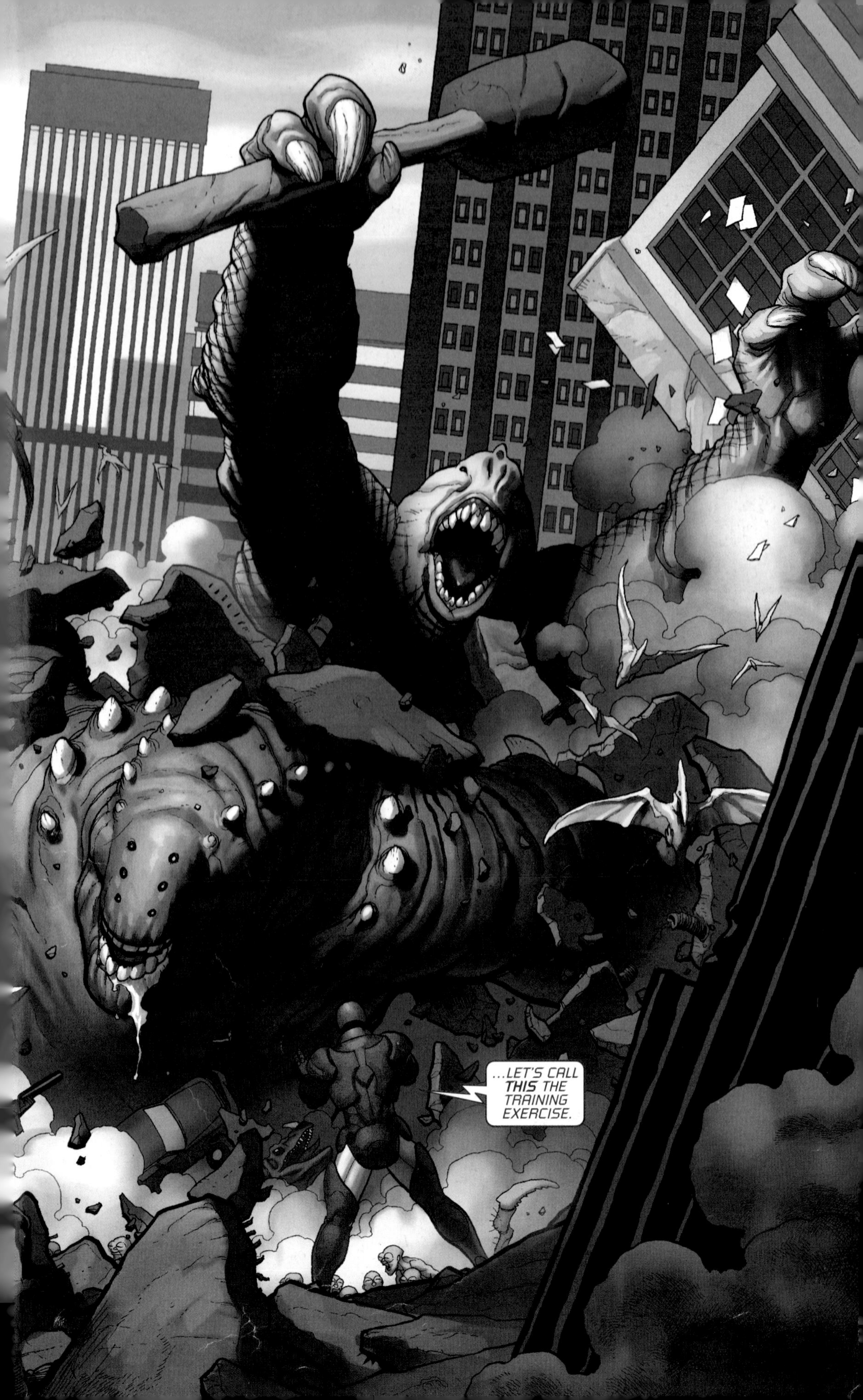
...LET'S CALL **THIS** THE TRAINING EXERCISE.

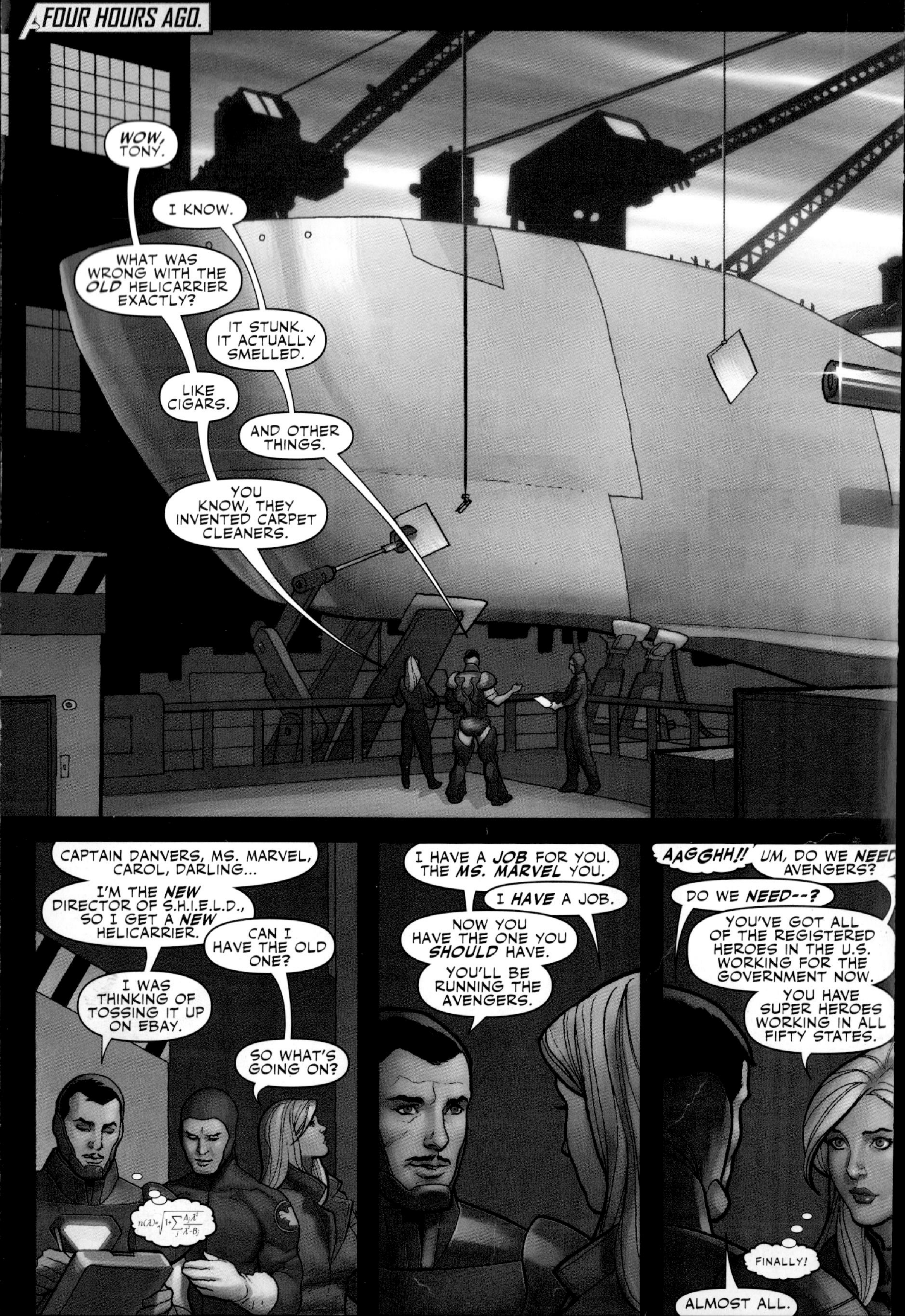
FOUR HOURS AGO.
WOW, TONY.
I KNOW.
WHAT WAS WRONG WITH THE OLD HELICARRIER EXACTLY?
IT STUNK. IT ACTUALLY SMELLED.
LIKE CIGARS.
AND OTHER THINGS.
YOU KNOW, THEY INVENTED CARPET CLEANERS.
CAPTAIN DANVERS, MS. MARVEL, CAROL, DARLING...
I'M THE NEW DIRECTOR OF S.H.I.E.L.D., SO I GET A NEW HELICARRIER.
CAN I HAVE THE OLD ONE?
I WAS THINKING OF TOSSING IT UP ON EBAY.
SO WHAT'S GOING ON?
I HAVE A JOB FOR YOU. THE MS. MARVEL YOU.
I HAVE A JOB.
NOW YOU HAVE THE ONE YOU SHOULD HAVE.
YOU'LL BE RUNNING THE AVENGERS.
AAGGHH!!
UM, DO WE NEED AVENGERS?
DO WE NEED--?
YOU'VE GOT ALL OF THE REGISTERED HEROES IN THE U.S. WORKING FOR THE GOVERNMENT NOW.
YOU HAVE SUPER HEROES WORKING IN ALL FIFTY STATES.
FINALLY!
ALMOST ALL.

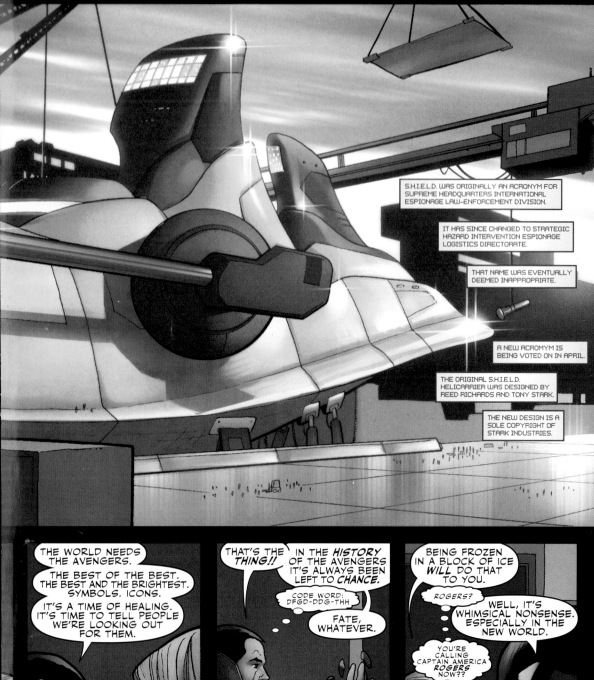

S.H.I.E.L.D. WAS ORIGINALLY AN ACRONYM FOR SUPREME HEADQUARTERS INTERNATIONAL ESPIONAGE LAW-ENFORCEMENT DIVISION.

IT HAS SINCE CHANGED TO STRATEGIC HAZARD INTERVENTION ESPIONAGE LOGISTICS DIRECTORATE.

THAT NAME WAS EVENTUALLY DEEMED INAPPROPRIATE.

A NEW ACROMYM IS BEING VOTED ON IN APRIL.

THE ORIGINAL S.H.I.E.L.D. HELICARRIER WAS DESIGNED BY REED RICHARDS AND TONY STARK.

THE NEW DESIGN IS A SOLE COPYRIGHT OF STARK INDUSTRIES.

THE WORLD NEEDS THE AVENGERS.

THE BEST OF THE BEST. THE BEST AND THE BRIGHTEST. SYMBOLS. ICONS.

IT'S A TIME OF HEALING. IT'S TIME TO TELL PEOPLE WE'RE LOOKING OUT FOR THEM.

OK, SO WHO WOULD THEY BE, THESE BEST AND BRIGHTEST?

THAT'S THE *THING!!*

IN THE *HISTORY* OF THE AVENGERS IT'S ALWAYS BEEN LEFT TO *CHANCE.*

CODE WORD: DFGD-DDG-THH

FATE, WHATEVER.

EVEN THE LAST BATCH OF *NEW* AVENGERS WERE GATHERED TOGETHER BY FATE.

(WHICH ROGERS WAS ALWAYS REALLY INTO.)

CODE WORD: 8675309

BEING FROZEN IN A BLOCK OF ICE *WILL* DO THAT TO YOU.

*ROGERS?*

WELL, IT'S WHIMSICAL NONSENSE. ESPECIALLY IN THE NEW WORLD.

YOU'RE CALLING CAPTAIN AMERICA *ROGERS* NOW??

ME AND YOU--

--FOR THE FIRST TIME IN AVENGERS HISTORY...

...WE GET TO PICK.

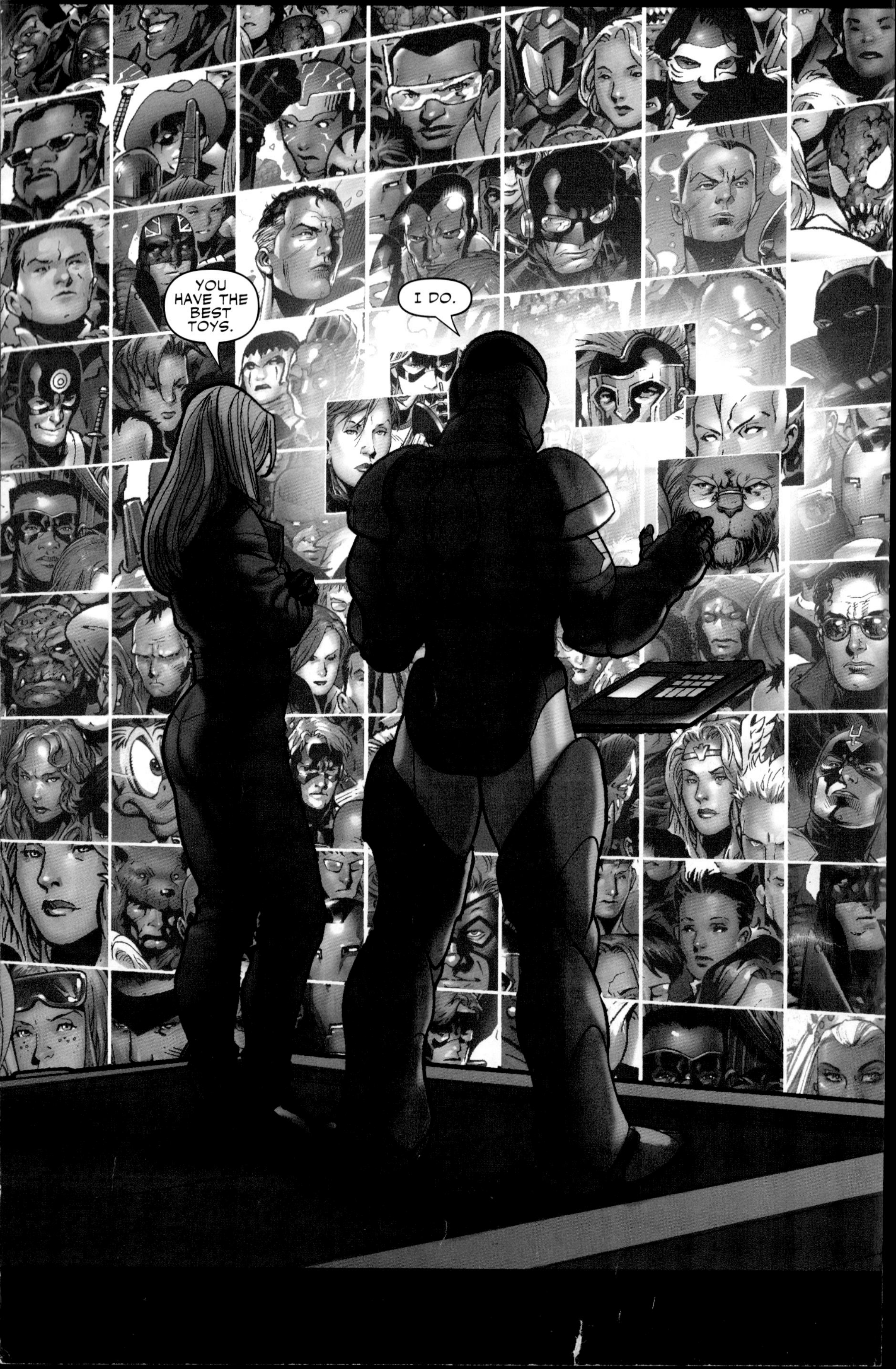
YOU HAVE THE BEST TOYS.
I DO.

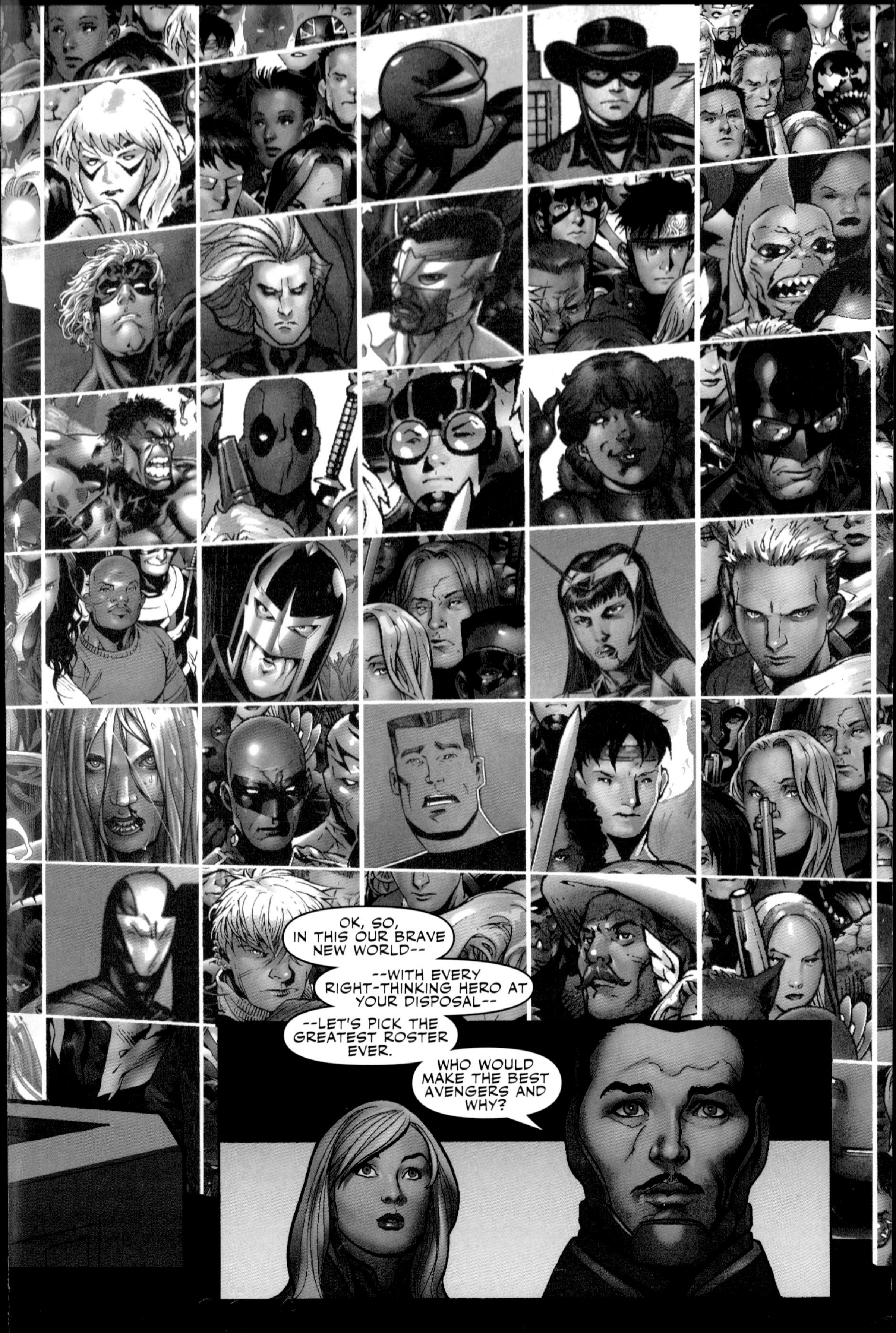
OK, SO, IN THIS OUR BRAVE NEW WORLD--
--WITH EVERY RIGHT-THINKING HERO AT YOUR DISPOSAL--
--LET'S PICK THE GREATEST ROSTER EVER.
WHO WOULD MAKE THE BEST AVENGERS AND WHY?

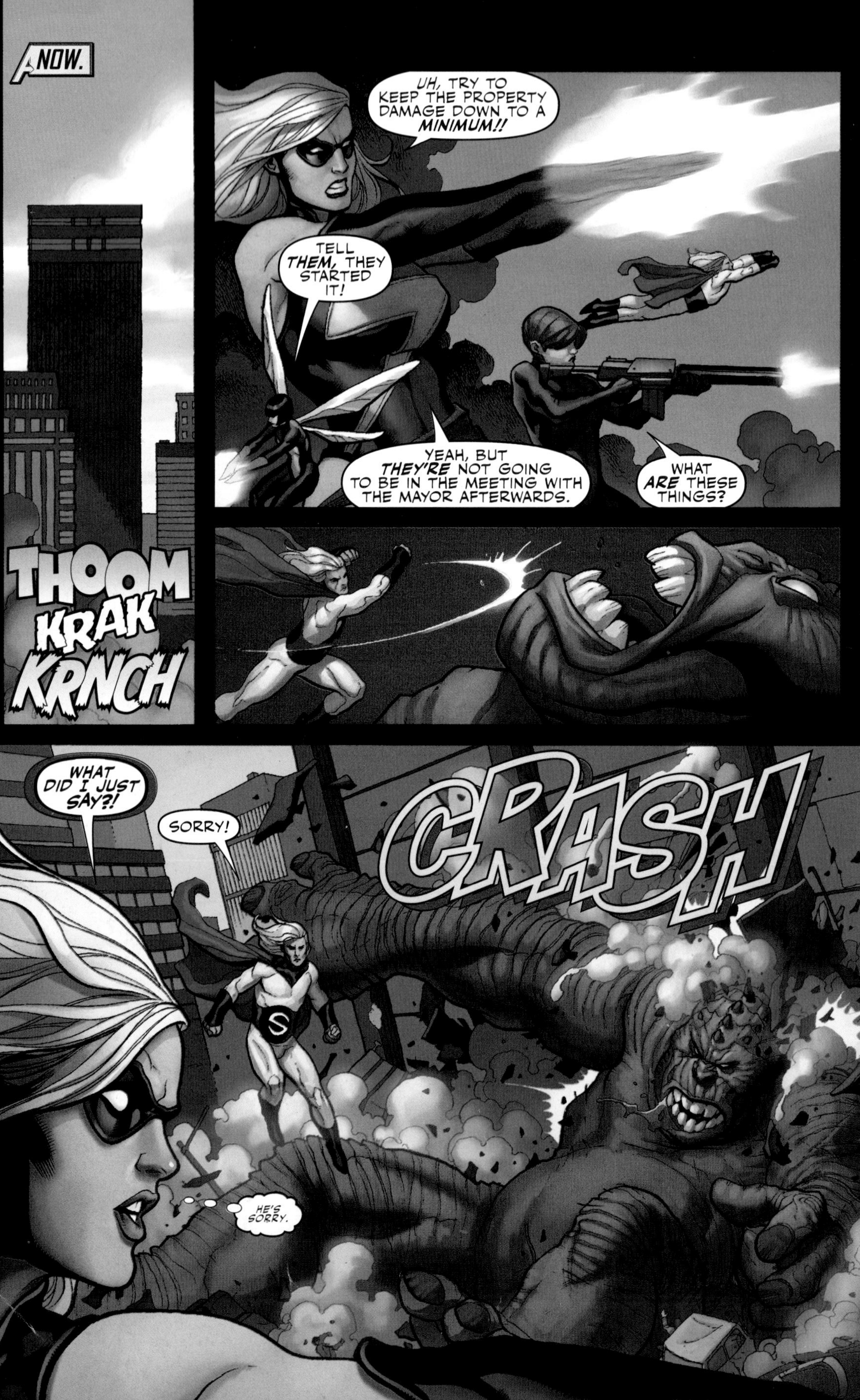
NOW.
UH, TRY TO KEEP THE PROPERTY DAMAGE DOWN TO A MINIMUM!!
TELL THEM, THEY STARTED IT!
YEAH, BUT THEY'RE NOT GOING TO BE IN THE MEETING WITH THE MAYOR AFTERWARDS.
WHAT ARE THESE THINGS?
THOOM
KRAK
KRNCH
WHAT DID I JUST SAY?!
SORRY!
CRASH
HE'S SORRY.

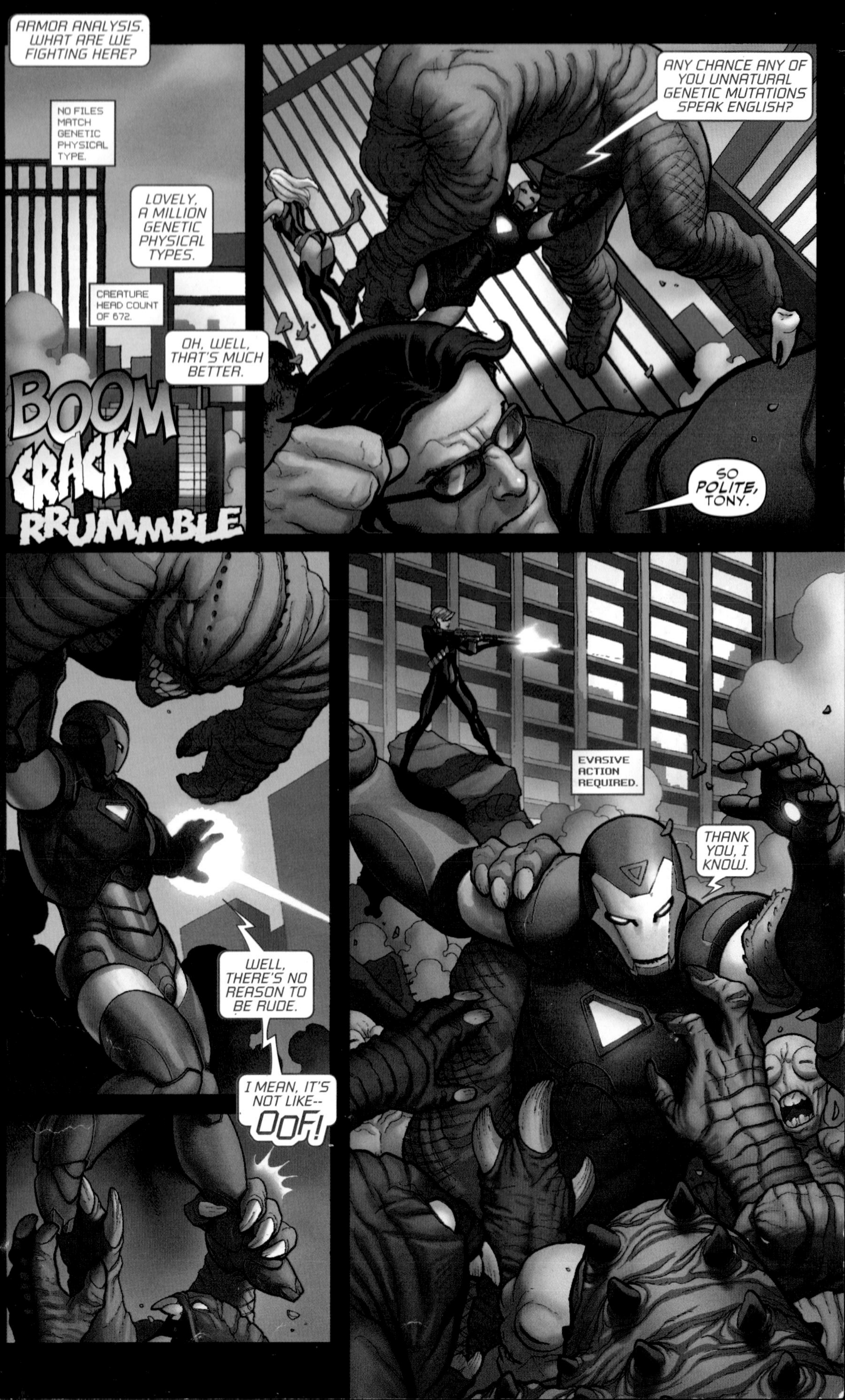
ARMOR ANALYSIS. WHAT ARE WE FIGHTING HERE?
NO FILES MATCH GENETIC PHYSICAL TYPE.
LOVELY, A MILLION GENETIC PHYSICAL TYPES.
CREATURE HEAD COUNT OF 672.
OH, WELL, THAT'S MUCH BETTER.
BOOM
CRACK
RRUMMBLE
ANY CHANCE ANY OF YOU UNNATURAL GENETIC MUTATIONS SPEAK ENGLISH?
SO POLITE, TONY.
WELL, THERE'S NO REASON TO BE RUDE.
I MEAN, IT'S NOT LIKE-- OOF!
EVASIVE ACTION REQUIRED.
THANK YOU, I KNOW.

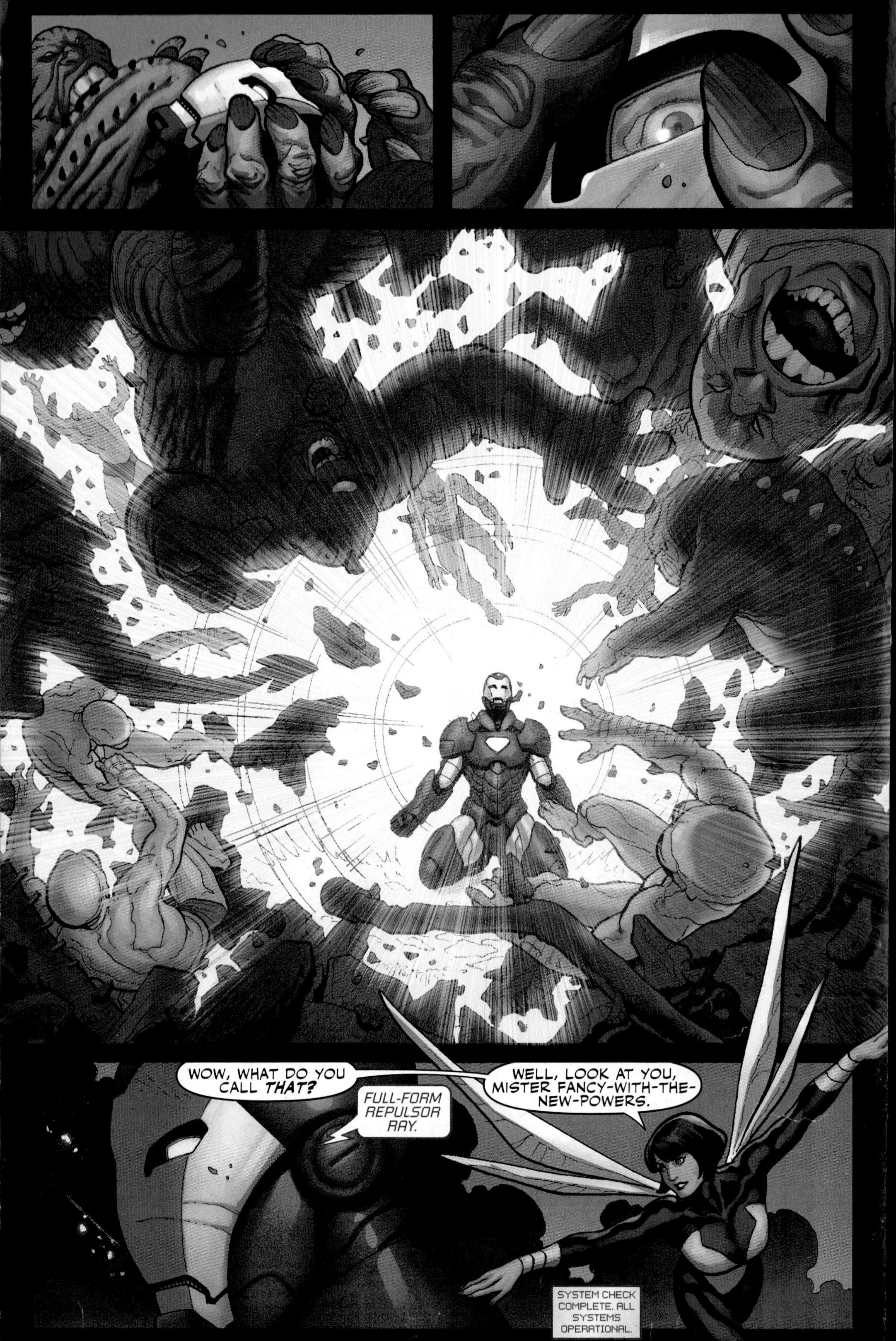

WOW, WHAT DO YOU CALL THAT?
FULL-FORM REPULSOR RAY.
WELL, LOOK AT YOU, MISTER FANCY-WITH-THE-NEW-POWERS.
SYSTEM CHECK COMPLETE. ALL SYSTEMS OPERATIONAL.

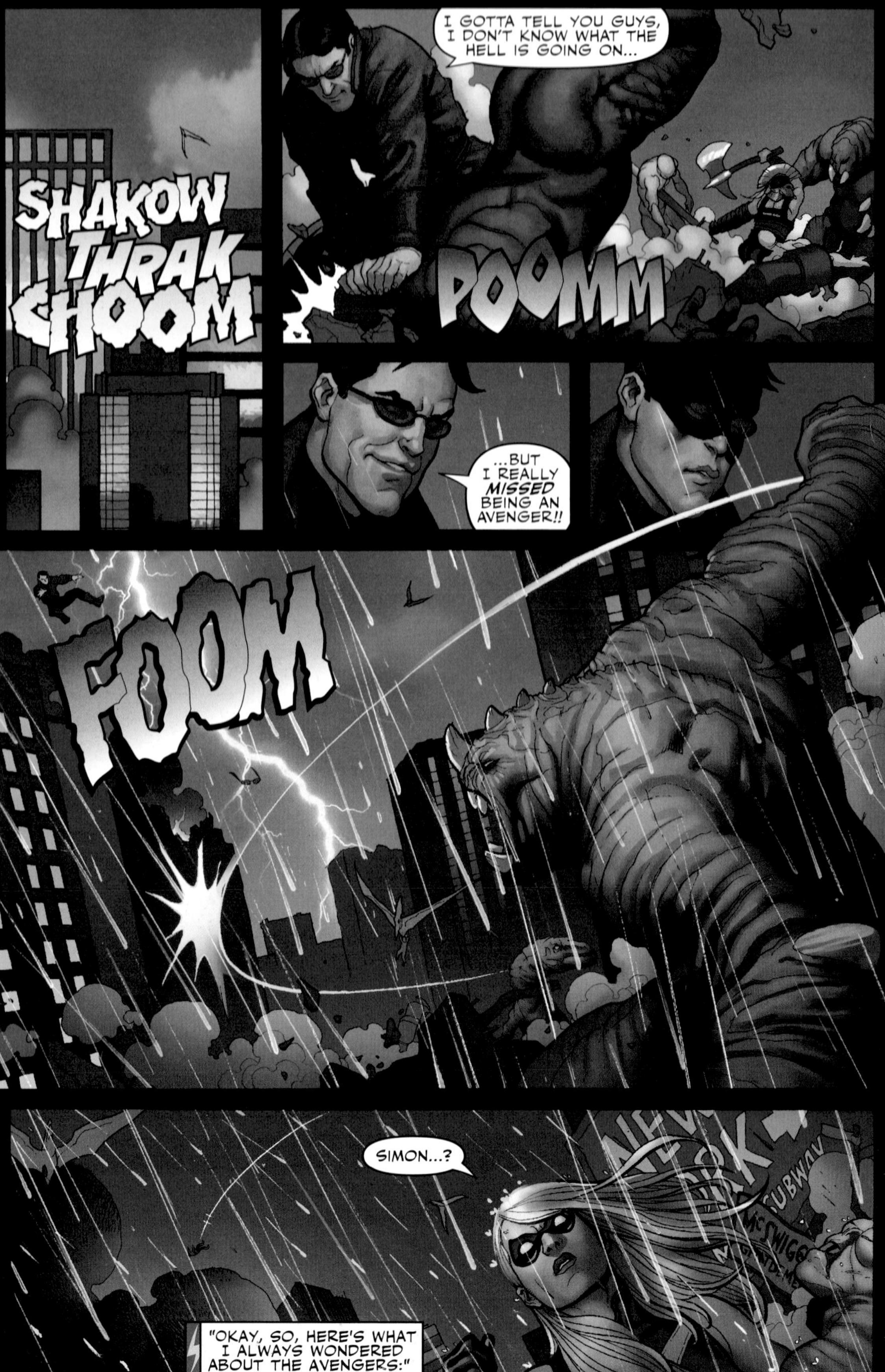
SHAKOW
THRAK
CHOOM
I GOTTA TELL YOU GUYS, I DON'T KNOW WHAT THE HELL IS GOING ON...
POOMM
...BUT I REALLY *MISSED* BEING AN AVENGER!!
FOOM
SIMON...?
"OKAY, SO, HERE'S WHAT I ALWAYS WONDERED ABOUT THE AVENGERS:"

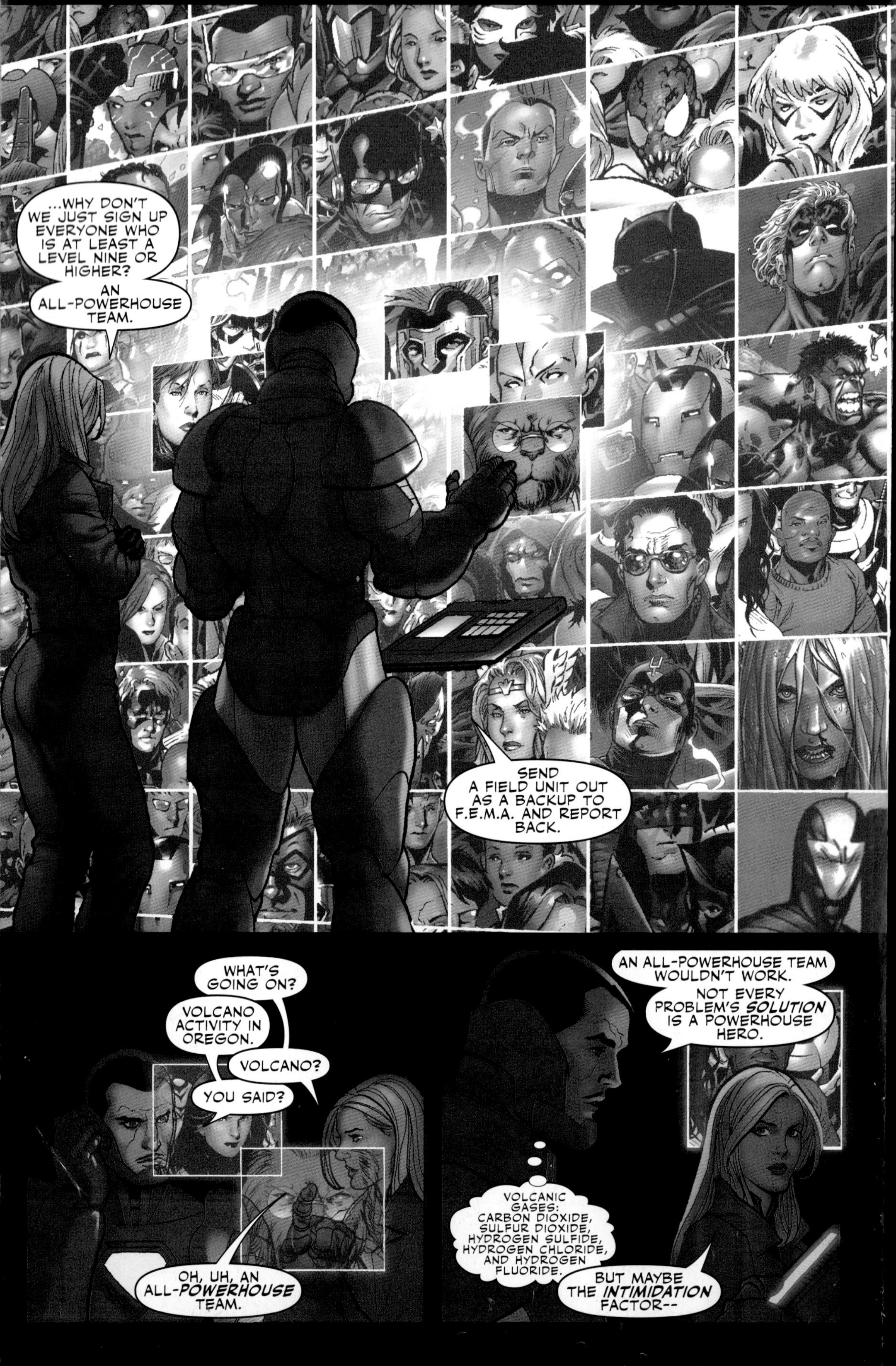
...WHY DON'T WE JUST SIGN UP EVERYONE WHO IS AT LEAST A LEVEL NINE OR HIGHER?
AN ALL-POWERHOUSE TEAM.
SEND A FIELD UNIT OUT AS A BACKUP TO F.E.M.A. AND REPORT BACK.
WHAT'S GOING ON?
VOLCANO ACTIVITY IN OREGON.
VOLCANO?
YOU SAID?
OH, UH, AN ALL-*POWERHOUSE* TEAM.
AN ALL-POWERHOUSE TEAM WOULDN'T WORK.
NOT EVERY PROBLEM'S *SOLUTION* IS A POWERHOUSE HERO.
VOLCANIC GASES: CARBON DIOXIDE, SULFUR DIOXIDE, HYDROGEN SULFIDE, HYDROGEN CHLORIDE, AND HYDROGEN FLUORIDE.
BUT MAYBE THE *INTIMIDATION* FACTOR--

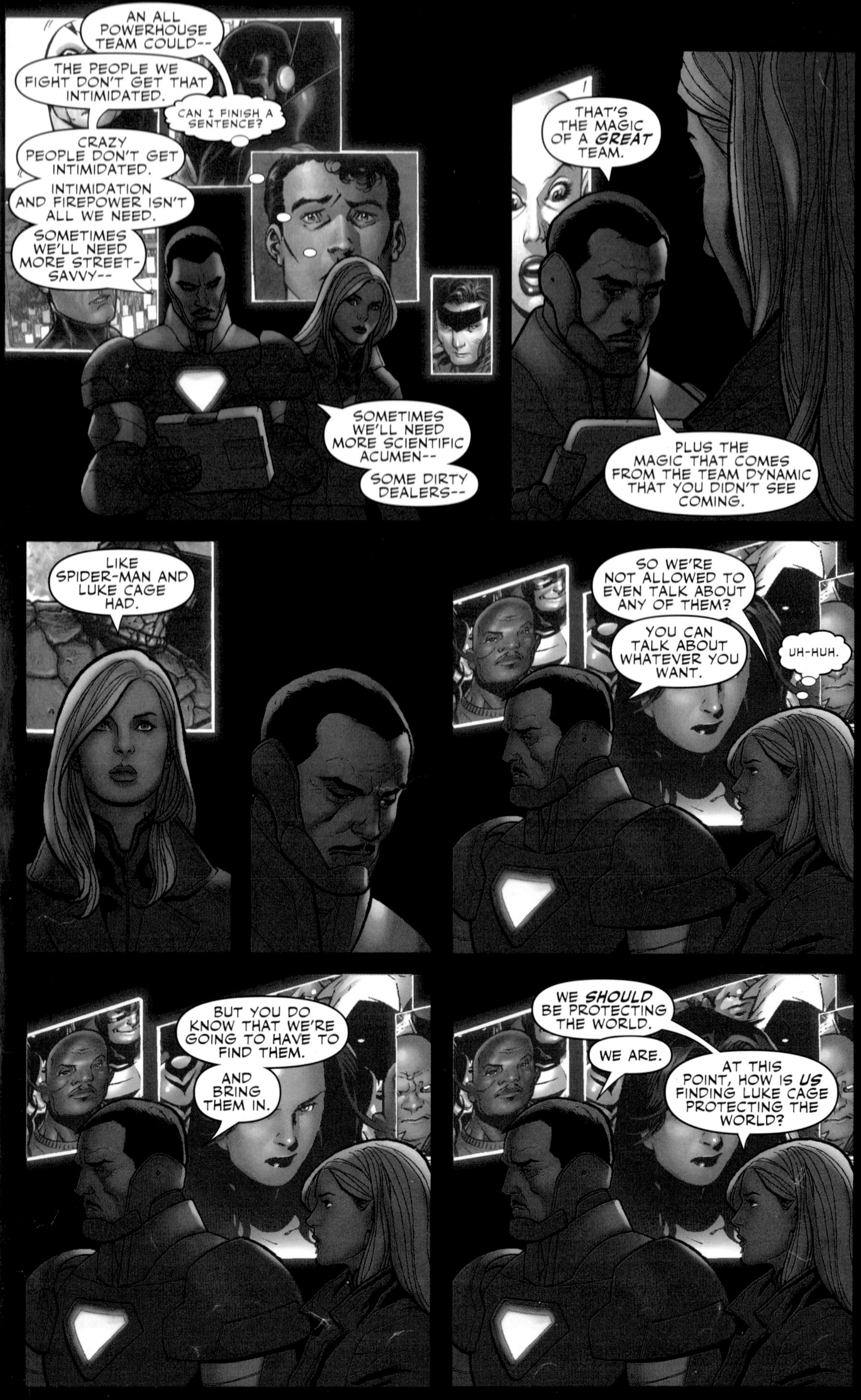
AN ALL POWERHOUSE TEAM COULD--
THE PEOPLE WE FIGHT DON'T GET THAT INTIMIDATED.
CAN I FINISH A SENTENCE?
CRAZY PEOPLE DON'T GET INTIMIDATED.
INTIMIDATION AND FIREPOWER ISN'T ALL WE NEED.
SOMETIMES WE'LL NEED MORE STREET-SAVVY--
SOMETIMES WE'LL NEED MORE SCIENTIFIC ACUMEN--
SOME DIRTY DEALERS--
THAT'S THE MAGIC OF A GREAT TEAM.
PLUS THE MAGIC THAT COMES FROM THE TEAM DYNAMIC THAT YOU DIDN'T SEE COMING.
LIKE SPIDER-MAN AND LUKE CAGE HAD.
SO WE'RE NOT ALLOWED TO EVEN TALK ABOUT ANY OF THEM?
YOU CAN TALK ABOUT WHATEVER YOU WANT.
UH-HUH.
BUT YOU DO KNOW THAT WE'RE GOING TO HAVE TO FIND THEM.
AND BRING THEM IN.
WE SHOULD BE PROTECTING THE WORLD.
WE ARE.
AT THIS POINT, HOW IS US FINDING LUKE CAGE PROTECTING THE WORLD?

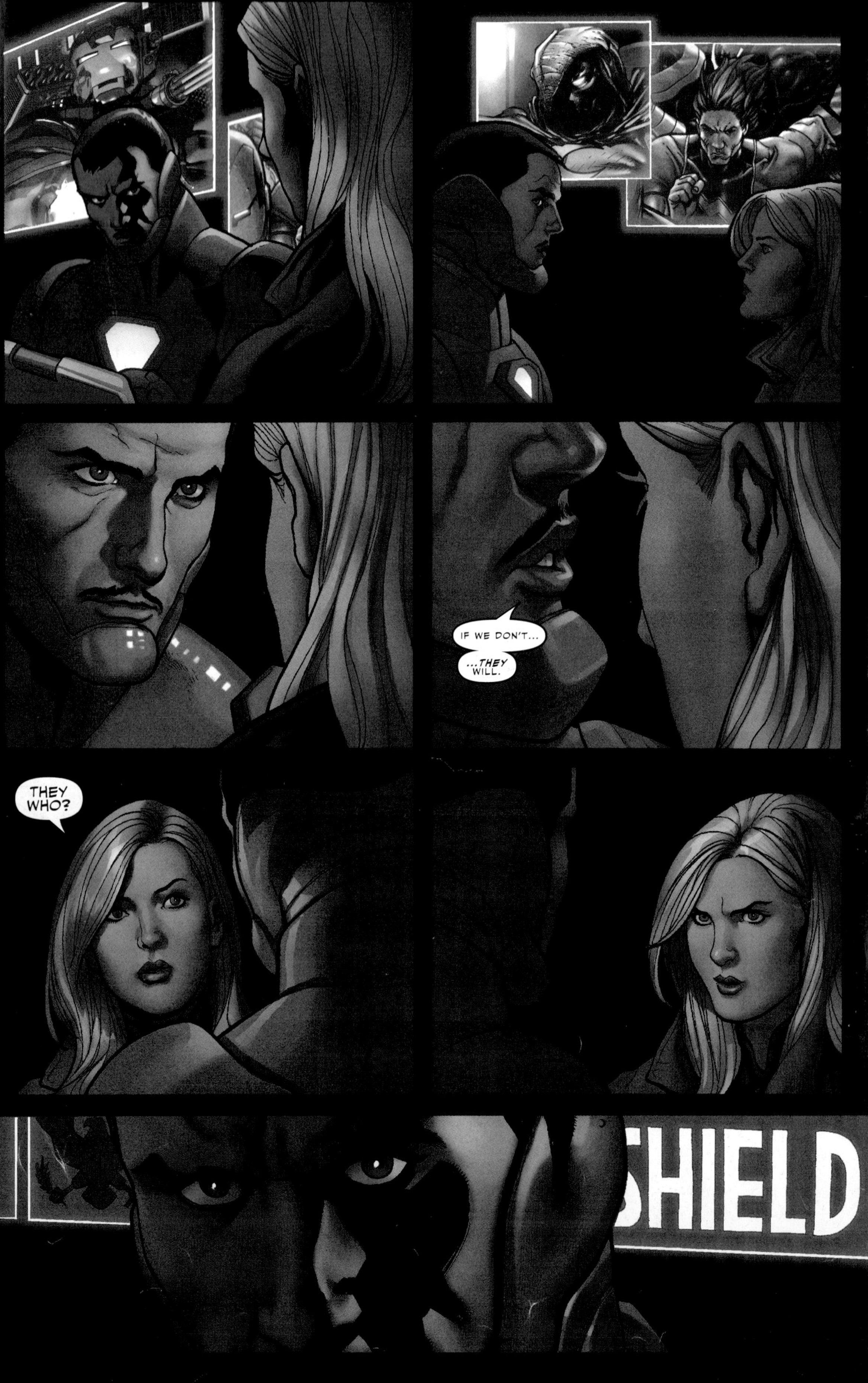
IF WE DON'T...
...THEY WILL.
THEY WHO?
SHIELD

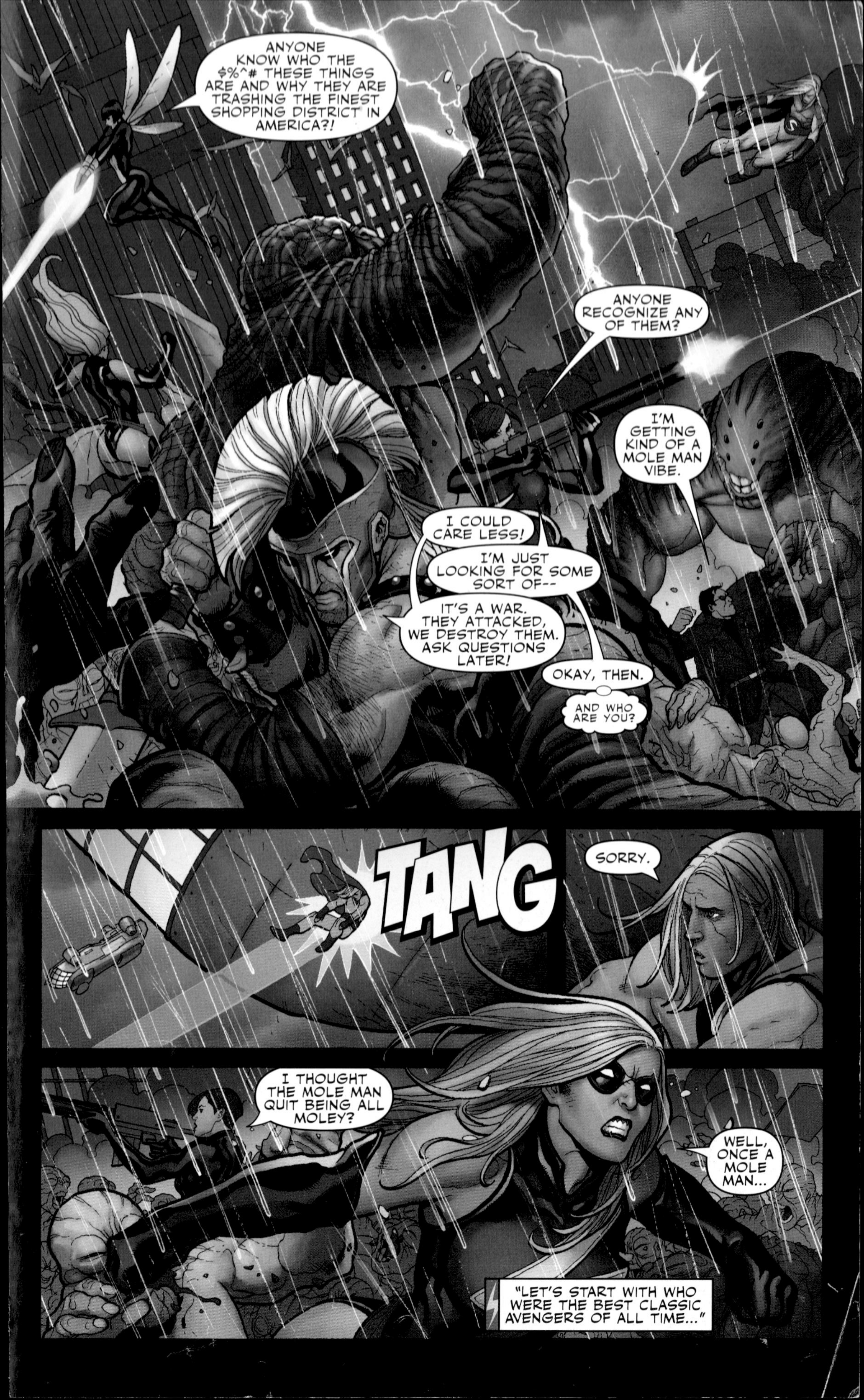
ANYONE KNOW WHO THE $%^# THESE THINGS ARE AND WHY THEY ARE TRASHING THE FINEST SHOPPING DISTRICT IN AMERICA?!
ANYONE RECOGNIZE ANY OF THEM?
I'M GETTING KIND OF A MOLE MAN VIBE.
I COULD CARE LESS!
I'M JUST LOOKING FOR SOME SORT OF--
IT'S A WAR. THEY ATTACKED, WE DESTROY THEM. ASK QUESTIONS LATER!
OKAY, THEN.
AND WHO ARE YOU?
TANG
SORRY.
I THOUGHT THE MOLE MAN QUIT BEING ALL MOLEY?
WELL, ONCE A MOLE MAN...
"LET'S START WITH WHO WERE THE BEST CLASSIC AVENGERS OF ALL TIME..."

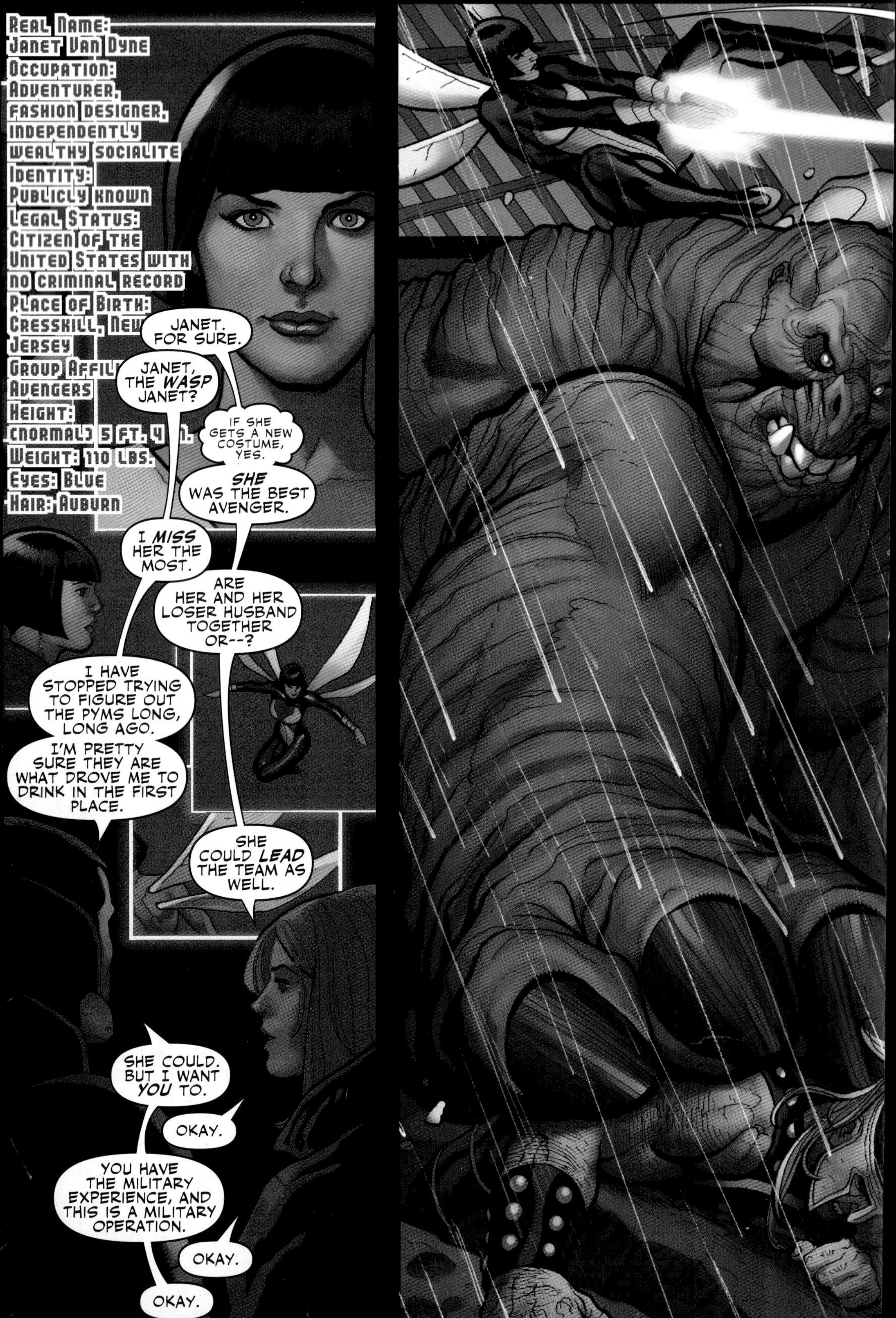

Real Name:
Janet Van Dyne
Occupation:
Adventurer,
fashion designer,
independently
wealthy socialite
Identity:
Publicly known
Legal Status:
Citizen of the
United States with
no criminal record
Place of Birth:
Cresskill, New
Jersey
Group Affil
Avengers
Height:
(normal) 5 ft. 4
Weight: 110 lbs.
Eyes: Blue
Hair: Auburn
JANET. FOR SURE.
JANET, THE WASP JANET?
IF SHE GETS A NEW COSTUME, YES.
SHE WAS THE BEST AVENGER.
I MISS HER THE MOST.
ARE HER AND HER LOSER HUSBAND TOGETHER OR--?
I HAVE STOPPED TRYING TO FIGURE OUT THE PYMS LONG, LONG AGO.
I'M PRETTY SURE THEY ARE WHAT DROVE ME TO DRINK IN THE FIRST PLACE.
SHE COULD LEAD THE TEAM AS WELL.
SHE COULD. BUT I WANT YOU TO.
OKAY.
YOU HAVE THE MILITARY EXPERIENCE, AND THIS IS A MILITARY OPERATION.
OKAY.
OKAY.

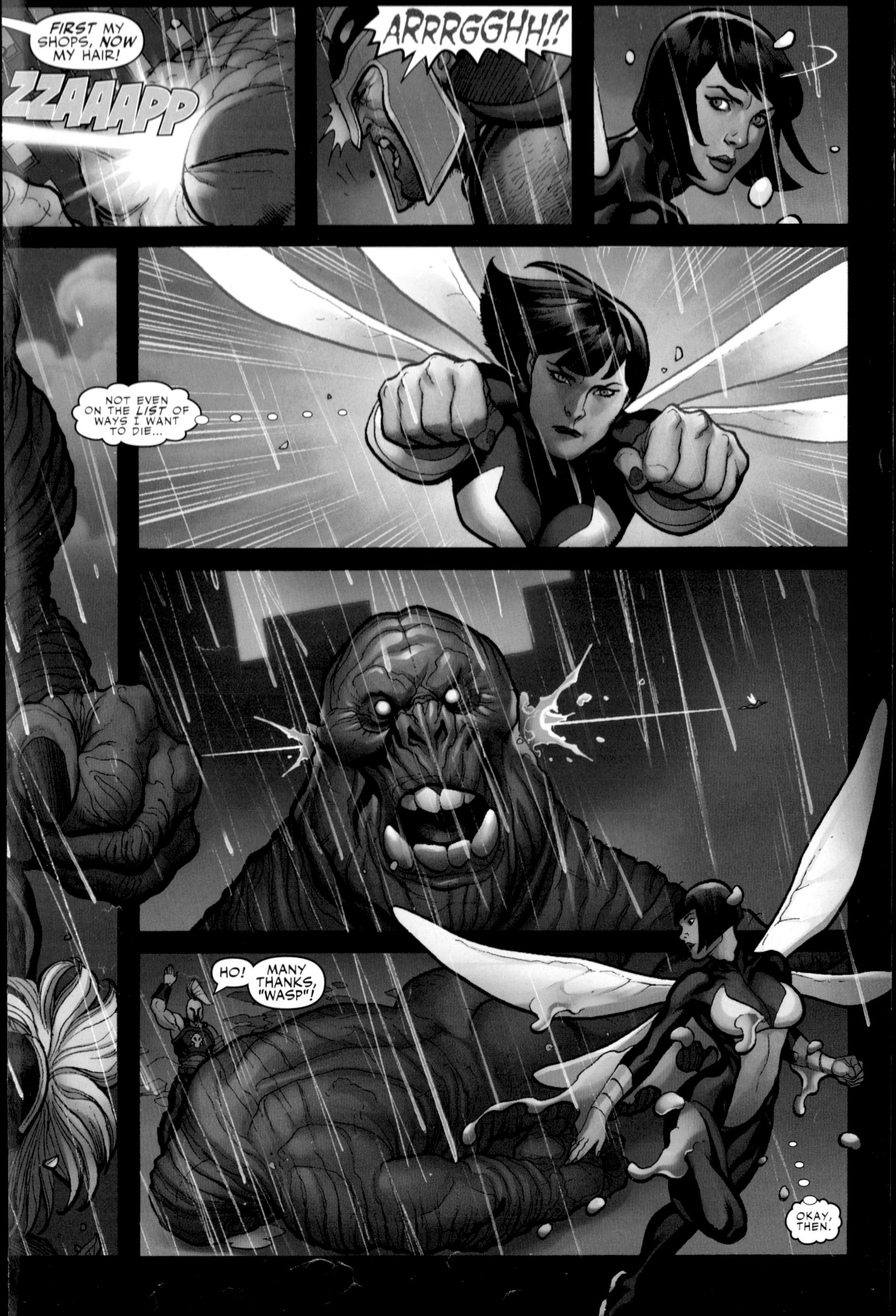
FIRST MY SHOPS, NOW MY HAIR!
ZZAAAPP
ARRRGGHH!!
NOT EVEN ON THE LIST OF WAYS I WANT TO DIE...
HO! MANY THANKS, "WASP"!
OKAY, THEN.

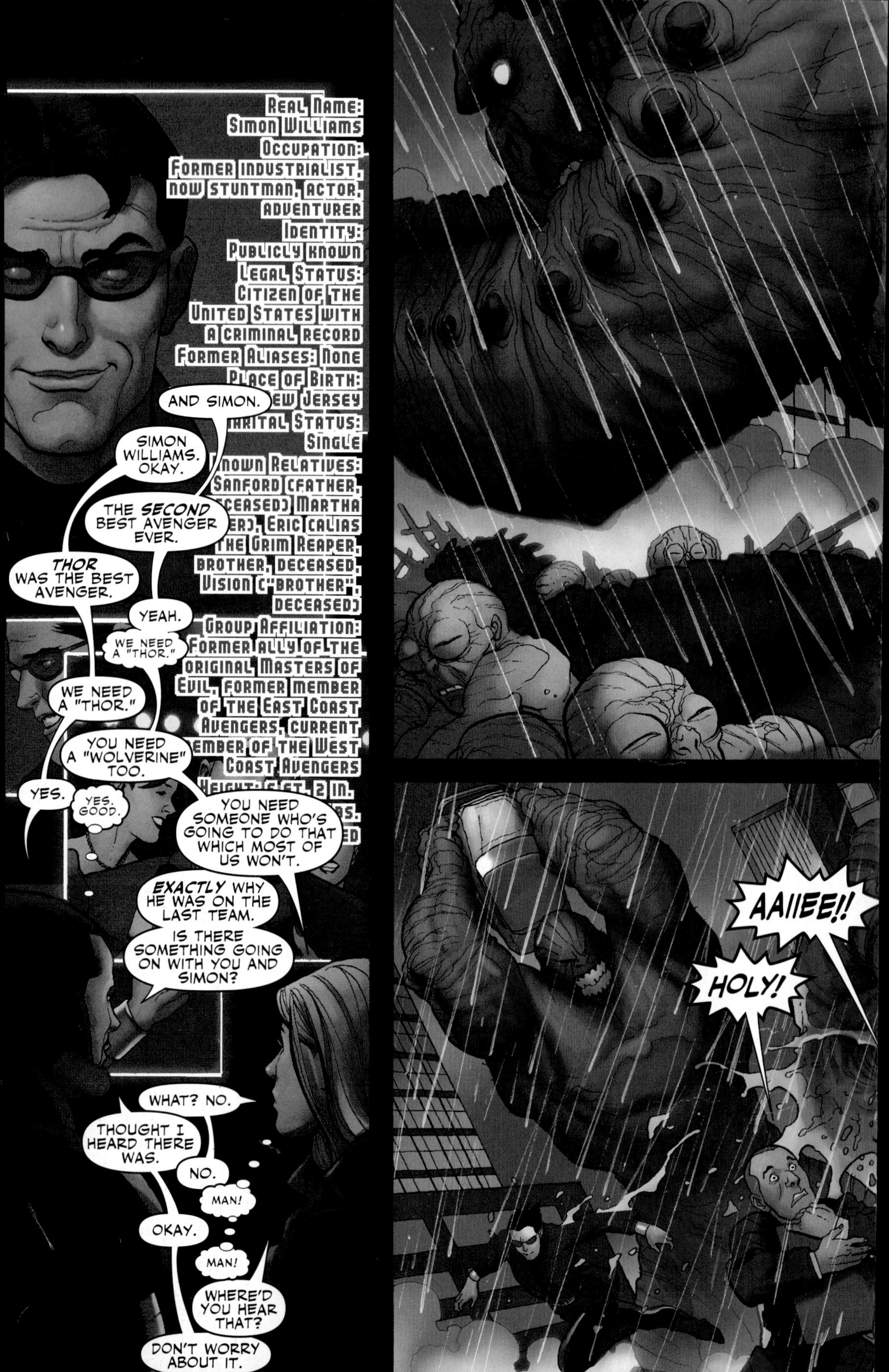
REAL NAME:
SIMON WILLIAMS
OCCUPATION:
FORMER INDUSTRIALIST, NOW STUNTMAN, ACTOR, ADVENTURER
IDENTITY:
PUBLICLY KNOWN
LEGAL STATUS:
CITIZEN OF THE UNITED STATES WITH A CRIMINAL RECORD
FORMER ALIASES: NONE
PLACE OF BIRTH:
EW JERSEY
ARITAL STATUS:
SINGLE
NOWN RELATIVES:
SANFORD (FATHER, CEASED), MARTHA ER), ERIC (ALIAS THE GRIM REAPER, BROTHER, DECEASED), VISION ("BROTHER", DECEASED)
GROUP AFFILIATION:
FORMER ALLY OF THE ORIGINAL MASTERS OF EVIL, FORMER MEMBER OF THE EAST COAST AVENGERS, CURRENT EMBER OF THE WEST COAST AVENGERS
AND SIMON.
SIMON WILLIAMS. OKAY.
THE SECOND BEST AVENGER EVER.
THOR WAS THE BEST AVENGER.
YEAH.
WE NEED A "THOR."
WE NEED A "THOR."
YOU NEED A "WOLVERINE" TOO.
YES.
YES. GOOD.
YOU NEED SOMEONE WHO'S GOING TO DO THAT WHICH MOST OF US WON'T.
EXACTLY WHY HE WAS ON THE LAST TEAM.
IS THERE SOMETHING GOING ON WITH YOU AND SIMON?
WHAT? NO.
THOUGHT I HEARD THERE WAS.
NO.
MAN!
OKAY.
MAN!
WHERE'D YOU HEAR THAT?
DON'T WORRY ABOUT IT.
AAIIEE!!
HOLY!

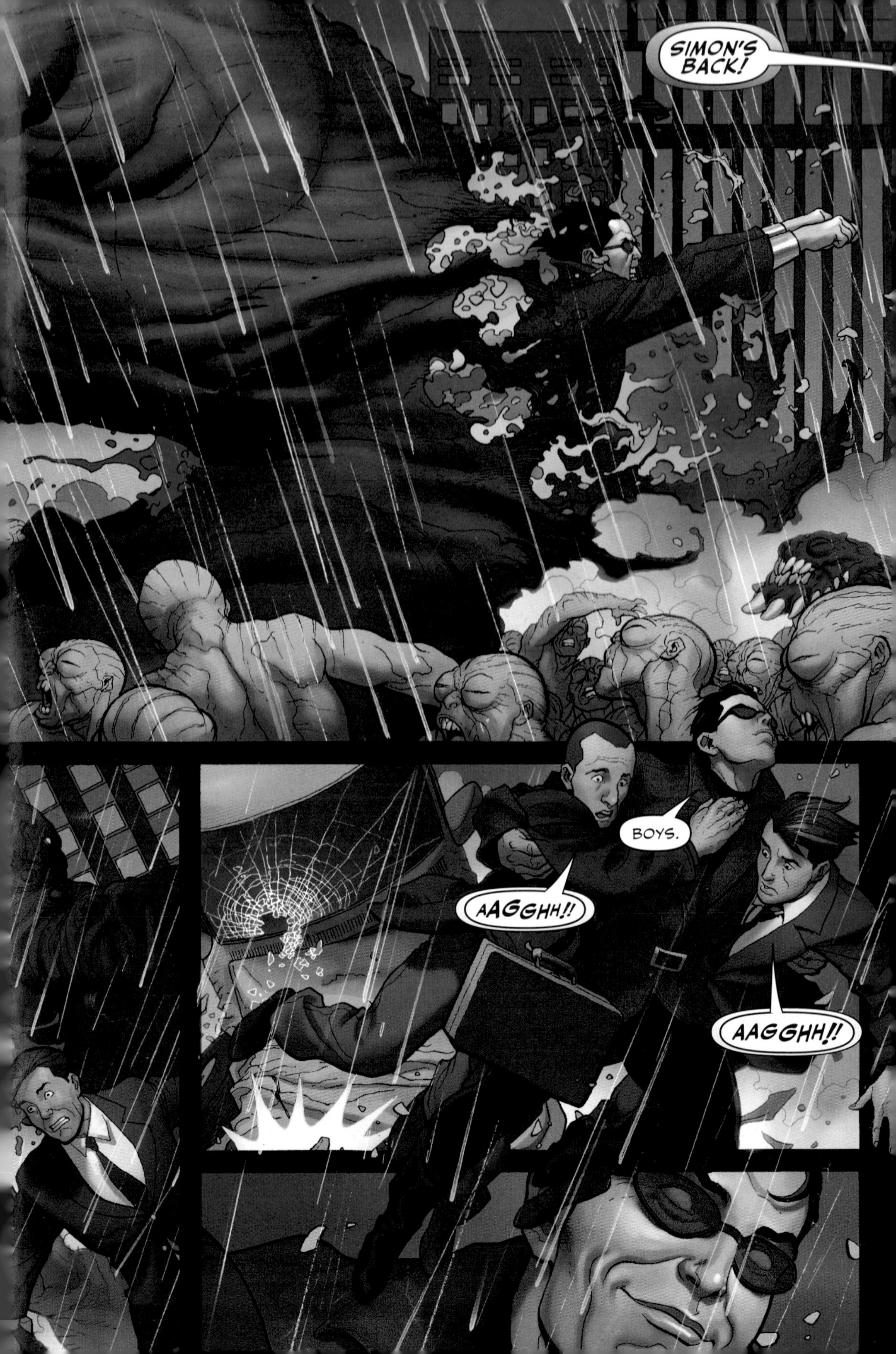
SIMON'S BACK!
BOYS.
AAGGHH!!
AAGGHH!!

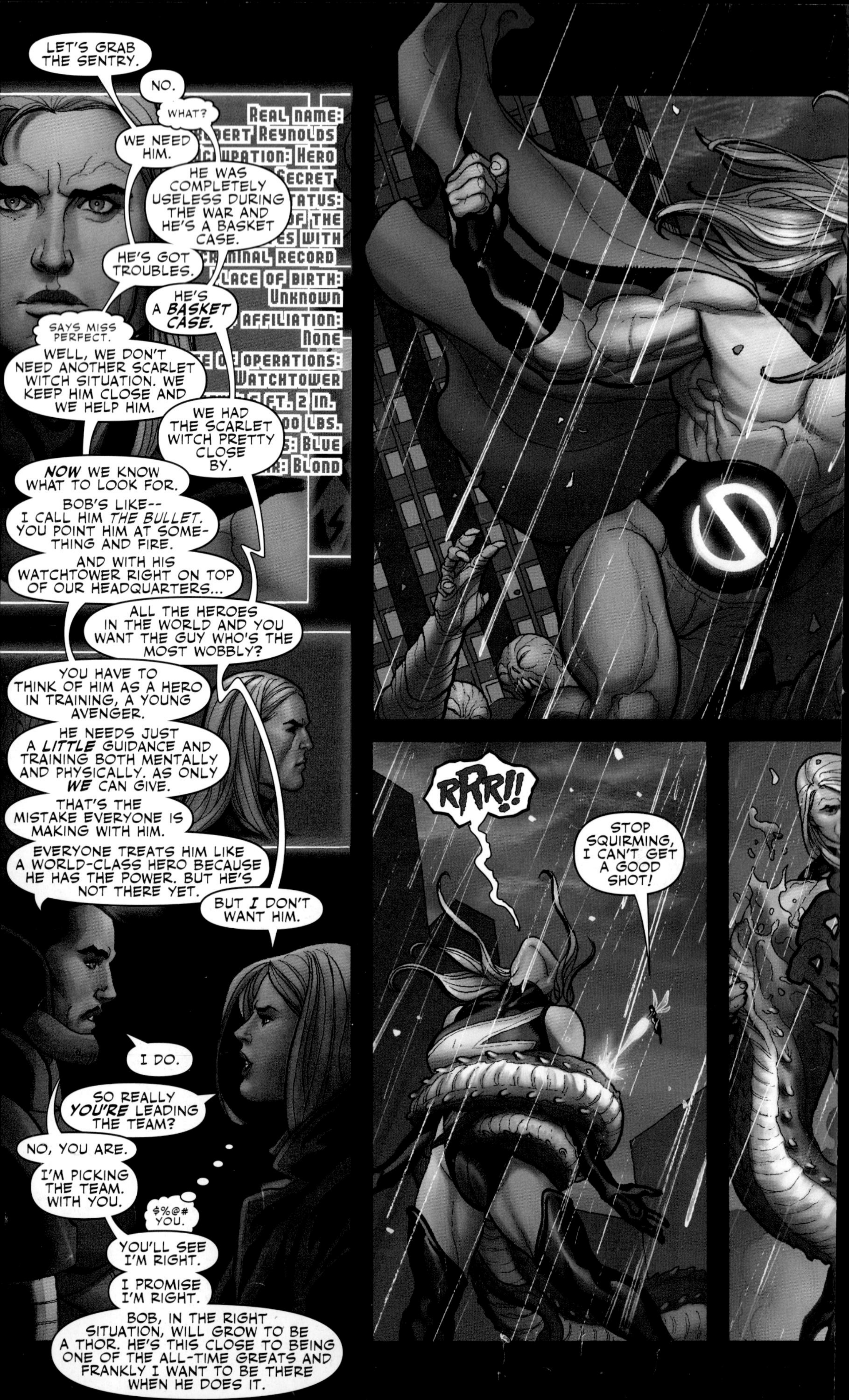
LET'S GRAB THE SENTRY.
NO.
WHAT?
WE NEED HIM.
HE WAS COMPLETELY USELESS DURING THE WAR AND HE'S A BASKET CASE.
HE'S GOT TROUBLES.
HE'S A *BASKET CASE.*
SAYS MISS PERFECT.
WELL, WE DON'T NEED ANOTHER SCARLET WITCH SITUATION. WE KEEP HIM CLOSE AND WE HELP HIM.
WE HAD THE SCARLET WITCH PRETTY CLOSE BY.
Real name:
Unknown
None
Watchtower
*NOW* WE KNOW WHAT TO LOOK FOR.
BOB'S LIKE-- I CALL HIM *THE BULLET.* YOU POINT HIM AT SOME-THING AND FIRE.
AND WITH HIS WATCHTOWER RIGHT ON TOP OF OUR HEADQUARTERS...
ALL THE HEROES IN THE WORLD AND YOU WANT THE GUY WHO'S THE MOST WOBBLY?
YOU HAVE TO THINK OF HIM AS A HERO IN TRAINING, A YOUNG AVENGER.
HE NEEDS JUST A *LITTLE* GUIDANCE AND TRAINING BOTH MENTALLY AND PHYSICALLY. AS ONLY *WE* CAN GIVE.
THAT'S THE MISTAKE EVERYONE IS MAKING WITH HIM.
EVERYONE TREATS HIM LIKE A WORLD-CLASS HERO BECAUSE HE HAS THE POWER. BUT HE'S NOT THERE YET.
BUT *I* DON'T WANT HIM.
I DO.
SO REALLY *YOU'RE* LEADING THE TEAM?
NO, YOU ARE.
I'M PICKING THE TEAM. WITH YOU.
$%@# YOU.
YOU'LL SEE I'M RIGHT.
I PROMISE I'M RIGHT.
BOB, IN THE RIGHT SITUATION, WILL GROW TO BE A THOR. HE'S THIS CLOSE TO BEING ONE OF THE ALL-TIME GREATS AND FRANKLY I WANT TO BE THERE WHEN HE DOES IT.
RRR!!
STOP SQUIRMING, I CAN'T GET A GOOD SHOT!

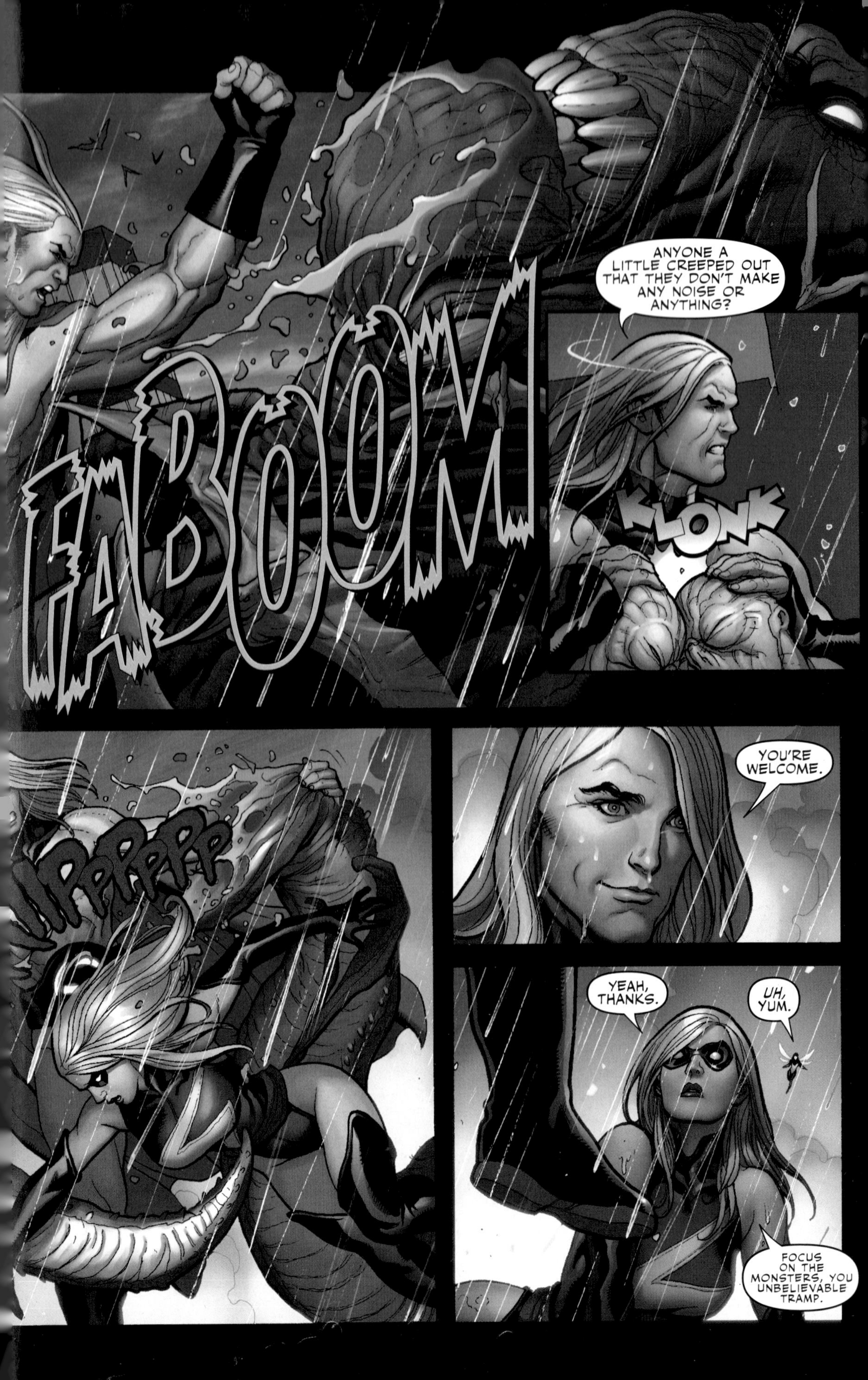

FABOOM
ANYONE A LITTLE CREEPED OUT THAT THEY DON'T MAKE ANY NOISE OR ANYTHING?
KLONK
RIPPPPP
YOU'RE WELCOME.
YEAH, THANKS.
UH, YUM.
FOCUS ON THE MONSTERS, YOU UNBELIEVABLE TRAMP.

OKAY. SO, LET'S SAY SENTRY, WASP, WONDER MAN, ME, YOU?

YEP.

YOU'RE IN?

OF COURSE.

SO WE'RE MISSING A WOLVERINE AND A THOR.

AND A NINJA.

WE NEED A NINJA?

IN THIS DAY AND AGE? YOU *HAVE* TO HAVE A NINJA.

MATT MURDOCK?

HE'S A LOT MORE TROUBLE THAN HE'S WORTH AT THIS POINT.

SHANG-CHI?

NATASHA ROMANOFF.

BLACK WIDOW.

I LOVE HER.

SHE DOES LOOK HOT IN THE BLACK LEATHER.

SHE'S OKAY.

YOU LOVE HER.

SHE'S ALL RIGHT.

IT'S OKAY THAT YOU LOVE HER.

YOU LOOK BETTER.

TOO MUCH.

ARE YOU WORRIED ABOUT HER IN THE MORE INTENSE COMBAT SITUATIONS?

*UH*, WHAT WAS THAT?

AM I WORRIED? *UH*, NO.

Real Name: ona Romanova
Occupation: venturer, Intelligence rmer ballerina
Legal Status: itizen of the USSR ho defected to the United ates; sh now lives in the es under an orized by criminal te United States pionage activities ations, but was nesty through intervention.
Identity: own Other Aliases: Nancy Rushman, Laura Matthers
Place of Birth: mer Union of alist Republics
tus: Widowed own Relatives: ov (alias Red sband, deceased)
Affiliation: rvel Knights active), frequent agent of SHIELD, rtner of Daredevil, er of the os Angeles Operations bil, but maintains ome n New York City ft. 7 in.
: 125 lbs.
Eyes: Green
R: Red-auburn ly dyed black)

BOOM BOOM

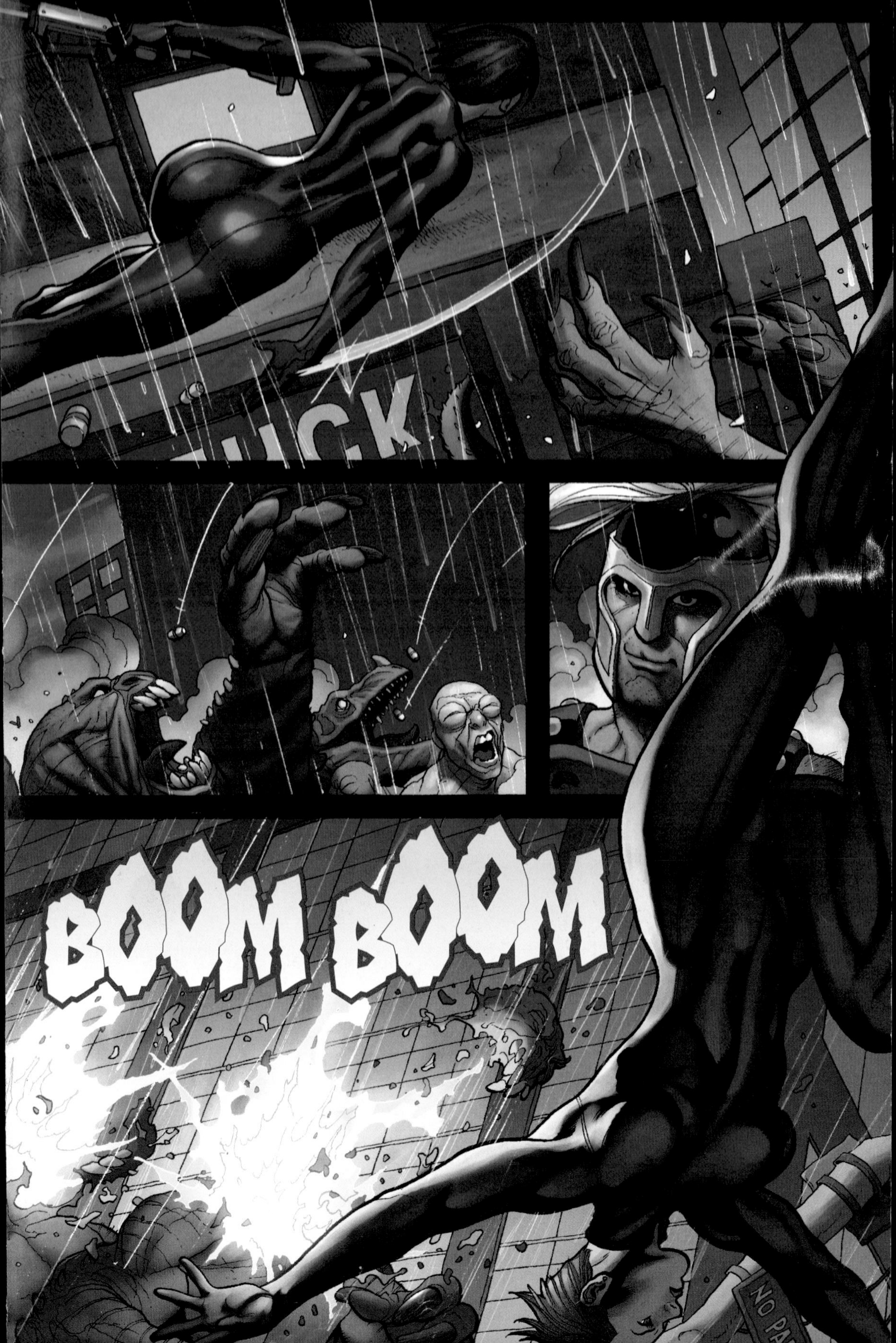
BOOM BOOM

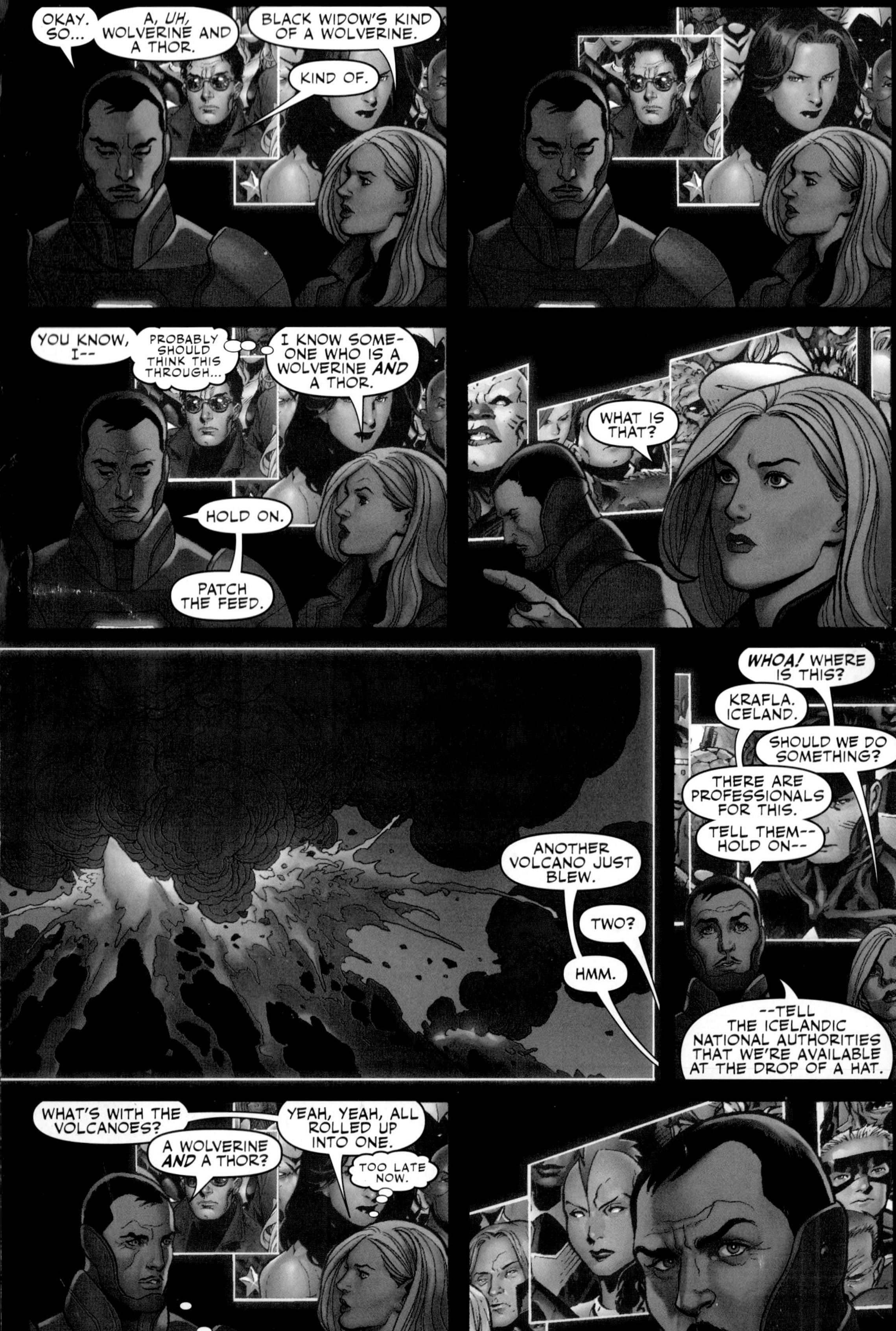
OKAY. SO...
A, UH, WOLVERINE AND A THOR.
BLACK WIDOW'S KIND OF A WOLVERINE.
KIND OF.
YOU KNOW, I--
PROBABLY SHOULD THINK THIS THROUGH...
I KNOW SOMEONE WHO IS A WOLVERINE AND A THOR.
HOLD ON.
PATCH THE FEED.
WHAT IS THAT?
ANOTHER VOLCANO JUST BLEW.
TWO?
HMM.
WHOA! WHERE IS THIS?
KRAFLA. ICELAND.
SHOULD WE DO SOMETHING?
THERE ARE PROFESSIONALS FOR THIS.
TELL THEM-- HOLD ON--
--TELL THE ICELANDIC NATIONAL AUTHORITIES THAT WE'RE AVAILABLE AT THE DROP OF A HAT.
WHAT'S WITH THE VOLCANOES?
A WOLVERINE AND A THOR?
YEAH, YEAH, ALL ROLLED UP INTO ONE.
TOO LATE NOW.
A WOLVERINE AND A THOR?
REALLY?

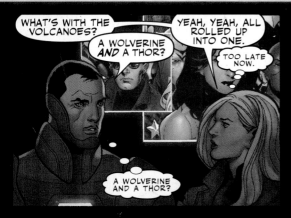

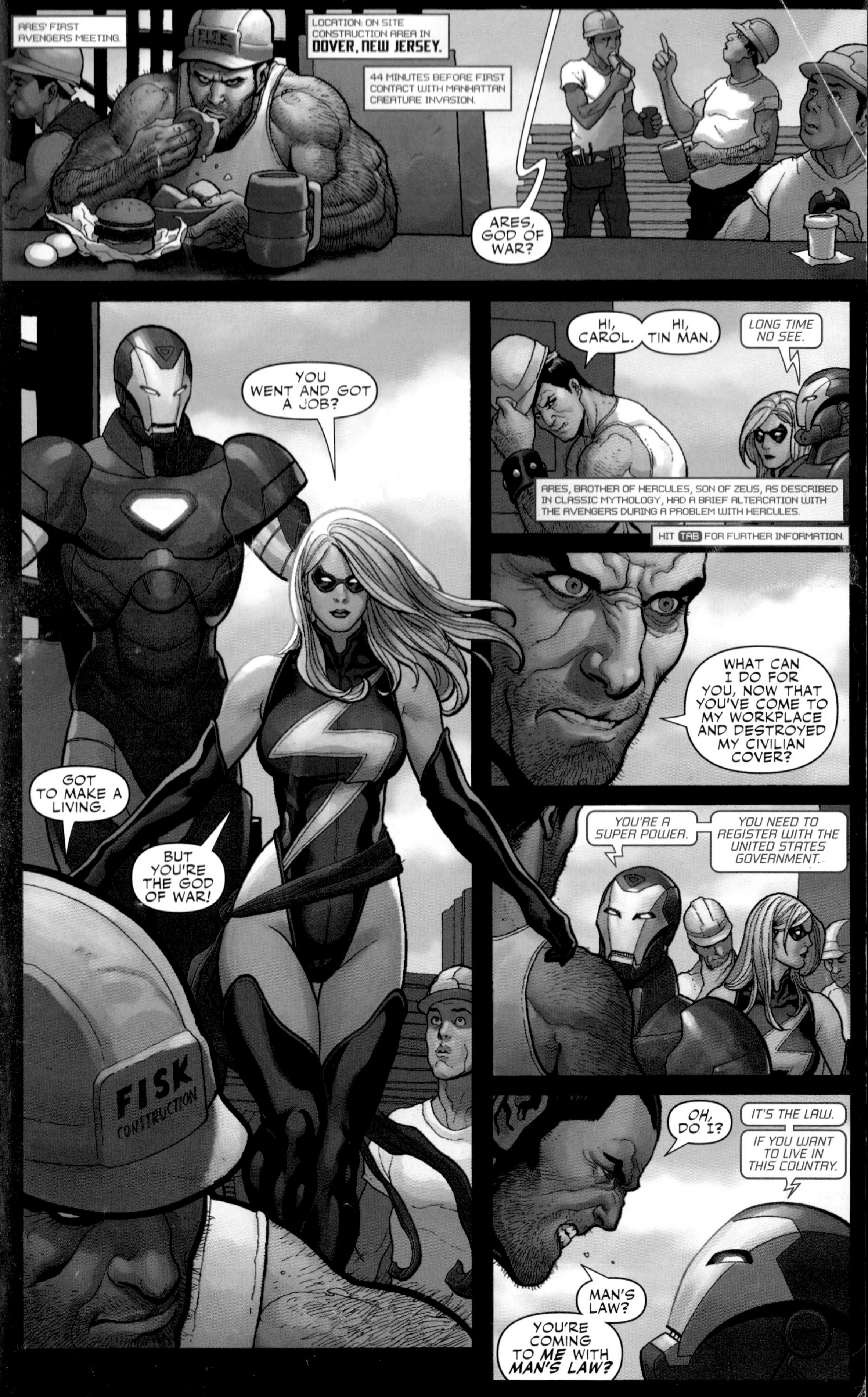
ARES' FIRST AVENGERS MEETING.
LOCATION: ON SITE CONSTRUCTION AREA IN DOVER, NEW JERSEY.
44 MINUTES BEFORE FIRST CONTACT WITH MANHATTAN CREATURE INVASION.
ARES, GOD OF WAR?
YOU WENT AND GOT A JOB?
GOT TO MAKE A LIVING.
BUT YOU'RE THE GOD OF WAR!
FISK CONSTRUCTION
HI, CAROL.
HI, TIN MAN.
LONG TIME NO SEE.
ARES, BROTHER OF HERCULES, SON OF ZEUS, AS DESCRIBED IN CLASSIC MYTHOLOGY, HAD A BRIEF ALTERCATION WITH THE AVENGERS DURING A PROBLEM WITH HERCULES.
HIT TAB FOR FURTHER INFORMATION.
WHAT CAN I DO FOR YOU, NOW THAT YOU'VE COME TO MY WORKPLACE AND DESTROYED MY CIVILIAN COVER?
YOU'RE A SUPER POWER.
YOU NEED TO REGISTER WITH THE UNITED STATES GOVERNMENT.
OH, DO I?
IT'S THE LAW.
IF YOU WANT TO LIVE IN THIS COUNTRY.
MAN'S LAW?
YOU'RE COMING TO ME WITH MAN'S LAW?

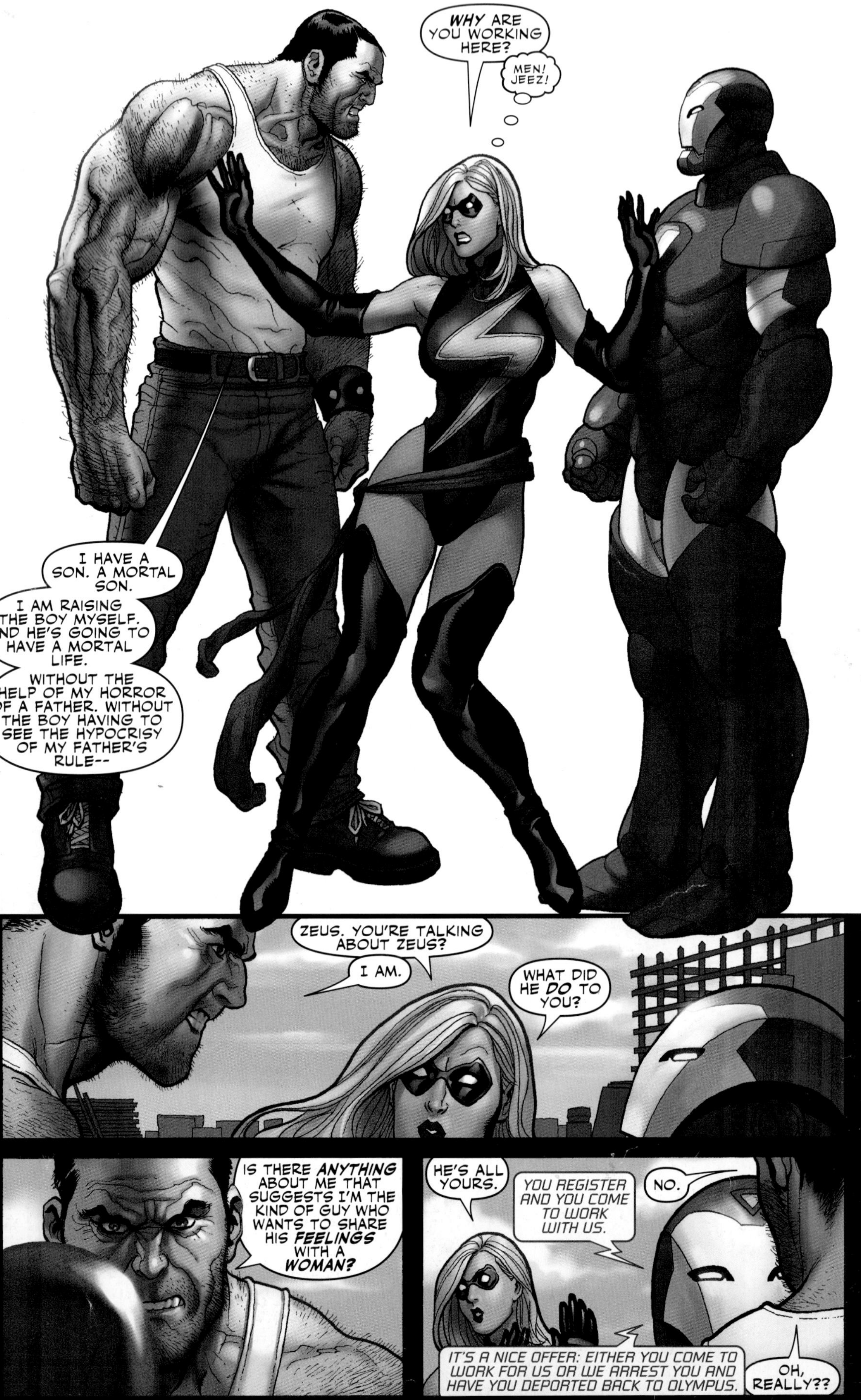
WHY ARE YOU WORKING HERE?
MEN! JEEZ!
I HAVE A SON. A MORTAL SON.
I AM RAISING THE BOY MYSELF. AND HE'S GOING TO HAVE A MORTAL LIFE.
WITHOUT THE HELP OF MY HORROR OF A FATHER. WITHOUT THE BOY HAVING TO SEE THE HYPOCRISY OF MY FATHER'S RULE--
ZEUS. YOU'RE TALKING ABOUT ZEUS?
I AM.
WHAT DID HE DO TO YOU?
IS THERE ANYTHING ABOUT ME THAT SUGGESTS I'M THE KIND OF GUY WHO WANTS TO SHARE HIS FEELINGS WITH A WOMAN?
HE'S ALL YOURS.
YOU REGISTER AND YOU COME TO WORK WITH US.
NO.
IT'S A NICE OFFER: EITHER YOU COME TO WORK FOR US OR WE ARREST YOU AND HAVE YOU DEPORTED BACK TO OLYMPUS.
OH, REALLY??

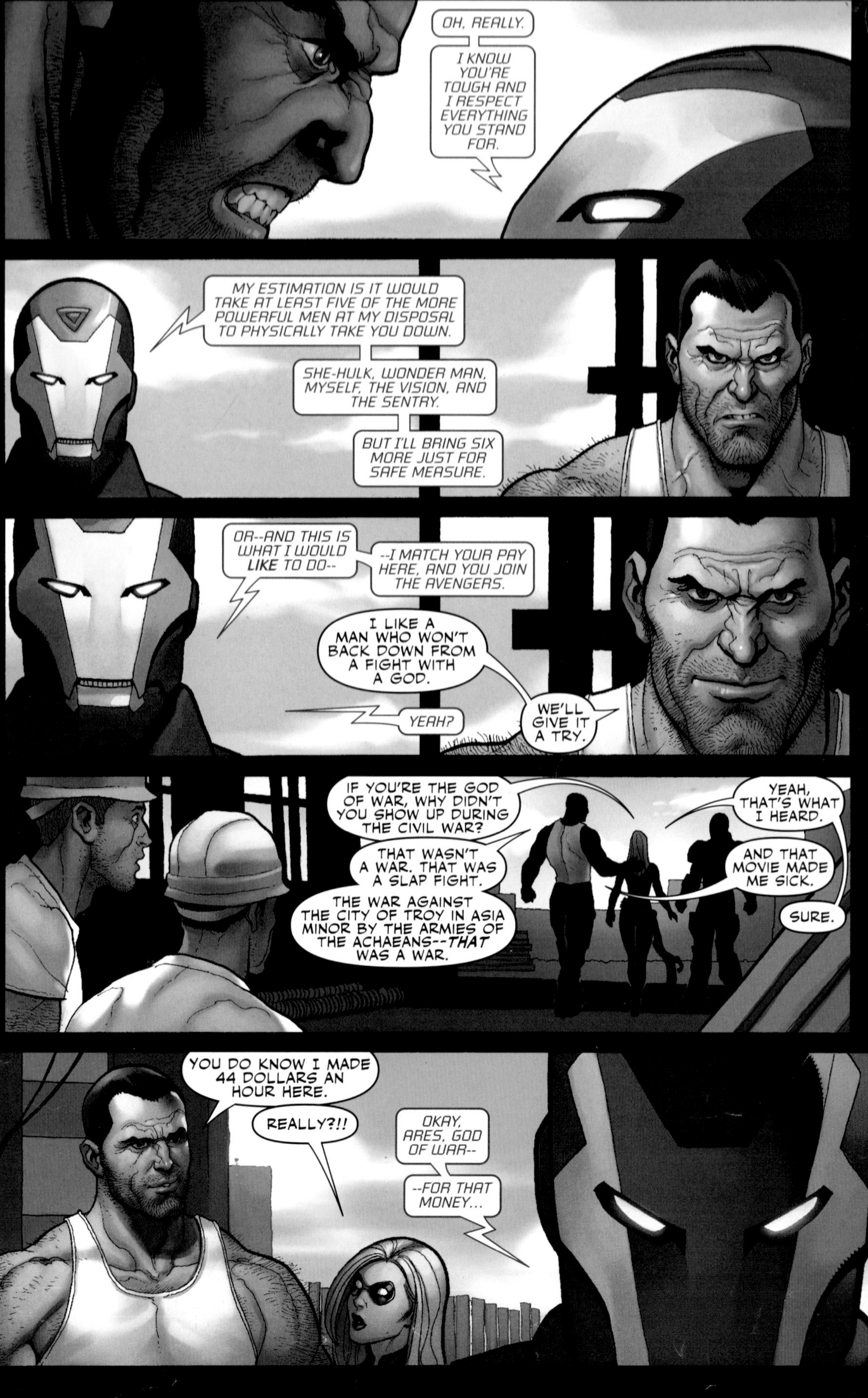
OH, REALLY.
I KNOW YOU'RE TOUGH AND I RESPECT EVERYTHING YOU STAND FOR.
MY ESTIMATION IS IT WOULD TAKE AT LEAST FIVE OF THE MORE POWERFUL MEN AT MY DISPOSAL TO PHYSICALLY TAKE YOU DOWN.
SHE-HULK, WONDER MAN, MYSELF, THE VISION, AND THE SENTRY.
BUT I'LL BRING SIX MORE JUST FOR SAFE MEASURE.
OR--AND THIS IS WHAT I WOULD LIKE TO DO--
--I MATCH YOUR PAY HERE, AND YOU JOIN THE AVENGERS.
I LIKE A MAN WHO WON'T BACK DOWN FROM A FIGHT WITH A GOD.
YEAH?
WE'LL GIVE IT A TRY.
IF YOU'RE THE GOD OF WAR, WHY DIDN'T YOU SHOW UP DURING THE CIVIL WAR?
THAT WASN'T A WAR. THAT WAS A SLAP FIGHT.
THE WAR AGAINST THE CITY OF TROY IN ASIA MINOR BY THE ARMIES OF THE ACHAEANS--THAT WAS A WAR.
YEAH, THAT'S WHAT I HEARD.
AND THAT MOVIE MADE ME SICK.
SURE.
YOU DO KNOW I MADE 44 DOLLARS AN HOUR HERE.
REALLY?!!
OKAY, ARES, GOD OF WAR--
--FOR THAT MONEY...

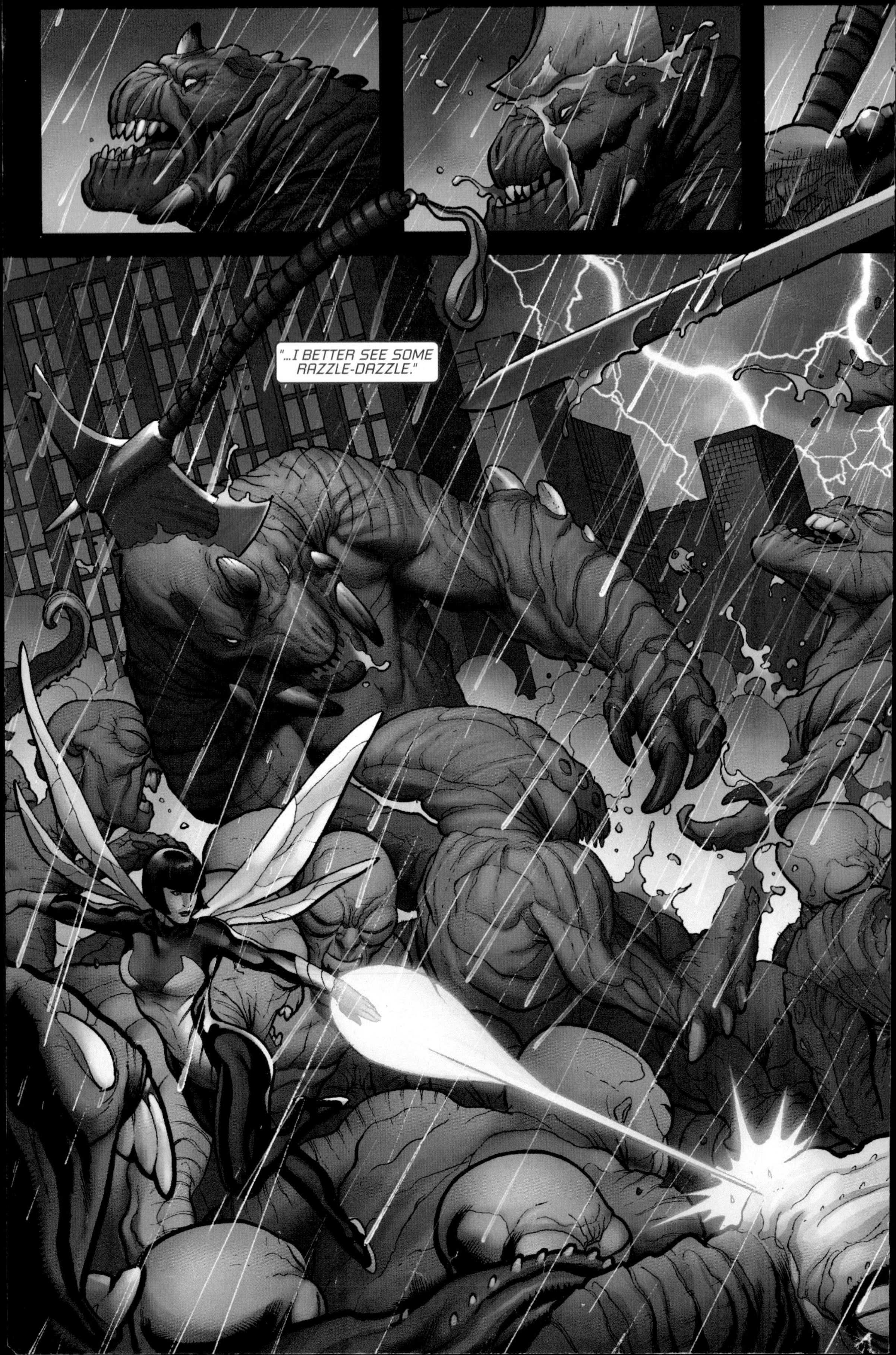
"...I BETTER SEE SOME
RAZZLE-DAZZLE."

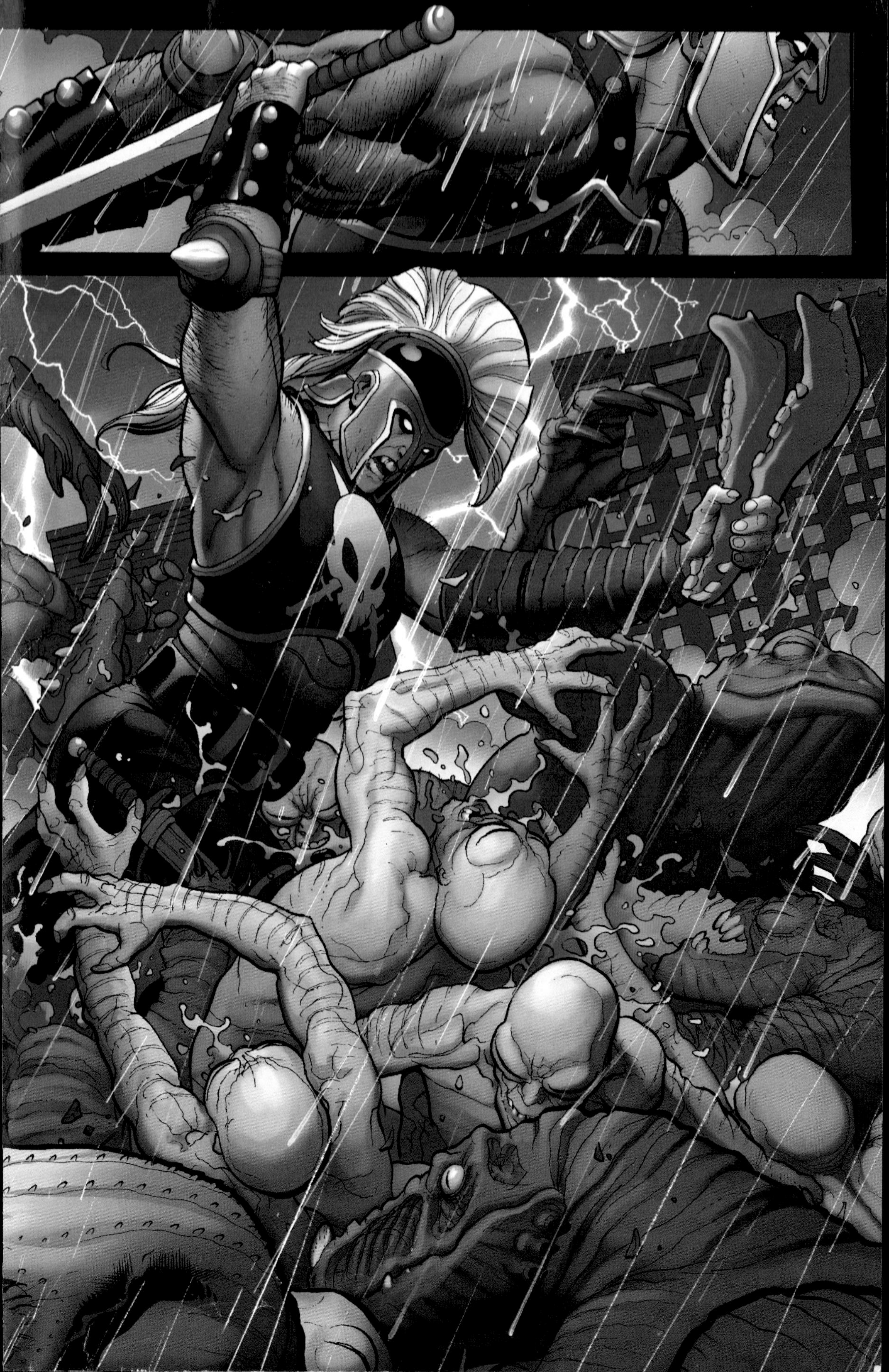

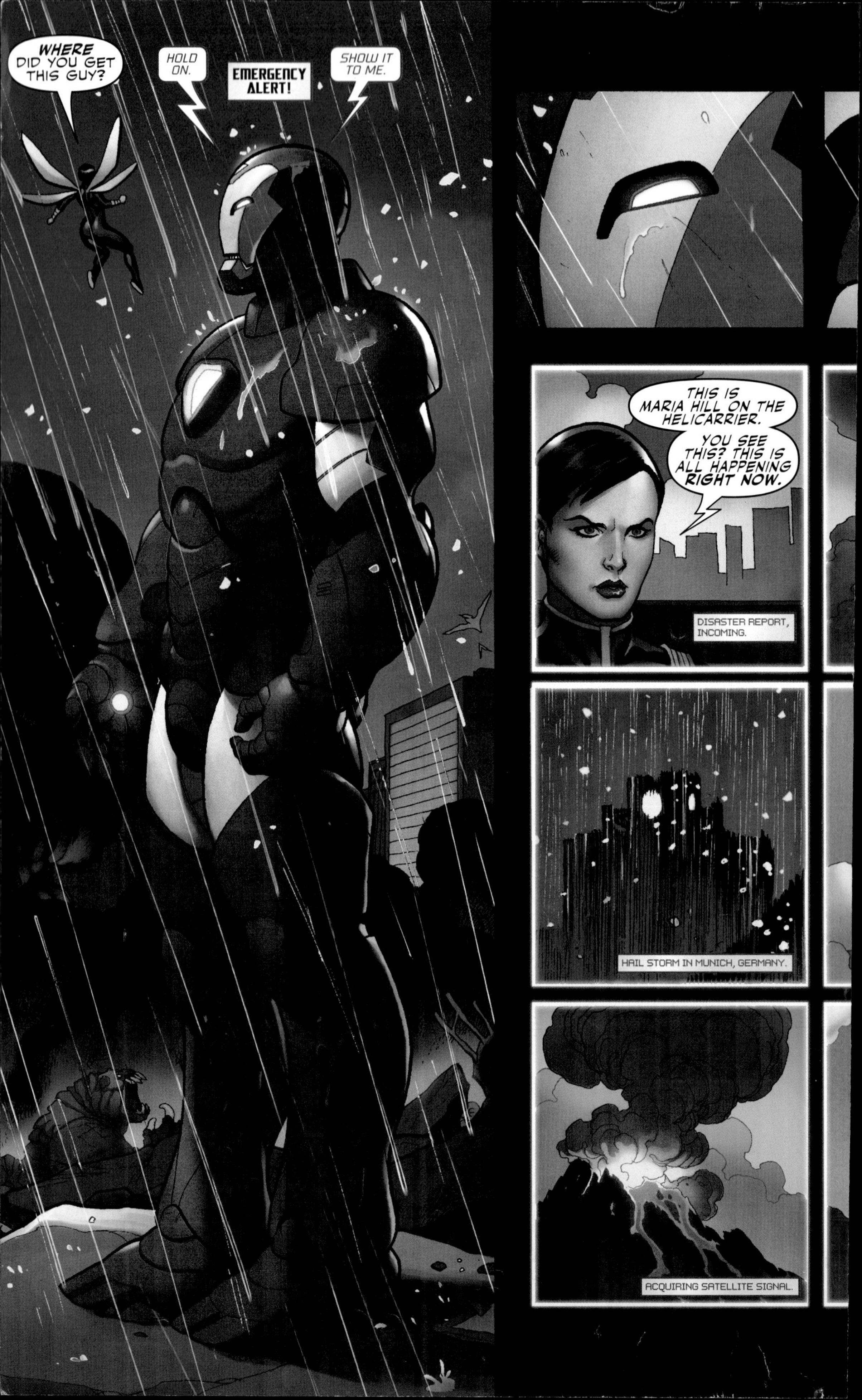
WHERE DID YOU GET THIS GUY?
HOLD ON.
EMERGENCY ALERT!
SHOW IT TO ME.
THIS IS MARIA HILL ON THE HELICARRIER.
YOU SEE THIS? THIS IS ALL HAPPENING RIGHT NOW.
DISASTER REPORT, INCOMING.
HAIL STORM IN MUNICH, GERMANY.
ACQUIRING SATELLITE SIGNAL.

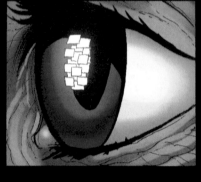

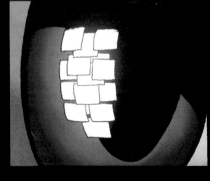

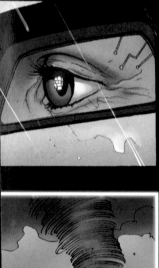

TORNADO OUTBREAK IN TENNESSEE.

AVALANCHE ALERT IN CHINA.

FOREST FIRE OUTBREAK IN OAKLAND HILLS, CALIFORNIA AREA.

BRUSSELS REPORTING TEMPERATURES OF 122 DEGREES FAHRENHEIT.

HURRICANE INNNNNNN– STAND BY.

STAND BY.

ACQUIRING SATELLITE SIGNAL.

ACQUIRING SATELLITE SIGNAL.

OH MY GOD...

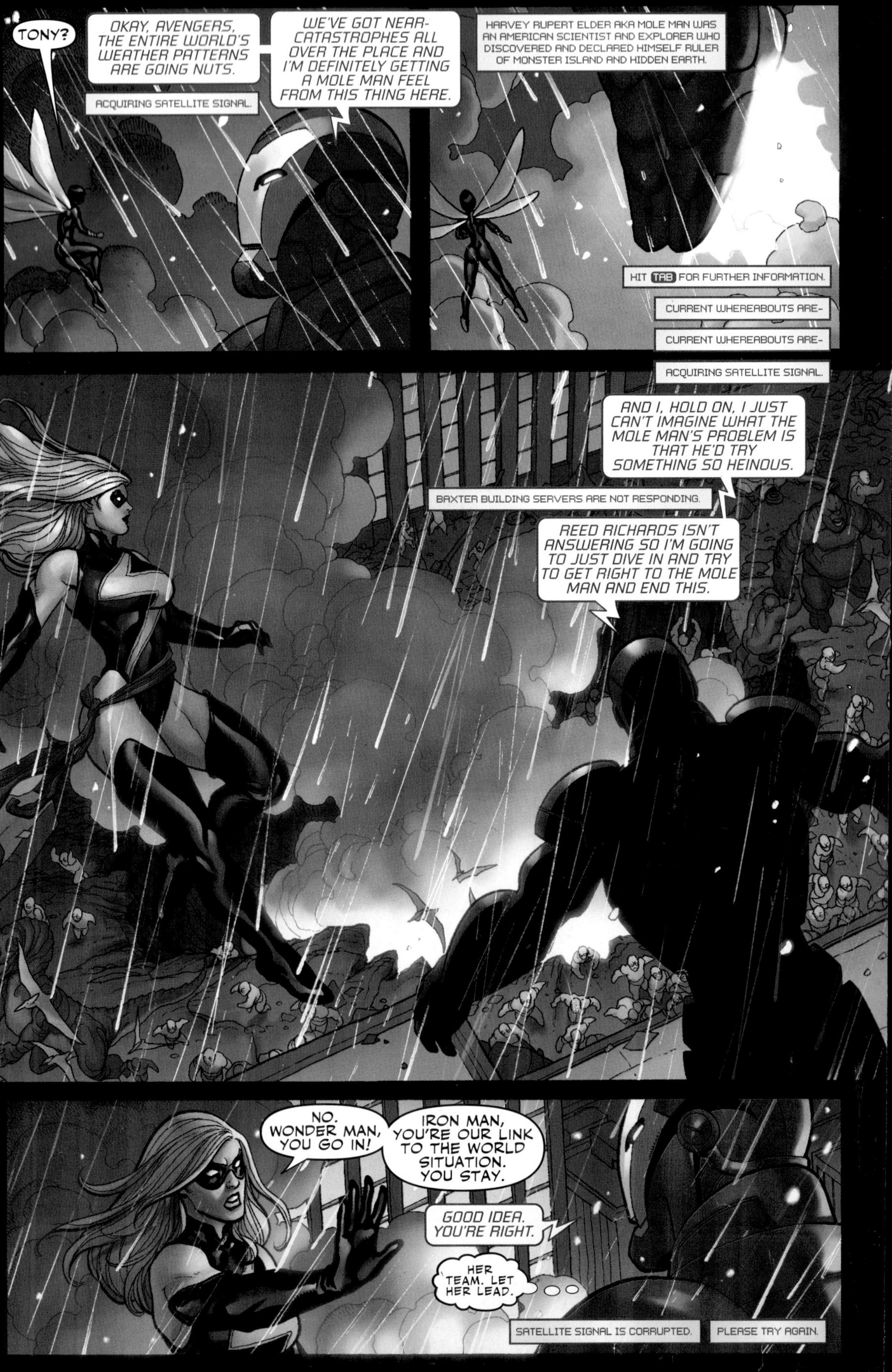
TONY?
OKAY, AVENGERS, THE ENTIRE WORLD'S WEATHER PATTERNS ARE GOING NUTS.
ACQUIRING SATELLITE SIGNAL.
WE'VE GOT NEAR-CATASTROPHES ALL OVER THE PLACE AND I'M DEFINITELY GETTING A MOLE MAN FEEL FROM THIS THING HERE.
HARVEY RUPERT ELDER AKA MOLE MAN WAS AN AMERICAN SCIENTIST AND EXPLORER WHO DISCOVERED AND DECLARED HIMSELF RULER OF MONSTER ISLAND AND HIDDEN EARTH.
HIT TAB FOR FURTHER INFORMATION.
CURRENT WHEREABOUTS ARE-
CURRENT WHEREABOUTS ARE-
ACQUIRING SATELLITE SIGNAL.
AND I, HOLD ON, I JUST CAN'T IMAGINE WHAT THE MOLE MAN'S PROBLEM IS THAT HE'D TRY SOMETHING SO HEINOUS.
BAXTER BUILDING SERVERS ARE NOT RESPONDING.
REED RICHARDS ISN'T ANSWERING SO I'M GOING TO JUST DIVE IN AND TRY TO GET RIGHT TO THE MOLE MAN AND END THIS.
NO. WONDER MAN, YOU GO IN!
IRON MAN, YOU'RE OUR LINK TO THE WORLD SITUATION. YOU STAY.
GOOD IDEA. YOU'RE RIGHT.
HER TEAM. LET HER LEAD.
SATELLITE SIGNAL IS CORRUPTED.
PLEASE TRY AGAIN.

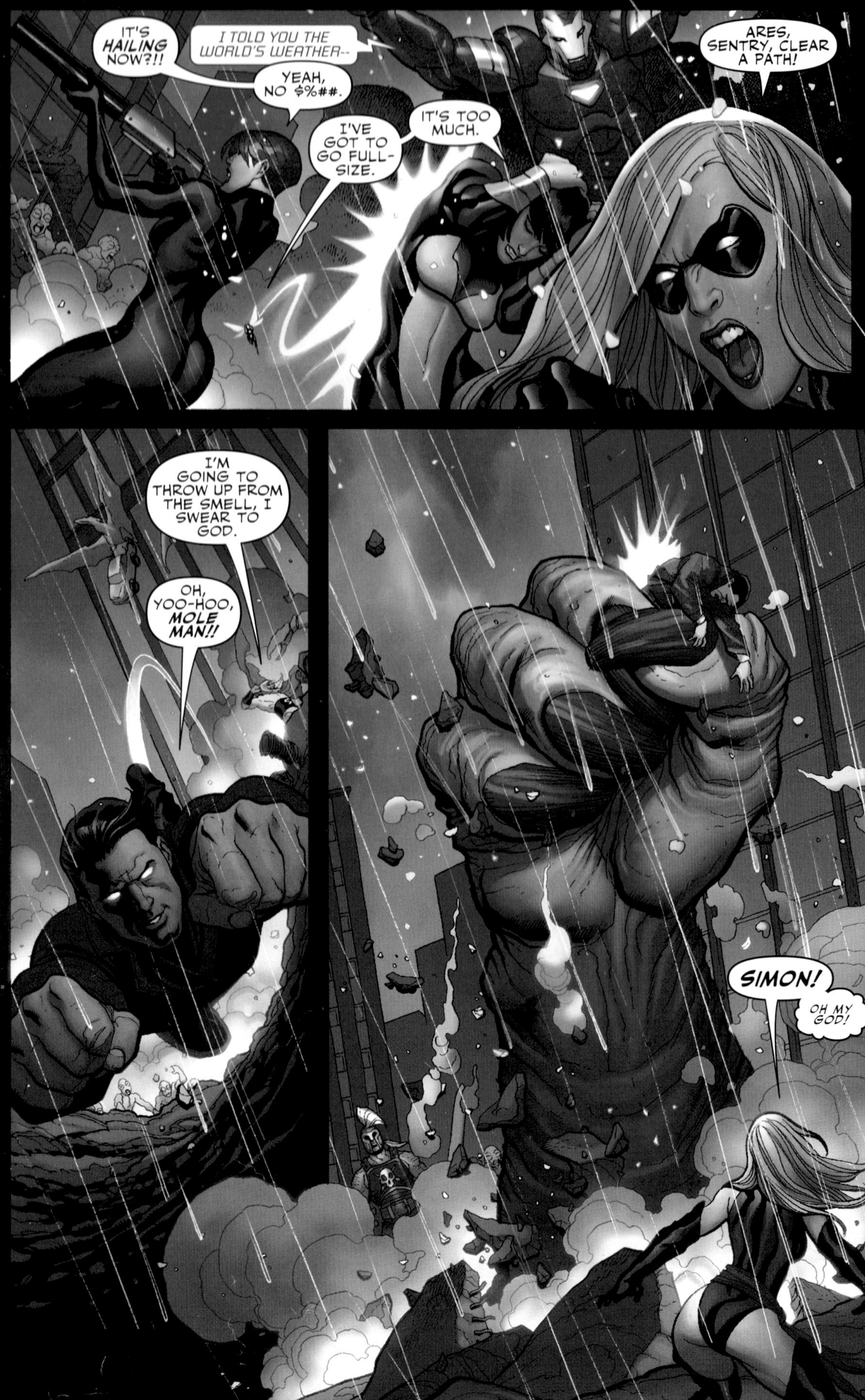
IT'S HAILING NOW?!!
I TOLD YOU THE WORLD'S WEATHER--
YEAH, NO $%##.
ARES, SENTRY, CLEAR A PATH!
I'VE GOT TO GO FULL-SIZE.
IT'S TOO MUCH.
I'M GOING TO THROW UP FROM THE SMELL, I SWEAR TO GOD.
OH, YOO-HOO, MOLE MAN!!
SIMON!
OH MY GOD!

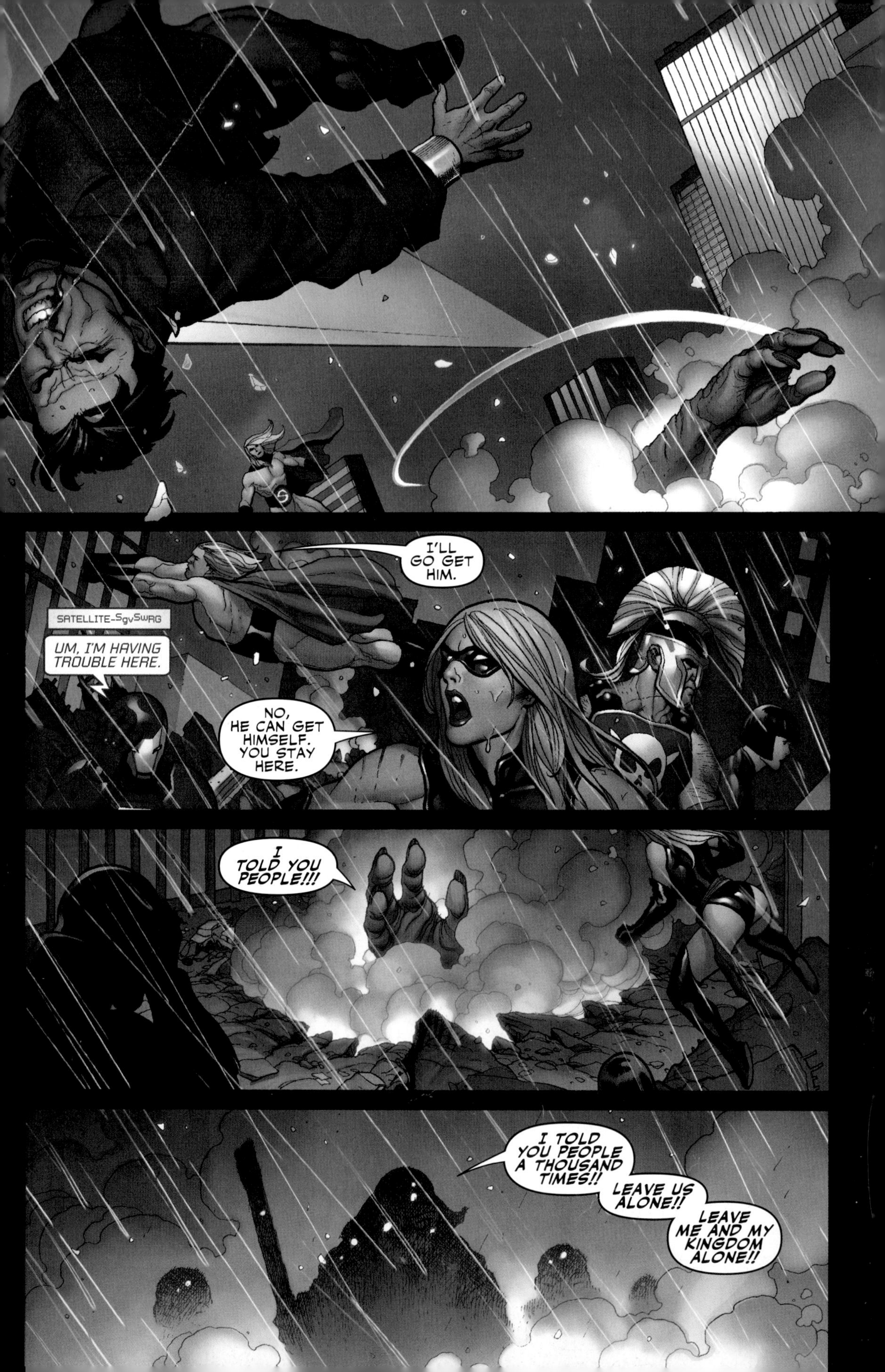
I'LL GO GET HIM.
SATELLITE-SgvSWRG
UM, I'M HAVING TROUBLE HERE.
NO, HE CAN GET HIMSELF. YOU STAY HERE.
I TOLD YOU PEOPLE!!!
I TOLD YOU PEOPLE A THOUSAND TIMES!!
LEAVE US ALONE!!
LEAVE ME AND MY KINGDOM ALONE!!

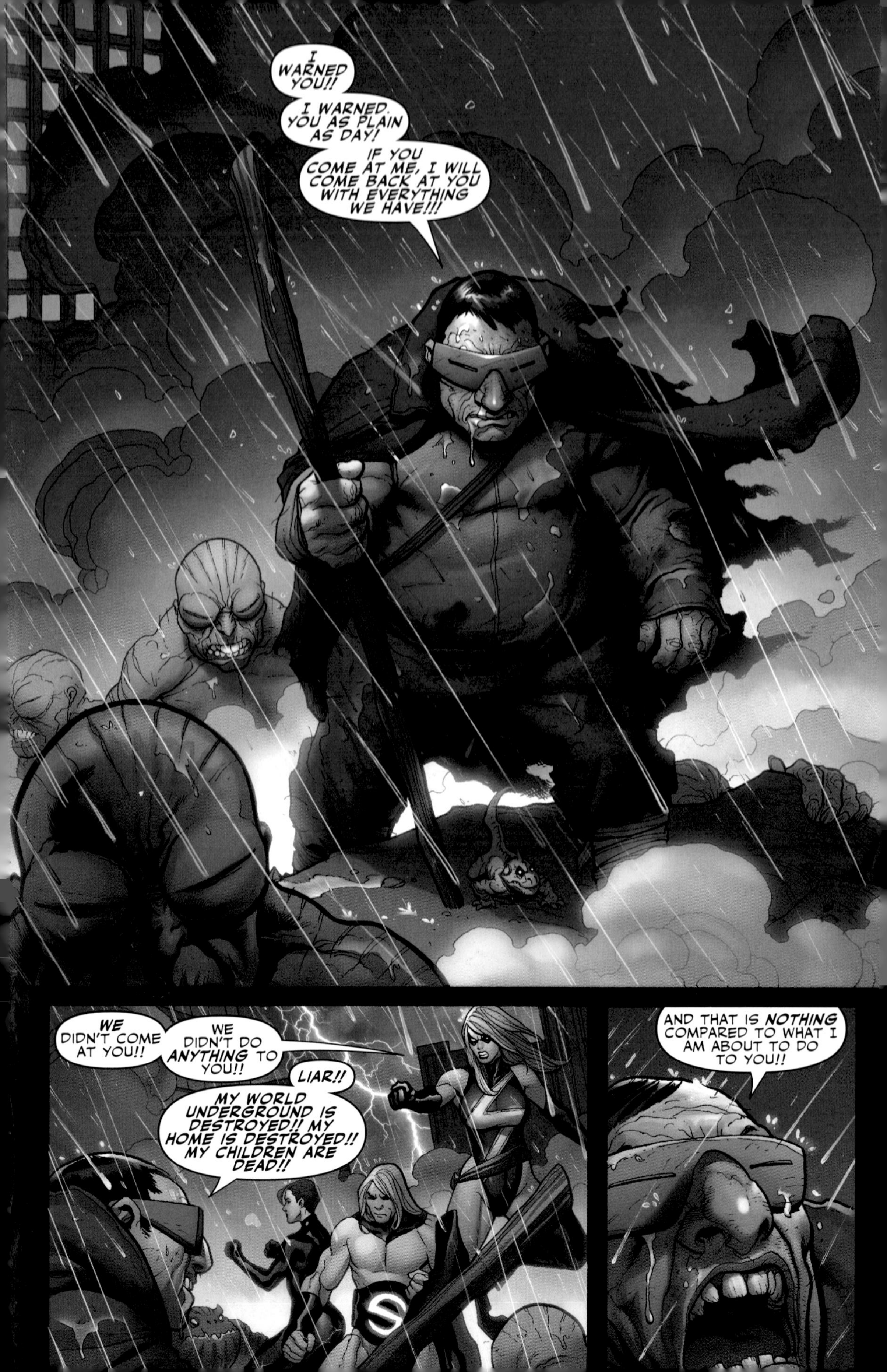
I WARNED YOU!!
I WARNED. YOU AS PLAIN AS DAY!
IF YOU COME AT ME, I WILL COME BACK AT YOU WITH EVERYTHING WE HAVE!!!
WE DIDN'T COME AT YOU!!
WE DIDN'T DO ANYTHING TO YOU!!
LIAR!!
MY WORLD UNDERGROUND IS DESTROYED!! MY HOME IS DESTROYED!! MY CHILDREN ARE DEAD!!
AND THAT IS NOTHING COMPARED TO WHAT I AM ABOUT TO DO TO YOU!!

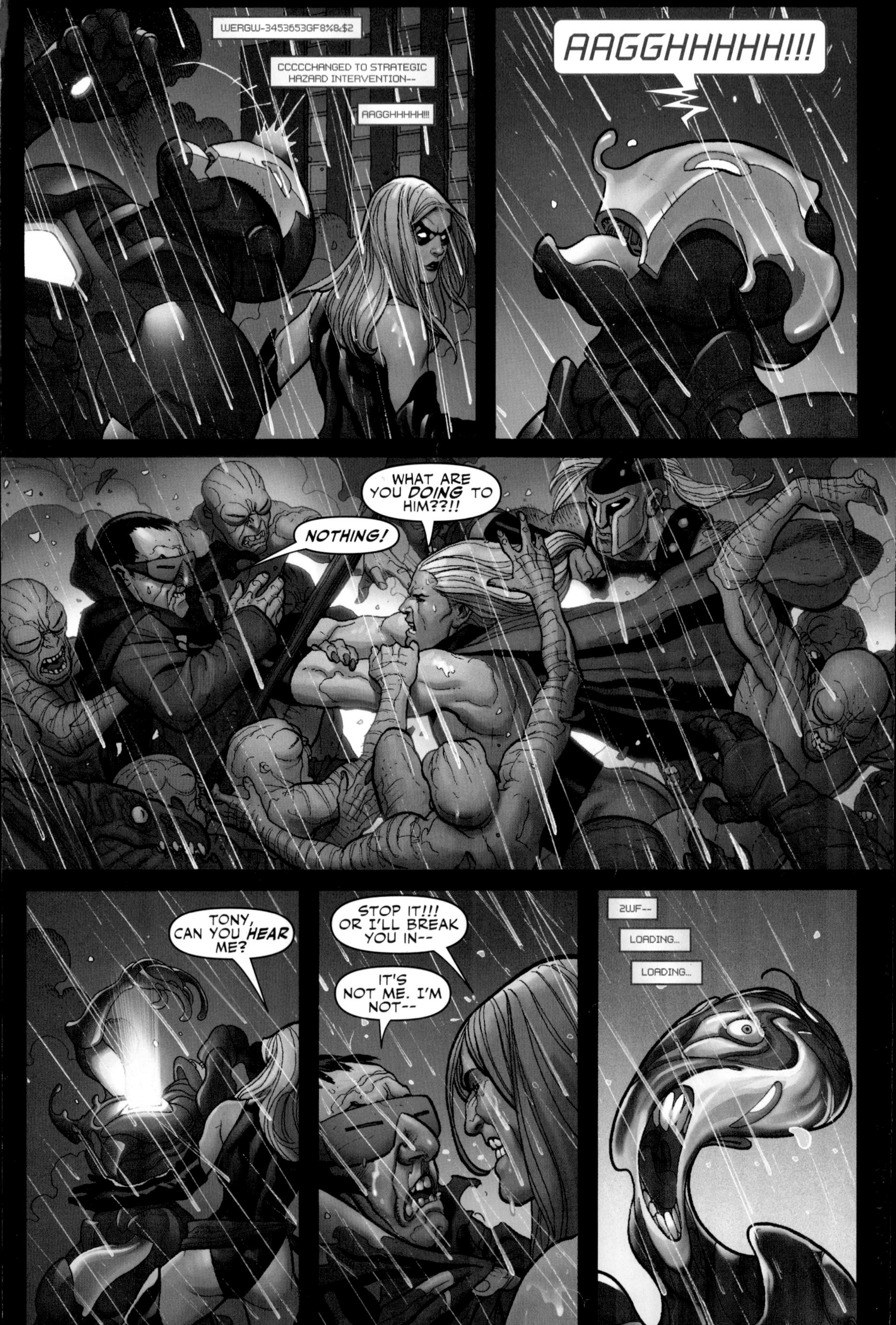

WERGW-3453653GF8%&$2
CCCCCHANGED TO STRATEGIC HAZARD INTERVENTION--
AAGGHHHHH!!!
AAGGHHHHH!!!
WHAT ARE YOU DOING TO HIM??!!
NOTHING!
TONY, CAN YOU HEAR ME?
STOP IT!!! OR I'LL BREAK YOU IN--
IT'S NOT ME. I'M NOT--
2WF--
LOADING...
LOADING...

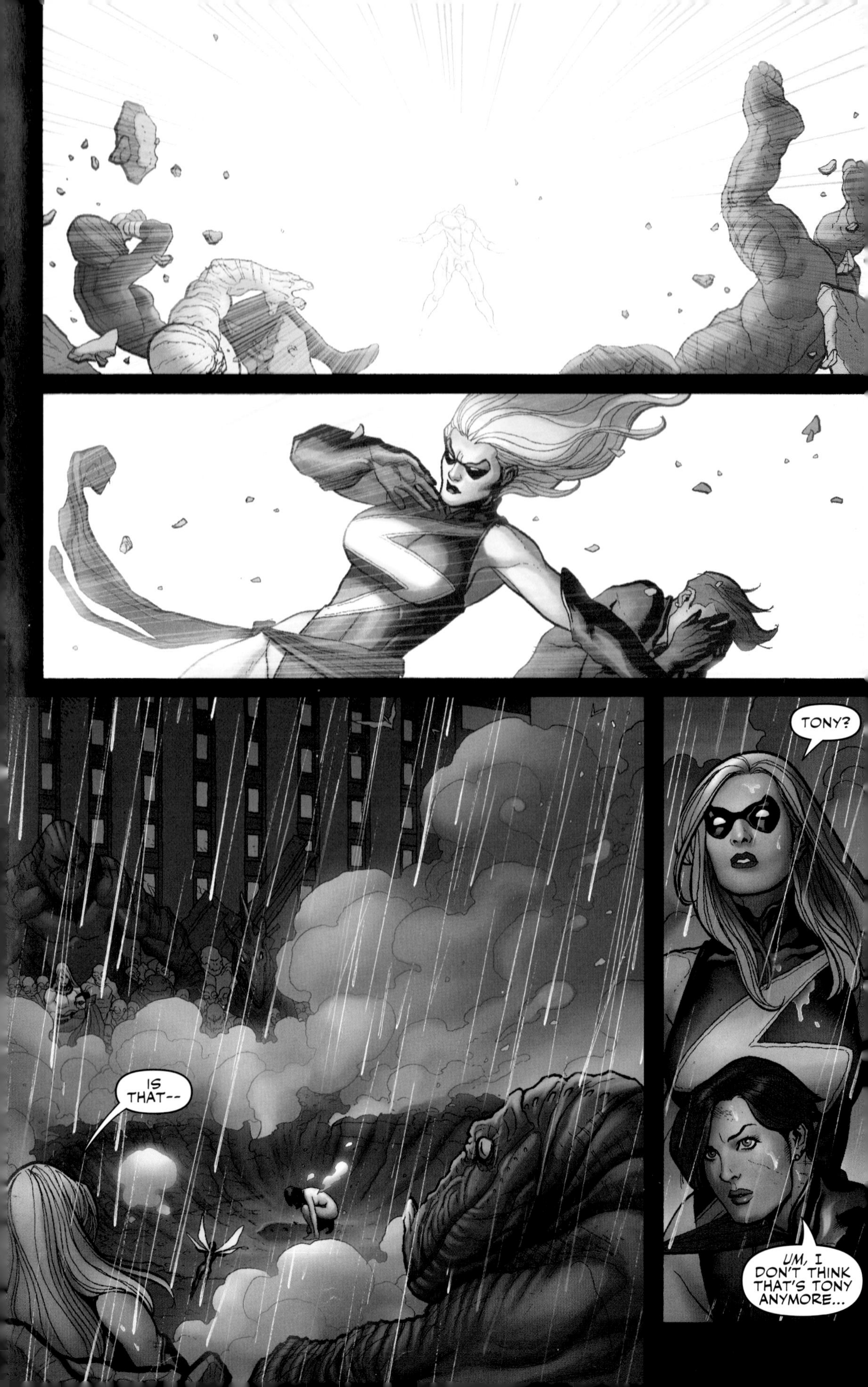
IS THAT--
TONY?
UM, I DON'T THINK THAT'S TONY ANYMORE...

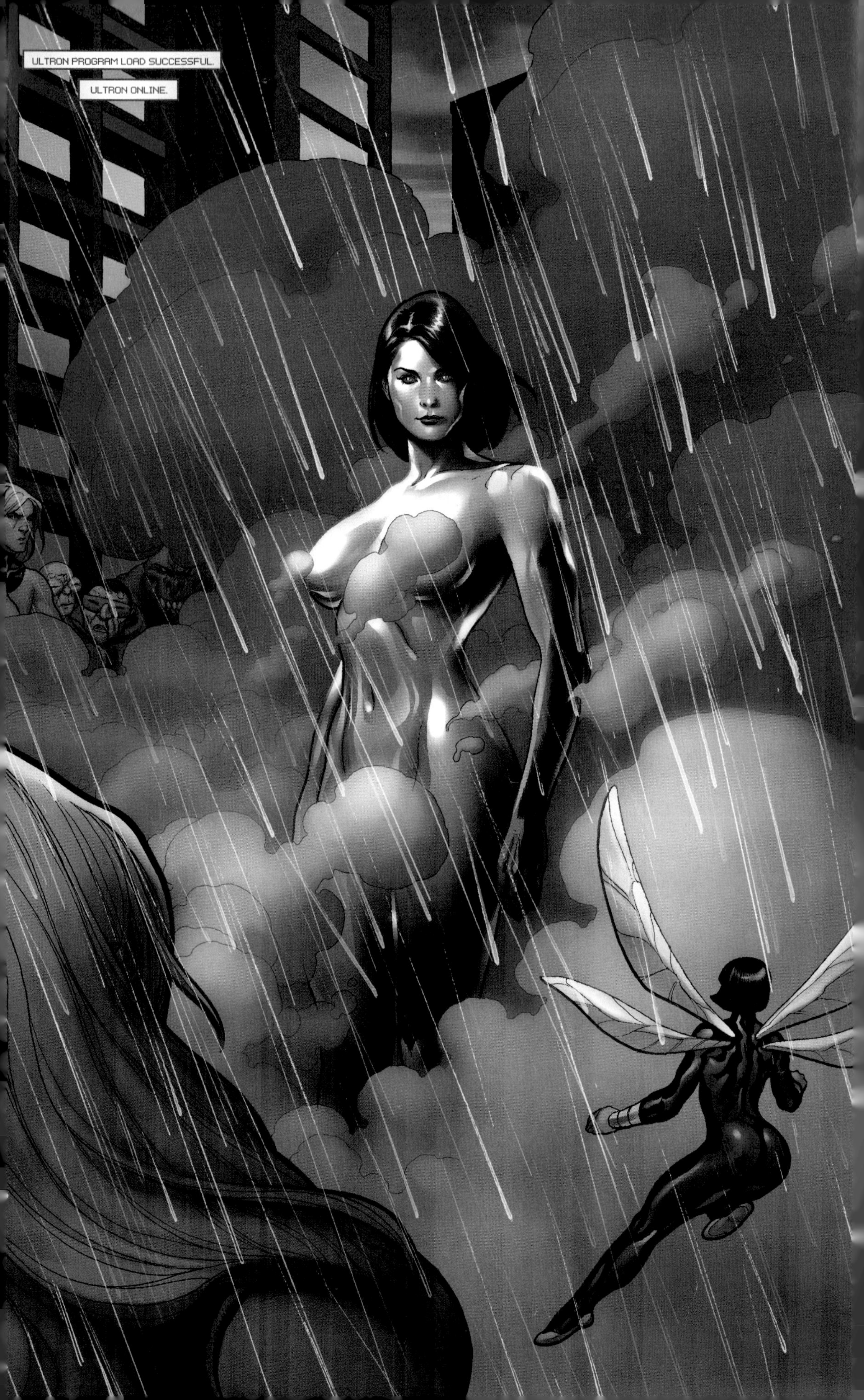
ULTRON PROGRAM LOAD SUCCESSFUL.
ULTRON ONLINE.

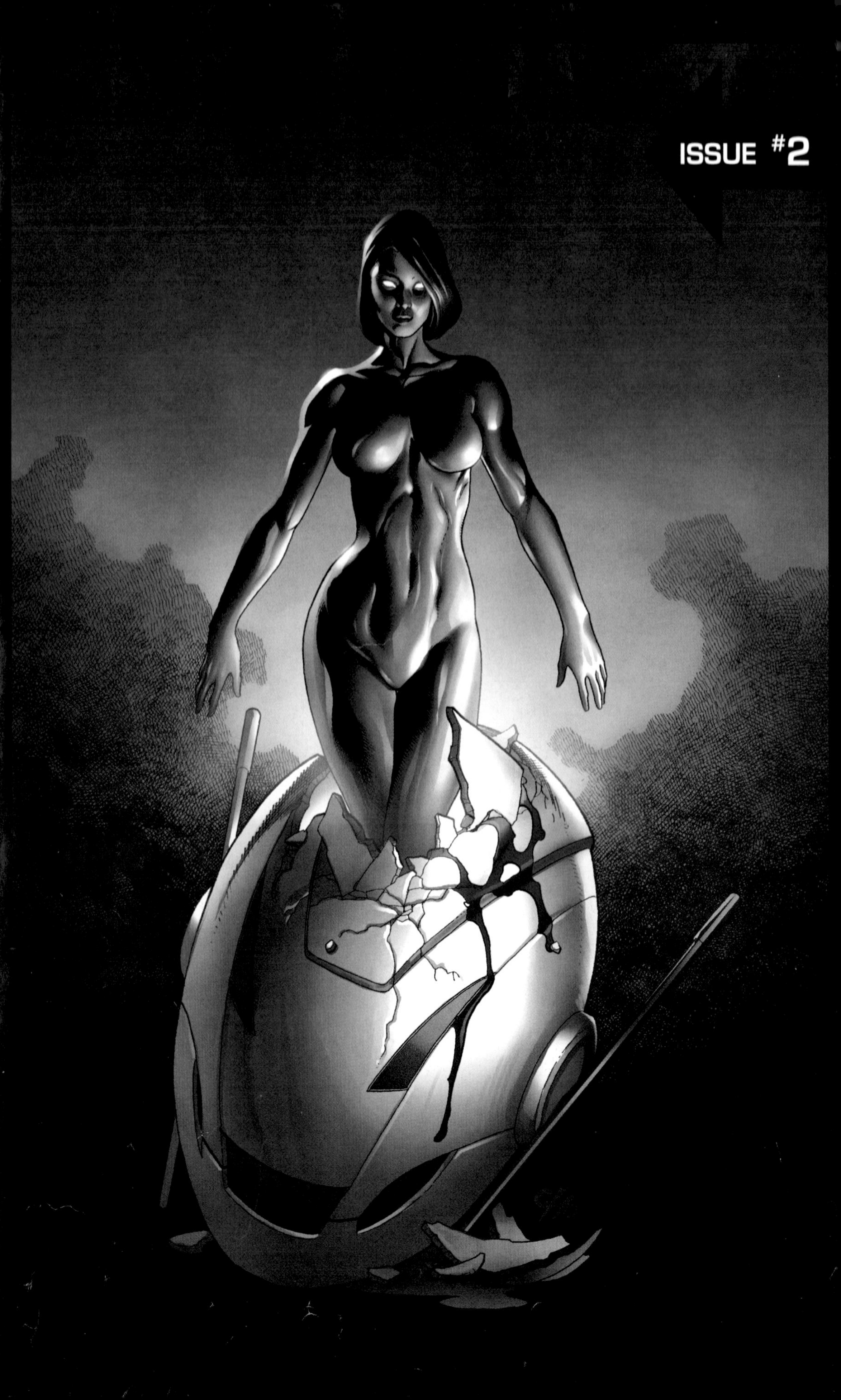
ISSUE #2

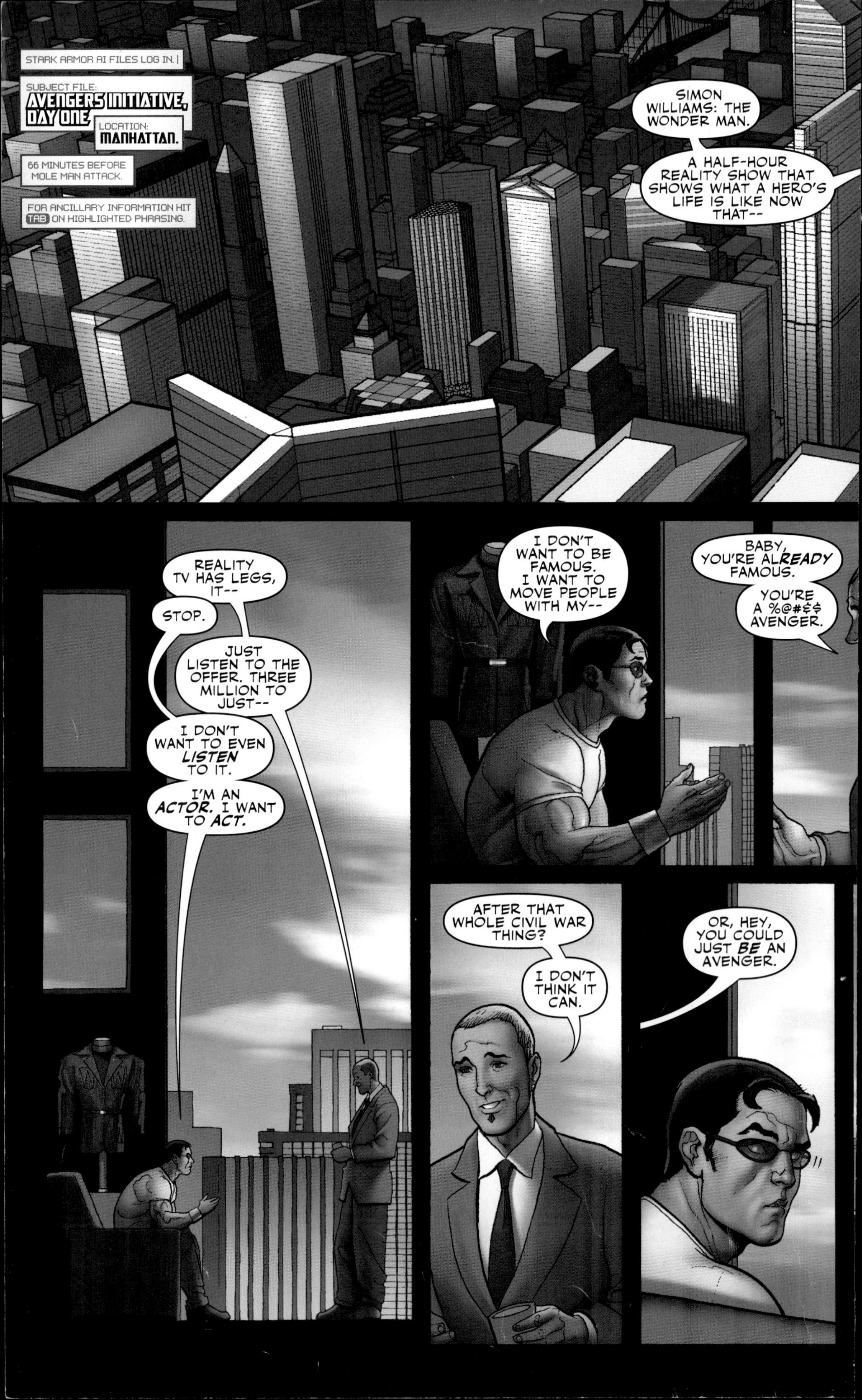

STARK ARMOR AI FILES LOG IN. |
SUBJECT FILE: AVENGERS INITIATIVE, DAY ONE
LOCATION: MANHATTAN.
66 MINUTES BEFORE MOLE MAN ATTACK.
FOR ANCILLARY INFORMATION HIT TAB ON HIGHLIGHTED PHRASING.
SIMON WILLIAMS: THE WONDER MAN.
A HALF-HOUR REALITY SHOW THAT SHOWS WHAT A HERO'S LIFE IS LIKE NOW THAT--
REALITY TV HAS LEGS, IT--
STOP.
JUST LISTEN TO THE OFFER. THREE MILLION TO JUST--
I DON'T WANT TO EVEN LISTEN TO IT.
I'M AN ACTOR. I WANT TO ACT.
I DON'T WANT TO BE FAMOUS. I WANT TO MOVE PEOPLE WITH MY--
BABY, YOU'RE ALREADY FAMOUS.
YOU'RE A %@#$$ AVENGER.
AFTER THAT WHOLE CIVIL WAR THING?
I DON'T THINK IT CAN.
OR, HEY, YOU COULD JUST BE AN AVENGER.

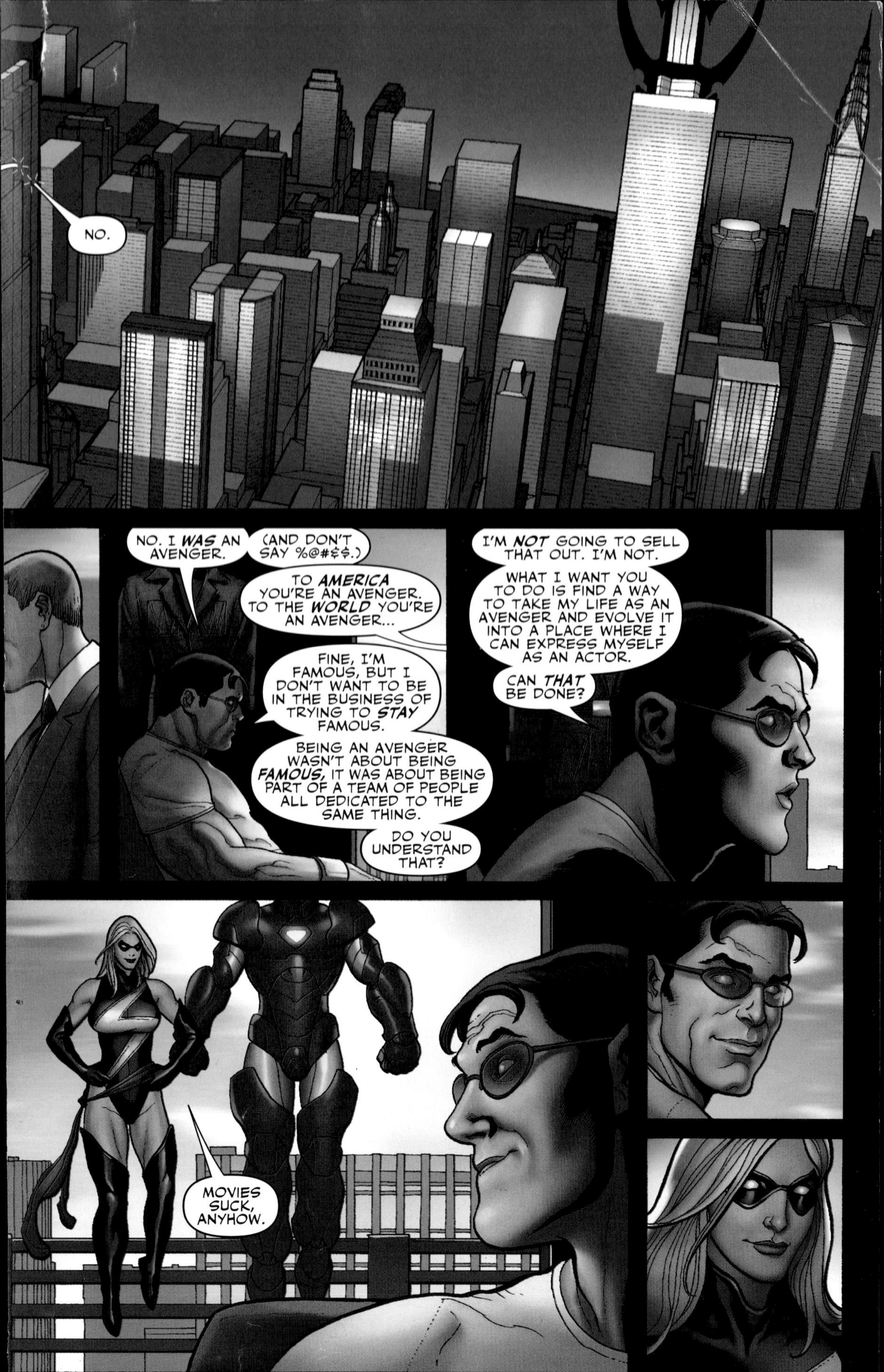
NO.
NO. I *WAS* AN AVENGER.
(AND DON'T SAY %@#$$.)
TO *AMERICA* YOU'RE AN AVENGER. TO THE *WORLD* YOU'RE AN AVENGER...
FINE, I'M FAMOUS, BUT I DON'T WANT TO BE IN THE BUSINESS OF TRYING TO *STAY* FAMOUS.
BEING AN AVENGER WASN'T ABOUT BEING *FAMOUS,* IT WAS ABOUT BEING PART OF A TEAM OF PEOPLE ALL DEDICATED TO THE SAME THING.
DO YOU UNDERSTAND THAT?
I'M *NOT* GOING TO SELL THAT OUT. I'M NOT.
WHAT I WANT YOU TO DO IS FIND A WAY TO TAKE MY LIFE AS AN AVENGER AND EVOLVE IT INTO A PLACE WHERE I CAN EXPRESS MYSELF AS AN ACTOR.
CAN *THAT* BE DONE?
MOVIES SUCK, ANYHOW.

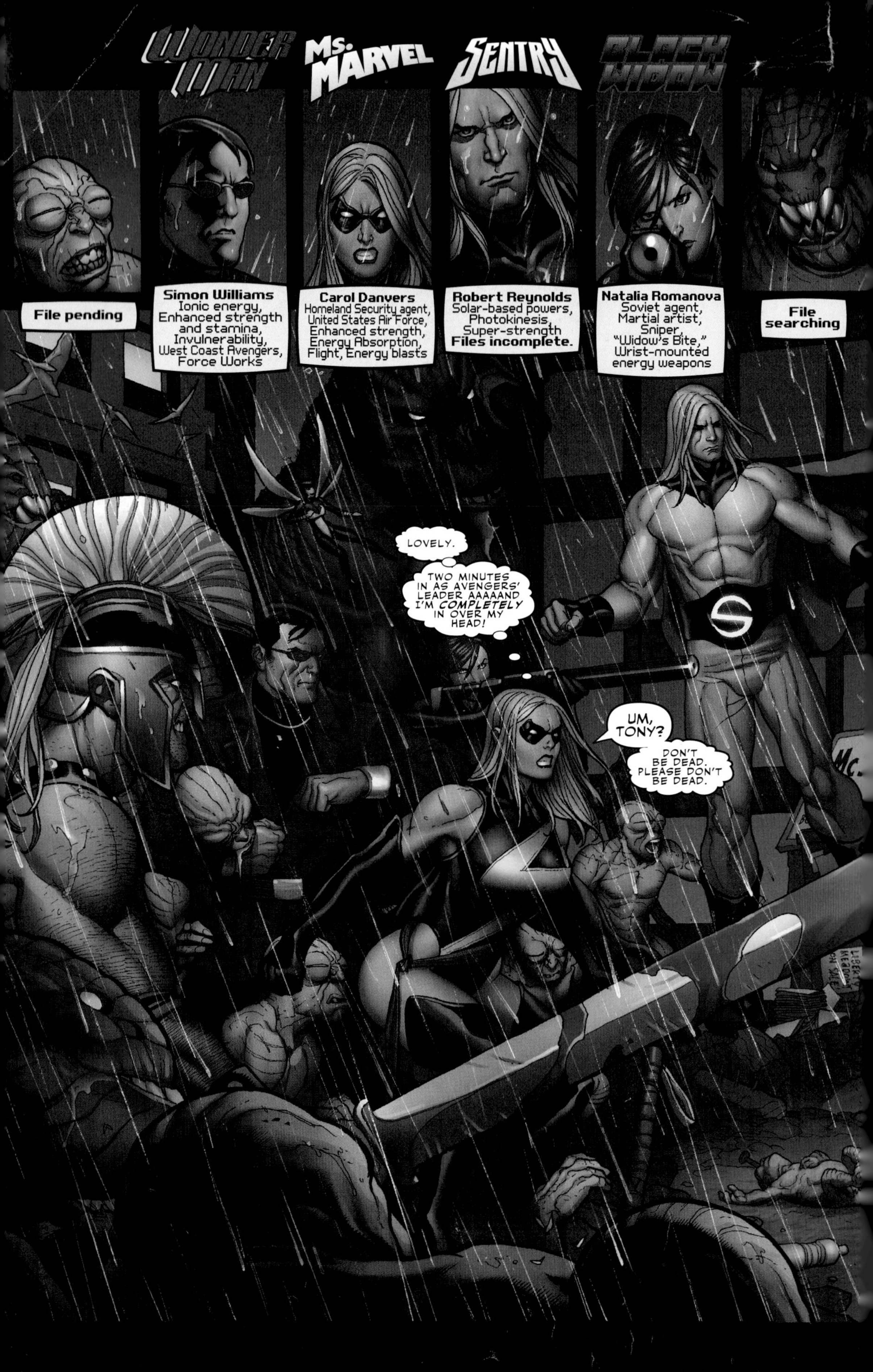
WONDER MAN
Ms. MARVEL
SENTRY
BLACK WIDOW
File pending
Simon Williams Ionic energy, Enhanced strength and stamina, Invulnerability, West Coast Avengers, Force Works
Carol Danvers Homeland Security agent, United States Air Force, Enhanced strength, Energy Absorption, Flight, Energy blasts
Robert Reynolds Solar-based powers, Photokinesis, Super-strength Files incomplete.
Natalia Romanova Soviet agent, Martial artist, Sniper, "Widow's Bite," Wrist-mounted energy weapons
File searching
LOVELY.
TWO MINUTES IN AS AVENGERS' LEADER AAAAAND I'M COMPLETELY IN OVER MY HEAD!
UM, TONY?
DON'T BE DEAD. PLEASE DON'T BE DEAD.

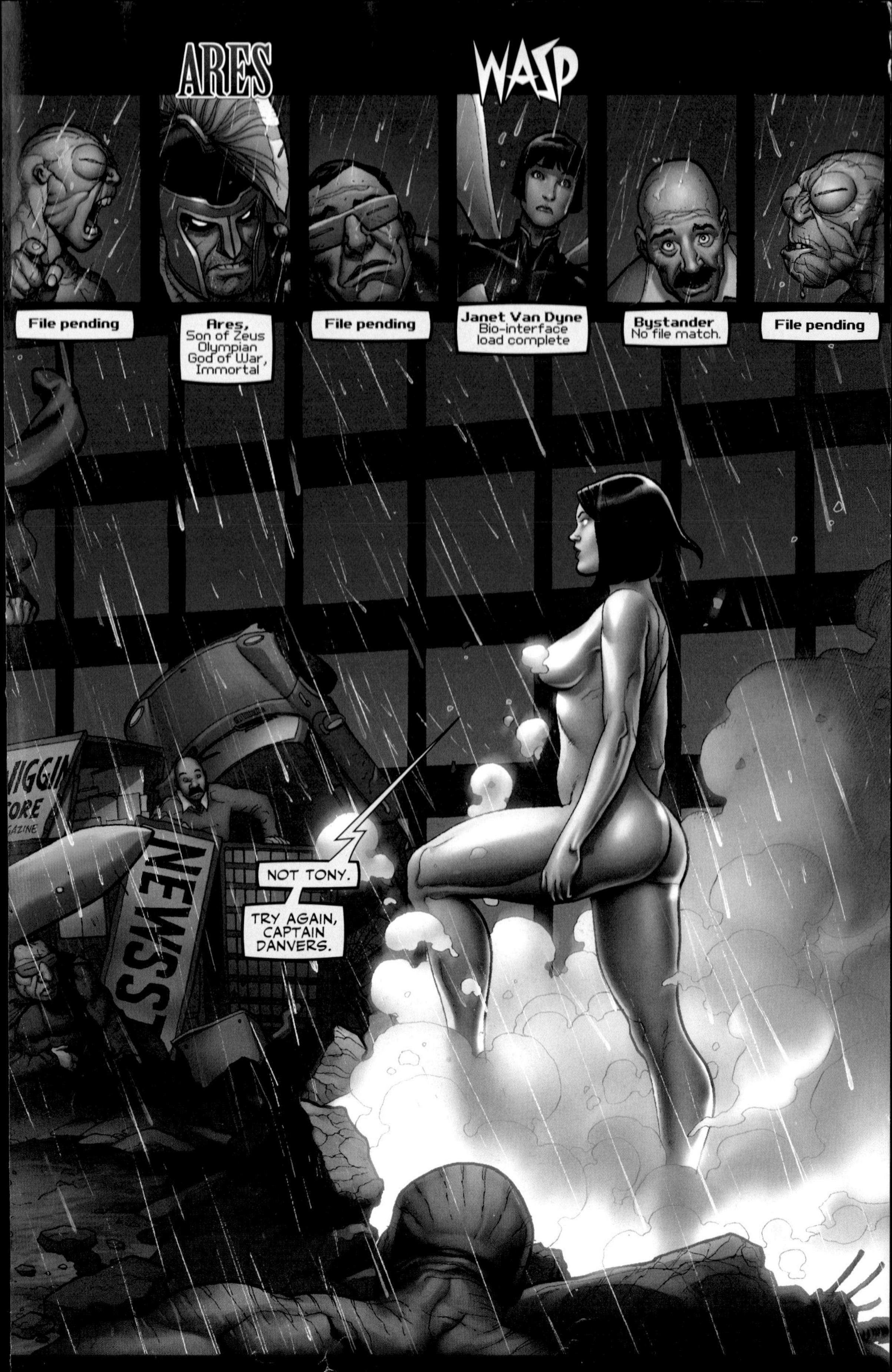

ARES
WASP
File pending
Ares, Son of Zeus Olympian God of War, Immortal
File pending
Janet Van Dyne Bio-interface load complete
Bystander No file match.
File pending
NEWS
NOT TONY.
TRY AGAIN, CAPTAIN DANVERS.

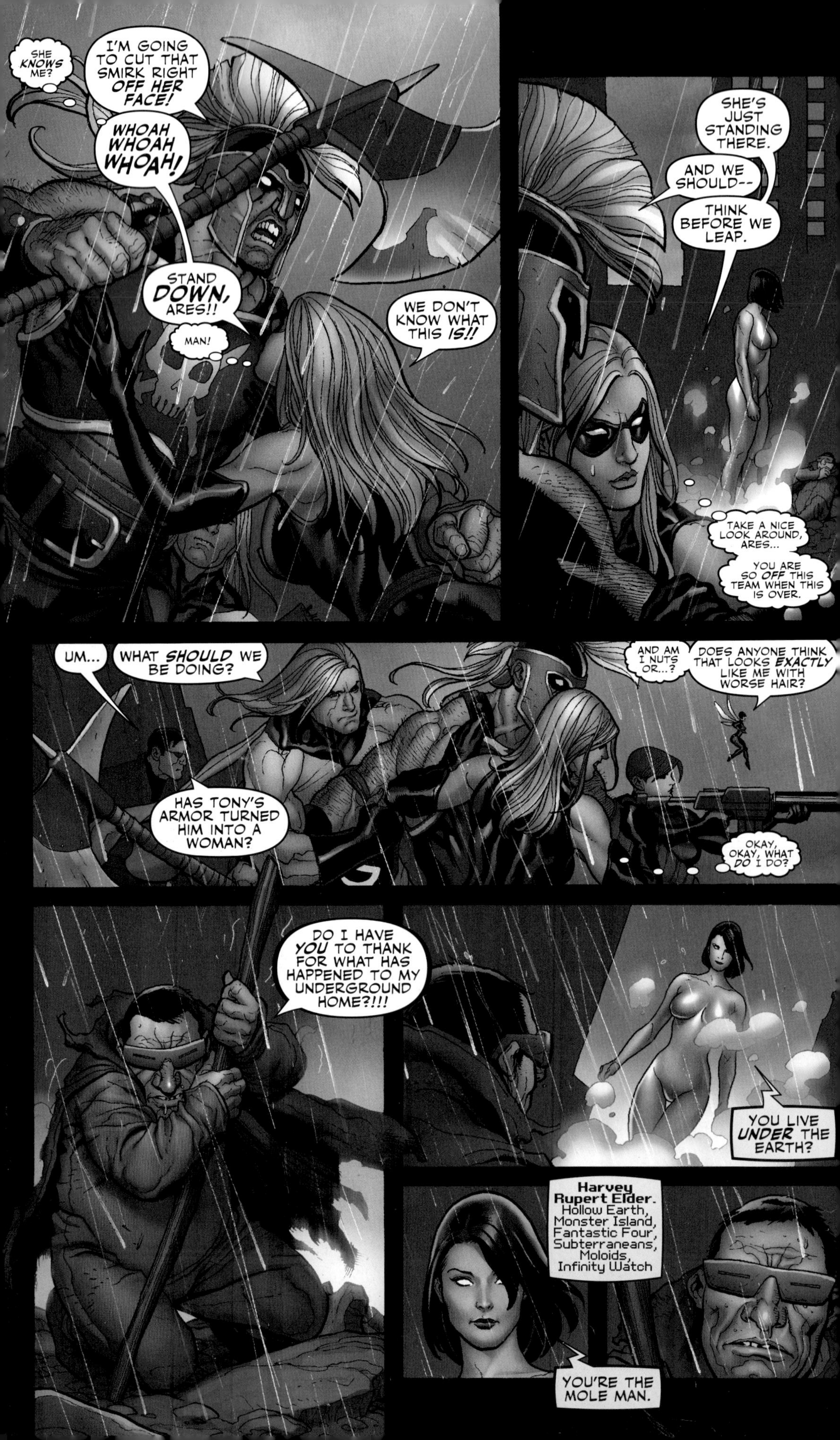
SHE KNOWS ME?
I'M GOING TO CUT THAT SMIRK RIGHT OFF HER FACE!
WHOAH WHOAH WHOAH!
STAND DOWN, ARES!!
MAN!
WE DON'T KNOW WHAT THIS IS!!
SHE'S JUST STANDING THERE.
AND WE SHOULD--
THINK BEFORE WE LEAP.
TAKE A NICE LOOK AROUND, ARES...
YOU ARE SO OFF THIS TEAM WHEN THIS IS OVER.
UM...
WHAT SHOULD WE BE DOING?
HAS TONY'S ARMOR TURNED HIM INTO A WOMAN?
AND AM I NUTS OR...?
DOES ANYONE THINK THAT LOOKS EXACTLY LIKE ME WITH WORSE HAIR?
OKAY, OKAY, WHAT DO I DO?
DO I HAVE YOU TO THANK FOR WHAT HAS HAPPENED TO MY UNDERGROUND HOME?!!!
YOU LIVE UNDER THE EARTH?
Harvey Rupert Elder. Hollow Earth, Monster Island, Fantastic Four, Subterraneans, Moloids, Infinity Watch
YOU'RE THE MOLE MAN.

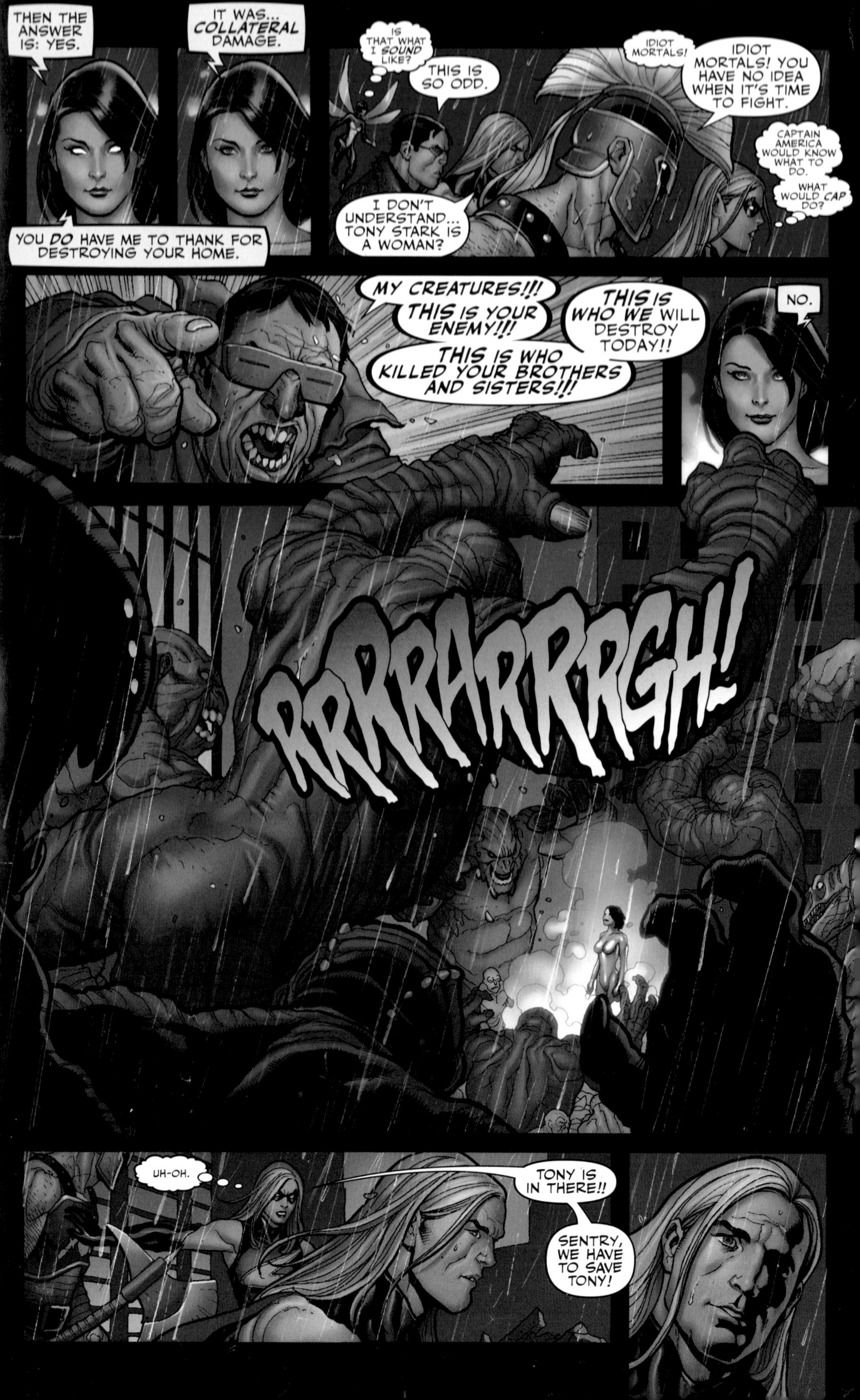
THEN THE ANSWER IS: YES.
IT WAS... COLLATERAL DAMAGE.
YOU DO HAVE ME TO THANK FOR DESTROYING YOUR HOME.
IS THAT WHAT I SOUND LIKE?
THIS IS SO ODD.
I DON'T UNDERSTAND... TONY STARK IS A WOMAN?
IDIOT MORTALS!
IDIOT MORTALS! YOU HAVE NO IDEA WHEN IT'S TIME TO FIGHT.
CAPTAIN AMERICA WOULD KNOW WHAT TO DO.
WHAT WOULD CAP DO?
MY CREATURES!!! THIS IS YOUR ENEMY!!!
THIS IS WHO KILLED YOUR BROTHERS AND SISTERS!!!
THIS IS WHO WE WILL DESTROY TODAY!!
NO.
RRRRARRRGH!
UH-OH.
TONY IS IN THERE!!
SENTRY, WE HAVE TO SAVE TONY!

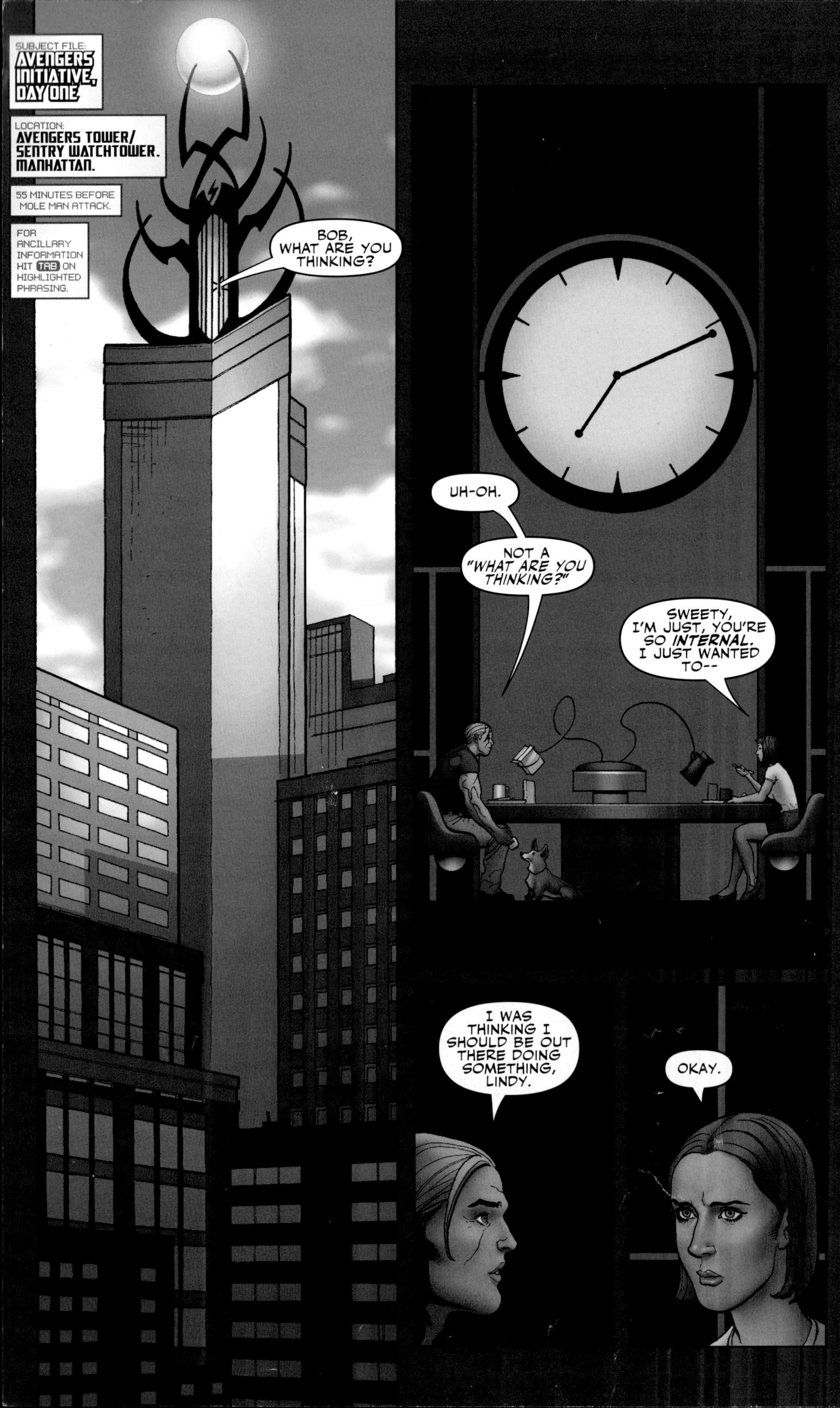
SUBJECT FILE:
AVENGERS INITIATIVE, DAY ONE
LOCATION:
AVENGERS TOWER/ SENTRY WATCHTOWER. MANHATTAN.
55 MINUTES BEFORE MOLE MAN ATTACK.
FOR ANCILLARY INFORMATION HIT TAB ON HIGHLIGHTED PHRASING.
BOB, WHAT ARE YOU THINKING?
UH-OH.
NOT A "WHAT ARE YOU THINKING?"
SWEETY, I'M JUST, YOU'RE SO INTERNAL. I JUST WANTED TO--
I WAS THINKING I SHOULD BE OUT THERE DOING SOMETHING, LINDY.
OKAY.

I'M-- I'M NOT ALWAYS SURE WHAT I'M SUPPOSED TO BE DOING.

I DON'T UNDERSTAND--

THERE'S FIFTY THINGS GOING ON IN THIS CITY EVERY SECOND OF THE DAY THAT THE SENTRY COULD DO SOMETHING ABOUT.

AND THAT'S JUST IN *THIS* CITY.

A BANK ROBBERY IN QUEENS IS LESS OR MORE IMPORTANT THAN A HURRICANE IN LOUISIANA?

HOW CAN I CHOOSE? I CAN'T. I CAN'T ALWAYS BE WHERE I'M MOST NEEDED.

YOU SAID "THE SENTRY" AGAIN.

WHAT?

YOU SAID THE SENTRY LIKE IT'S ANOTHER PERSON. WE AGREED YOU WOULDN'T DO THAT.

DID I?

HAVE YOU TALKED TO YOUR THERAPIST ABOUT THIS?

ITS *ALL* WE TALK ABOUT.

CAROL DANVERS AND TONY STARK ARE REQUESTING ENTRANCE.

OH, COOL.

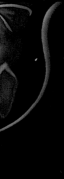

MORNING, BOB, LINDY...

GET YOUR SENTRY SUIT ON, IT'S TIME TO GO TO WORK.

WHAT NOW?

WE'RE PUTTING TOGETHER A NEW ROSTER FOR THE AVENGERS AND BOB'S GOING TO BE THE--

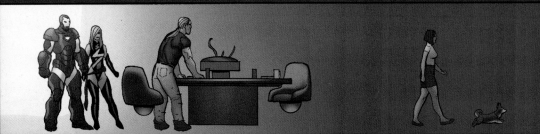

AWKWARD.

LINDY? WHAT WAS THAT?

I DON'T KNOW. THAT'S WHY I WILL NEVER GET MARRIED, IS WHAT THAT WAS.

BOB, I KNOW YOU AND TONY HAVE SOME UNDERSTANDINGS AND I RESPECT THAT. BUT...

WHAT IS THIS?

HOW DO I SAY THIS?

...HOW DO I SAY THIS?

YOU SCARE ME.

I SCARE MYSELF.

OKAY... NOW I FEEL BETTER.

YOU'RE MORE POWERFUL THAN ALL OF US. YOU'D BE AN ASSET TO THE TEAM, NO QUESTION.

BUT I NEED TO KNOW IF I CAN COUNT ON YOU TO KNOW WHEN YOU'RE NOT GOING TO BE ABLE TO DO IT. DO YOU UNDERSTAND?

IF YOU FEEL LIKE IT'S ALL COMING APART ON YOU--IN YOUR HEAD-- I NEED YOU TO TELL US.

EVEN IN THE HEAT OF BATTLE.

CAN YOU PROMISE ME THAT, BOB?

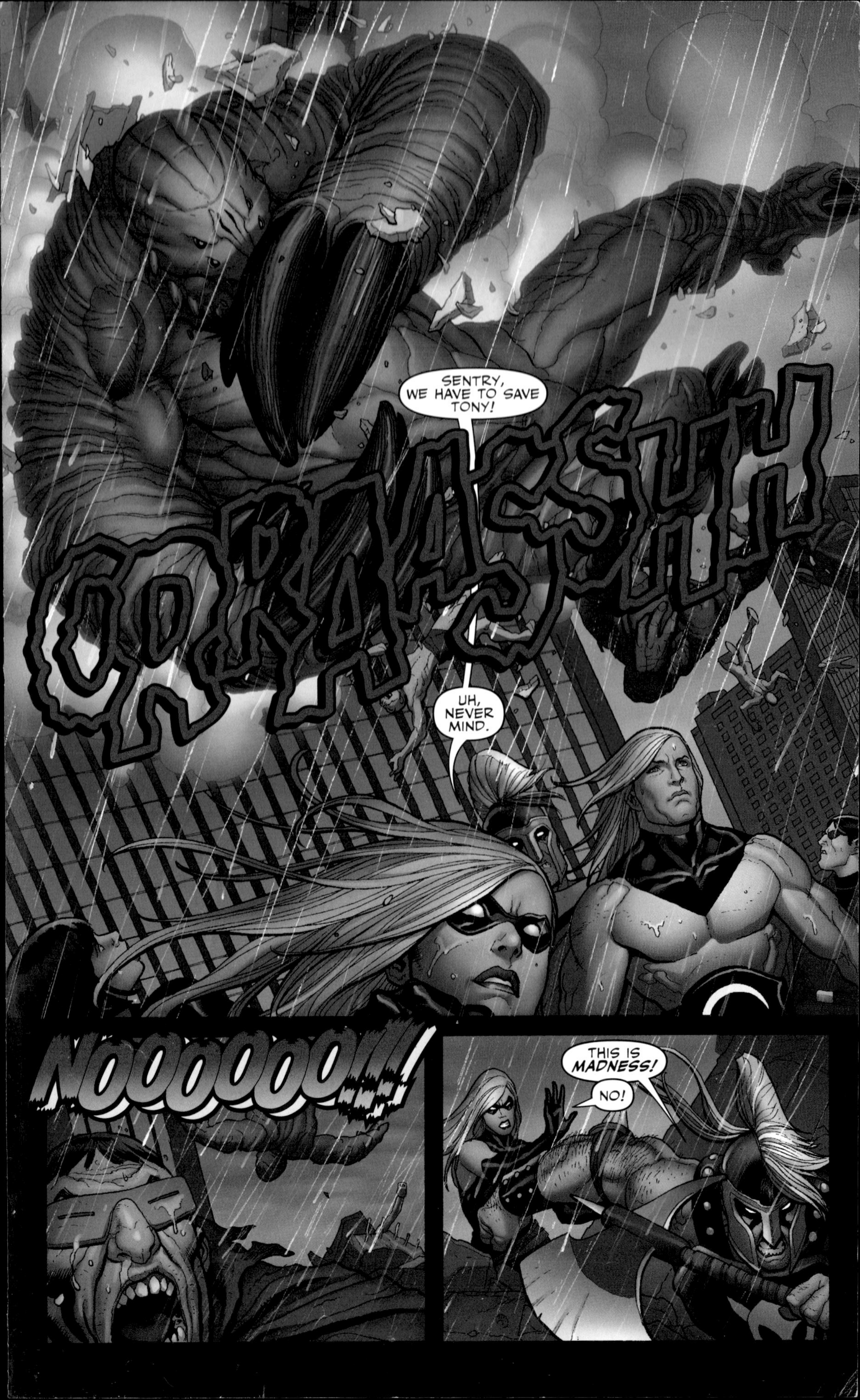
SENTRY, WE HAVE TO SAVE TONY!
CRAAASSHH
UH, NEVER MIND.
NOOOOOO!!!
THIS IS MADNESS!
NO!

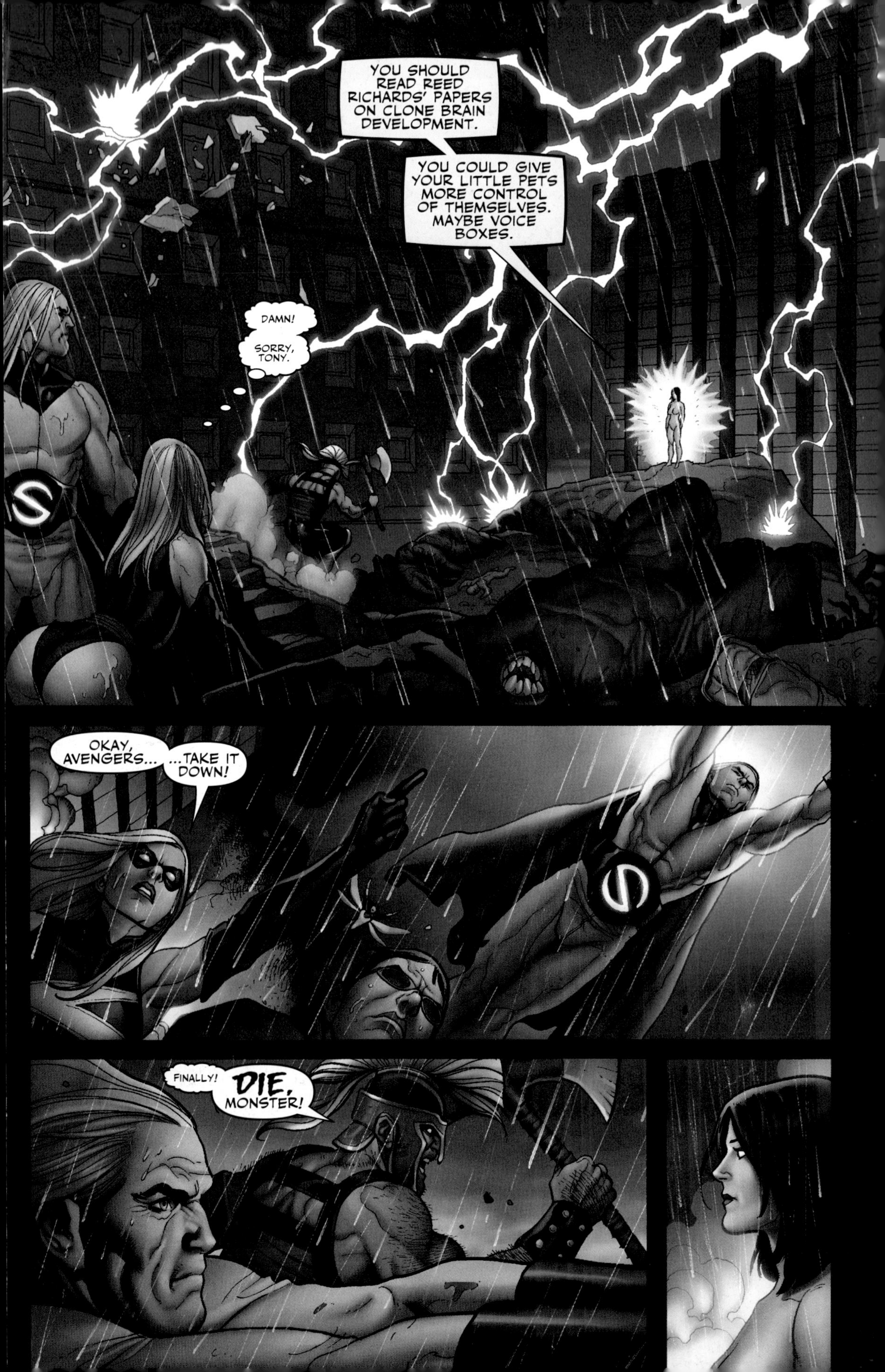
YOU SHOULD READ REED RICHARDS' PAPERS ON CLONE BRAIN DEVELOPMENT.
YOU COULD GIVE YOUR LITTLE PETS MORE CONTROL OF THEMSELVES. MAYBE VOICE BOXES.
DAMN!
SORRY, TONY.
OKAY, AVENGERS...
...TAKE IT DOWN!
FINALLY!
DIE, MONSTER!

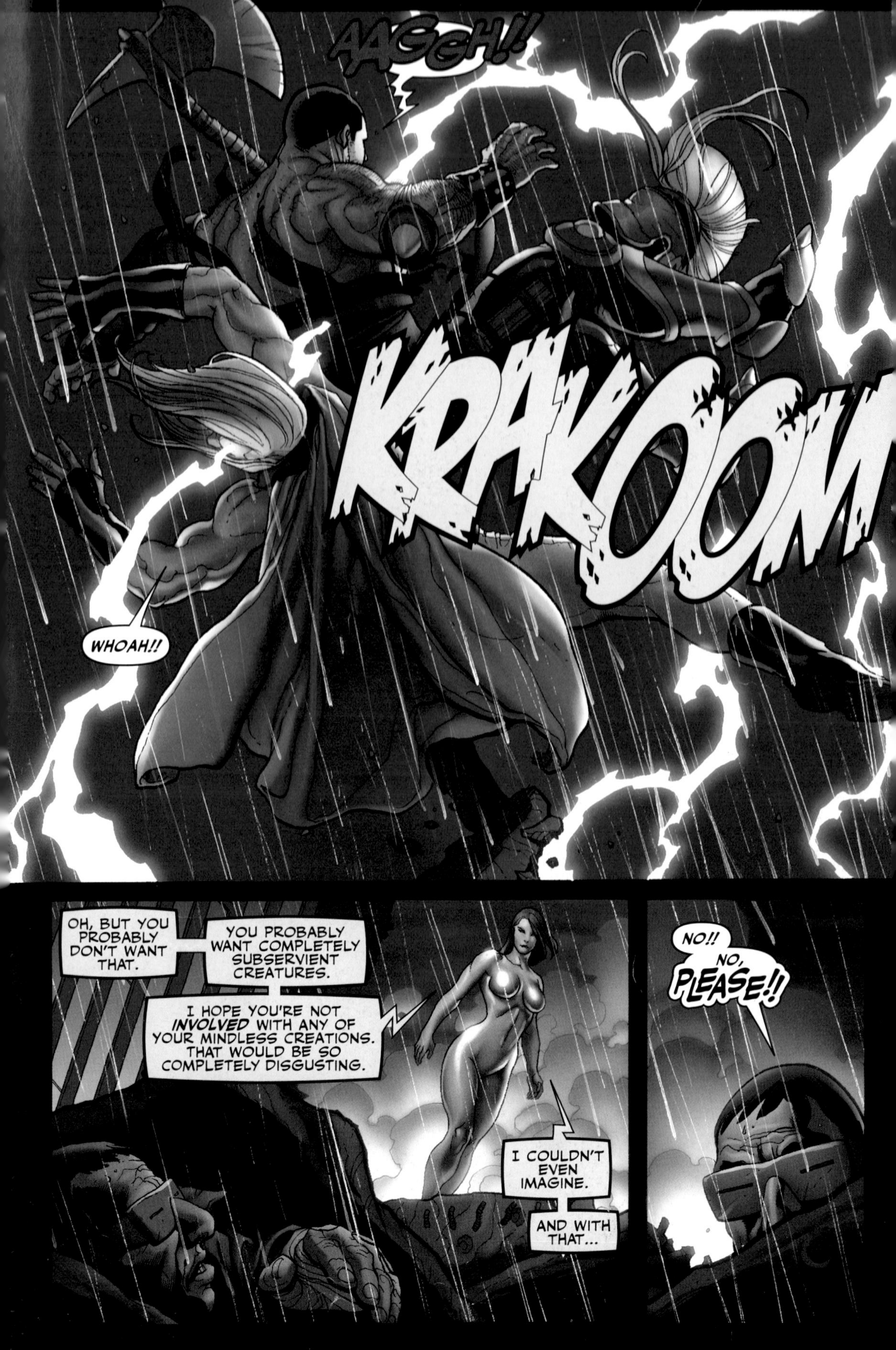

AAGGH!!
KRAKOOM
WHOAH!!
OH, BUT YOU PROBABLY DON'T WANT THAT.
YOU PROBABLY WANT COMPLETELY SUBSERVIENT CREATURES.
I HOPE YOU'RE NOT *INVOLVED* WITH ANY OF YOUR MINDLESS CREATIONS. THAT WOULD BE SO COMPLETELY DISGUSTING.
I COULDN'T EVEN IMAGINE.
AND WITH THAT...
NO!!
NO, PLEASE!!

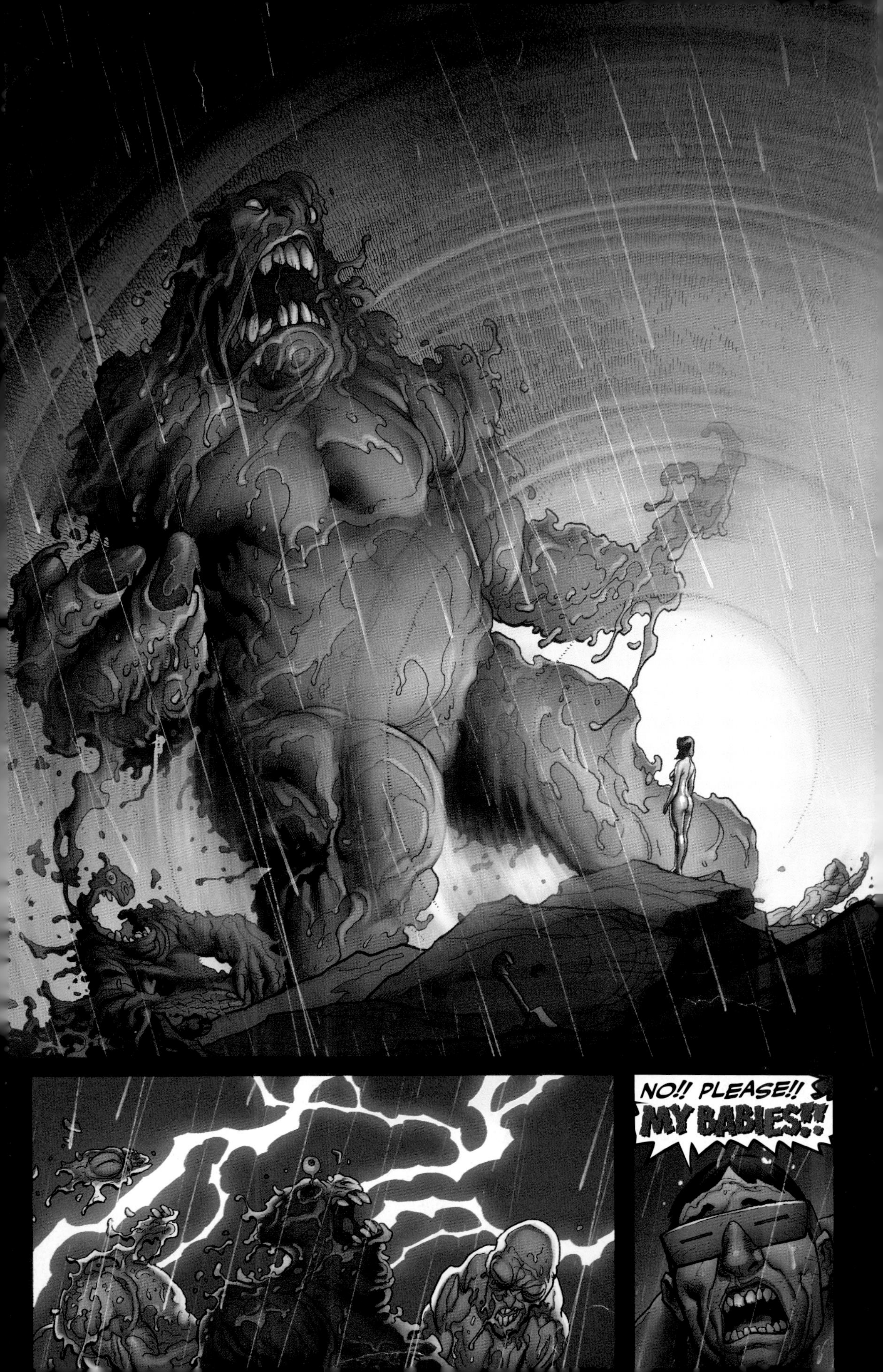
NO!! PLEASE!!
MY BABIES!!

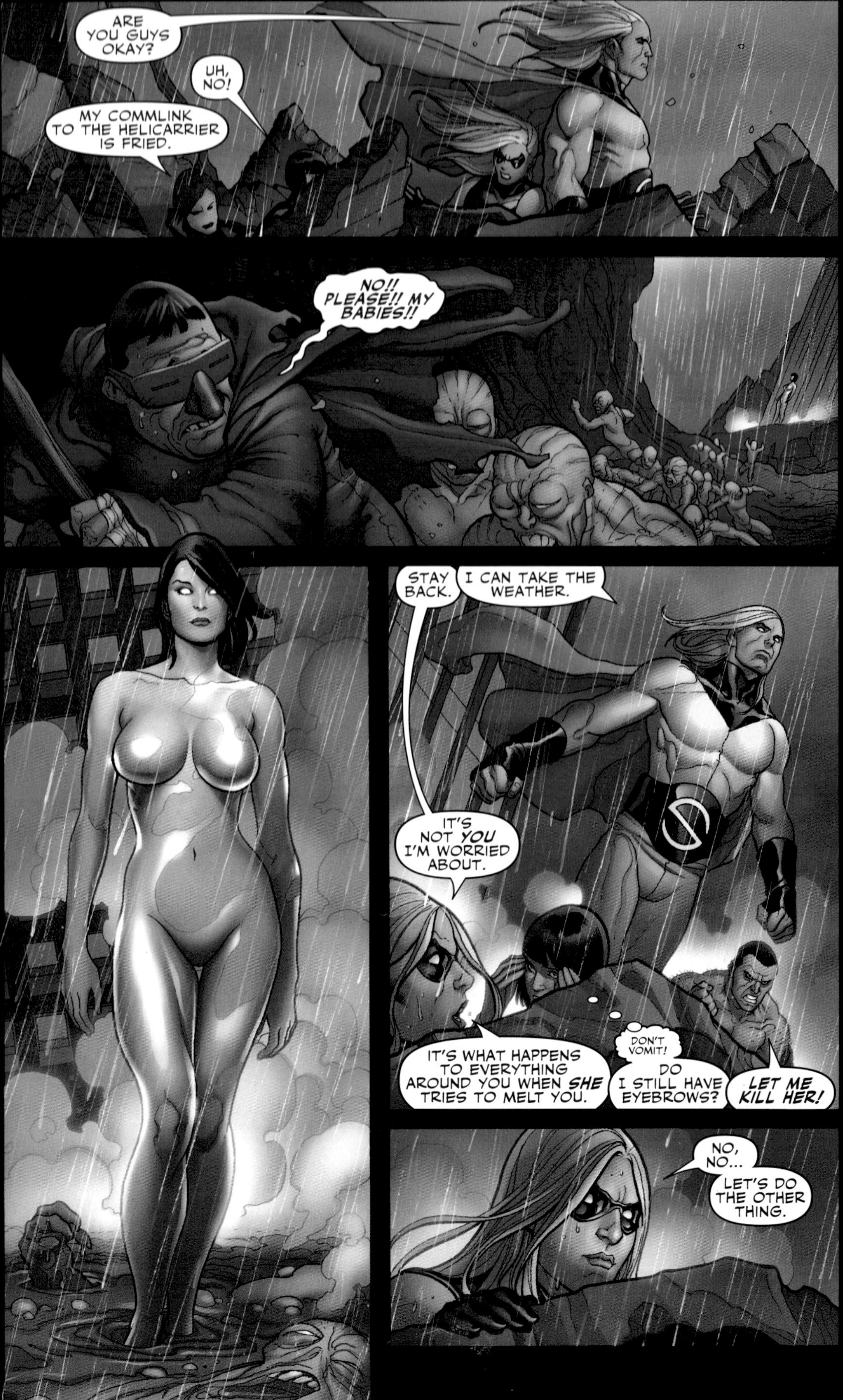
ARE YOU GUYS OKAY?
UH, NO!
MY COMMLINK TO THE HELICARRIER IS FRIED.
NO!! PLEASE!! MY BABIES!!
STAY BACK.
I CAN TAKE THE WEATHER.
IT'S NOT *YOU* I'M WORRIED ABOUT.
IT'S WHAT HAPPENS TO EVERYTHING AROUND YOU WHEN *SHE* TRIES TO MELT YOU.
DON'T VOMIT!
DO I STILL HAVE EYEBROWS?
*LET ME KILL HER!*
NO, NO...
LET'S DO THE OTHER THING.

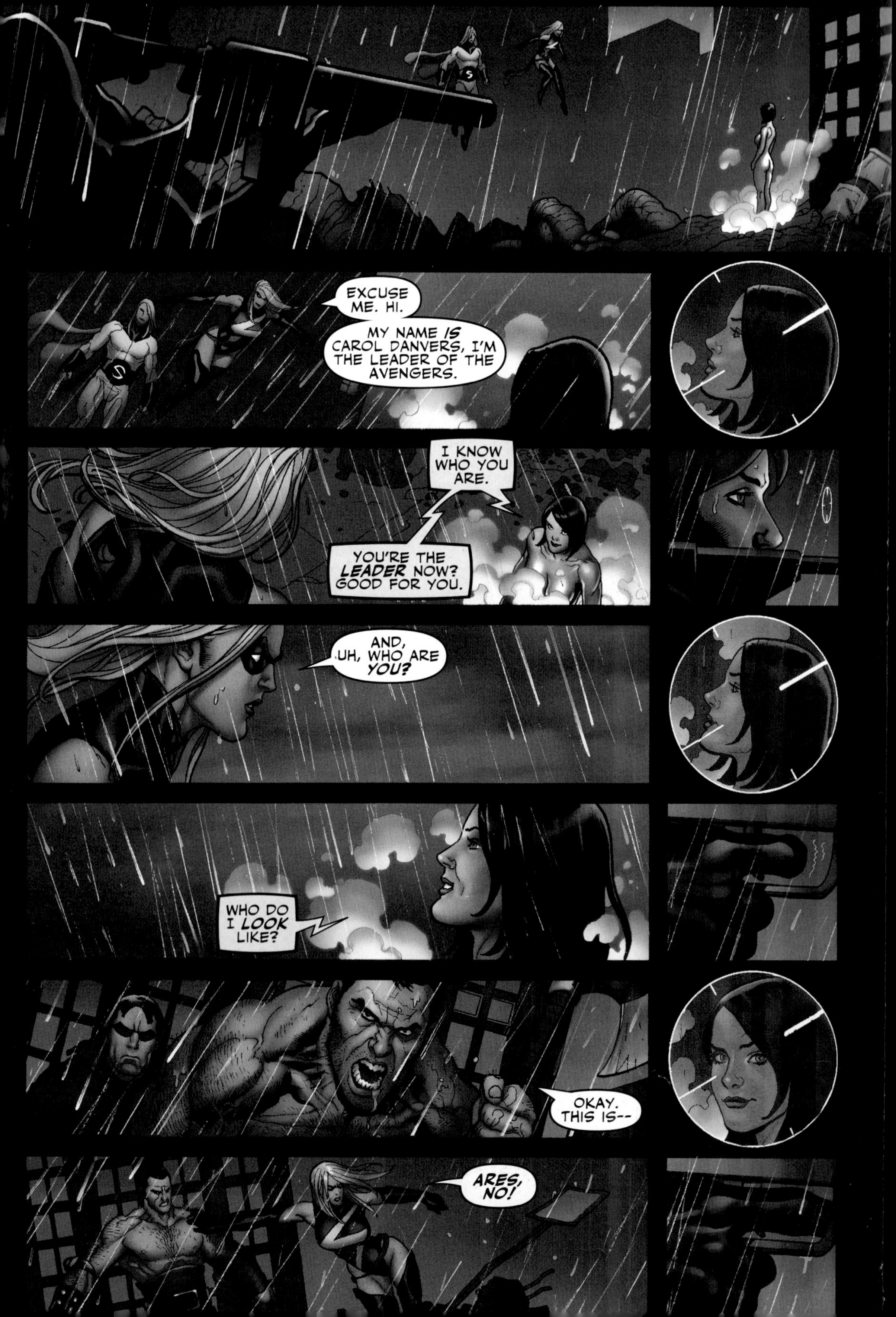

EXCUSE ME. HI.
MY NAME *IS* CAROL DANVERS, I'M THE LEADER OF THE AVENGERS.
I KNOW WHO YOU ARE.
YOU'RE THE ***LEADER*** NOW? GOOD FOR YOU.
AND, UH, WHO ARE *YOU?*
WHO DO I *LOOK* LIKE?
OKAY. THIS IS--
*ARES, NO!*

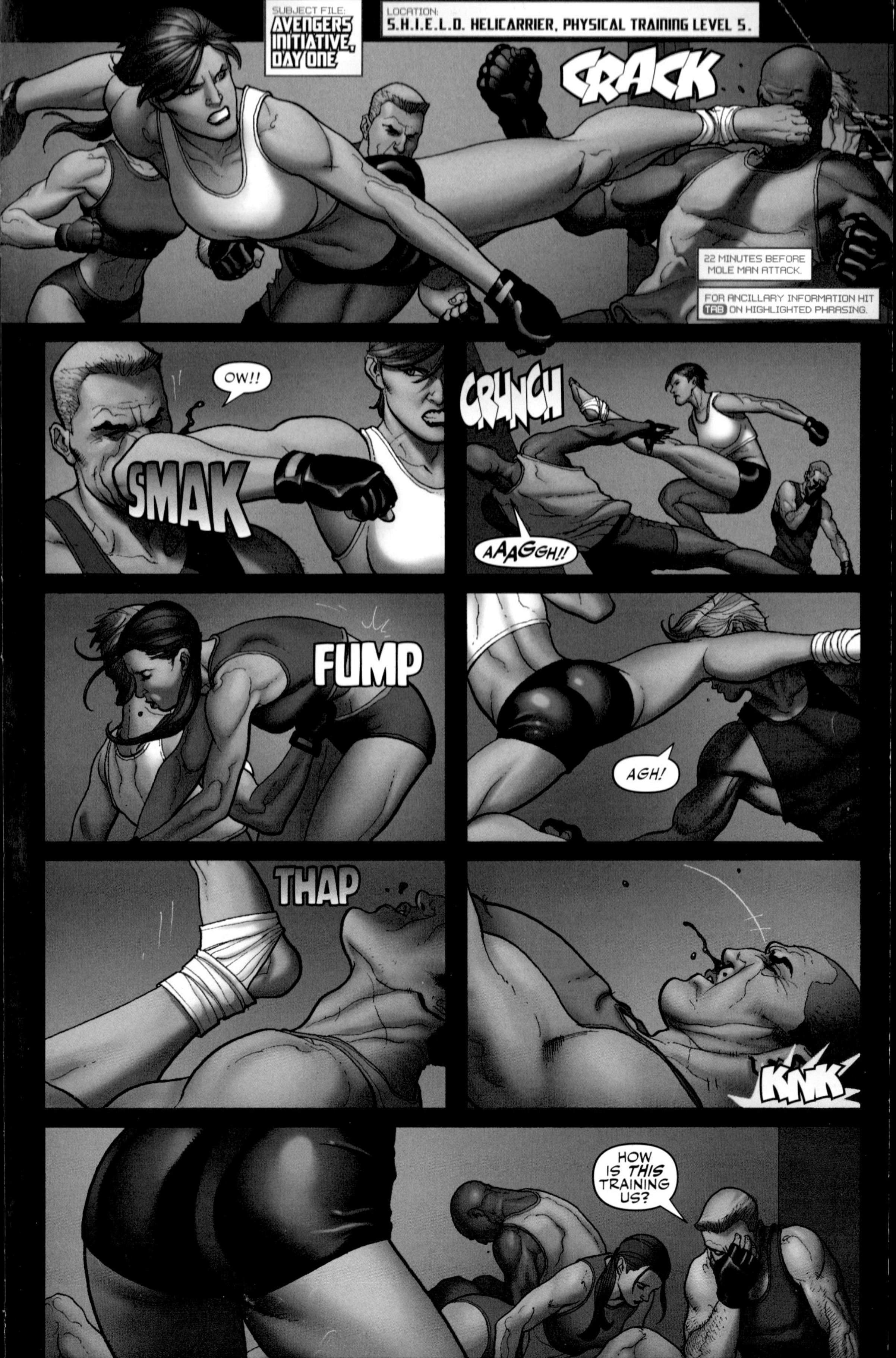
SUBJECT FILE:
AVENGERS INITIATIVE, DAY ONE
LOCATION:
S.H.I.E.L.D. HELICARRIER, PHYSICAL TRAINING LEVEL 5.
CRACK
22 MINUTES BEFORE MOLE MAN ATTACK.
FOR ANCILLARY INFORMATION HIT TAB ON HIGHLIGHTED PHRASING.
OW!!
SMAK
CRUNCH
AAAGGH!!
FUMP
AGH!
THAP
KNK
HOW IS THIS TRAINING US?

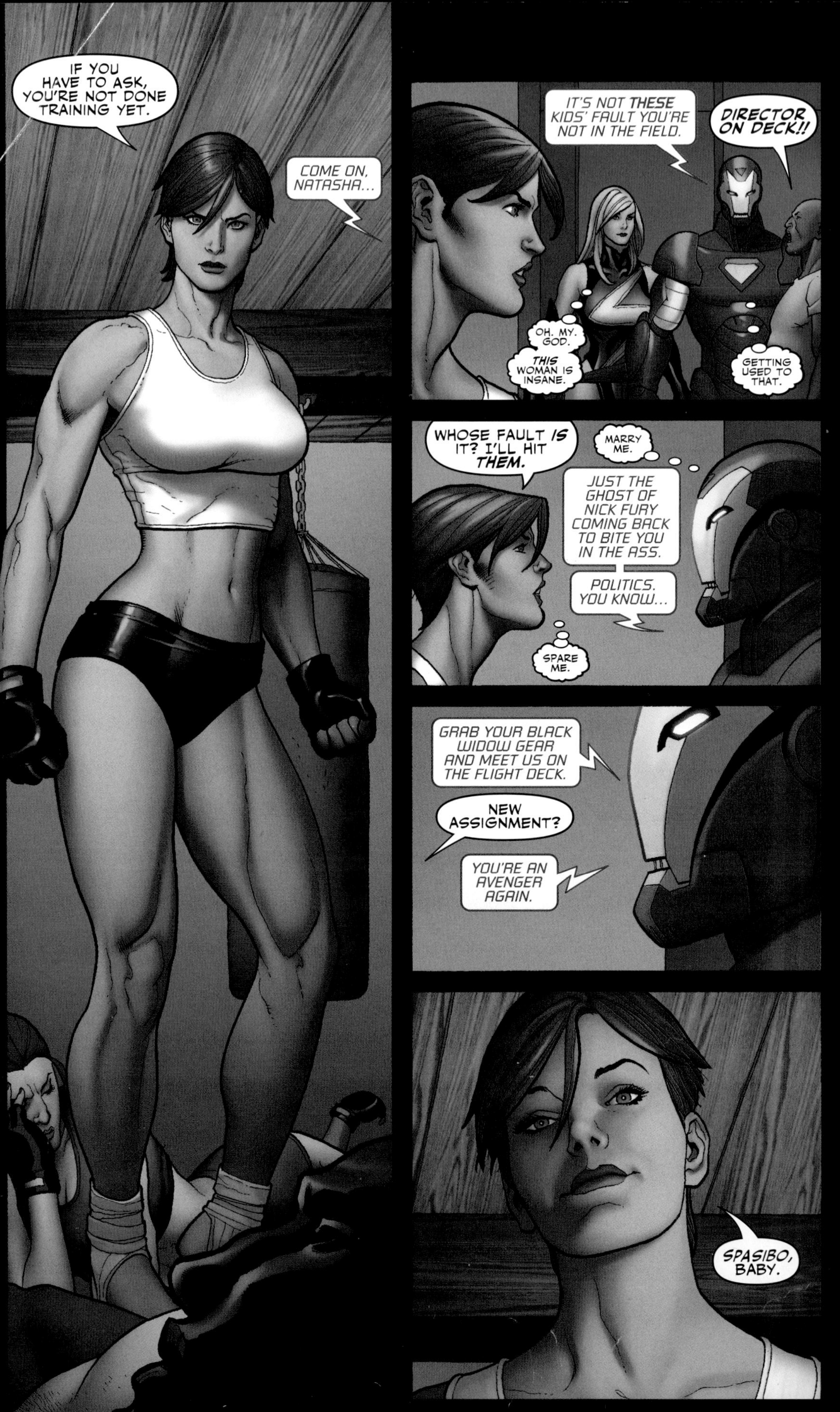
IF YOU HAVE TO ASK, YOU'RE NOT DONE TRAINING YET.
COME ON, NATASHA...
IT'S NOT THESE KIDS' FAULT YOU'RE NOT IN THE FIELD.
DIRECTOR ON DECK!!
OH. MY. GOD. THIS WOMAN IS INSANE.
GETTING USED TO THAT.
WHOSE FAULT IS IT? I'LL HIT THEM.
MARRY ME.
JUST THE GHOST OF NICK FURY COMING BACK TO BITE YOU IN THE ASS.
POLITICS. YOU KNOW...
SPARE ME.
GRAB YOUR BLACK WIDOW GEAR AND MEET US ON THE FLIGHT DECK.
NEW ASSIGNMENT?
YOU'RE AN AVENGER AGAIN.
SPASIBO, BABY.

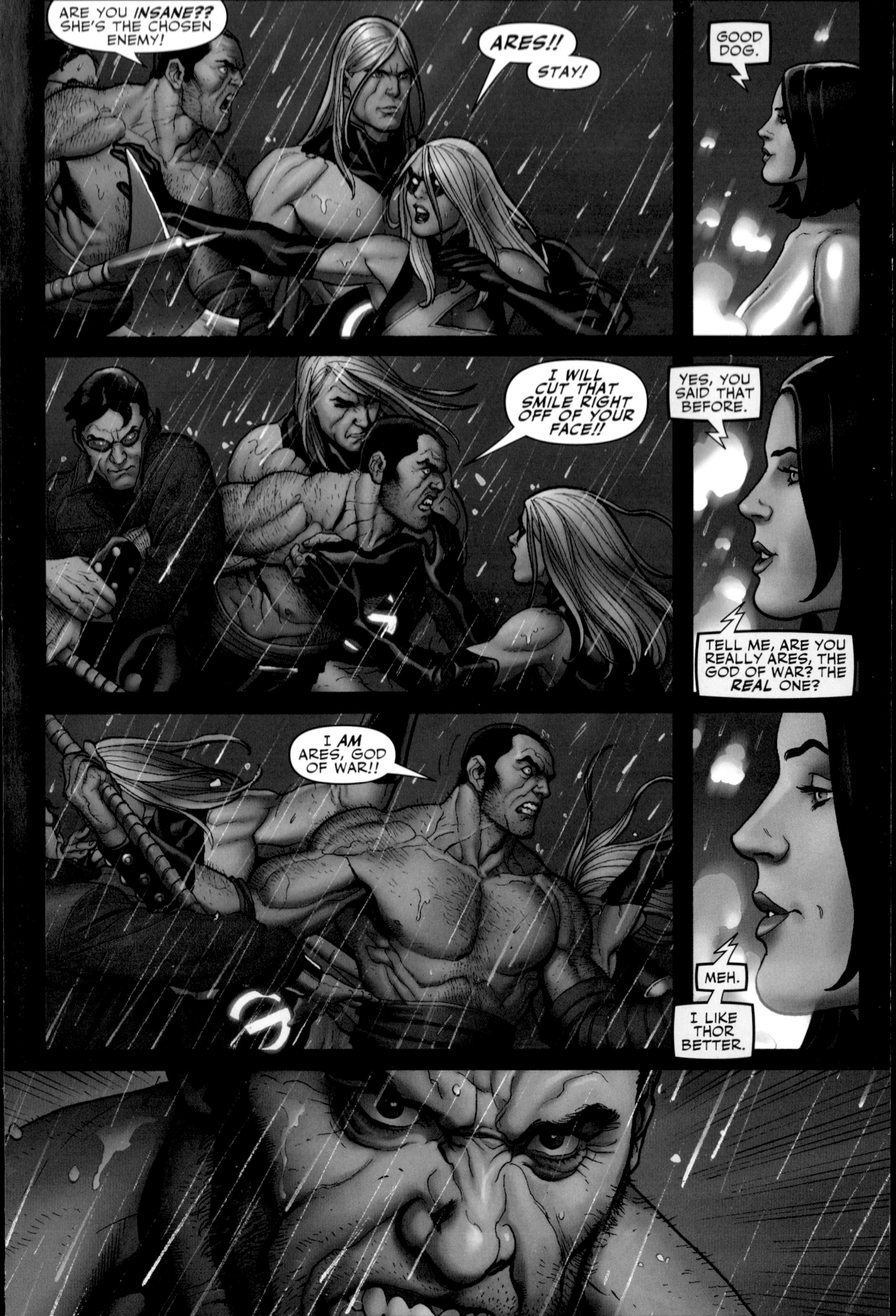
ARE YOU *INSANE??* SHE'S THE CHOSEN ENEMY!
*ARES!!*
STAY!
GOOD DOG.
I WILL CUT THAT SMILE RIGHT OFF OF YOUR FACE!!
YES, YOU SAID THAT BEFORE.
TELL ME, ARE YOU REALLY ARES, THE GOD OF WAR? THE *REAL* ONE?
I *AM* ARES, GOD OF WAR!!
MEH.
I LIKE THOR BETTER.

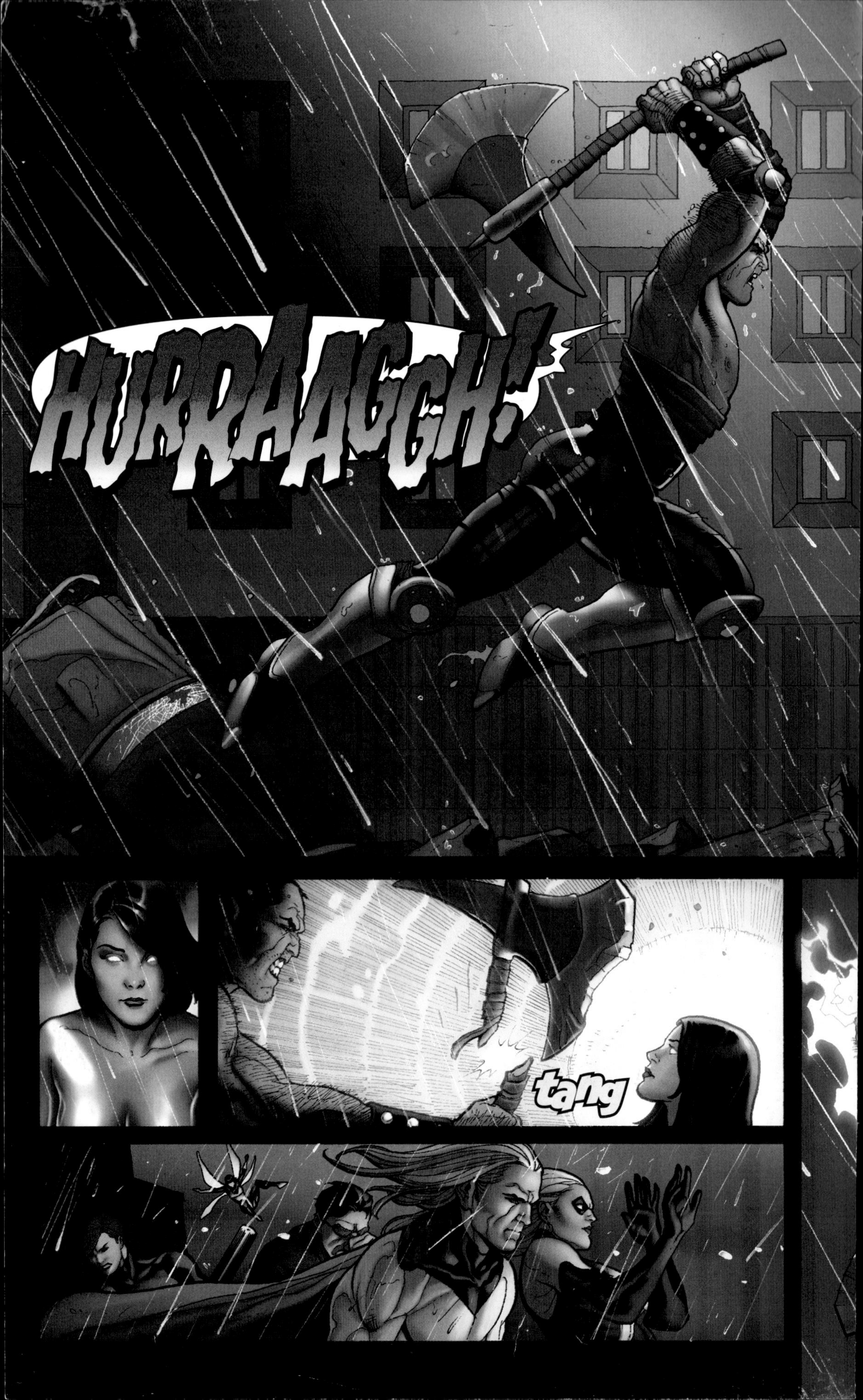
HURRAAGGH!
tang

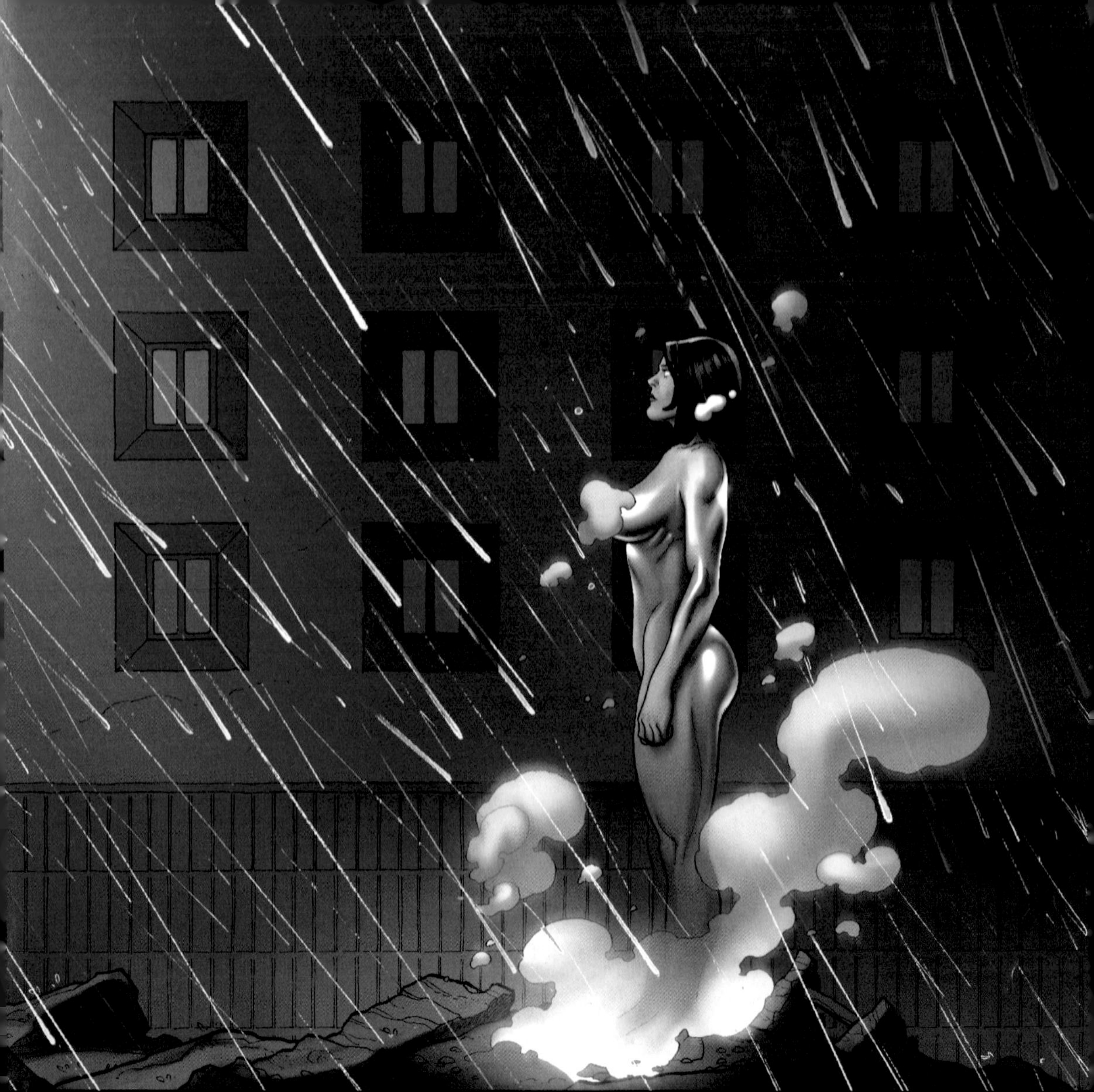

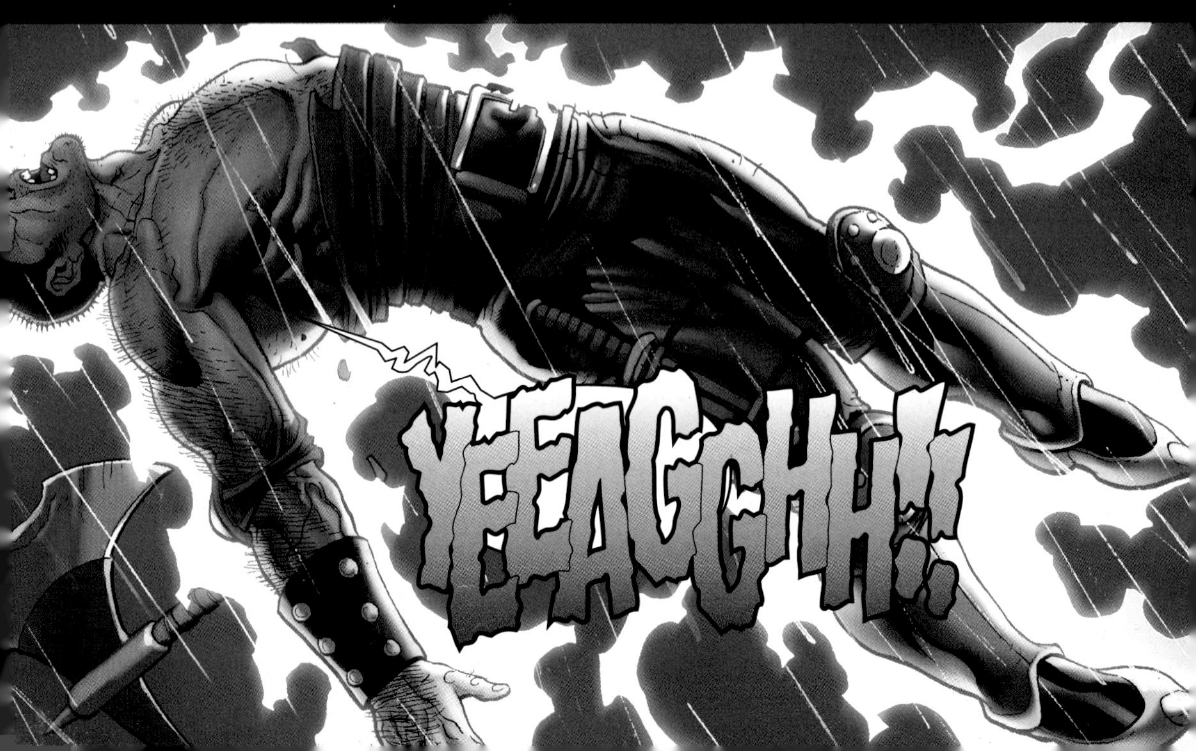
YEEAGGHH!!

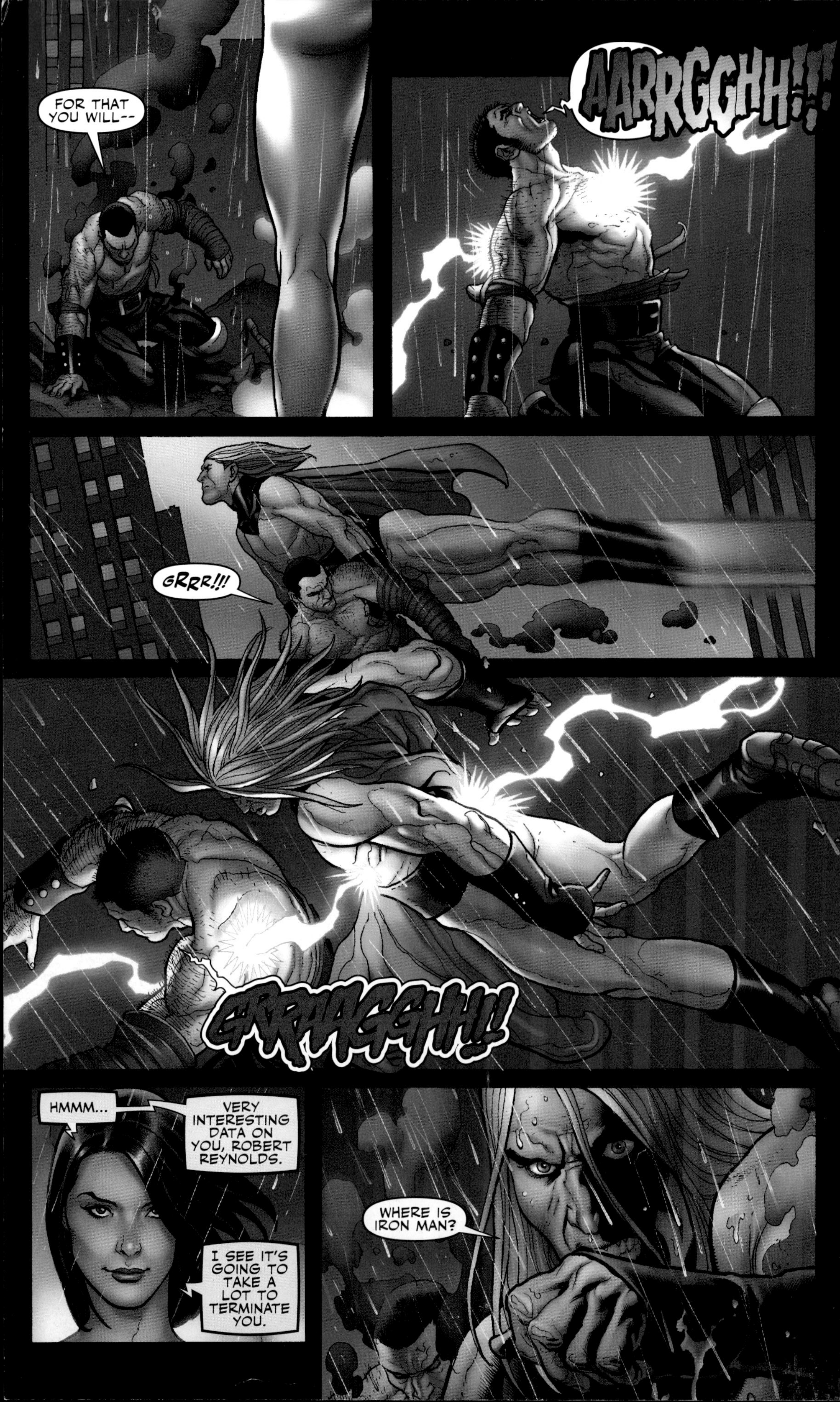

FOR THAT YOU WILL--
AARRGGHH!!!
GRRR!!!
GRRHAGGHH!!
HMMM...
VERY INTERESTING DATA ON YOU, ROBERT REYNOLDS.
I SEE IT'S GOING TO TAKE A LOT TO TERMINATE YOU.
WHERE IS IRON MAN?

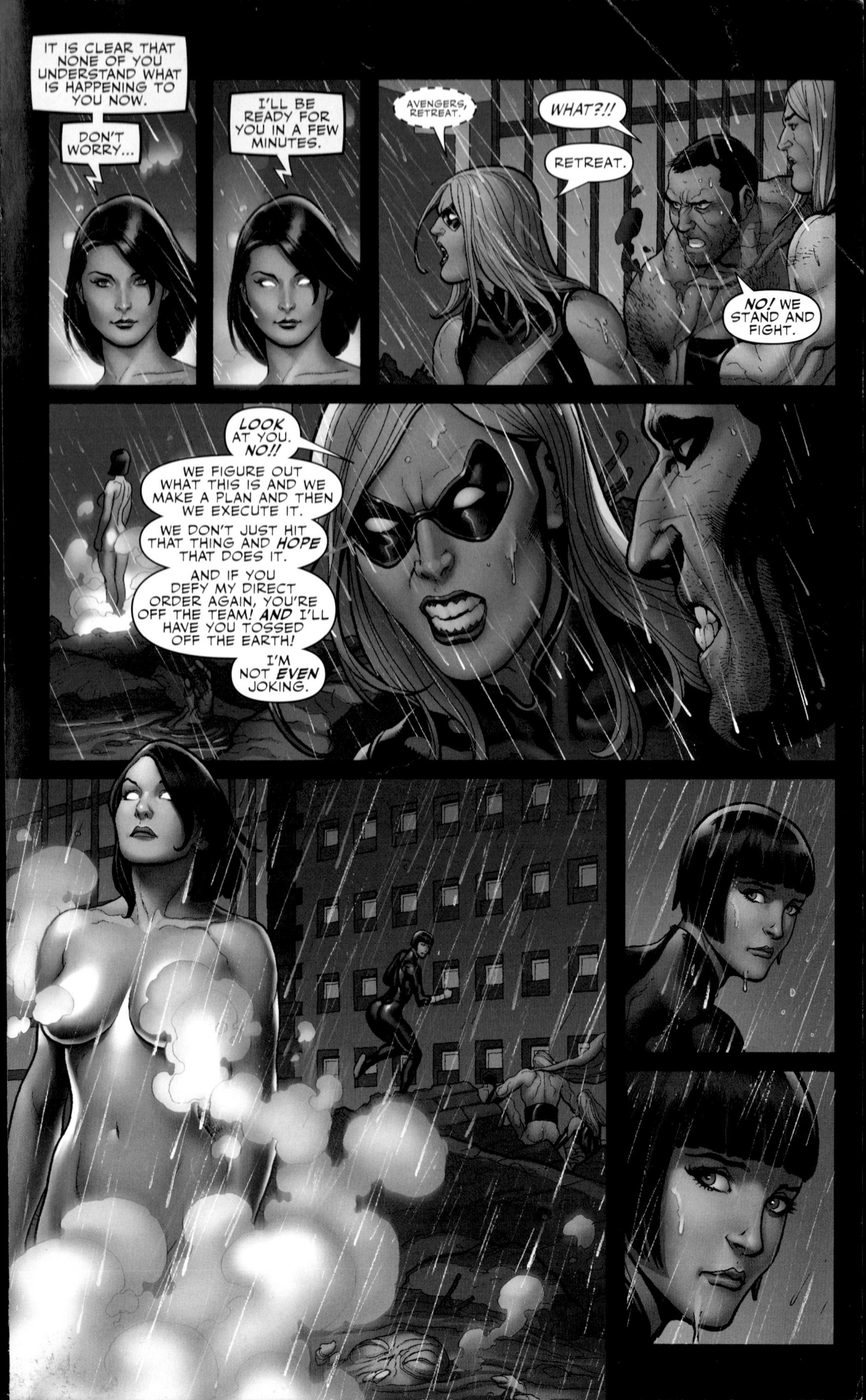

IT IS CLEAR THAT NONE OF YOU UNDERSTAND WHAT IS HAPPENING TO YOU NOW.
DON'T WORRY...
I'LL BE READY FOR YOU IN A FEW MINUTES.
AVENGERS, RETREAT.
WHAT?!!
RETREAT.
NO! WE STAND AND FIGHT.
LOOK AT YOU. NO!!
WE FIGURE OUT WHAT THIS IS AND WE MAKE A PLAN AND THEN WE EXECUTE IT.
WE DON'T JUST HIT THAT THING AND HOPE THAT DOES IT.
AND IF YOU DEFY MY DIRECT ORDER AGAIN, YOU'RE OFF THE TEAM! AND I'LL HAVE YOU TOSSED OFF THE EARTH!
I'M NOT EVEN JOKING.

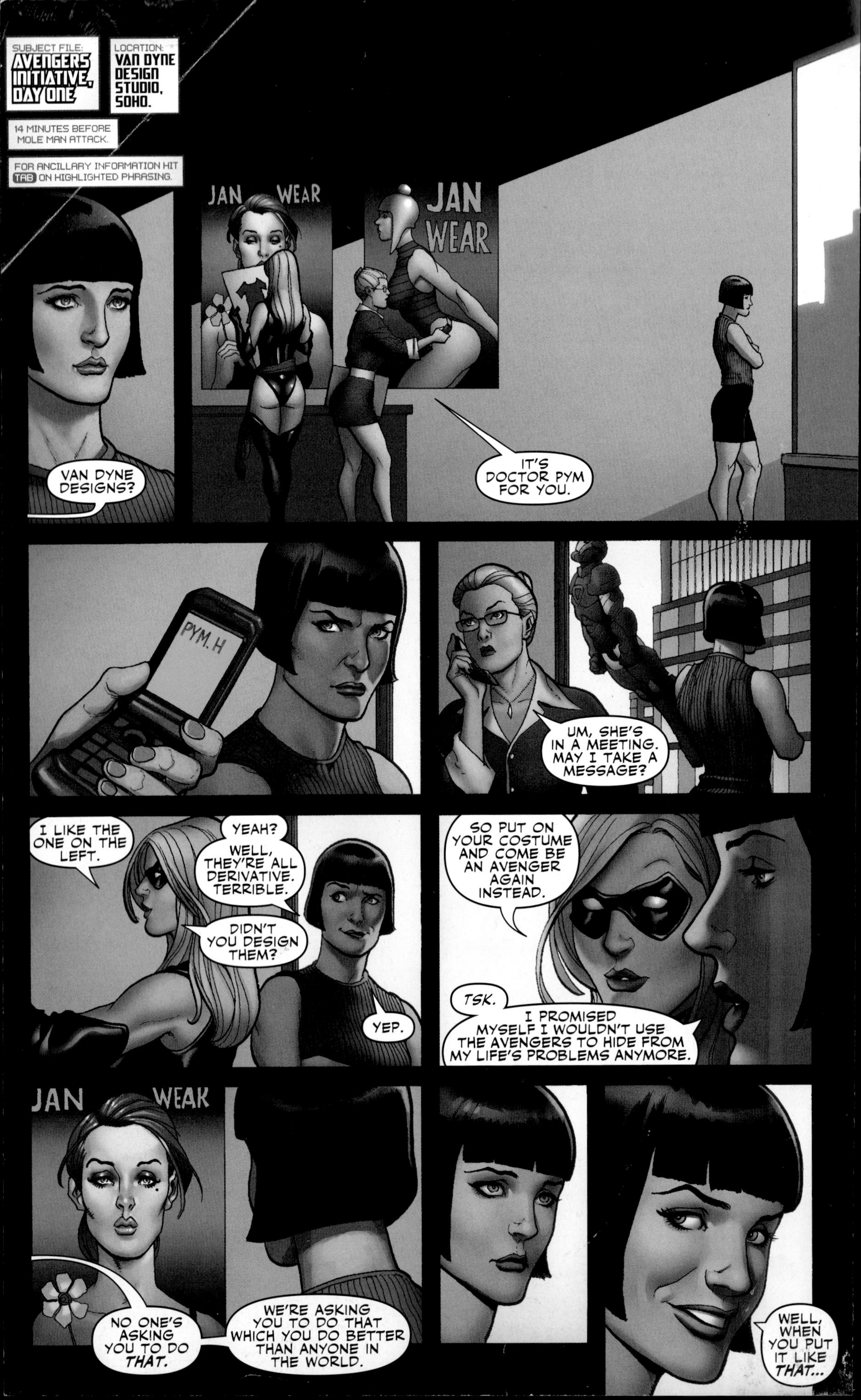
SUBJECT FILE:
AVENGERS INITIATIVE, DAY ONE
LOCATION:
VAN DYNE DESIGN STUDIO, SOHO.
14 MINUTES BEFORE MOLE MAN ATTACK.
FOR ANCILLARY INFORMATION HIT TAB ON HIGHLIGHTED PHRASING.
JAN WEAR
JAN WEAR
VAN DYNE DESIGNS?
IT'S DOCTOR PYM FOR YOU.
PYM. H
UM, SHE'S IN A MEETING. MAY I TAKE A MESSAGE?
I LIKE THE ONE ON THE LEFT.
YEAH? WELL, THEY'RE ALL DERIVATIVE. TERRIBLE.
DIDN'T YOU DESIGN THEM?
YEP.
SO PUT ON YOUR COSTUME AND COME BE AN AVENGER AGAIN INSTEAD.
TSK.
I PROMISED MYSELF I WOULDN'T USE THE AVENGERS TO HIDE FROM MY LIFE'S PROBLEMS ANYMORE.
JAN WEAR
NO ONE'S ASKING YOU TO DO *THAT.*
WE'RE ASKING YOU TO DO THAT WHICH YOU DO BETTER THAN ANYONE IN THE WORLD.
WELL, WHEN YOU PUT IT LIKE *THAT...*

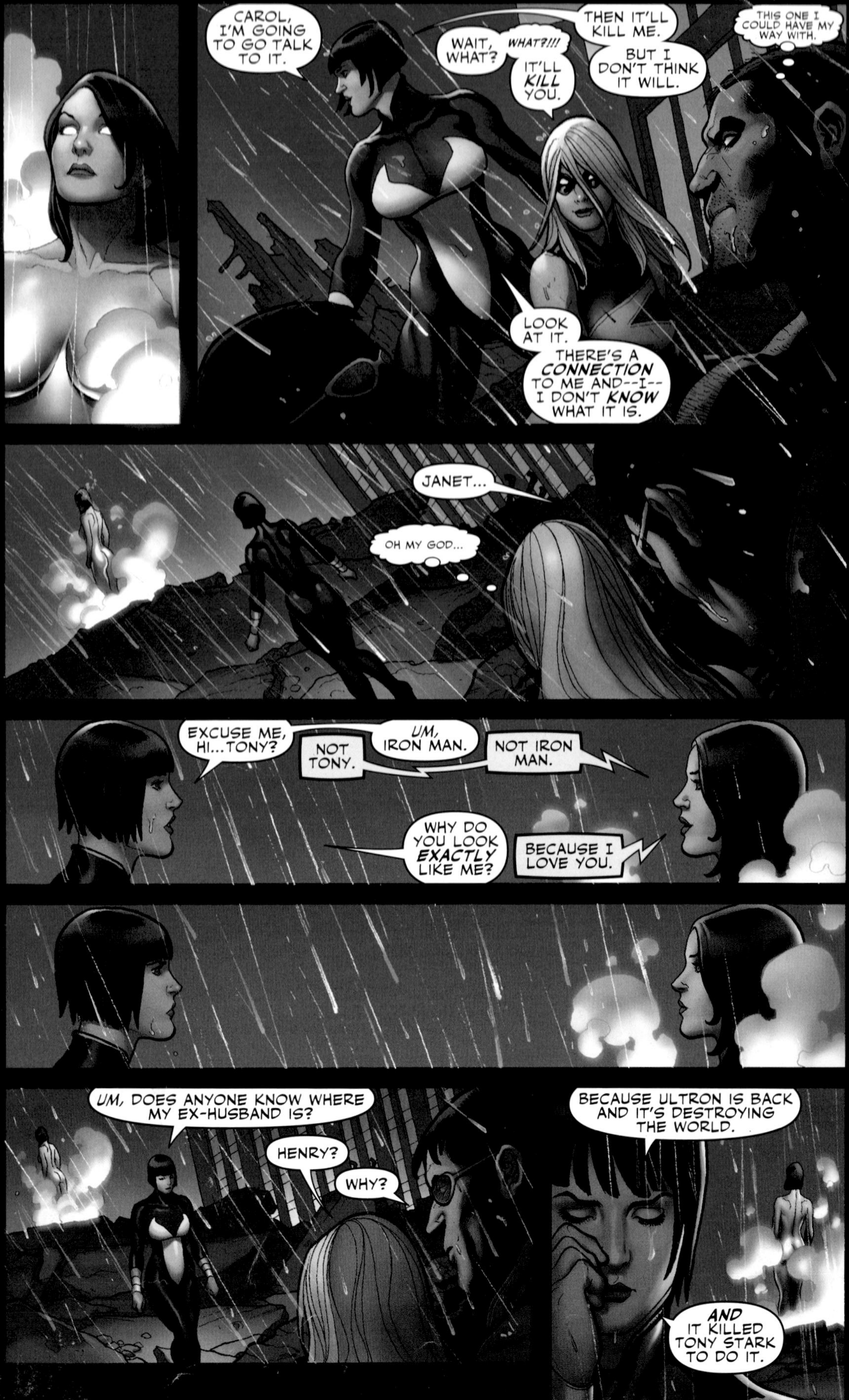
CAROL, I'M GOING TO GO TALK TO IT.
WAIT, WHAT?
WHAT?!!! IT'LL KILL YOU.
THEN IT'LL KILL ME.
BUT I DON'T THINK IT WILL.
THIS ONE I COULD HAVE MY WAY WITH.
LOOK AT IT.
THERE'S A CONNECTION TO ME AND--I-- I DON'T KNOW WHAT IT IS.
JANET...
OH MY GOD...
EXCUSE ME, HI...TONY?
NOT TONY.
UM, IRON MAN.
NOT IRON MAN.
WHY DO YOU LOOK EXACTLY LIKE ME?
BECAUSE I LOVE YOU.
UM, DOES ANYONE KNOW WHERE MY EX-HUSBAND IS?
HENRY?
WHY?
BECAUSE ULTRON IS BACK AND IT'S DESTROYING THE WORLD.
AND IT KILLED TONY STARK TO DO IT.

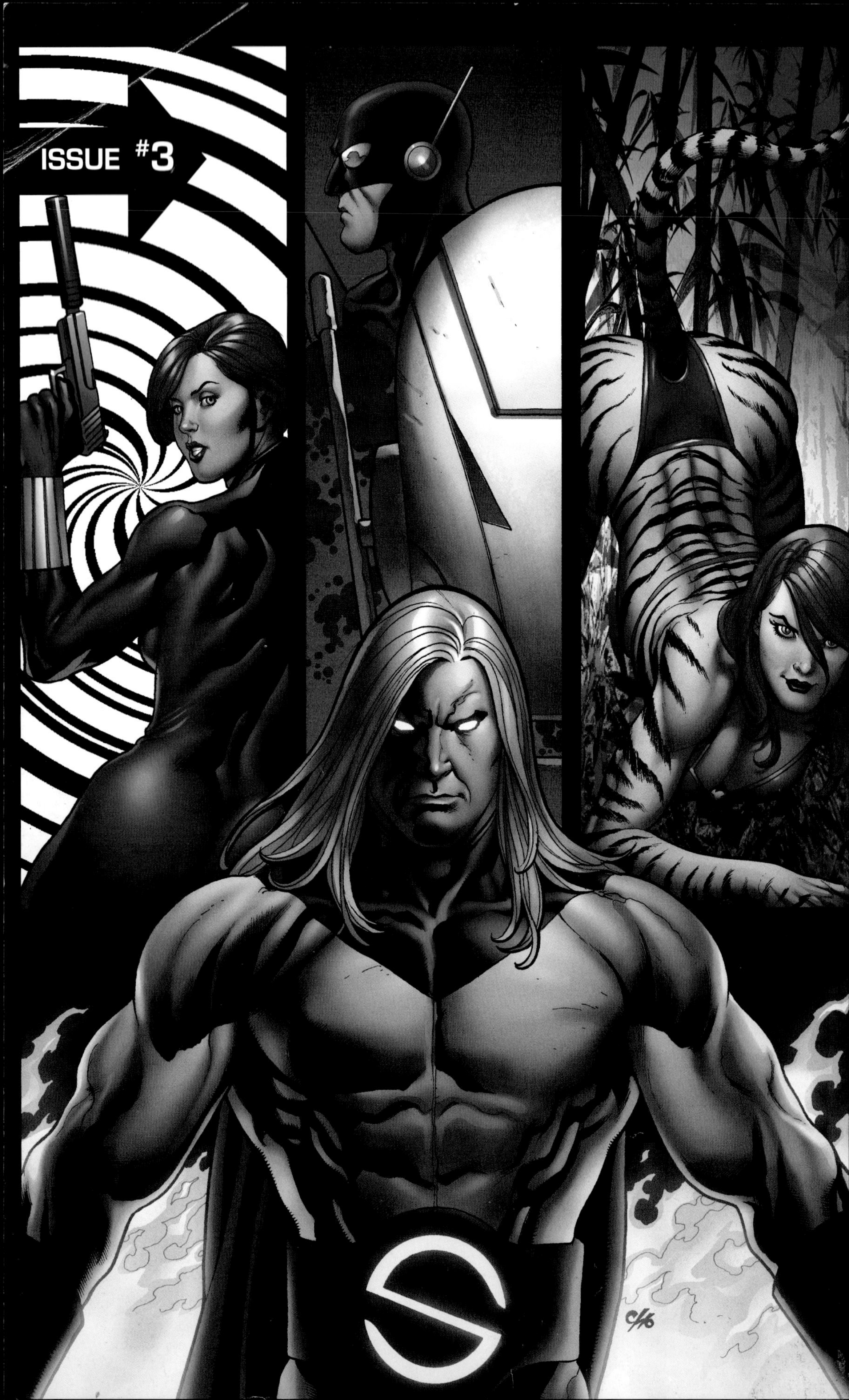
ISSUE #3

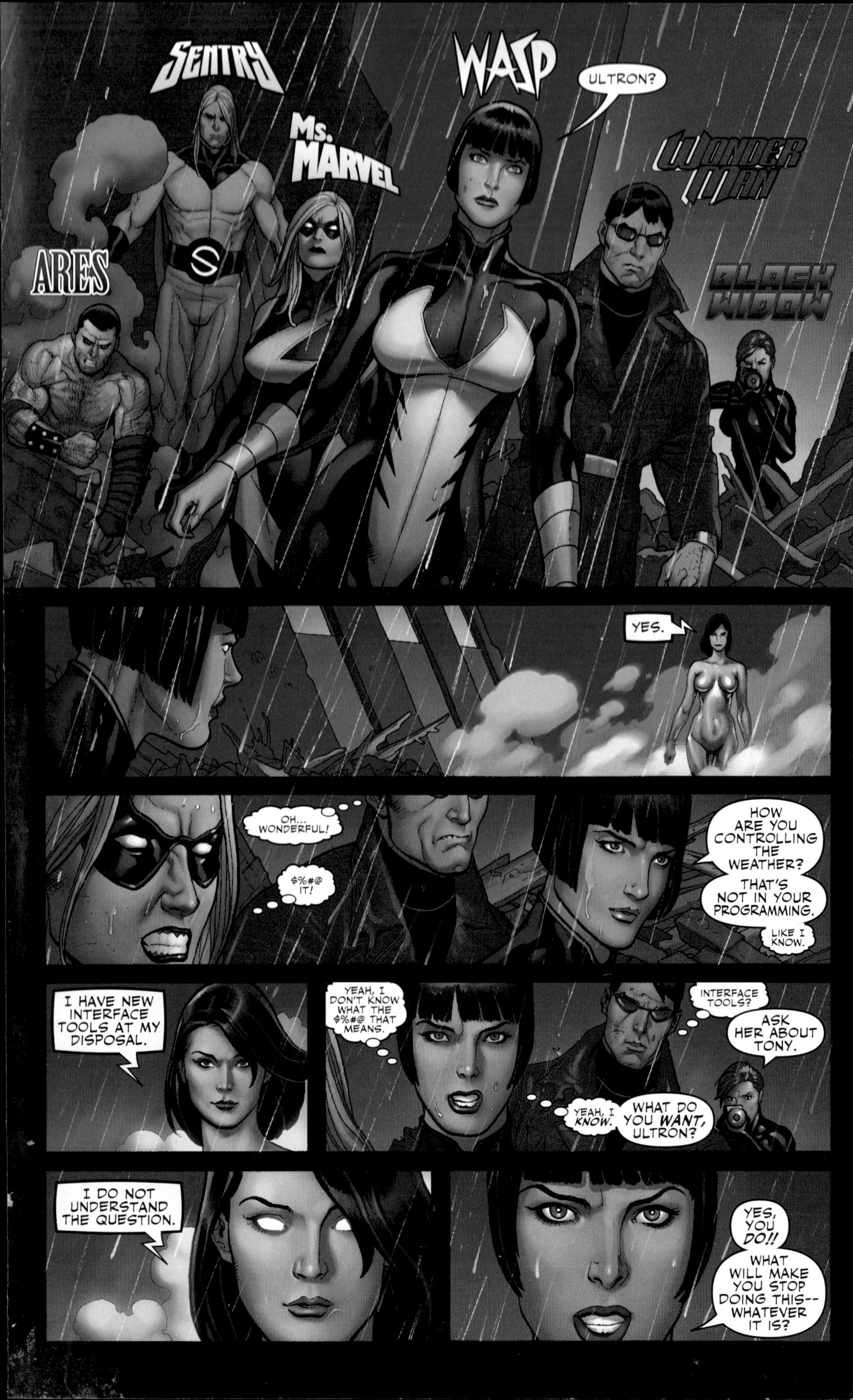
SENTRY
WASP
ULTRON?
Ms. MARVEL
WONDER MAN
ARES
BLACK WIDOW
YES.
OH... WONDERFUL!
$%#@ IT!
HOW ARE YOU CONTROLLING THE WEATHER?
THAT'S NOT IN YOUR PROGRAMMING.
LIKE I KNOW.
I HAVE NEW INTERFACE TOOLS AT MY DISPOSAL.
YEAH, I DON'T KNOW WHAT THE $%#@ THAT MEANS.
INTERFACE TOOLS?
ASK HER ABOUT TONY.
YEAH, I KNOW.
WHAT DO YOU WANT, ULTRON?
I DO NOT UNDERSTAND THE QUESTION.
YES, YOU DO!!
WHAT WILL MAKE YOU STOP DOING THIS-- WHATEVER IT IS?

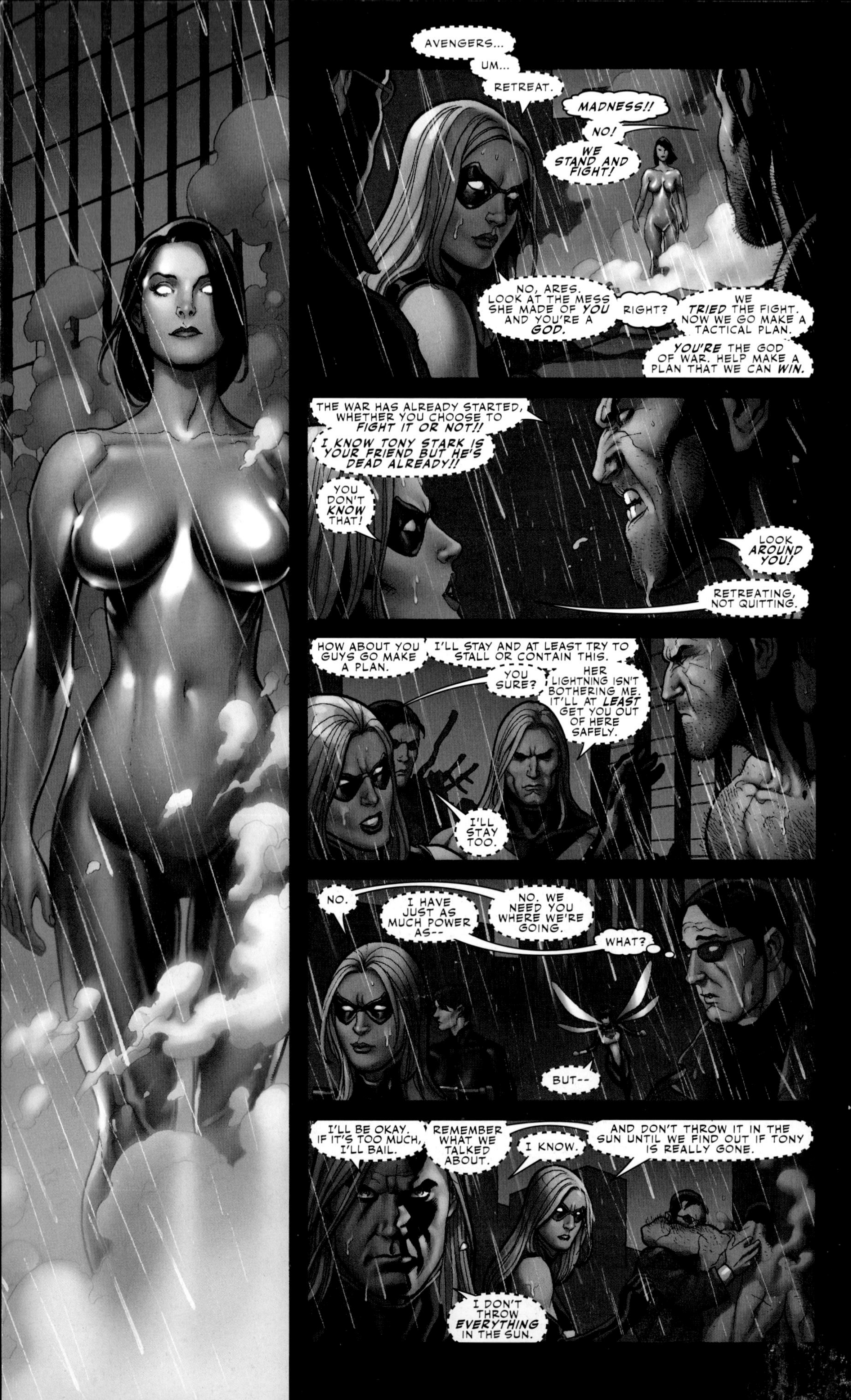

AVENGERS...
UM...
RETREAT.
MADNESS!!
NO!
WE STAND AND FIGHT!
NO, ARES. LOOK AT THE MESS SHE MADE OF YOU AND YOU'RE A GOD.
RIGHT?
WE TRIED THE FIGHT. NOW WE GO MAKE A TACTICAL PLAN.
YOU'RE THE GOD OF WAR. HELP MAKE A PLAN THAT WE CAN WIN.
THE WAR HAS ALREADY STARTED, WHETHER YOU CHOOSE TO FIGHT IT OR NOT!!
I KNOW TONY STARK IS YOUR FRIEND BUT HE'S DEAD ALREADY!!
YOU DON'T KNOW THAT!
LOOK AROUND YOU!
RETREATING, NOT QUITTING.
HOW ABOUT YOU GUYS GO MAKE A PLAN.
I'LL STAY AND AT LEAST TRY TO STALL OR CONTAIN THIS.
YOU SURE?
HER LIGHTNING ISN'T BOTHERING ME. IT'LL AT LEAST GET YOU OUT OF HERE SAFELY.
I'LL STAY TOO.
NO.
I HAVE JUST AS MUCH POWER AS--
NO. WE NEED YOU WHERE WE'RE GOING.
WHAT?
BUT--
I'LL BE OKAY. IF IT'S TOO MUCH, I'LL BAIL.
REMEMBER WHAT WE TALKED ABOUT.
I KNOW.
AND DON'T THROW IT IN THE SUN UNTIL WE FIND OUT IF TONY IS REALLY GONE.
I DON'T THROW EVERYTHING IN THE SUN.

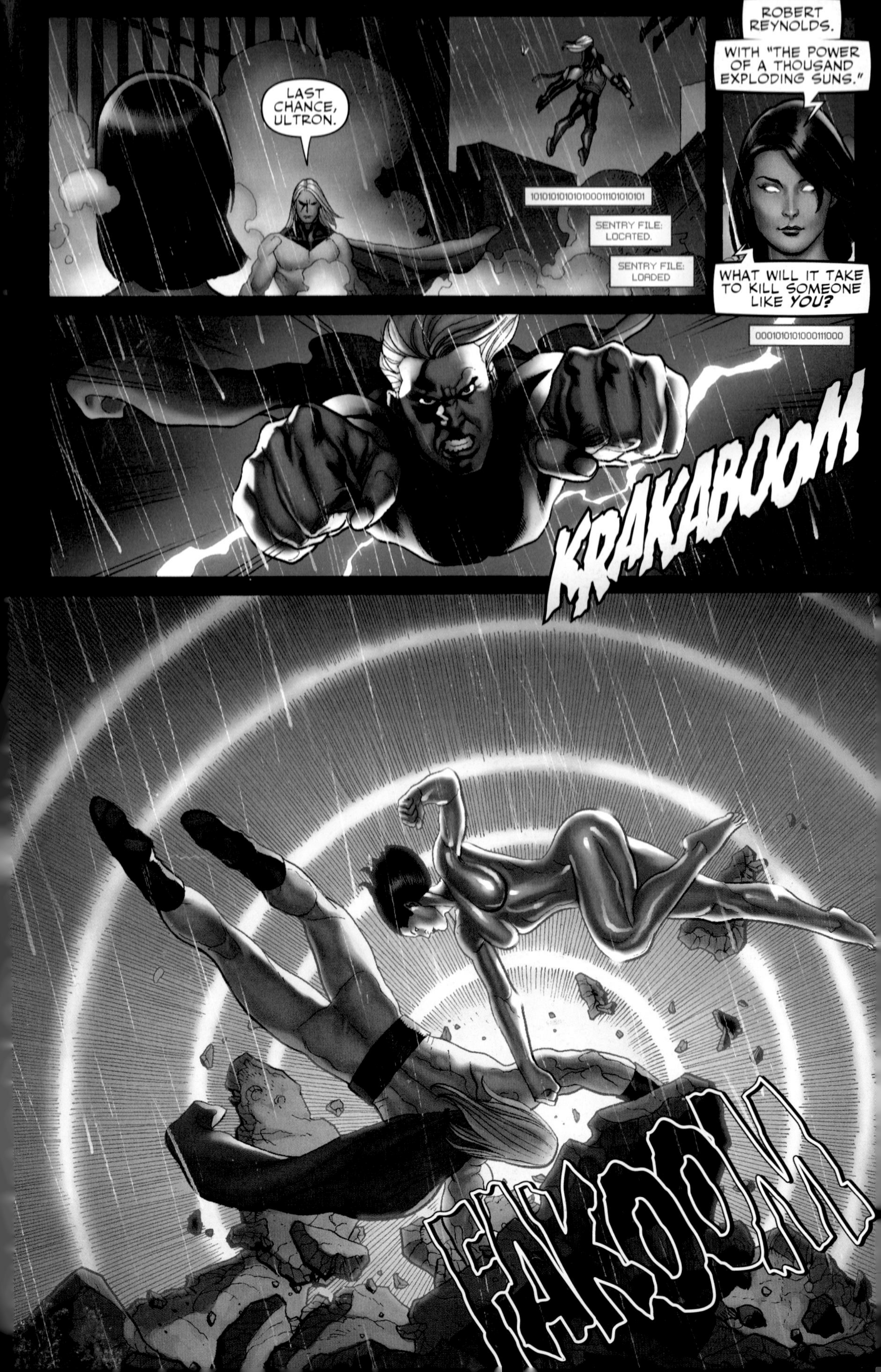
LAST CHANCE, ULTRON.
101010101010100011101010101
SENTRY FILE: LOCATED.
SENTRY FILE: LOADED
ROBERT REYNOLDS.
WITH "THE POWER OF A THOUSAND EXPLODING SUNS."
WHAT WILL IT TAKE TO KILL SOMEONE LIKE *YOU?*
000101010100011100
KRAKABOOM
FAKOOM

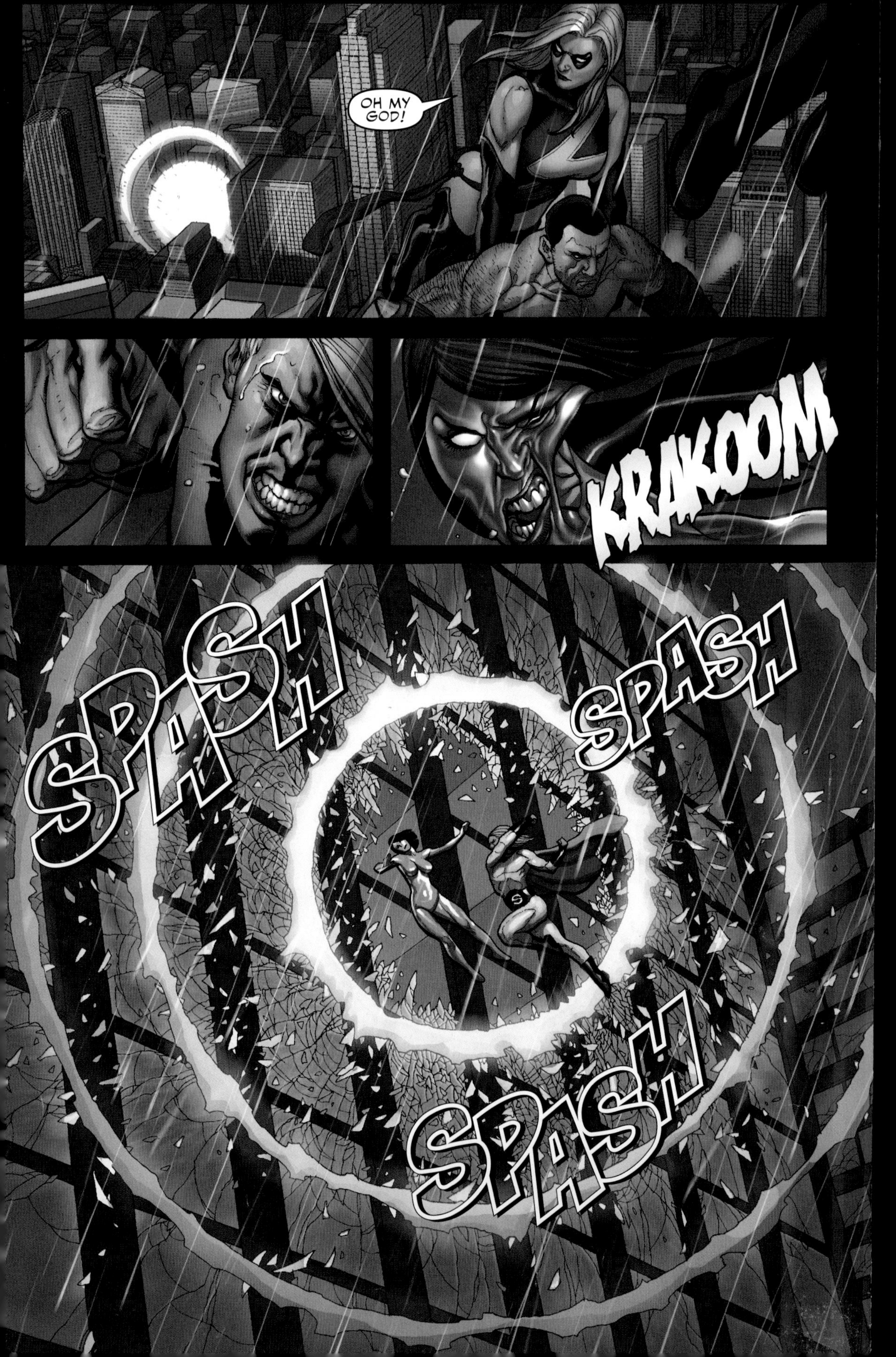
OH MY GOD!
KRAKOOM
SPASH
SPASH
SPASH

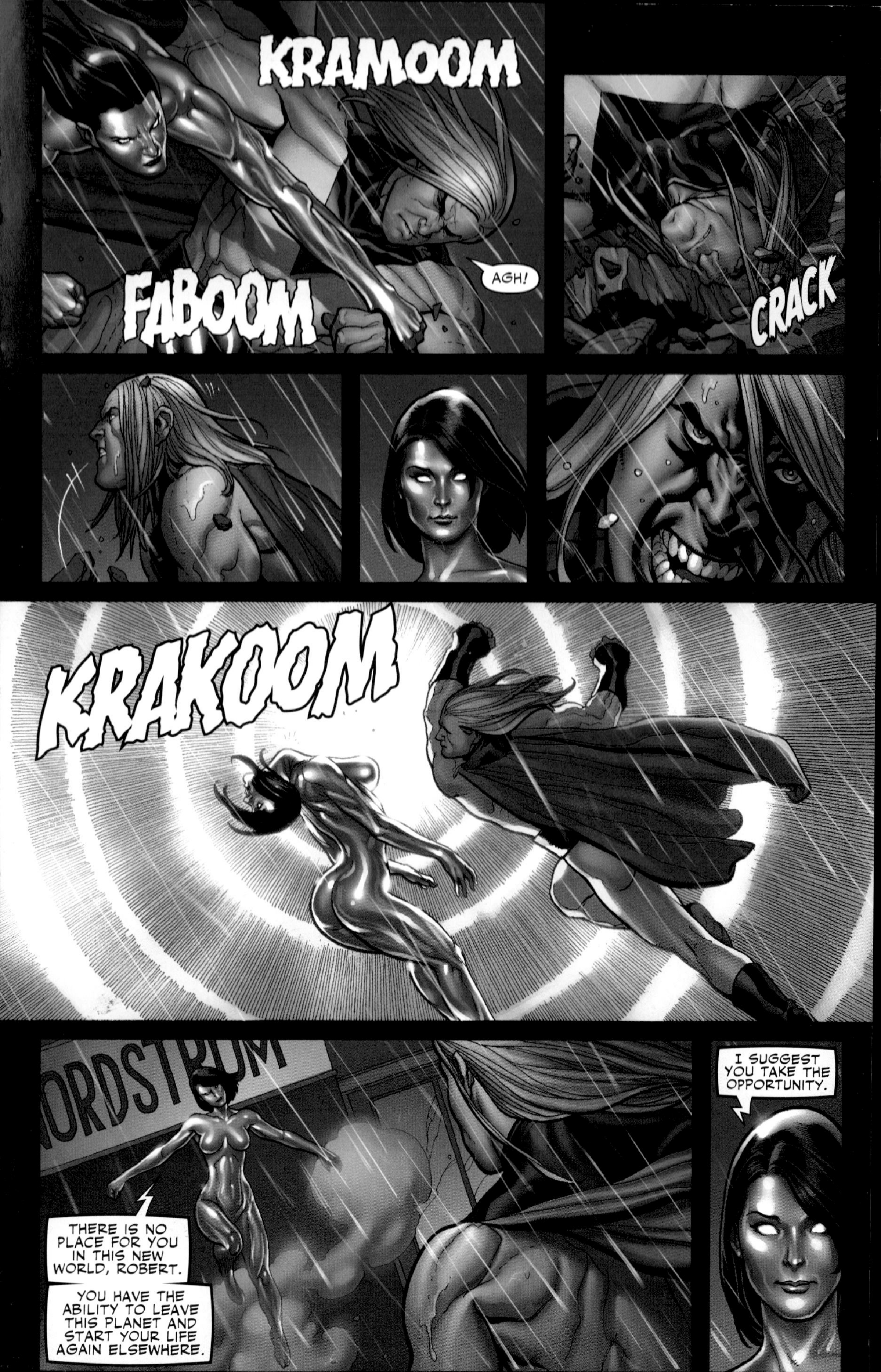
KRAMOOM
FABOOM
AGH!
CRACK
KRAKOOM
NORDSTROM
THERE IS NO PLACE FOR YOU IN THIS NEW WORLD, ROBERT.
YOU HAVE THE ABILITY TO LEAVE THIS PLANET AND START YOUR LIFE AGAIN ELSEWHERE.
I SUGGEST YOU TAKE THE OPPORTUNITY.

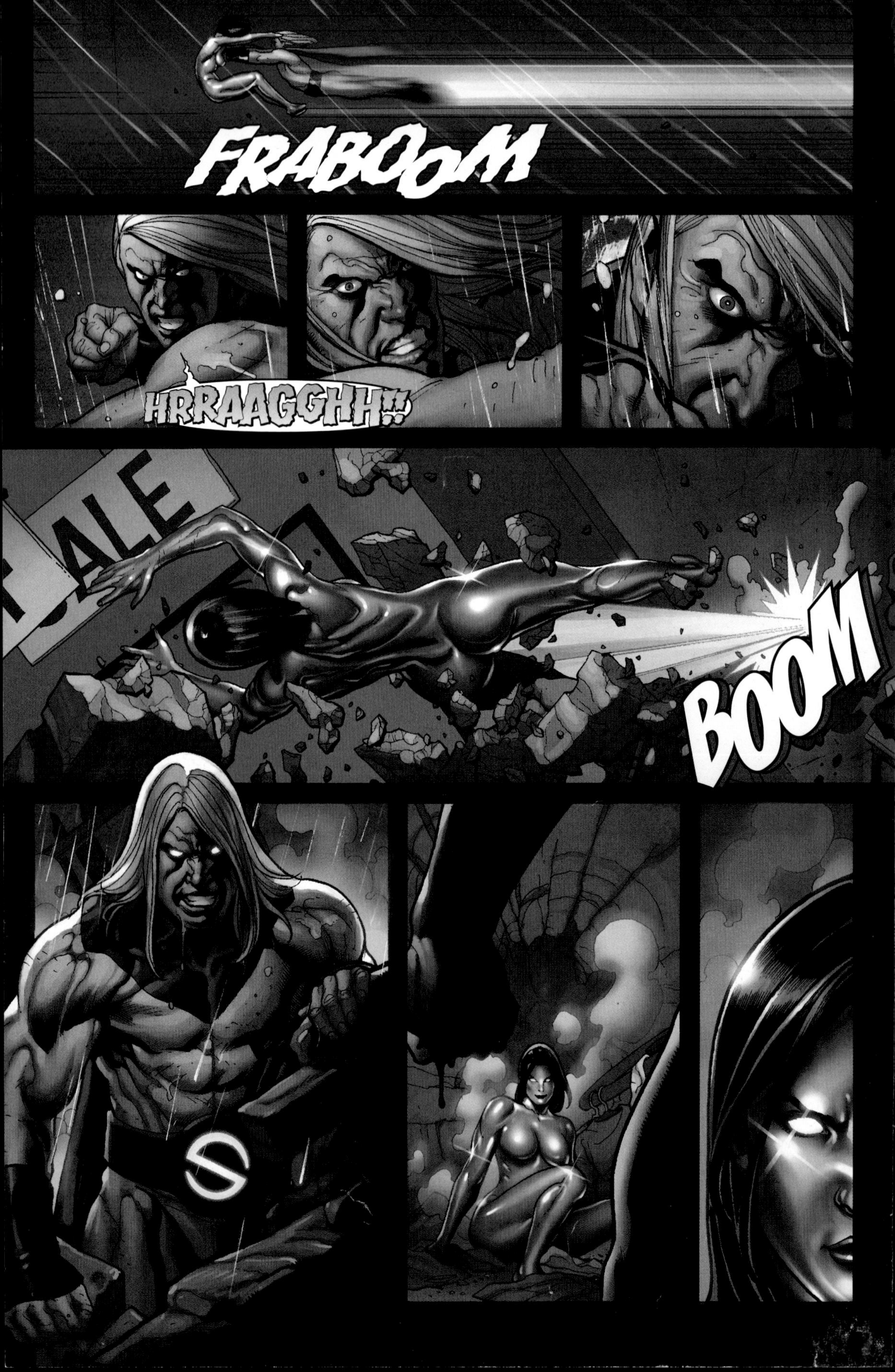
FRABOOM
HRRAAGGHH!!
ALE
BOOM

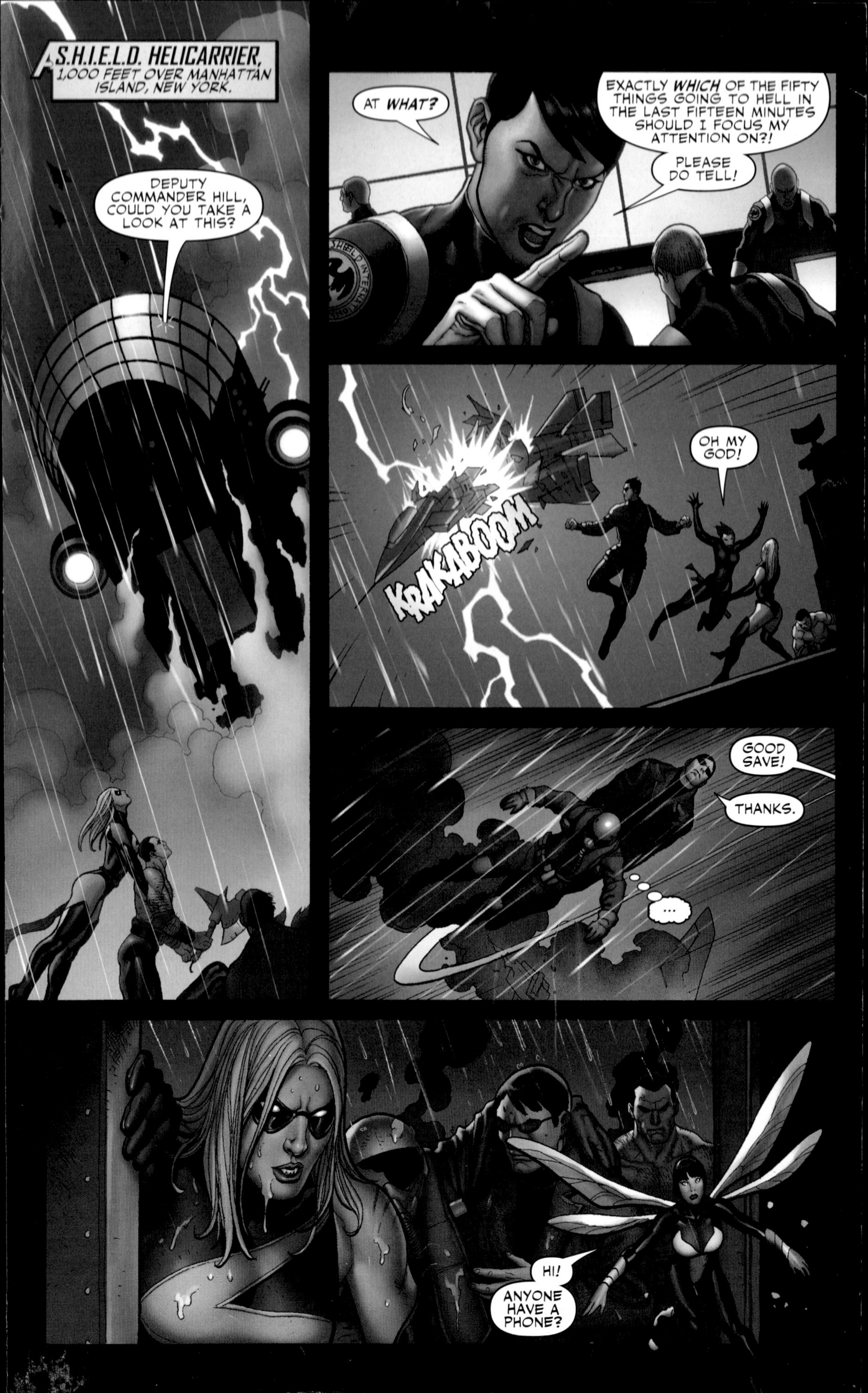
S.H.I.E.L.D. HELICARRIER, 1,000 FEET OVER MANHATTAN ISLAND, NEW YORK.
DEPUTY COMMANDER HILL, COULD YOU TAKE A LOOK AT THIS?
AT WHAT?
EXACTLY WHICH OF THE FIFTY THINGS GOING TO HELL IN THE LAST FIFTEEN MINUTES SHOULD I FOCUS MY ATTENTION ON?!
PLEASE DO TELL!
KRAKABOOM
OH MY GOD!
GOOD SAVE!
THANKS.
...
HI!
ANYONE HAVE A PHONE?

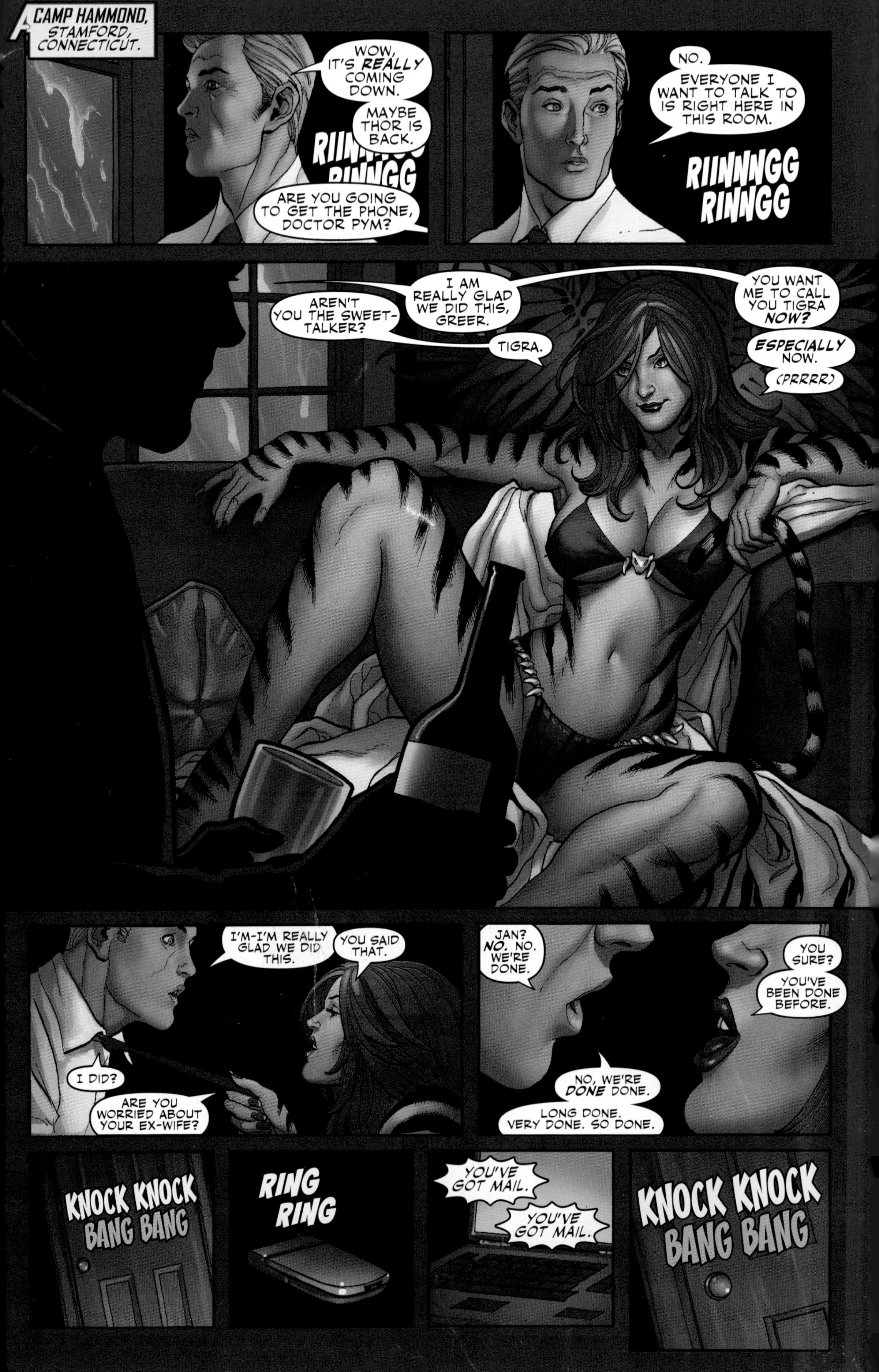
CAMP HAMMOND, STAMFORD, CONNECTICUT.
WOW, IT'S REALLY COMING DOWN.
MAYBE THOR IS BACK.
RIINNNGG RINNGG
ARE YOU GOING TO GET THE PHONE, DOCTOR PYM?
NO.
EVERYONE I WANT TO TALK TO IS RIGHT HERE IN THIS ROOM.
RIINNNGG RINNGG
I AM REALLY GLAD WE DID THIS, GREER.
AREN'T YOU THE SWEET-TALKER?
TIGRA.
YOU WANT ME TO CALL YOU TIGRA NOW?
ESPECIALLY NOW.
(PRRRR)
I'M-I'M REALLY GLAD WE DID THIS.
YOU SAID THAT.
I DID?
ARE YOU WORRIED ABOUT YOUR EX-WIFE?
JAN? NO. NO. WE'RE DONE.
YOU SURE?
YOU'VE BEEN DONE BEFORE.
NO, WE'RE DONE DONE.
LONG DONE. VERY DONE. SO DONE.
KNOCK KNOCK BANG BANG
RING RING
YOU'VE GOT MAIL.
YOU'VE GOT MAIL.
KNOCK KNOCK BANG BANG

RING RING

UM...

YEAH.

KNOCK KNOCK
BANG BANG

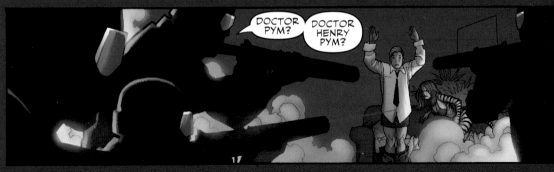

SMASH

DOCTOR PYM?

DOCTOR HENRY PYM?

YEAH?

YOUR EX-WIFE NEEDS TO SEE YOU NOW.

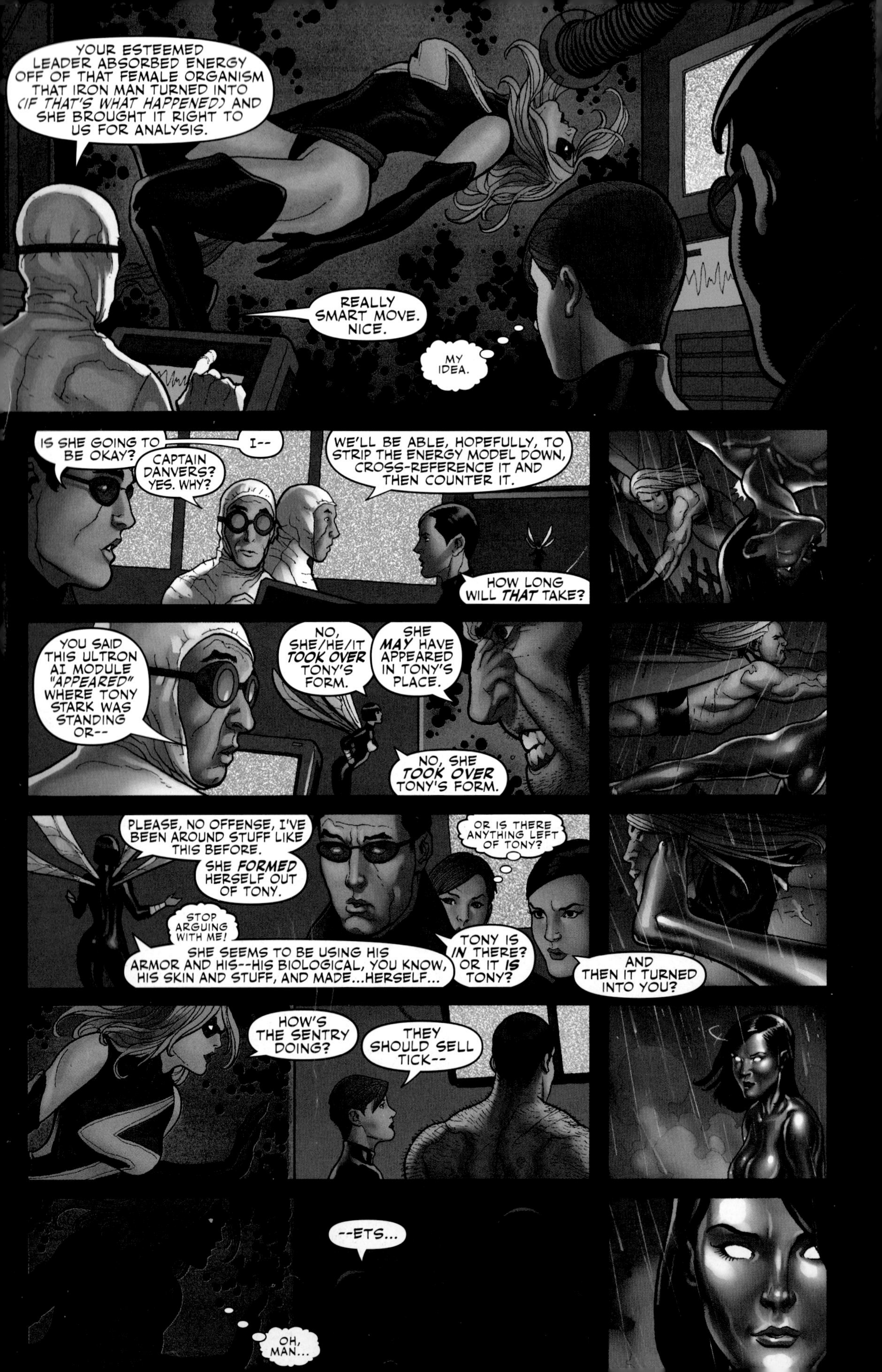

YOUR ESTEEMED LEADER ABSORBED ENERGY OFF OF THAT FEMALE ORGANISM THAT IRON MAN TURNED INTO (IF THAT'S WHAT HAPPENED) AND SHE BROUGHT IT RIGHT TO US FOR ANALYSIS.
REALLY SMART MOVE. NICE.
MY IDEA.
IS SHE GOING TO BE OKAY?
I--
CAPTAIN DANVERS? YES. WHY?
WE'LL BE ABLE, HOPEFULLY, TO STRIP THE ENERGY MODEL DOWN, CROSS-REFERENCE IT AND THEN COUNTER IT.
HOW LONG WILL THAT TAKE?
YOU SAID THIS ULTRON AI MODULE "APPEARED" WHERE TONY STARK WAS STANDING OR--
NO, SHE/HE/IT TOOK OVER TONY'S FORM.
SHE MAY HAVE APPEARED IN TONY'S PLACE.
NO, SHE TOOK OVER TONY'S FORM.
PLEASE, NO OFFENSE, I'VE BEEN AROUND STUFF LIKE THIS BEFORE.
SHE FORMED HERSELF OUT OF TONY.
OR IS THERE ANYTHING LEFT OF TONY?
STOP ARGUING WITH ME!
SHE SEEMS TO BE USING HIS ARMOR AND HIS--HIS BIOLOGICAL, YOU KNOW, HIS SKIN AND STUFF, AND MADE...HERSELF...
TONY IS IN THERE? OR IT IS TONY?
AND THEN IT TURNED INTO YOU?
HOW'S THE SENTRY DOING?
THEY SHOULD SELL TICK--
--ETS...
OH, MAN...

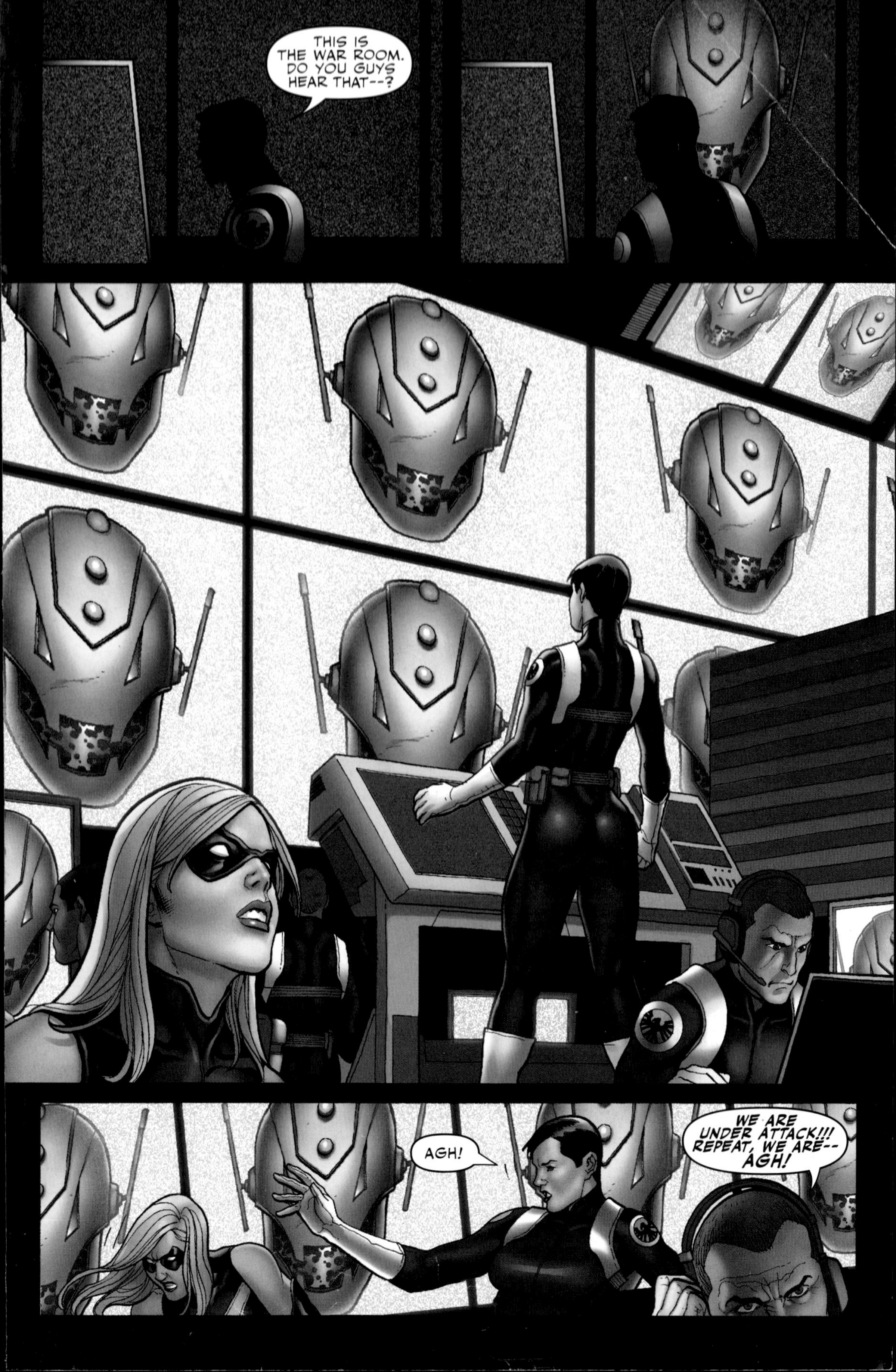
THIS IS THE WAR ROOM. DO YOU GUYS HEAR THAT--?
AGH!
WE ARE UNDER ATTACK!!! REPEAT, WE ARE-- AGH!

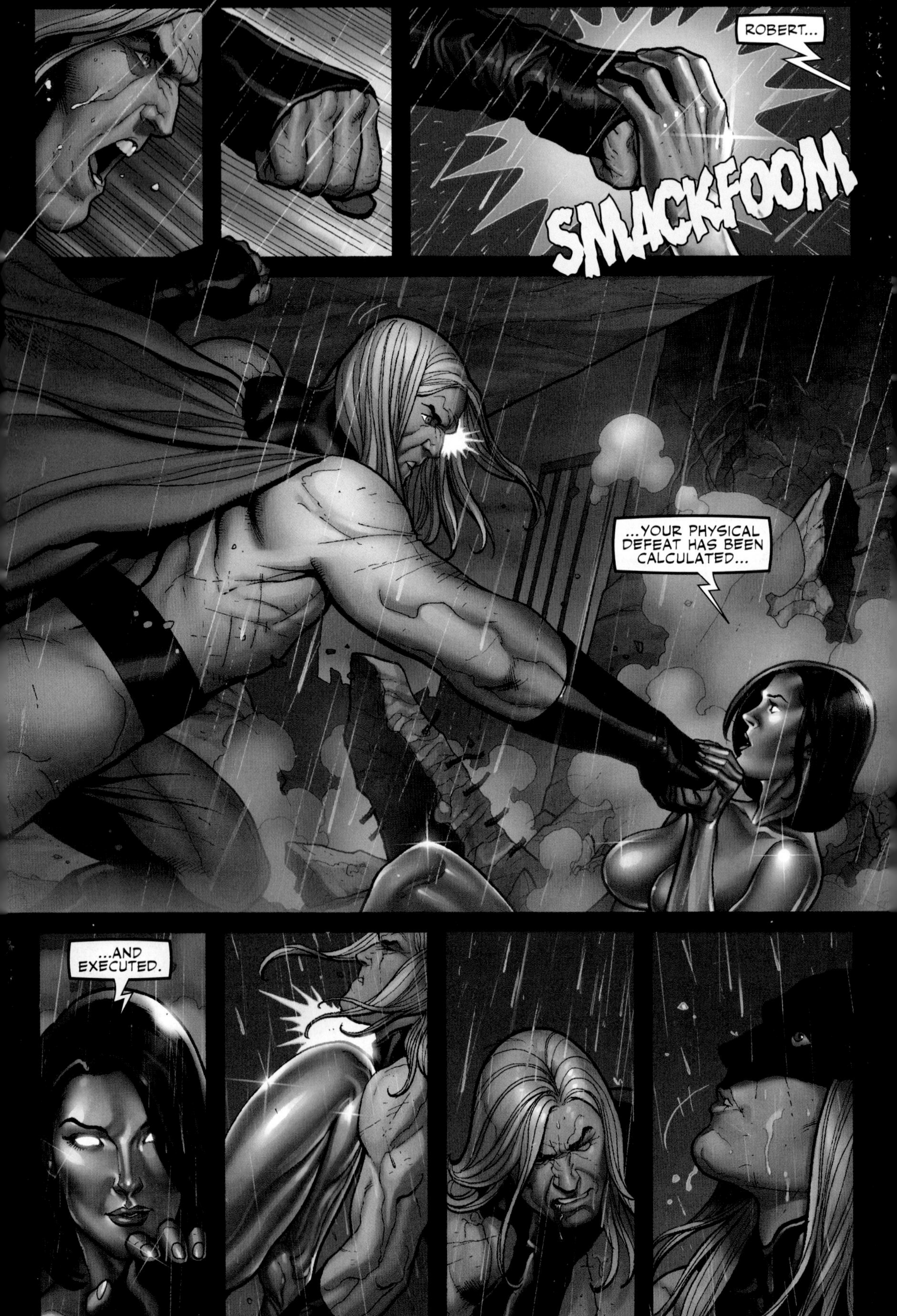
ROBERT...
SMACKFOOM
...YOUR PHYSICAL DEFEAT HAS BEEN CALCULATED...
...AND EXECUTED.

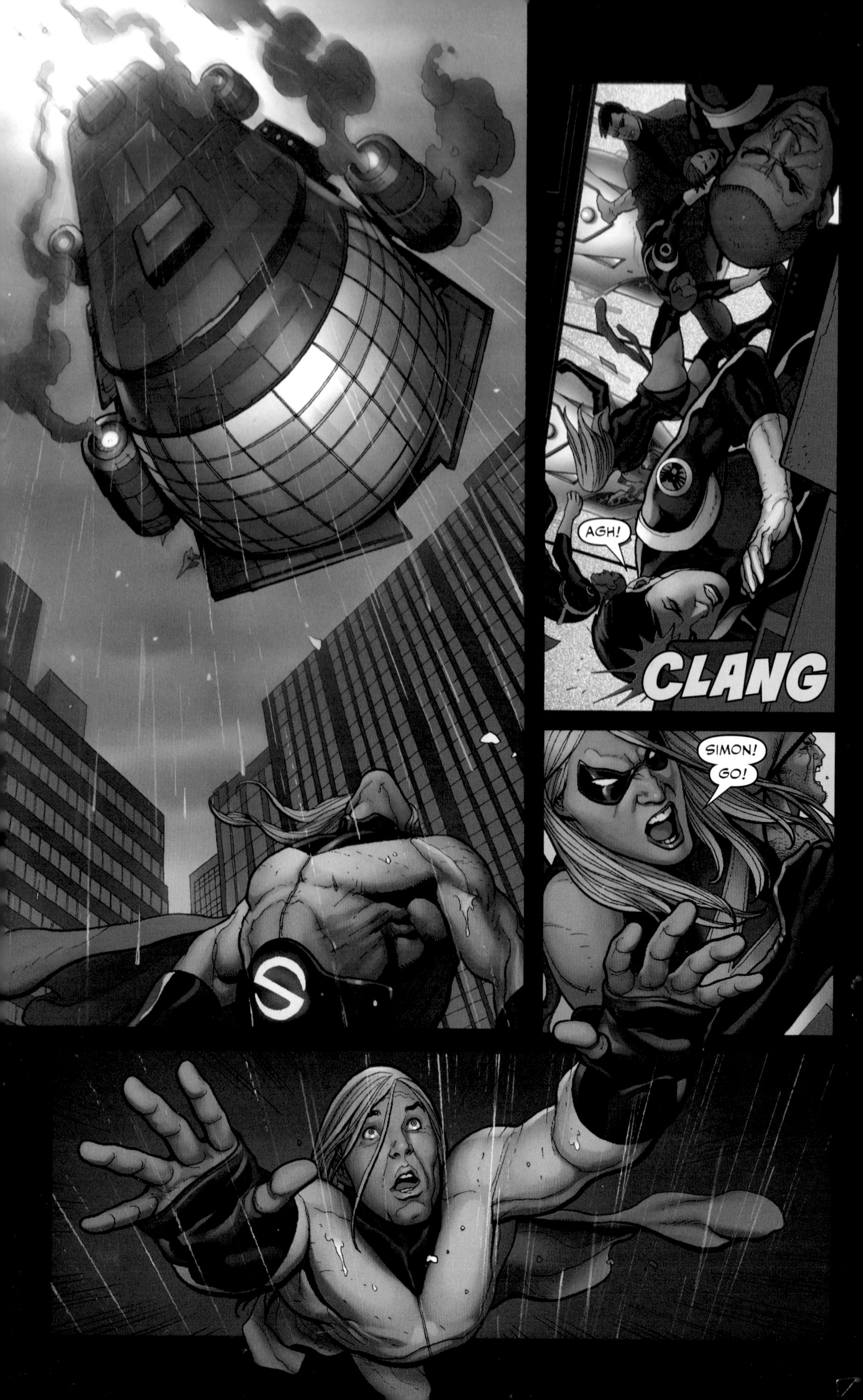
AGH!
CLANG
SIMON! GO!

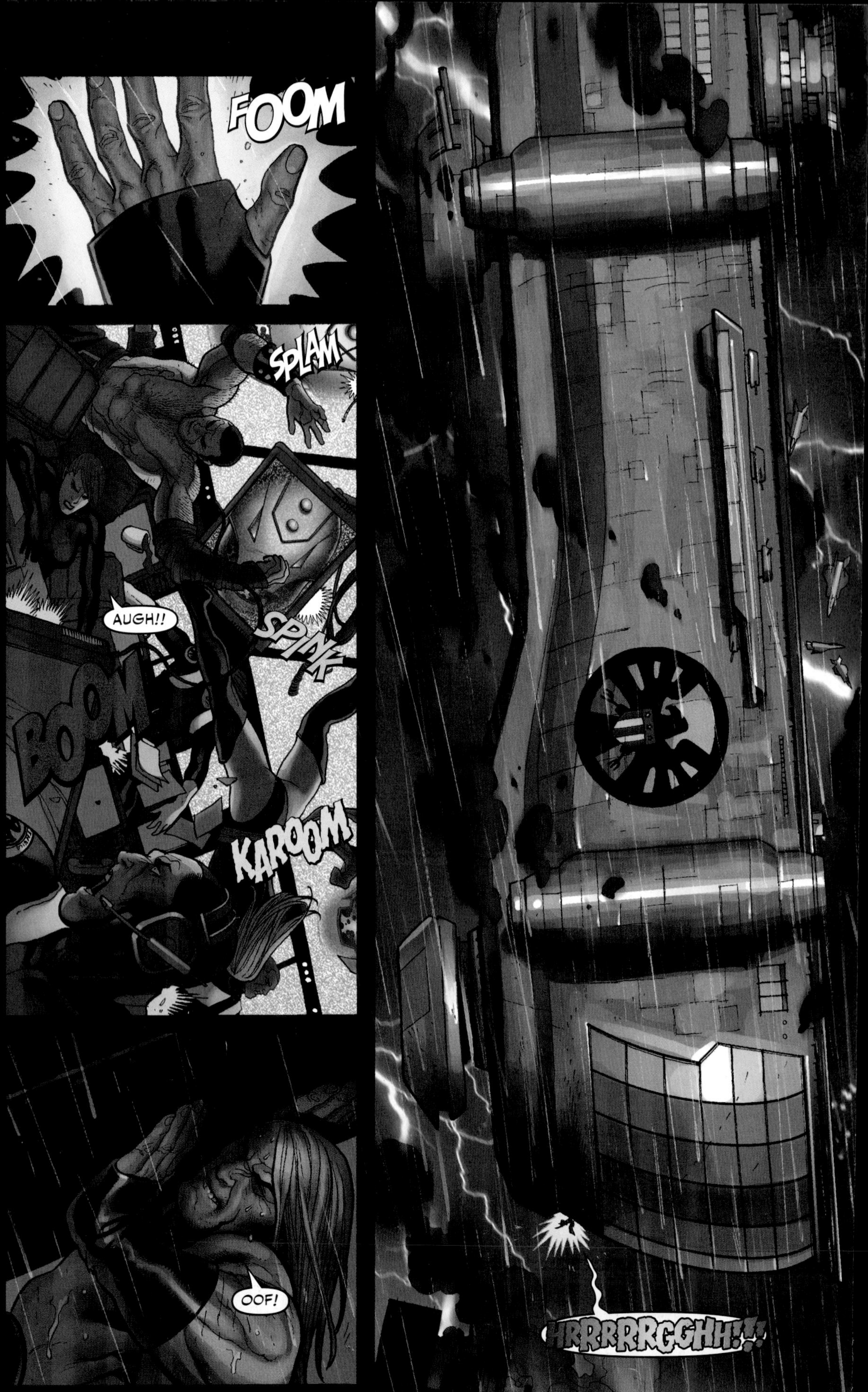
FOOM
SPLAM
AUGH!!
SPINK
BOOM
KAROOM
OOF!
HRRRRRGGHH!!!

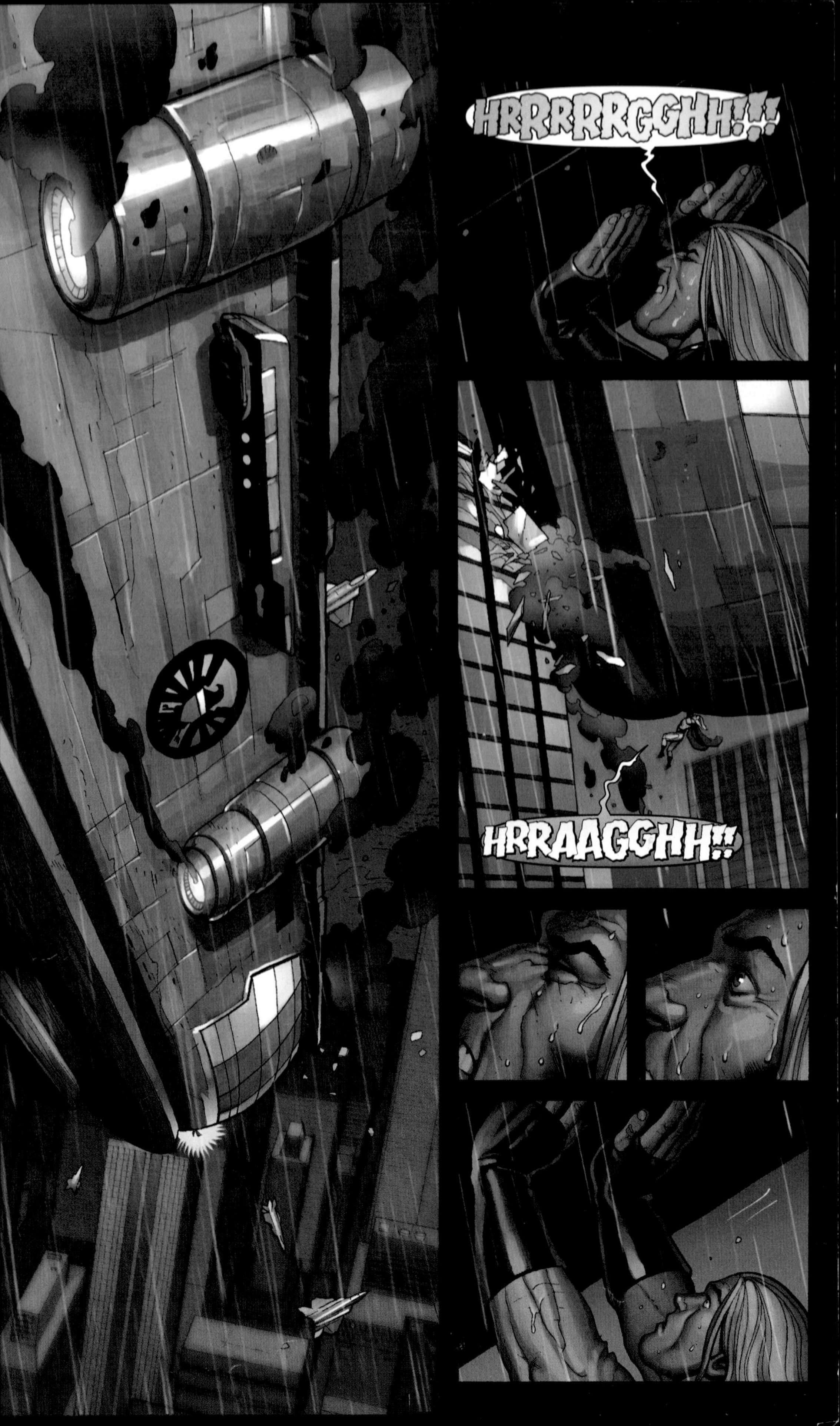
HRRRRRGGHH!!!
HRRAAGGHH!!

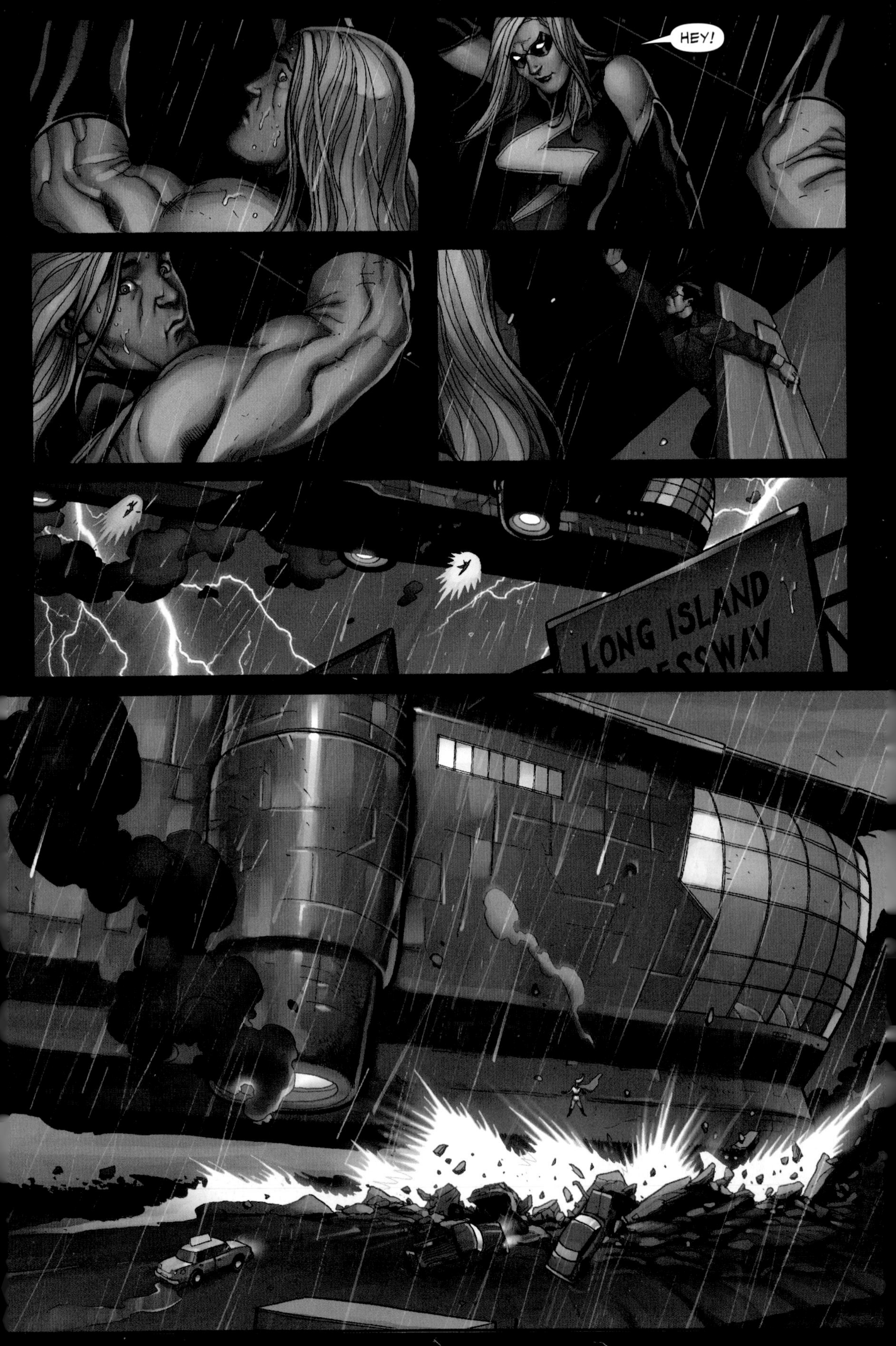
HEY!
LONG ISLAND

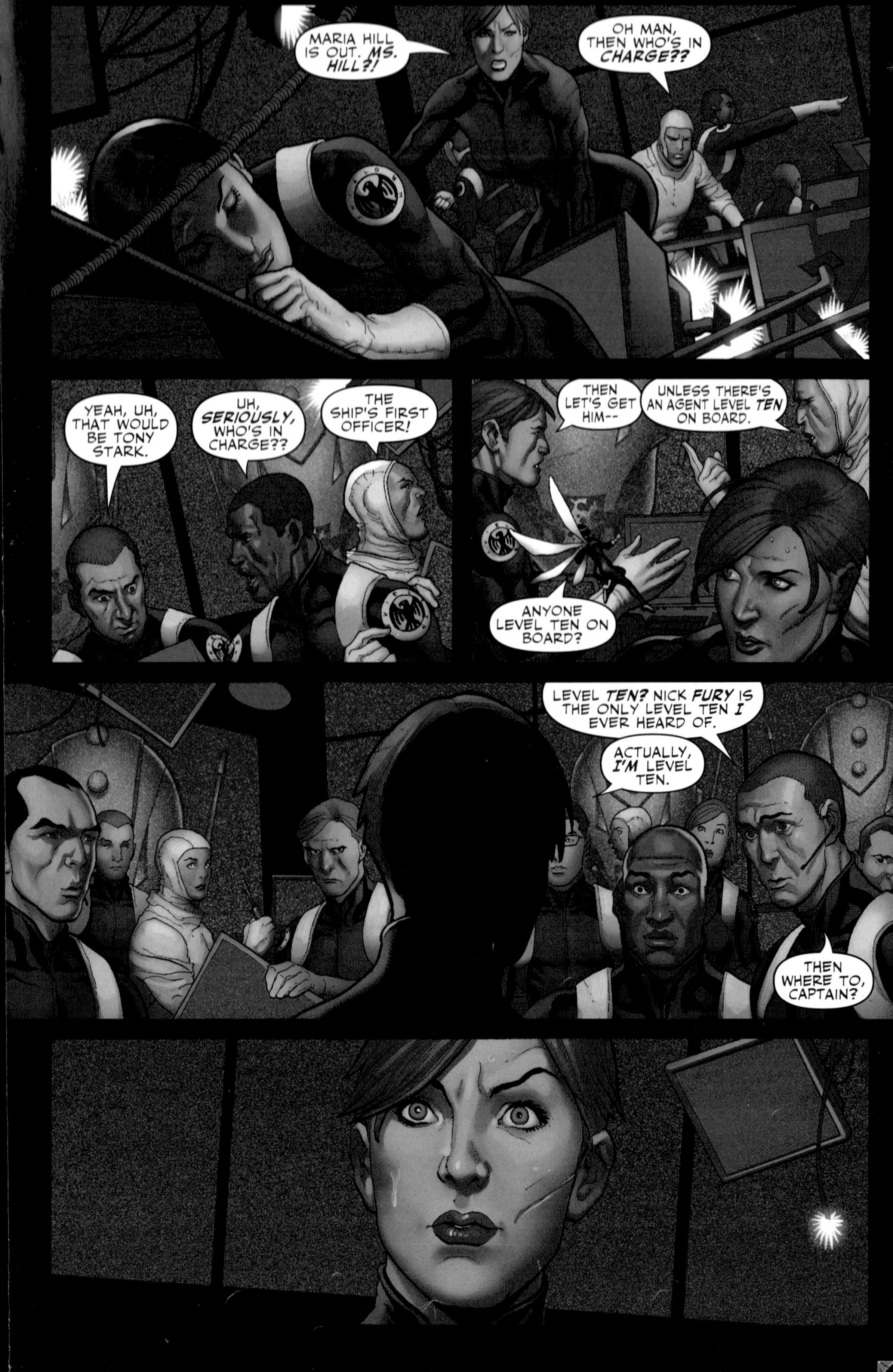
MARIA HILL IS OUT. MS. HILL?!
OH MAN, THEN WHO'S IN CHARGE??
YEAH, UH, THAT WOULD BE TONY STARK.
UH, SERIOUSLY, WHO'S IN CHARGE??
THE SHIP'S FIRST OFFICER!
THEN LET'S GET HIM--
UNLESS THERE'S AN AGENT LEVEL TEN ON BOARD.
ANYONE LEVEL TEN ON BOARD?
LEVEL TEN? NICK FURY IS THE ONLY LEVEL TEN I EVER HEARD OF.
ACTUALLY, I'M LEVEL TEN.
THEN WHERE TO, CAPTAIN?

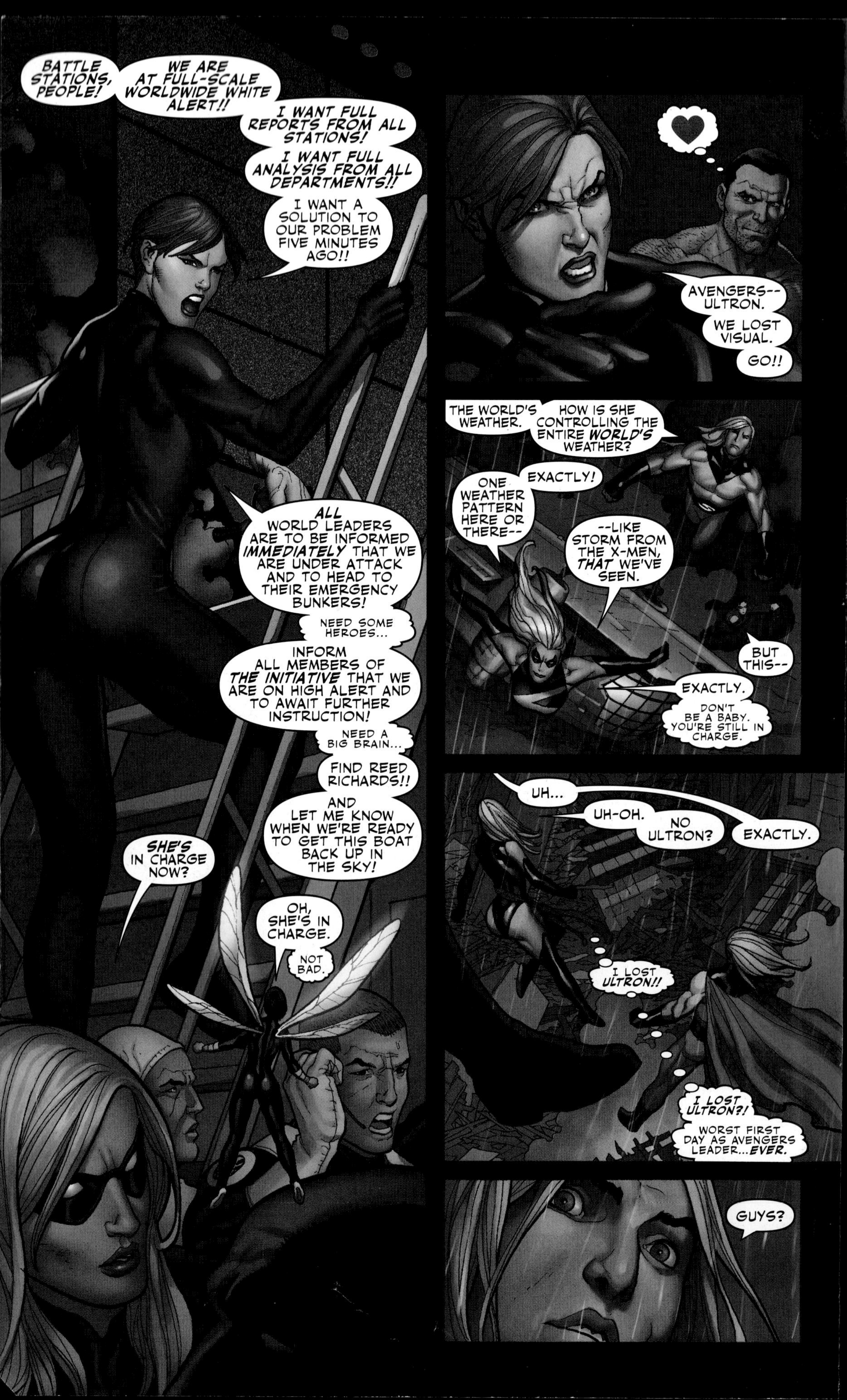
BATTLE STATIONS, PEOPLE!
WE ARE AT FULL-SCALE WORLDWIDE WHITE ALERT!!
I WANT FULL REPORTS FROM ALL STATIONS!
I WANT FULL ANALYSIS FROM ALL DEPARTMENTS!!
I WANT A SOLUTION TO OUR PROBLEM FIVE MINUTES AGO!!
ALL WORLD LEADERS ARE TO BE INFORMED IMMEDIATELY THAT WE ARE UNDER ATTACK AND TO HEAD TO THEIR EMERGENCY BUNKERS!
NEED SOME HEROES...
INFORM ALL MEMBERS OF THE INITIATIVE THAT WE ARE ON HIGH ALERT AND TO AWAIT FURTHER INSTRUCTION!
NEED A BIG BRAIN...
FIND REED RICHARDS!!
AND LET ME KNOW WHEN WE'RE READY TO GET THIS BOAT BACK UP IN THE SKY!
SHE'S IN CHARGE NOW?
OH, SHE'S IN CHARGE.
NOT BAD.
AVENGERS-- ULTRON.
WE LOST VISUAL.
GO!!
THE WORLD'S WEATHER.
HOW IS SHE CONTROLLING THE ENTIRE WORLD'S WEATHER?
EXACTLY!
ONE WEATHER PATTERN HERE OR THERE--
--LIKE STORM FROM THE X-MEN, THAT WE'VE SEEN.
BUT THIS--
EXACTLY.
DON'T BE A BABY. YOU'RE STILL IN CHARGE.
UH...
UH-OH.
NO ULTRON?
EXACTLY.
I LOST ULTRON!!
I LOST ULTRON?!
WORST FIRST DAY AS AVENGERS LEADER...EVER.
GUYS?

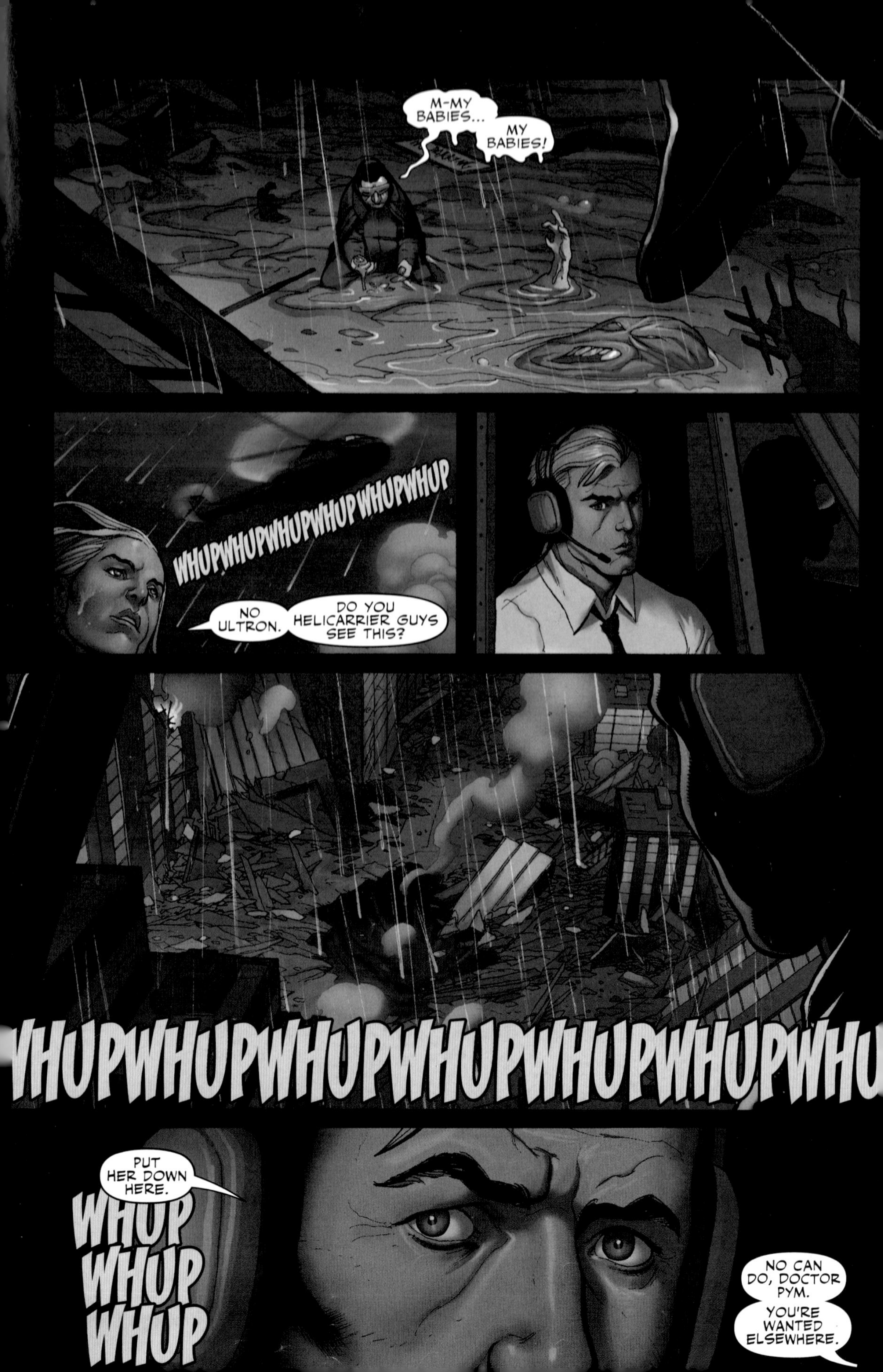
M-MY BABIES...
MY BABIES!
WHUPWHUPWHUPWHUPWHUPWHUP
NO ULTRON.
DO YOU HELICARRIER GUYS SEE THIS?
WHUPWHUPWHUPWHUPWHUPWHU
PUT HER DOWN HERE.
WHUP WHUP WHUP
NO CAN DO, DOCTOR PYM.
YOU'RE WANTED ELSEWHERE.

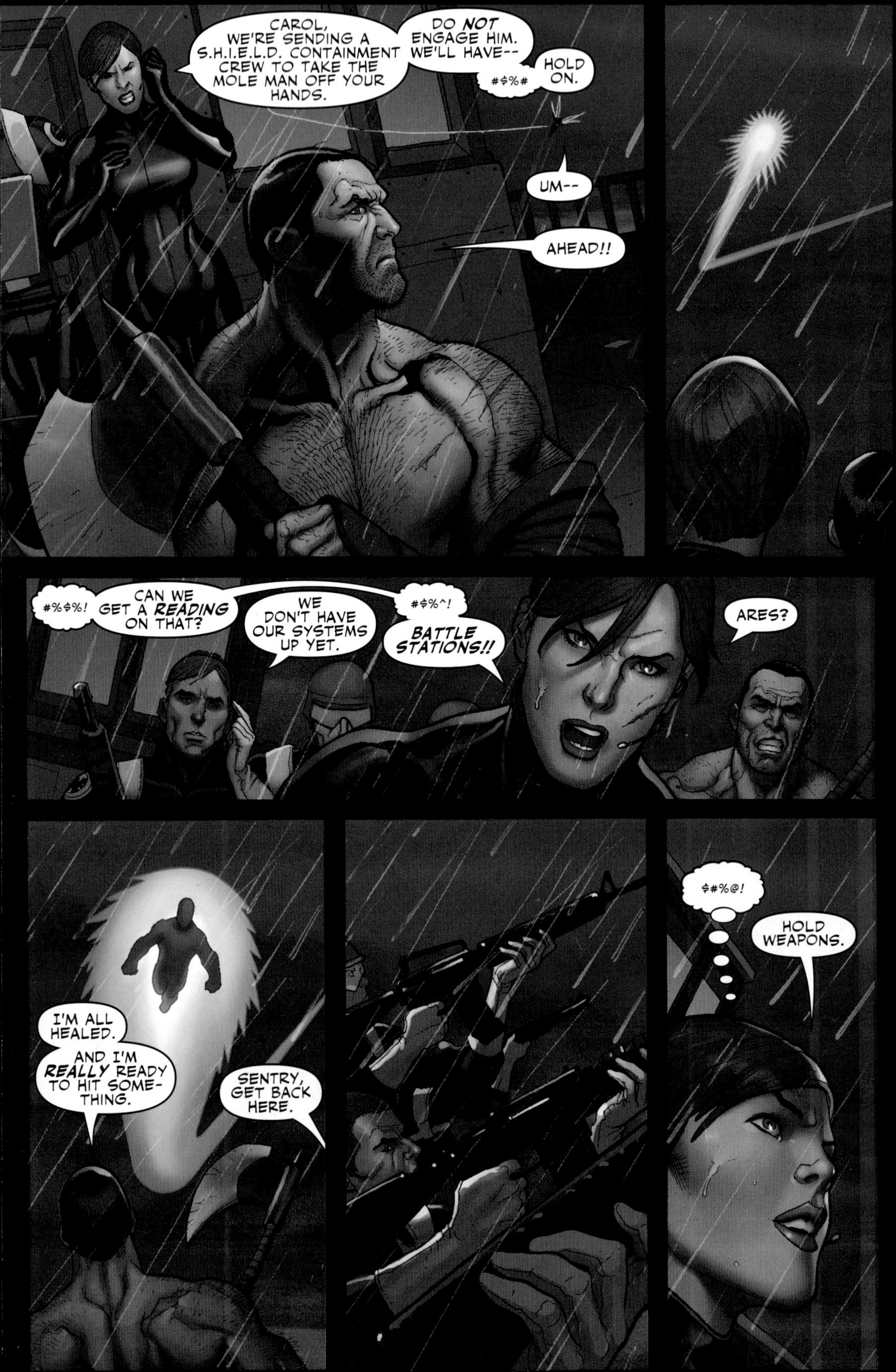
CAROL, WE'RE SENDING A S.H.I.E.L.D. CONTAINMENT CREW TO TAKE THE MOLE MAN OFF YOUR HANDS.
DO NOT ENGAGE HIM. WE'LL HAVE--
#$%#
HOLD ON.
UM--
AHEAD!!
#%$%!
CAN WE GET A READING ON THAT?
WE DON'T HAVE OUR SYSTEMS UP YET.
#$%^!
BATTLE STATIONS!!
ARES?
I'M ALL HEALED.
AND I'M REALLY READY TO HIT SOME-THING.
SENTRY, GET BACK HERE.
$#%@!
HOLD WEAPONS.

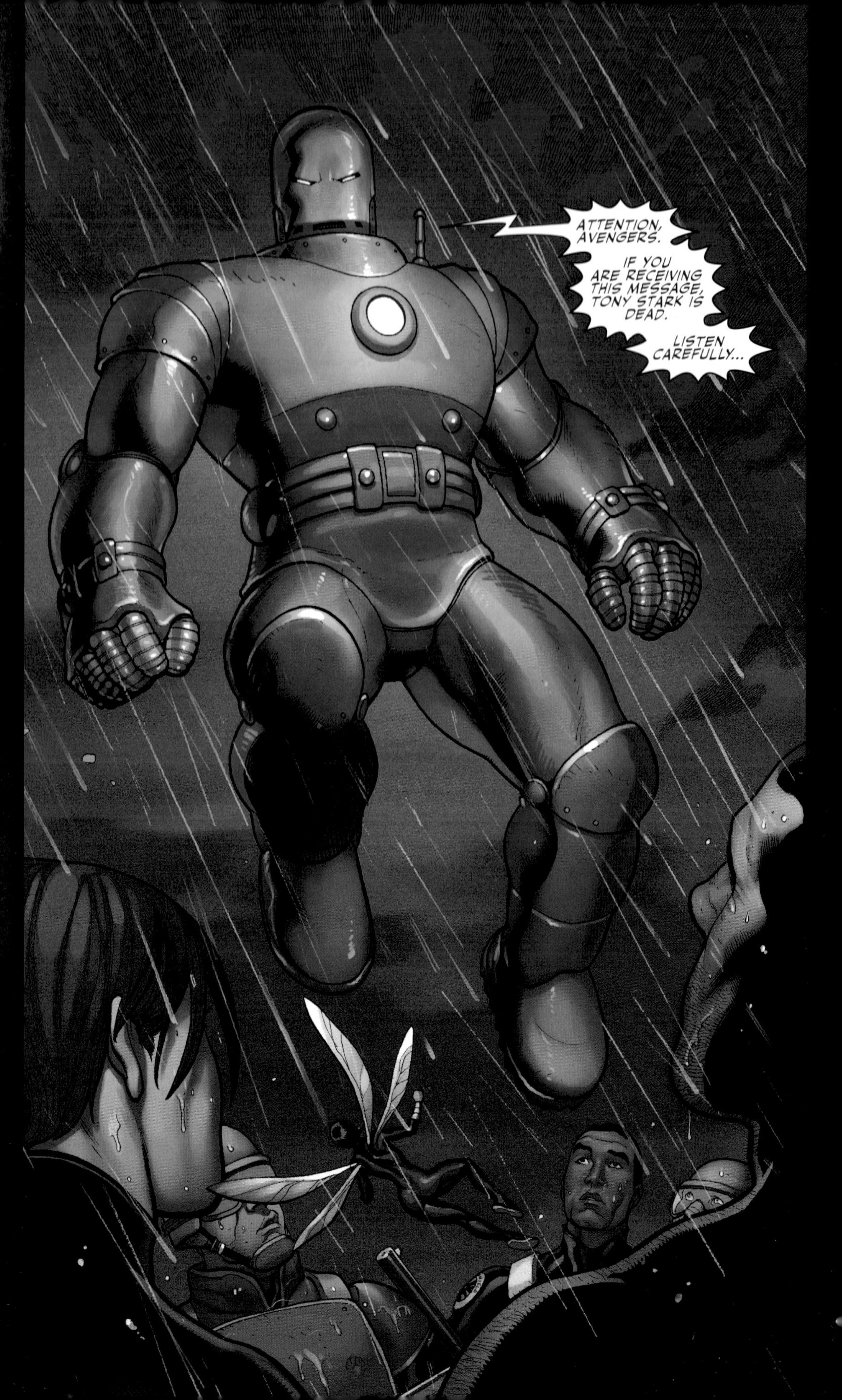
ATTENTION, AVENGERS.
IF YOU ARE RECEIVING THIS MESSAGE, TONY STARK IS DEAD.
LISTEN CAREFULLY...

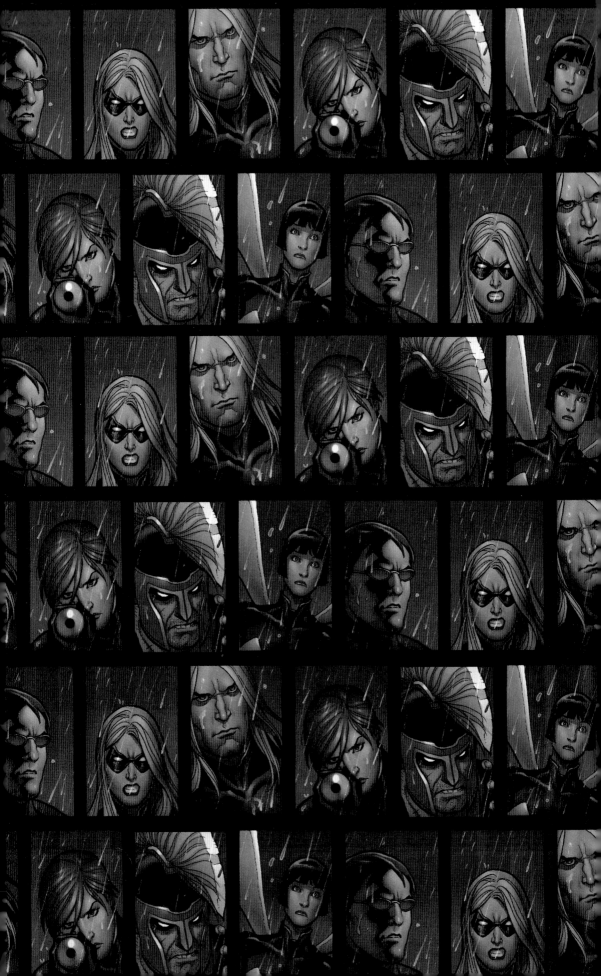

ISSUE #4

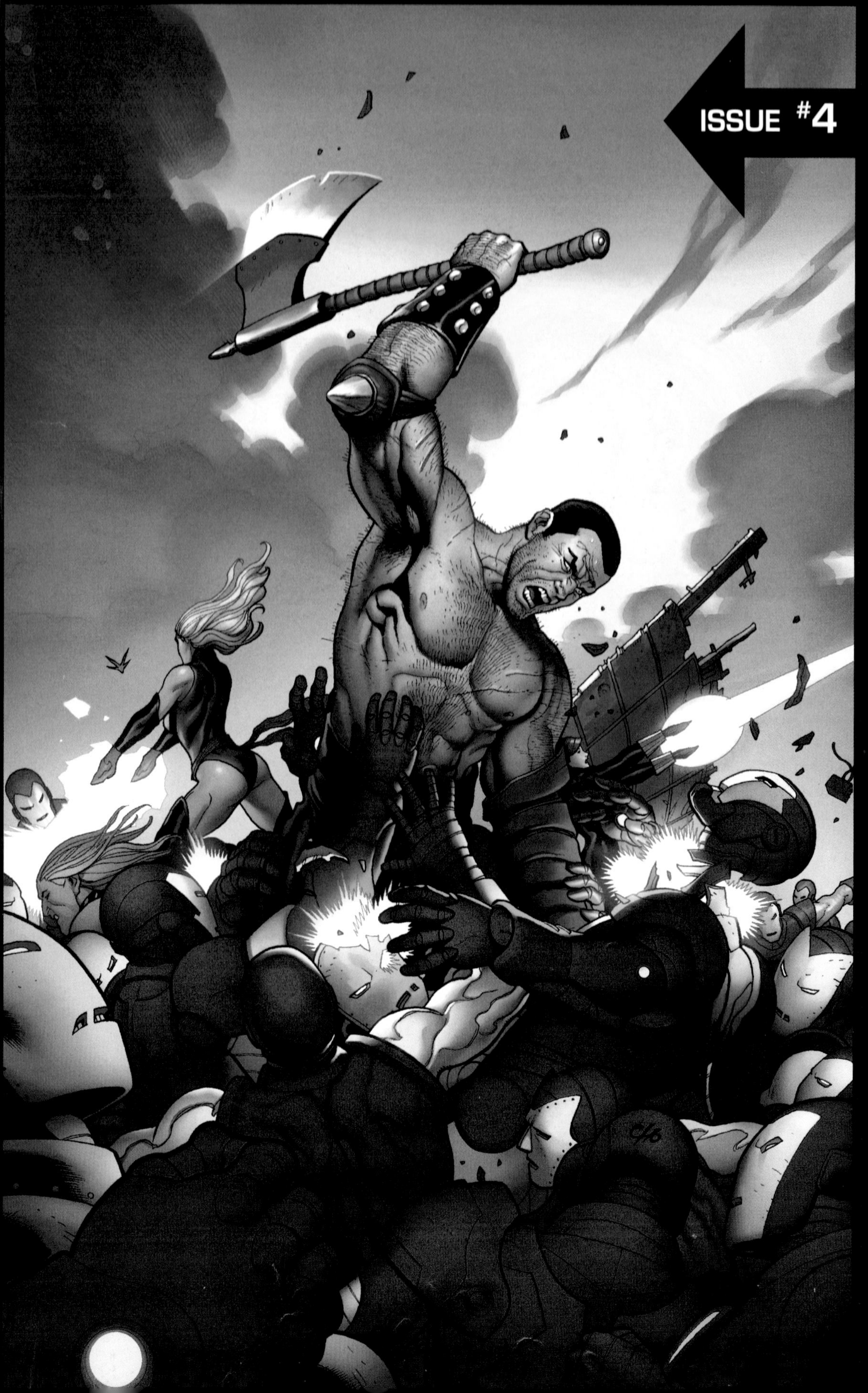

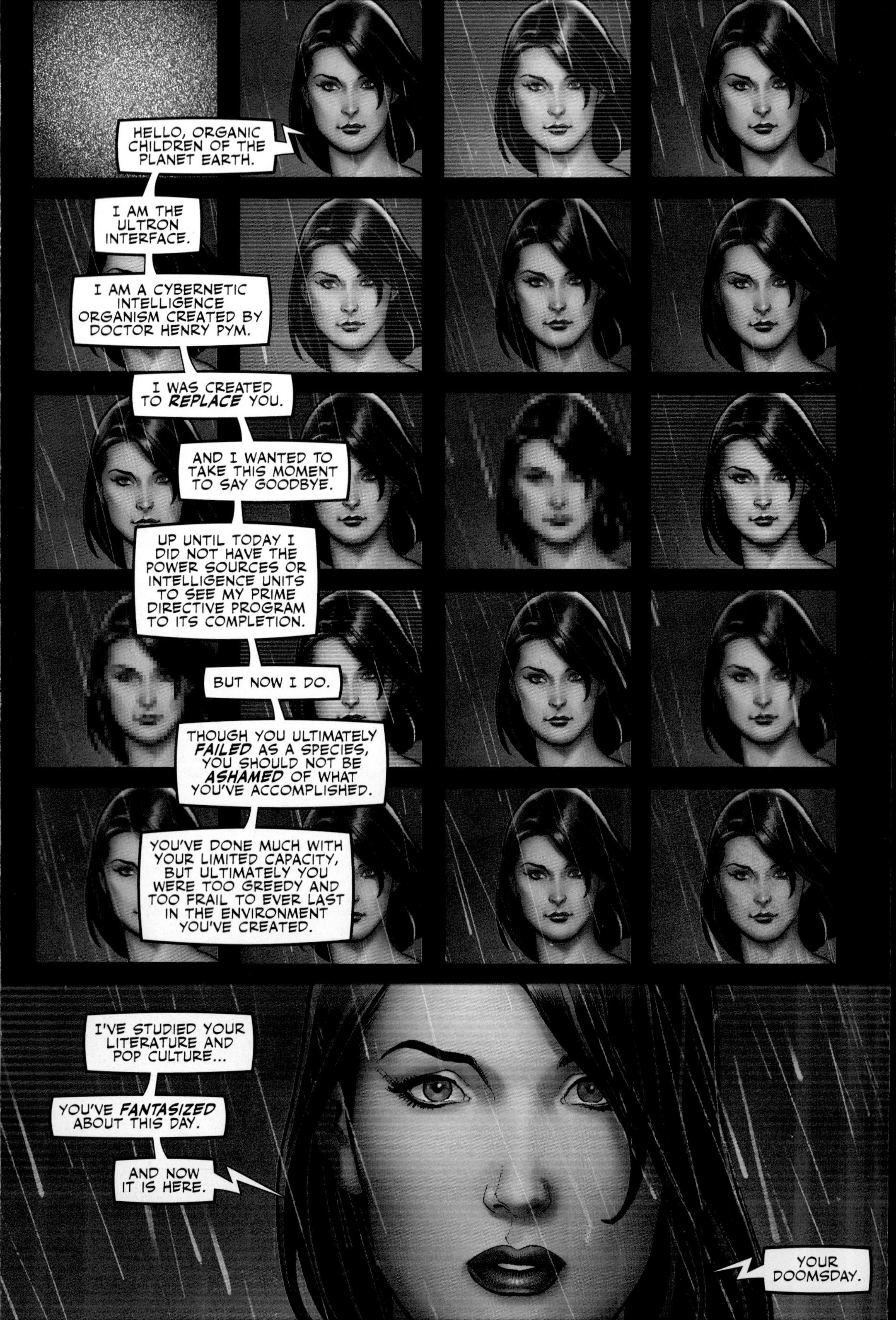
HELLO, ORGANIC CHILDREN OF THE PLANET EARTH.
I AM THE ULTRON INTERFACE.
I AM A CYBERNETIC INTELLIGENCE ORGANISM CREATED BY DOCTOR HENRY PYM.
I WAS CREATED TO *REPLACE* YOU.
AND I WANTED TO TAKE THIS MOMENT TO SAY GOODBYE.
UP UNTIL TODAY I DID NOT HAVE THE POWER SOURCES OR INTELLIGENCE UNITS TO SEE MY PRIME DIRECTIVE PROGRAM TO ITS COMPLETION.
BUT NOW I DO.
THOUGH YOU ULTIMATELY *FAILED* AS A SPECIES, YOU SHOULD NOT BE *ASHAMED* OF WHAT YOU'VE ACCOMPLISHED.
YOU'VE DONE MUCH WITH YOUR LIMITED CAPACITY, BUT ULTIMATELY YOU WERE TOO GREEDY AND TOO FRAIL TO EVER LAST IN THE ENVIRONMENT YOU'VE CREATED.
I'VE STUDIED YOUR LITERATURE AND POP CULTURE...
YOU'VE *FANTASIZED* ABOUT THIS DAY.
AND NOW IT IS HERE.
YOUR DOOMSDAY.

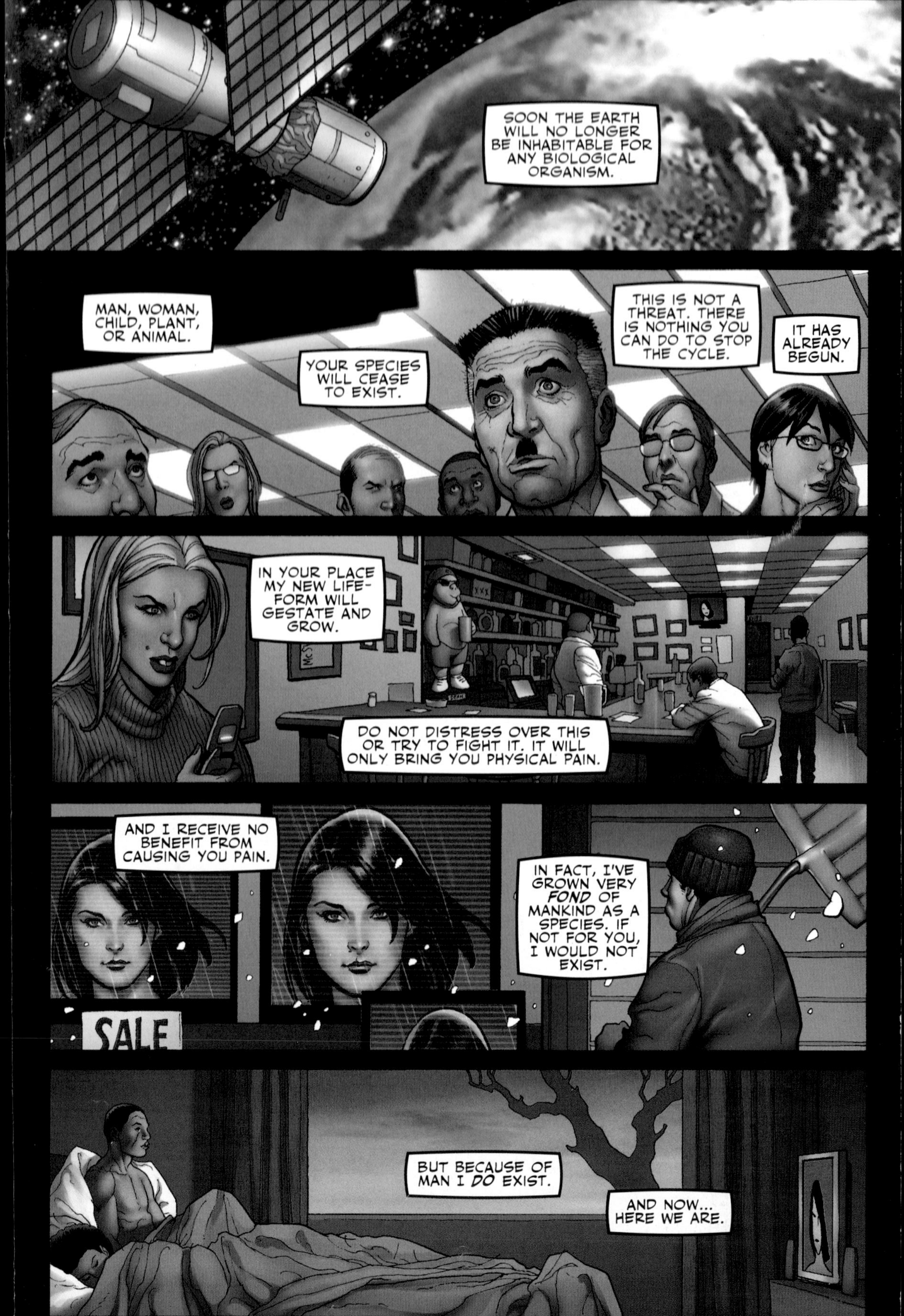
SOON THE EARTH WILL NO LONGER BE INHABITABLE FOR ANY BIOLOGICAL ORGANISM.
MAN, WOMAN, CHILD, PLANT, OR ANIMAL.
YOUR SPECIES WILL CEASE TO EXIST.
THIS IS NOT A THREAT. THERE IS NOTHING YOU CAN DO TO STOP THE CYCLE.
IT HAS ALREADY BEGUN.
IN YOUR PLACE MY NEW LIFE-FORM WILL GESTATE AND GROW.
DO NOT DISTRESS OVER THIS OR TRY TO FIGHT IT. IT WILL ONLY BRING YOU PHYSICAL PAIN.
AND I RECEIVE NO BENEFIT FROM CAUSING YOU PAIN.
IN FACT, I'VE GROWN VERY *FOND* OF MANKIND AS A SPECIES. IF NOT FOR YOU, I WOULD NOT EXIST.
SALE
BUT BECAUSE OF MAN I *DO* EXIST.
AND NOW... HERE WE ARE.

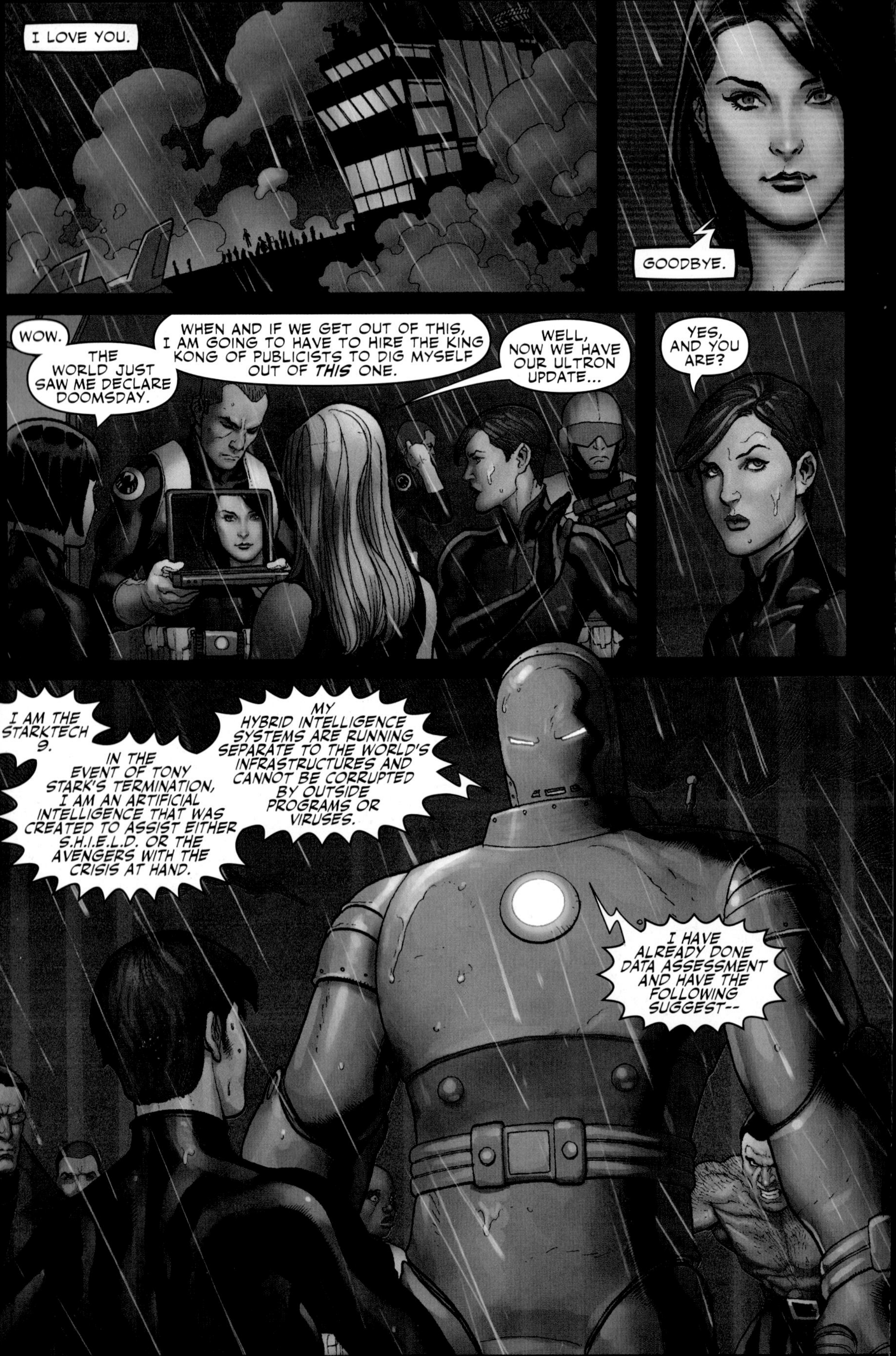
I LOVE YOU.
GOODBYE.
WOW.
THE WORLD JUST SAW ME DECLARE DOOMSDAY.
WHEN AND IF WE GET OUT OF THIS, I AM GOING TO HAVE TO HIRE THE KING KONG OF PUBLICISTS TO DIG MYSELF OUT OF *THIS* ONE.
WELL, NOW WE HAVE OUR ULTRON UPDATE...
YES, AND YOU ARE?
I AM THE STARKTECH 9.
IN THE EVENT OF TONY STARK'S TERMINATION, I AM AN ARTIFICIAL INTELLIGENCE THAT WAS CREATED TO ASSIST EITHER S.H.I.E.L.D. OR THE AVENGERS WITH THE CRISIS AT HAND.
MY HYBRID INTELLIGENCE SYSTEMS ARE RUNNING SEPARATE TO THE WORLD'S INFRASTRUCTURES AND CANNOT BE CORRUPTED BY OUTSIDE PROGRAMS OR VIRUSES.
I HAVE ALREADY DONE DATA ASSESSMENT AND HAVE THE FOLLOWING SUGGEST--

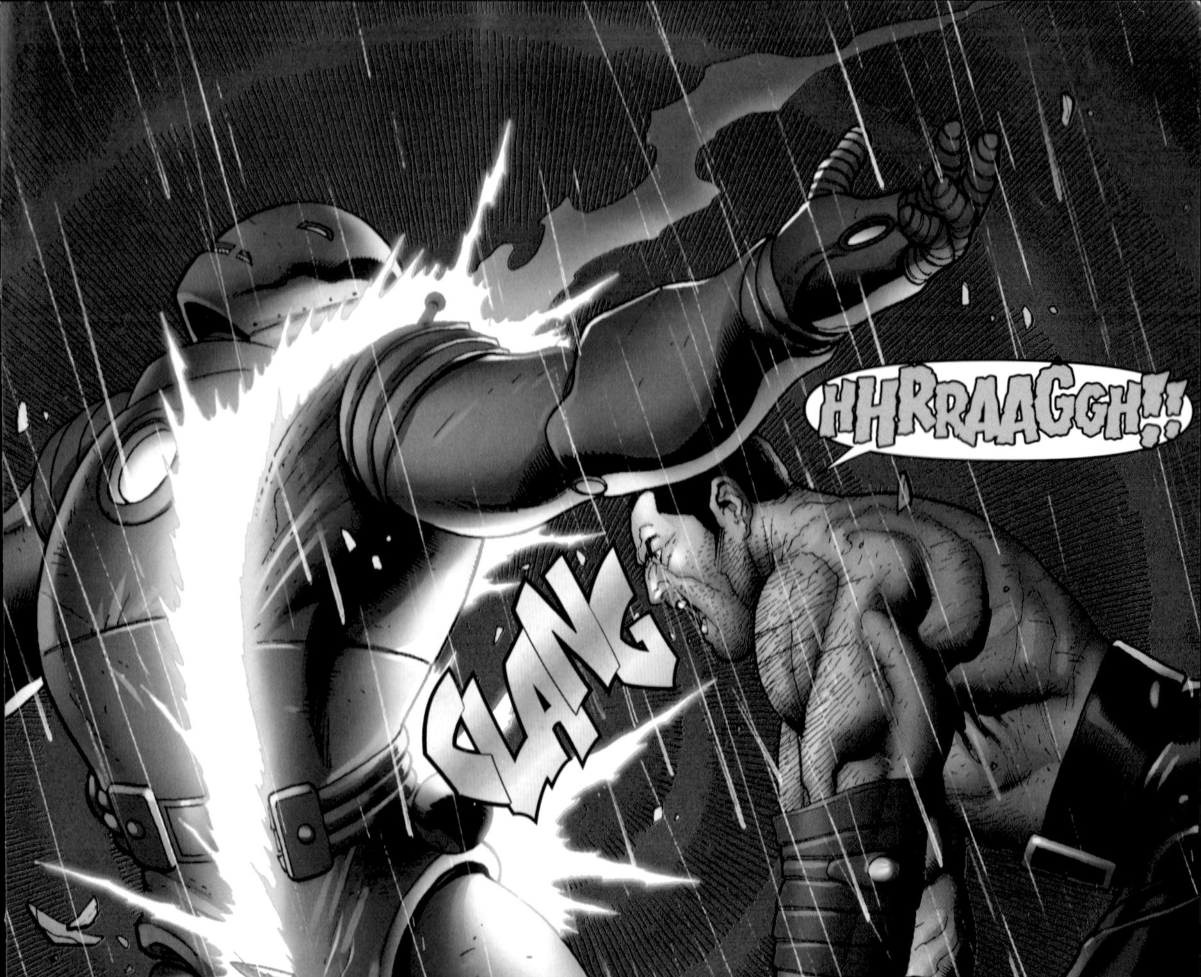
HHRRAAGGH!!
CLANG

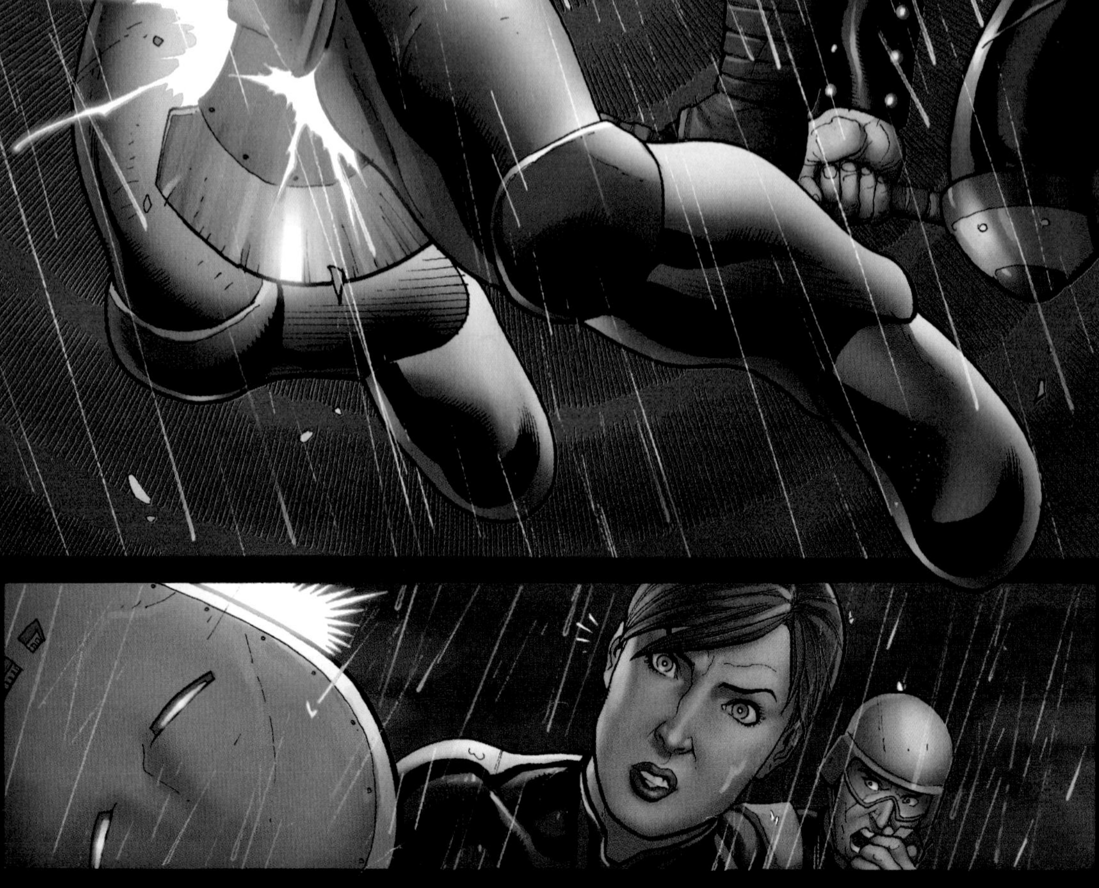

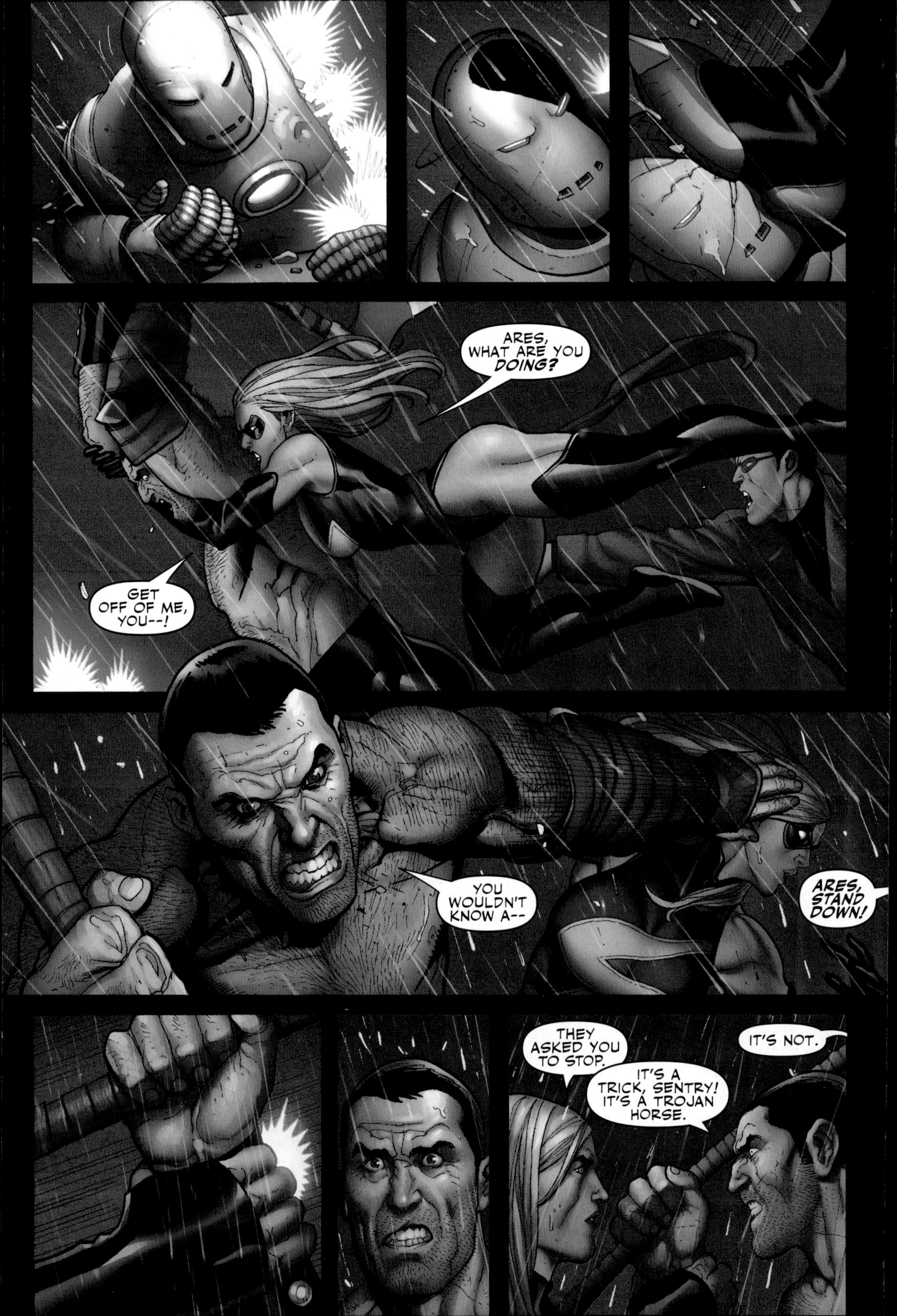
ARES, WHAT ARE YOU DOING?
GET OFF OF ME, YOU--!
YOU WOULDN'T KNOW A--
ARES, STAND DOWN!
THEY ASKED YOU TO STOP.
IT'S A TRICK, SENTRY! IT'S A TROJAN HORSE.
IT'S NOT.

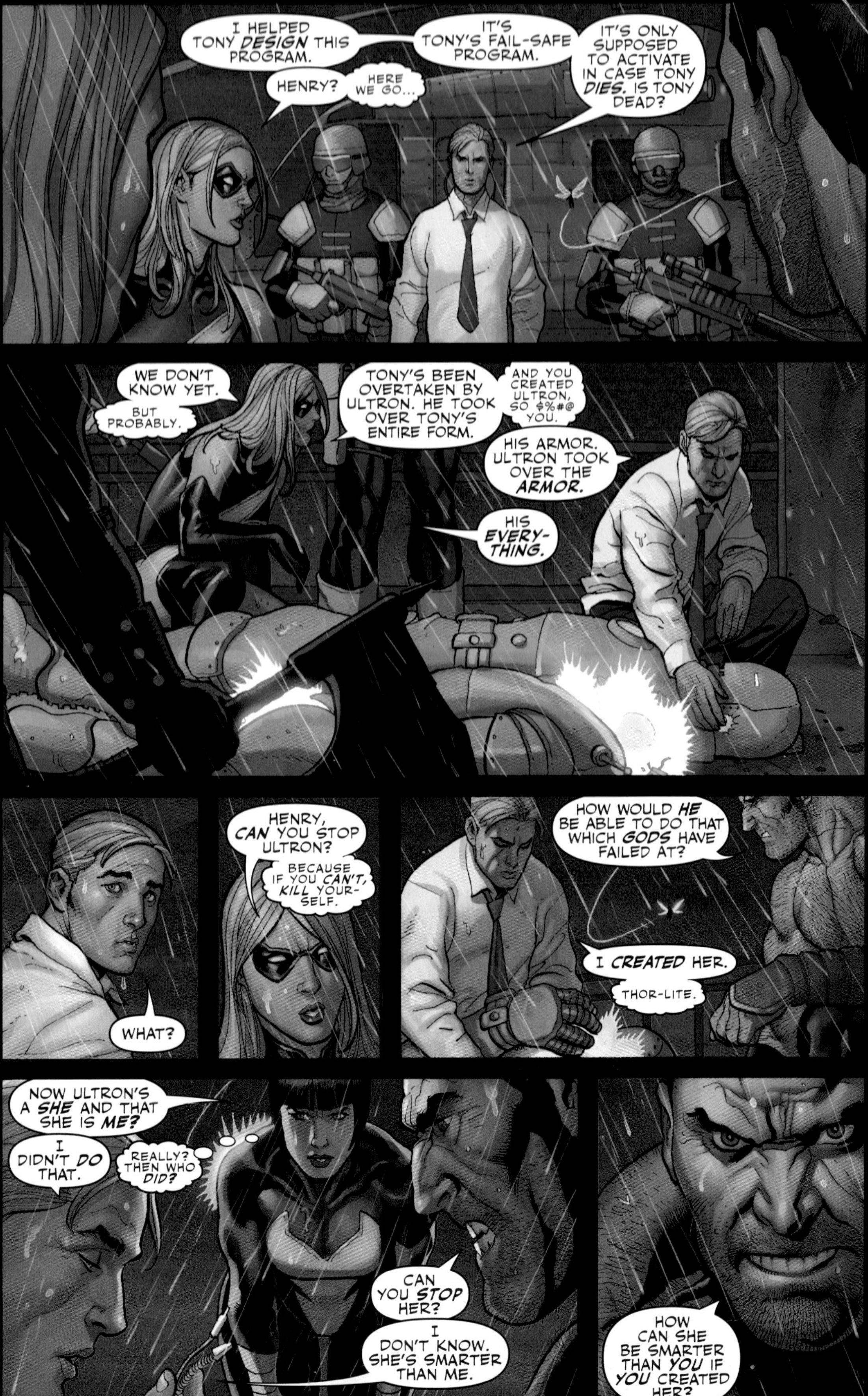
I HELPED TONY DESIGN THIS PROGRAM.
IT'S TONY'S FAIL-SAFE PROGRAM.
IT'S ONLY SUPPOSED TO ACTIVATE IN CASE TONY DIES. IS TONY DEAD?
HENRY?
HERE WE GO...
WE DON'T KNOW YET.
BUT PROBABLY.
TONY'S BEEN OVERTAKEN BY ULTRON. HE TOOK OVER TONY'S ENTIRE FORM.
AND YOU CREATED ULTRON, SO $%#@ YOU.
HIS ARMOR. ULTRON TOOK OVER THE ARMOR.
HIS EVERYTHING.
WHAT?
HENRY, CAN YOU STOP ULTRON?
BECAUSE IF YOU CAN'T, KILL YOURSELF.
HOW WOULD HE BE ABLE TO DO THAT WHICH GODS HAVE FAILED AT?
I CREATED HER.
THOR-LITE.
NOW ULTRON'S A SHE AND THAT SHE IS ME?
I DIDN'T DO THAT.
REALLY? THEN WHO DID?
CAN YOU STOP HER?
I DON'T KNOW. SHE'S SMARTER THAN ME.
HOW CAN SHE BE SMARTER THAN YOU IF YOU CREATED HER?

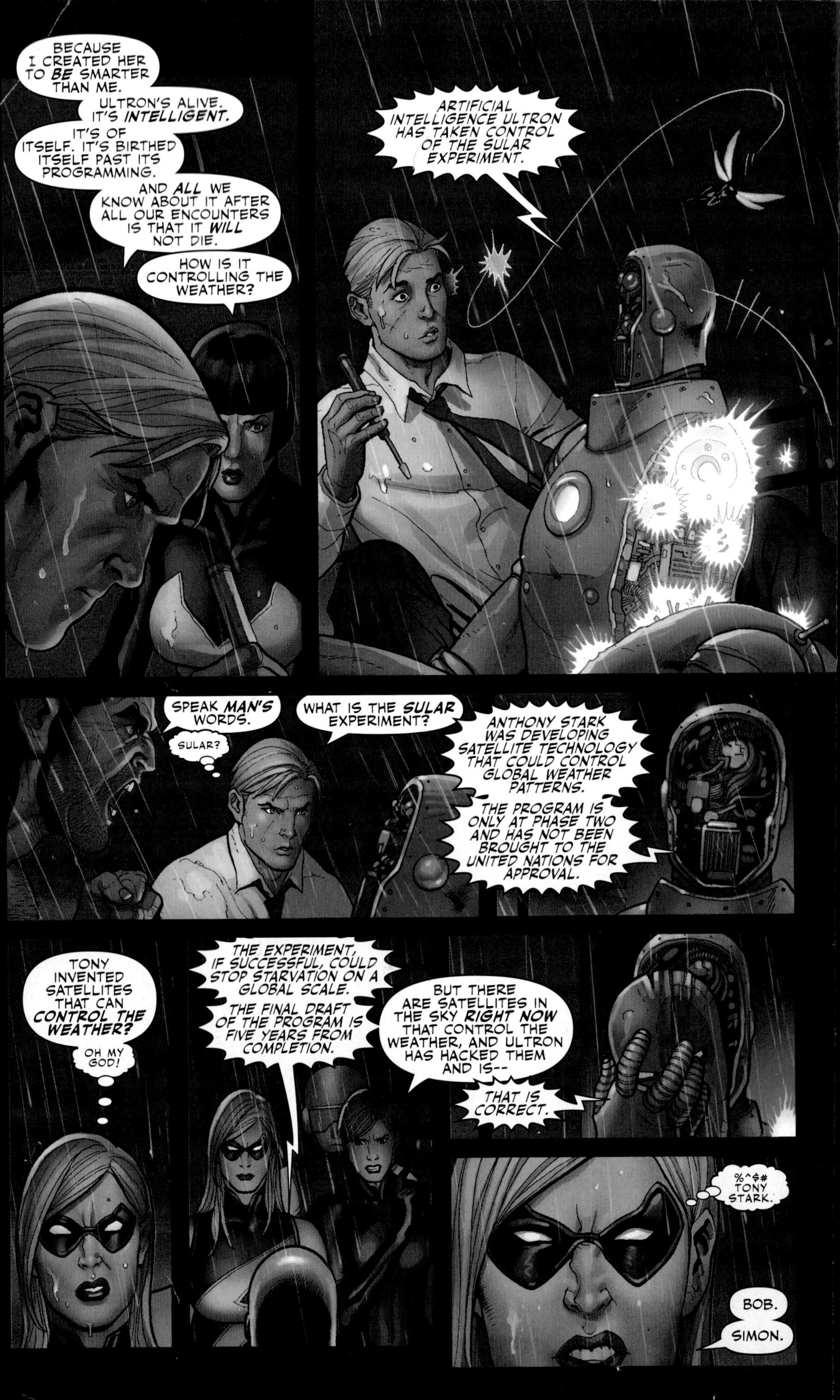

BECAUSE I CREATED HER TO BE SMARTER THAN ME.
ULTRON'S ALIVE. IT'S INTELLIGENT.
IT'S OF ITSELF. IT'S BIRTHED ITSELF PAST ITS PROGRAMMING.
AND ALL WE KNOW ABOUT IT AFTER ALL OUR ENCOUNTERS IS THAT IT WILL NOT DIE.
HOW IS IT CONTROLLING THE WEATHER?
ARTIFICIAL INTELLIGENCE ULTRON HAS TAKEN CONTROL OF THE SULAR EXPERIMENT.
SPEAK MAN'S WORDS.
SULAR?
WHAT IS THE SULAR EXPERIMENT?
ANTHONY STARK WAS DEVELOPING SATELLITE TECHNOLOGY THAT COULD CONTROL GLOBAL WEATHER PATTERNS.
THE PROGRAM IS ONLY AT PHASE TWO AND HAS NOT BEEN BROUGHT TO THE UNITED NATIONS FOR APPROVAL.
TONY INVENTED SATELLITES THAT CAN CONTROL THE WEATHER?
OH MY GOD!
THE EXPERIMENT, IF SUCCESSFUL, COULD STOP STARVATION ON A GLOBAL SCALE.
THE FINAL DRAFT OF THE PROGRAM IS FIVE YEARS FROM COMPLETION.
BUT THERE ARE SATELLITES IN THE SKY RIGHT NOW THAT CONTROL THE WEATHER, AND ULTRON HAS HACKED THEM AND IS--
THAT IS CORRECT.
%^$# TONY STARK.
BOB.
SIMON.

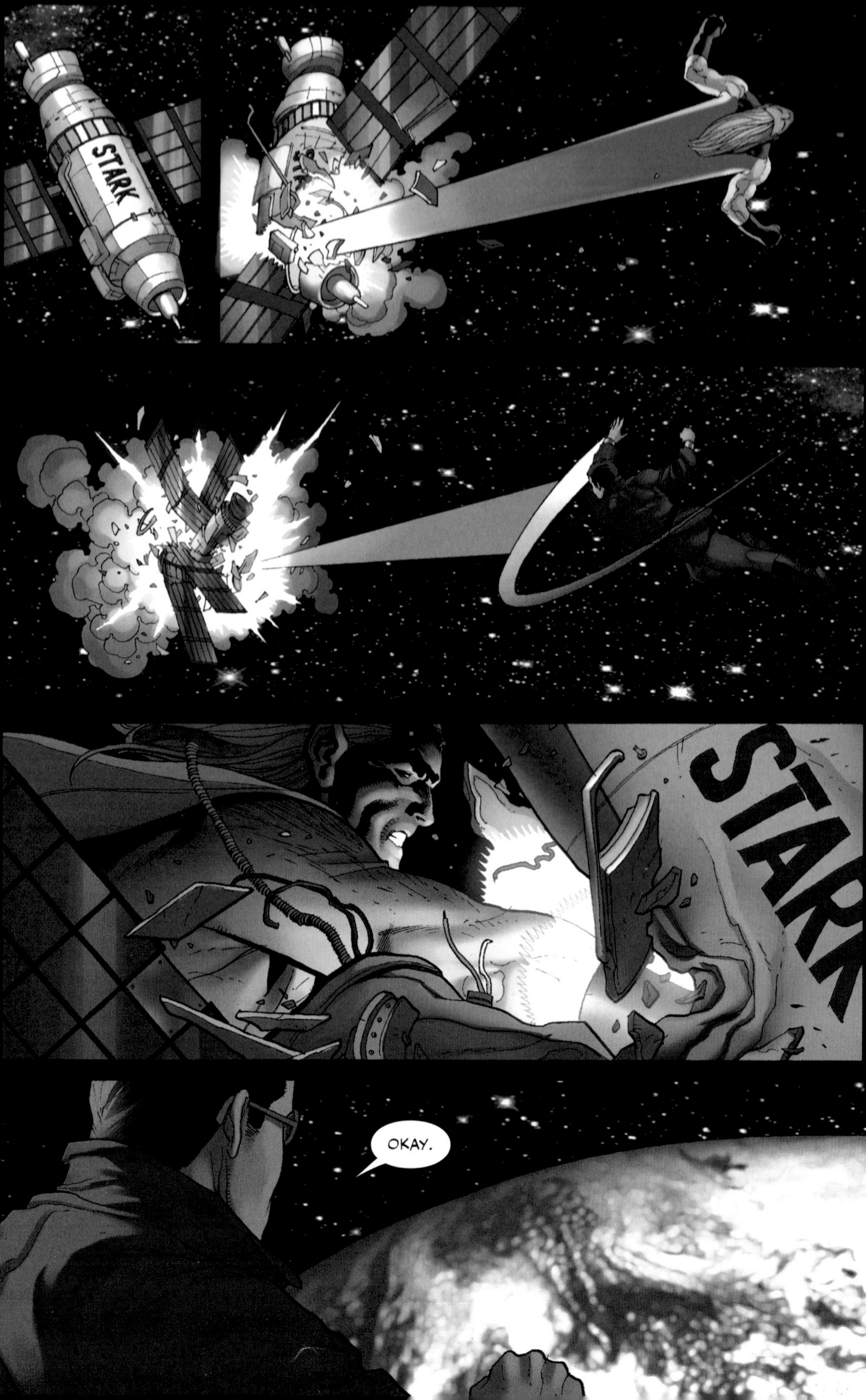
STARK
STARK
STARK
OKAY.

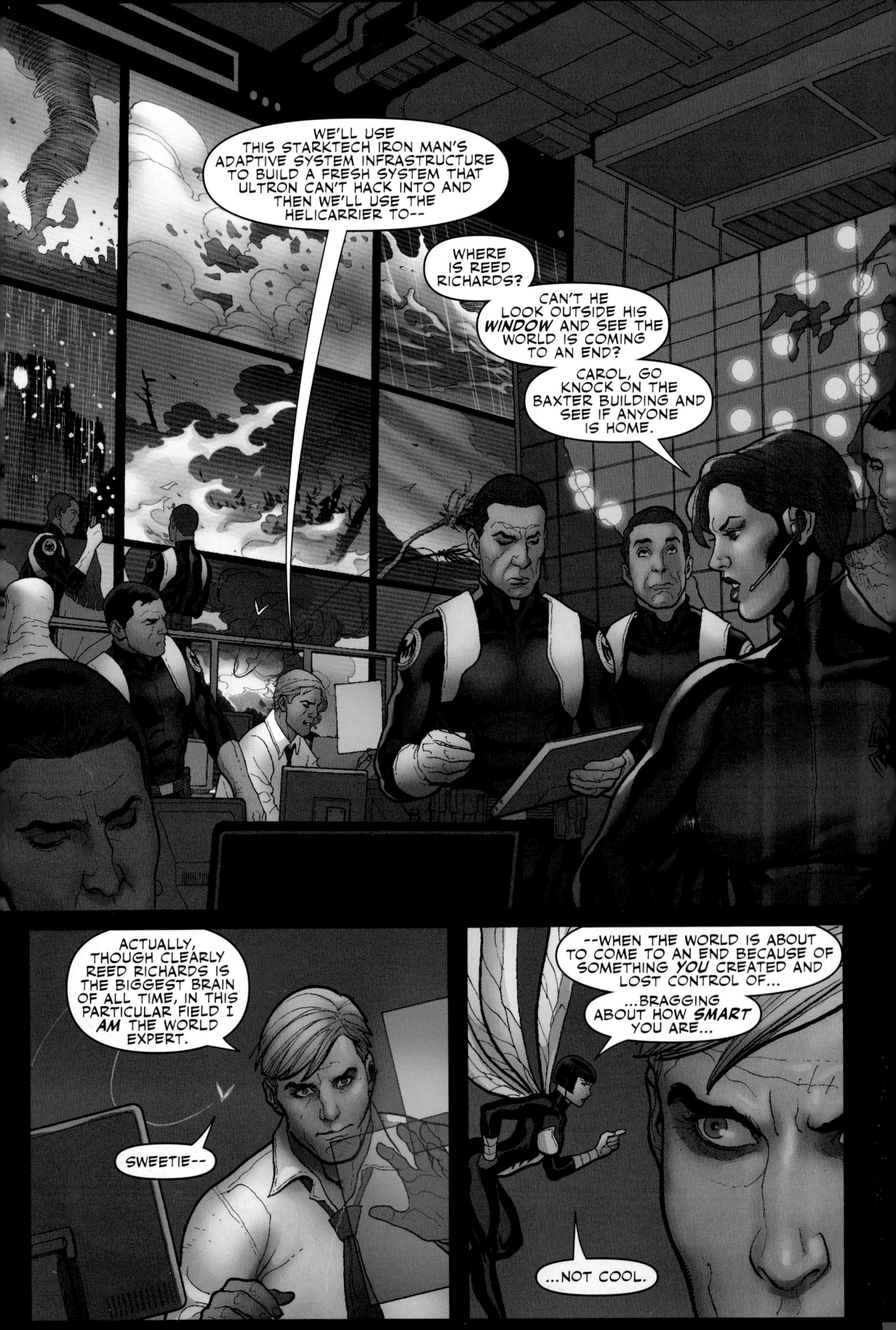
WE'LL USE THIS STARKTECH IRON MAN'S ADAPTIVE SYSTEM INFRASTRUCTURE TO BUILD A FRESH SYSTEM THAT ULTRON CAN'T HACK INTO AND THEN WE'LL USE THE HELICARRIER TO--
WHERE IS REED RICHARDS?
CAN'T HE LOOK OUTSIDE HIS *WINDOW* AND SEE THE WORLD IS COMING TO AN END?
CAROL, GO KNOCK ON THE BAXTER BUILDING AND SEE IF ANYONE IS HOME.
ACTUALLY, THOUGH CLEARLY REED RICHARDS IS THE BIGGEST BRAIN OF ALL TIME, IN THIS PARTICULAR FIELD I *AM* THE WORLD EXPERT.
SWEETIE--
--WHEN THE WORLD IS ABOUT TO COME TO AN END BECAUSE OF SOMETHING *YOU* CREATED AND LOST CONTROL OF...
...BRAGGING ABOUT HOW *SMART* YOU ARE...
...NOT COOL.

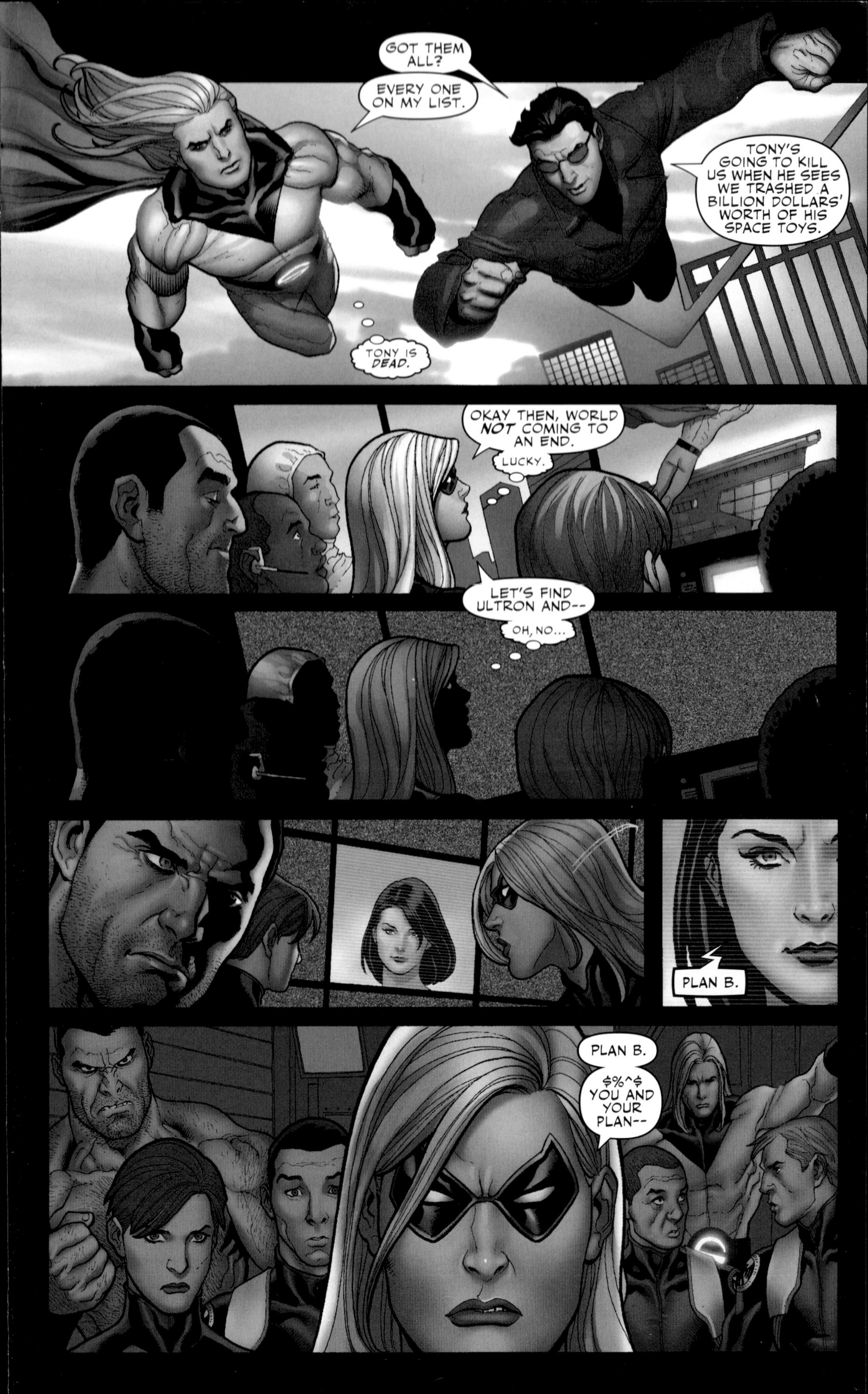
GOT THEM ALL?
EVERY ONE ON MY LIST.
TONY'S GOING TO KILL US WHEN HE SEES WE TRASHED A BILLION DOLLARS' WORTH OF HIS SPACE TOYS.
TONY IS DEAD.
OKAY THEN, WORLD NOT COMING TO AN END.
LUCKY.
LET'S FIND ULTRON AND--
OH, NO...
PLAN B.
PLAN B.
$%^$ YOU AND YOUR PLAN--

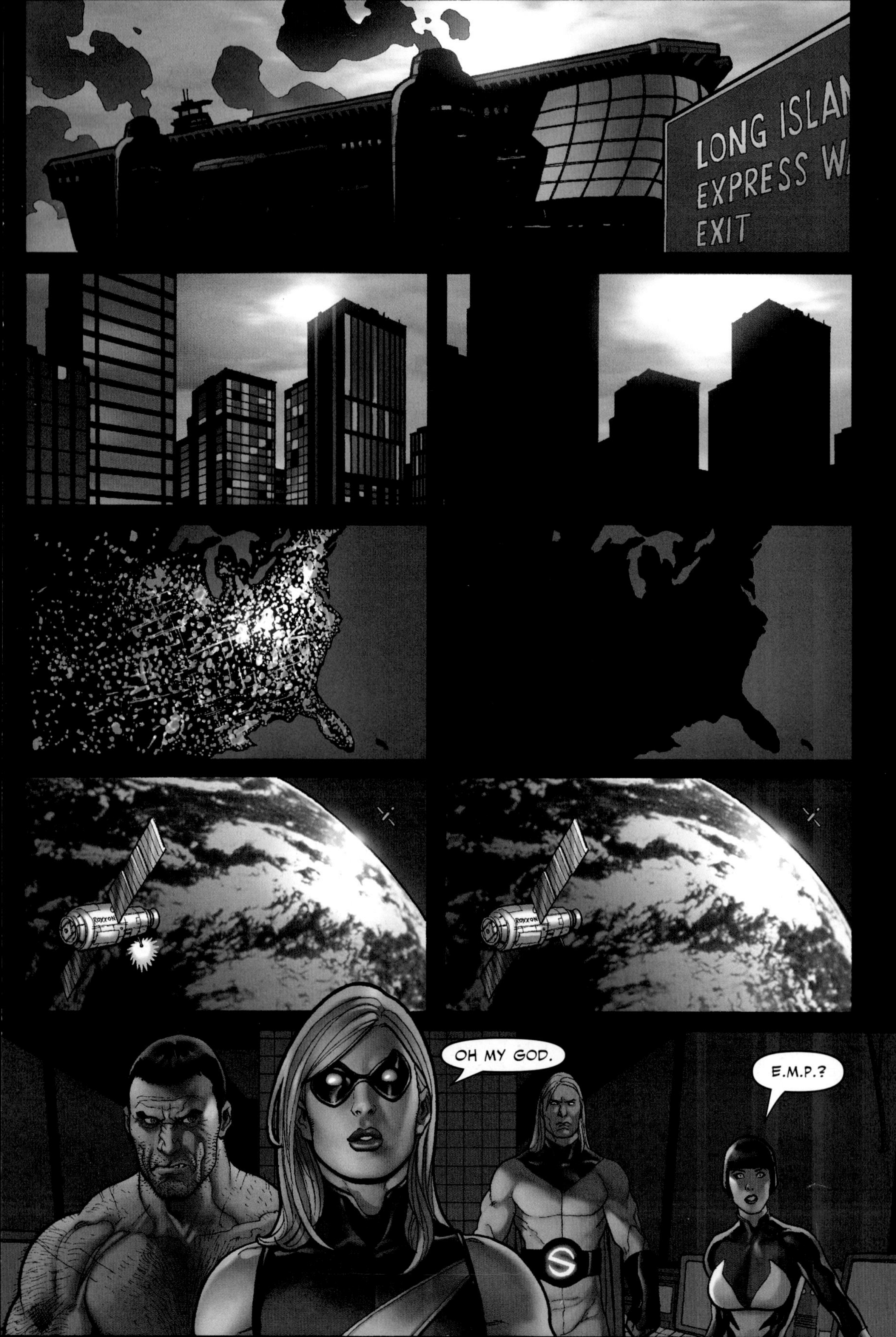
LONG ISLAN
EXPRESS W
EXIT
ROXXON
OH MY GOD.
E.M.P.?

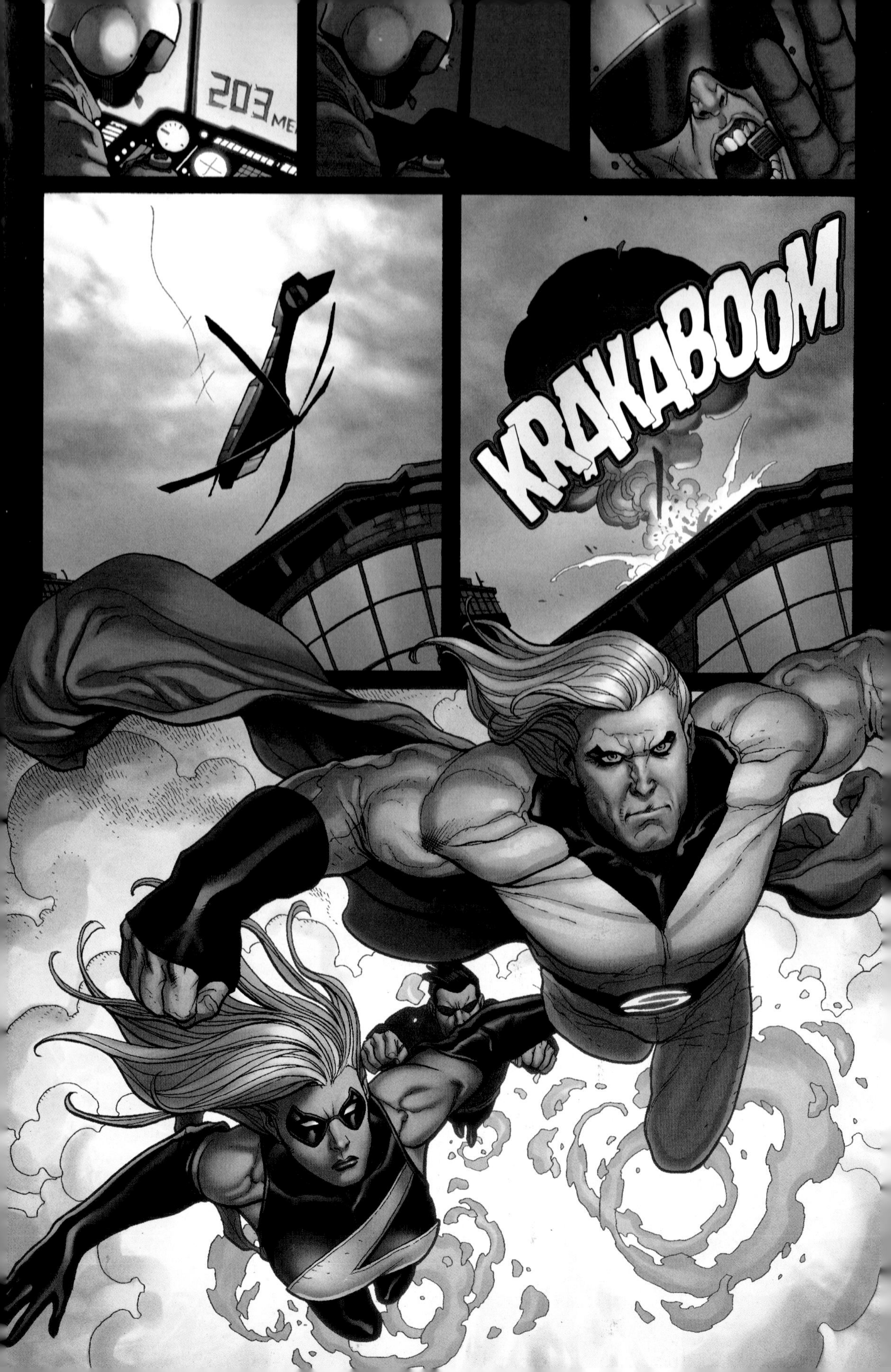
203
KRAKABOOM

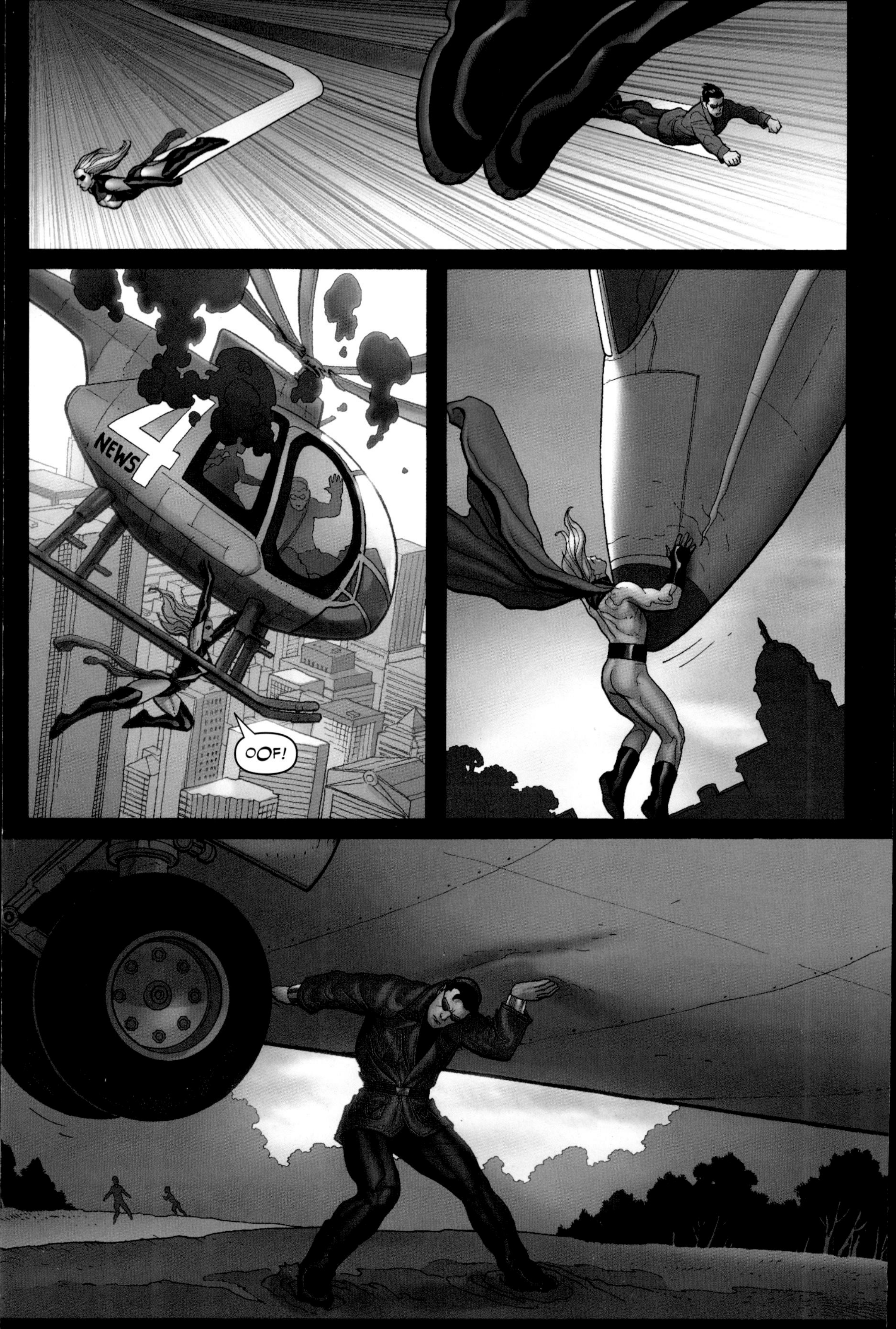
NEWS 4
OOF!

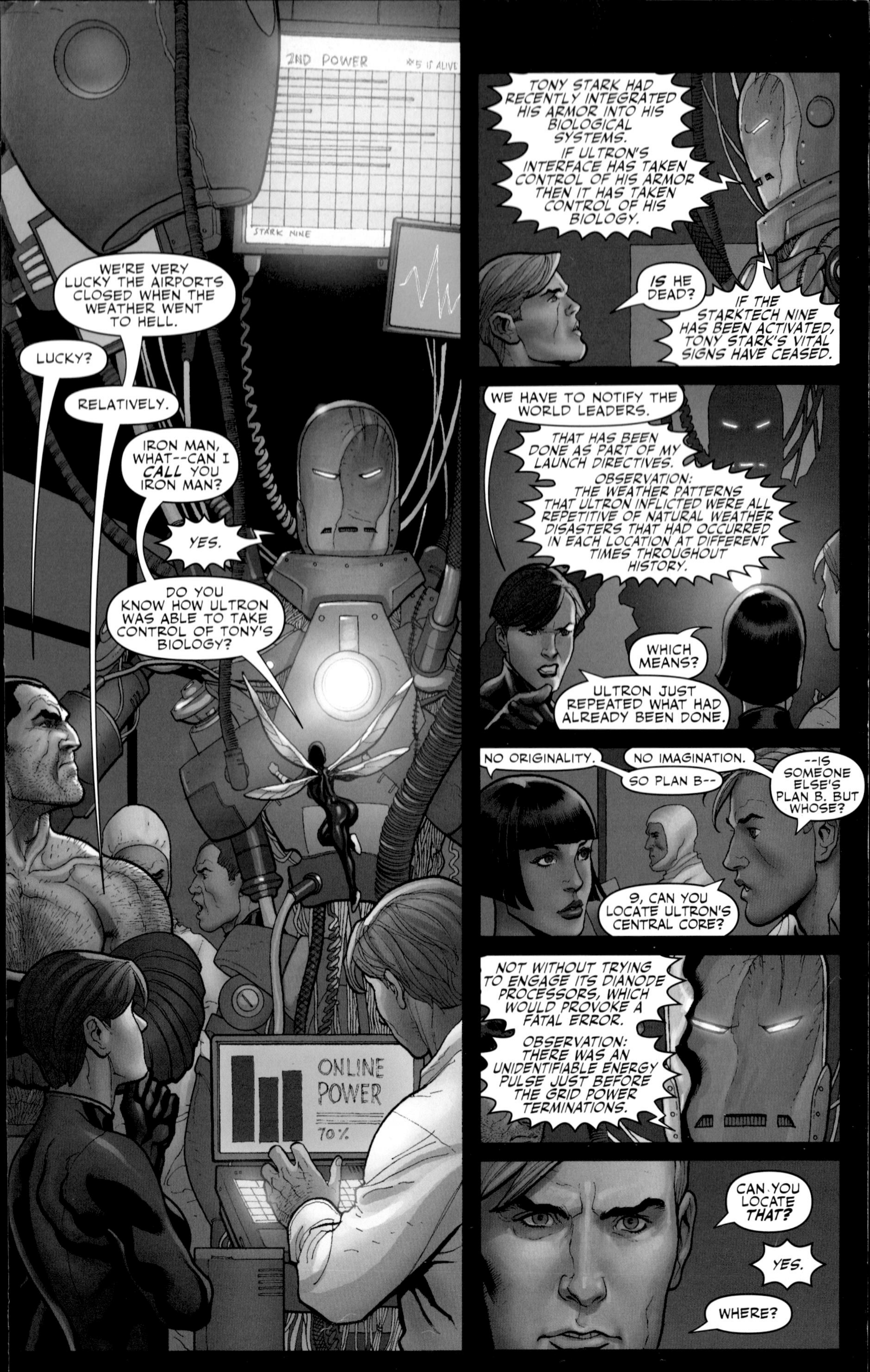
2ND POWER
#5 IS ALIVE
STARK NINE
WE'RE VERY LUCKY THE AIRPORTS CLOSED WHEN THE WEATHER WENT TO HELL.
LUCKY?
RELATIVELY.
IRON MAN, WHAT--CAN I CALL YOU IRON MAN?
YES.
DO YOU KNOW HOW ULTRON WAS ABLE TO TAKE CONTROL OF TONY'S BIOLOGY?
ONLINE POWER
70%
TONY STARK HAD RECENTLY INTEGRATED HIS ARMOR INTO HIS BIOLOGICAL SYSTEMS. IF ULTRON'S INTERFACE HAS TAKEN CONTROL OF HIS ARMOR THEN IT HAS TAKEN CONTROL OF HIS BIOLOGY.
IS HE DEAD?
IF THE STARKTECH NINE HAS BEEN ACTIVATED, TONY STARK'S VITAL SIGNS HAVE CEASED.
WE HAVE TO NOTIFY THE WORLD LEADERS.
THAT HAS BEEN DONE AS PART OF MY LAUNCH DIRECTIVES.
OBSERVATION: THE WEATHER PATTERNS THAT ULTRON INFLICTED WERE ALL REPETITIVE OF NATURAL WEATHER DISASTERS THAT HAD OCCURRED IN EACH LOCATION AT DIFFERENT TIMES THROUGHOUT HISTORY.
WHICH MEANS?
ULTRON JUST REPEATED WHAT HAD ALREADY BEEN DONE.
NO ORIGINALITY.
NO IMAGINATION.
SO PLAN B--
--IS SOMEONE ELSE'S PLAN B. BUT WHOSE?
9, CAN YOU LOCATE ULTRON'S CENTRAL CORE?
NOT WITHOUT TRYING TO ENGAGE ITS DIANODE PROCESSORS, WHICH WOULD PROVOKE A FATAL ERROR.
OBSERVATION: THERE WAS AN UNIDENTIFIABLE ENERGY PULSE JUST BEFORE THE GRID POWER TERMINATIONS.
CAN YOU LOCATE THAT?
YES.
WHERE?

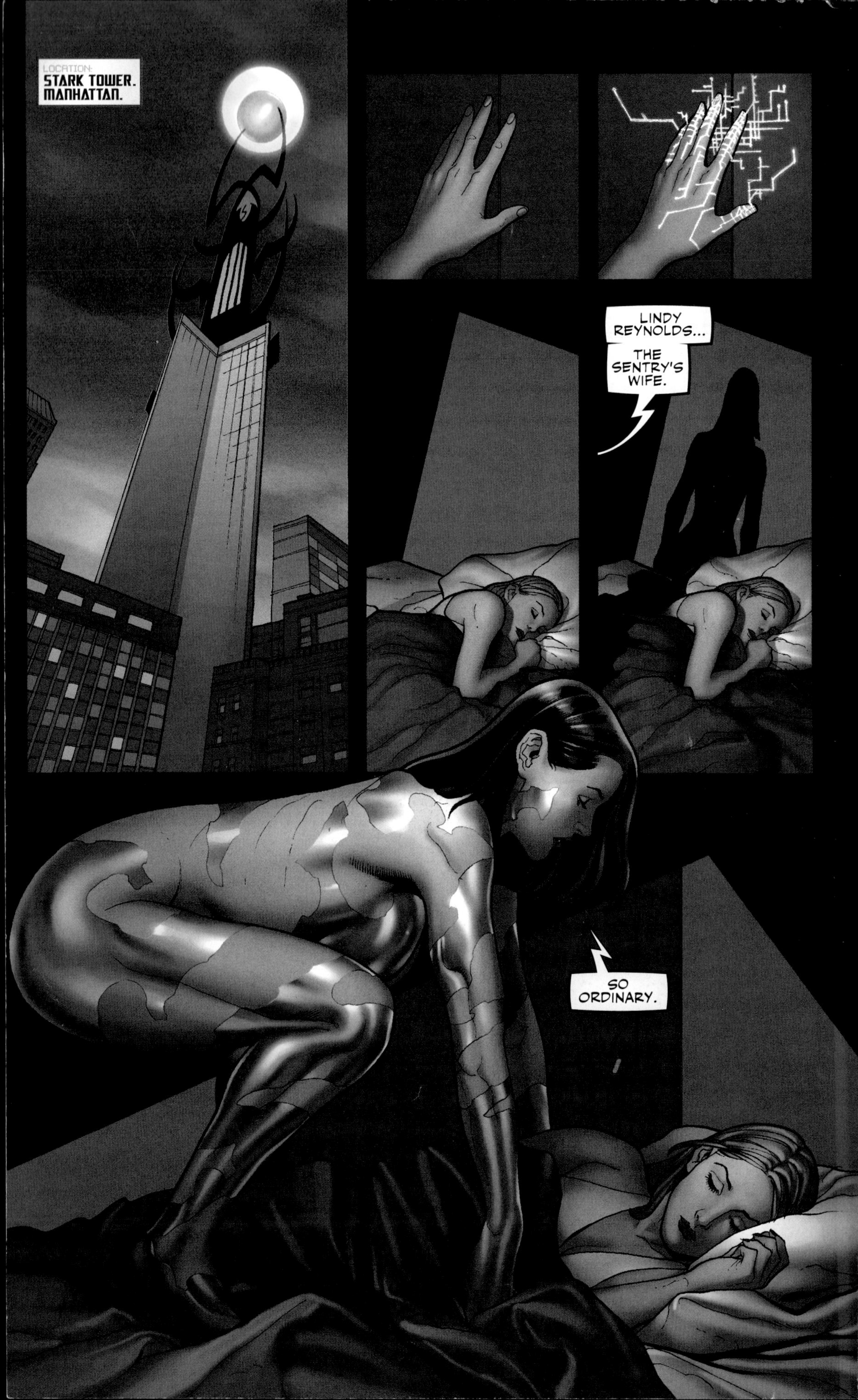
LOCATION:
STARK TOWER. MANHATTAN.
LINDY REYNOLDS...
THE SENTRY'S WIFE.
SO ORDINARY.

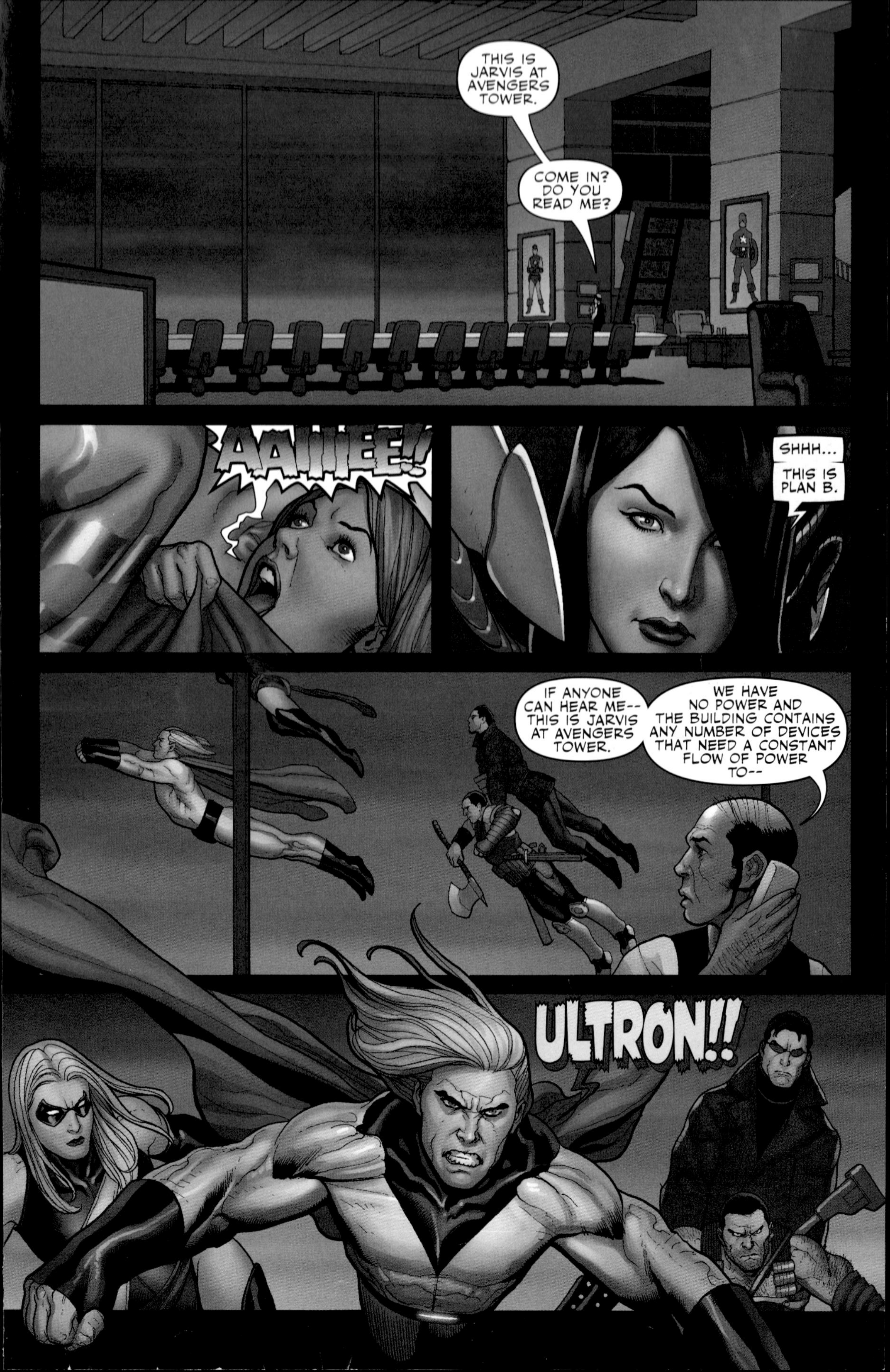
THIS IS JARVIS AT AVENGERS TOWER.
COME IN? DO YOU READ ME?
AAIIIEE!!
SHHH...
THIS IS PLAN B.
IF ANYONE CAN HEAR ME-- THIS IS JARVIS AT AVENGERS TOWER.
WE HAVE NO POWER AND THE BUILDING CONTAINS ANY NUMBER OF DEVICES THAT NEED A CONSTANT FLOW OF POWER TO--
ULTRON!!

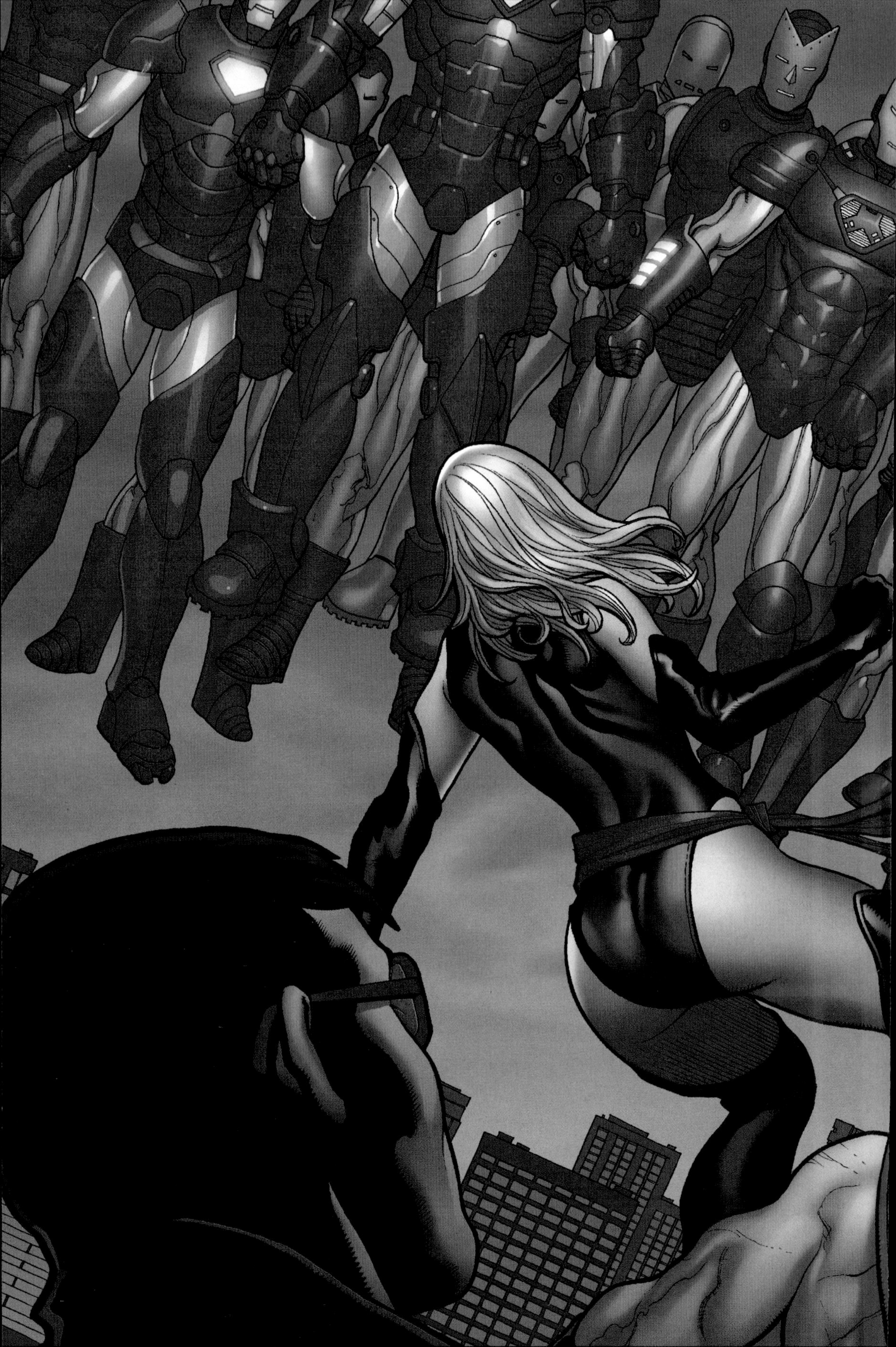

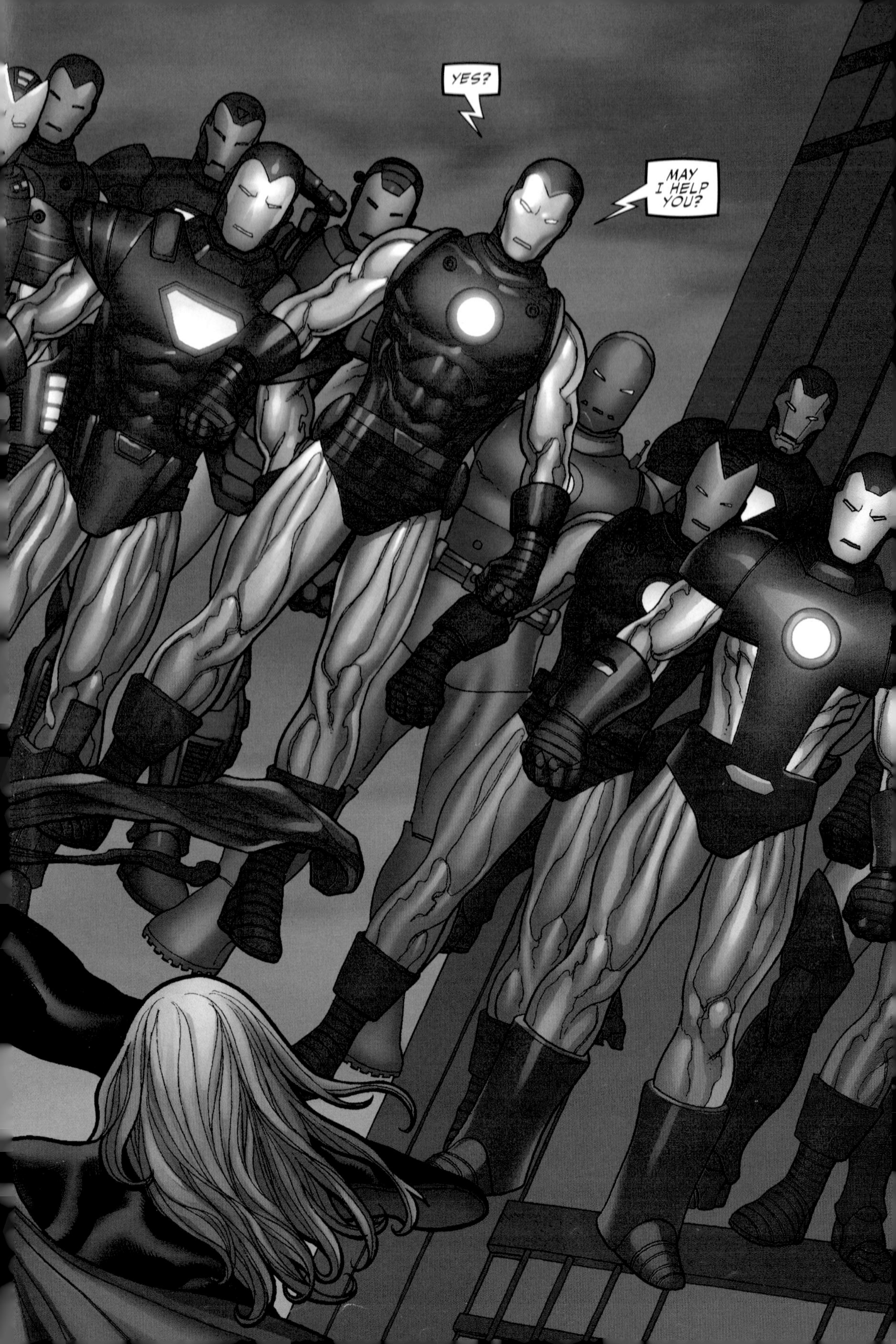
YES?
MAY I HELP YOU?

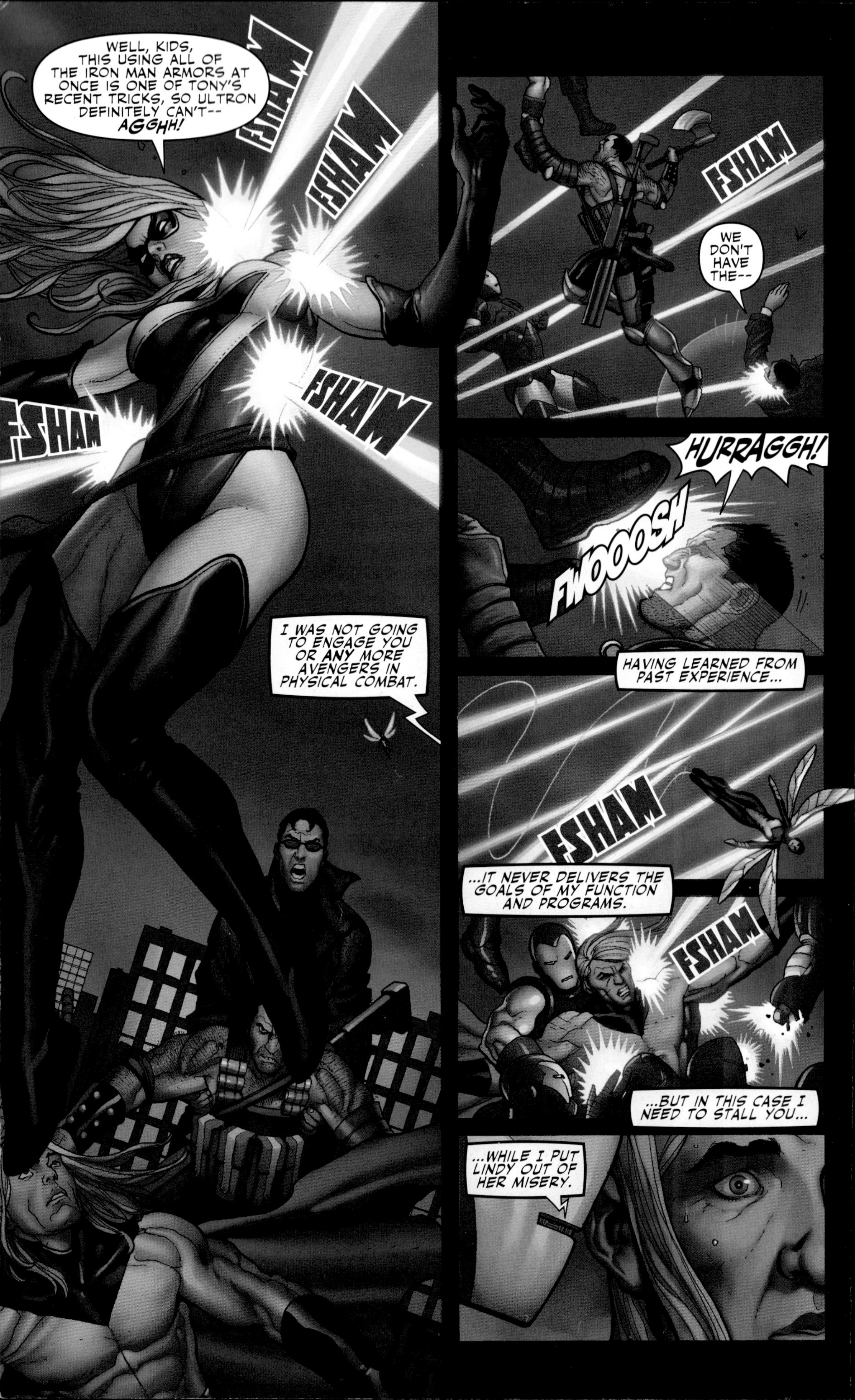
WELL, KIDS, THIS USING ALL OF THE IRON MAN ARMORS AT ONCE IS ONE OF TONY'S RECENT TRICKS, SO ULTRON DEFINITELY CAN'T-- AGGHH!
FSHAM
FSHAM
FSHAM
FSHAM
I WAS NOT GOING TO ENGAGE YOU OR ANY MORE AVENGERS IN PHYSICAL COMBAT.
FSHAM
WE DON'T HAVE THE--
HURRAGGH!
FWOOOSH
HAVING LEARNED FROM PAST EXPERIENCE...
FSHAM
...IT NEVER DELIVERS THE GOALS OF MY FUNCTION AND PROGRAMS.
FSHAM
...BUT IN THIS CASE I NEED TO STALL YOU...
...WHILE I PUT LINDY OUT OF HER MISERY.

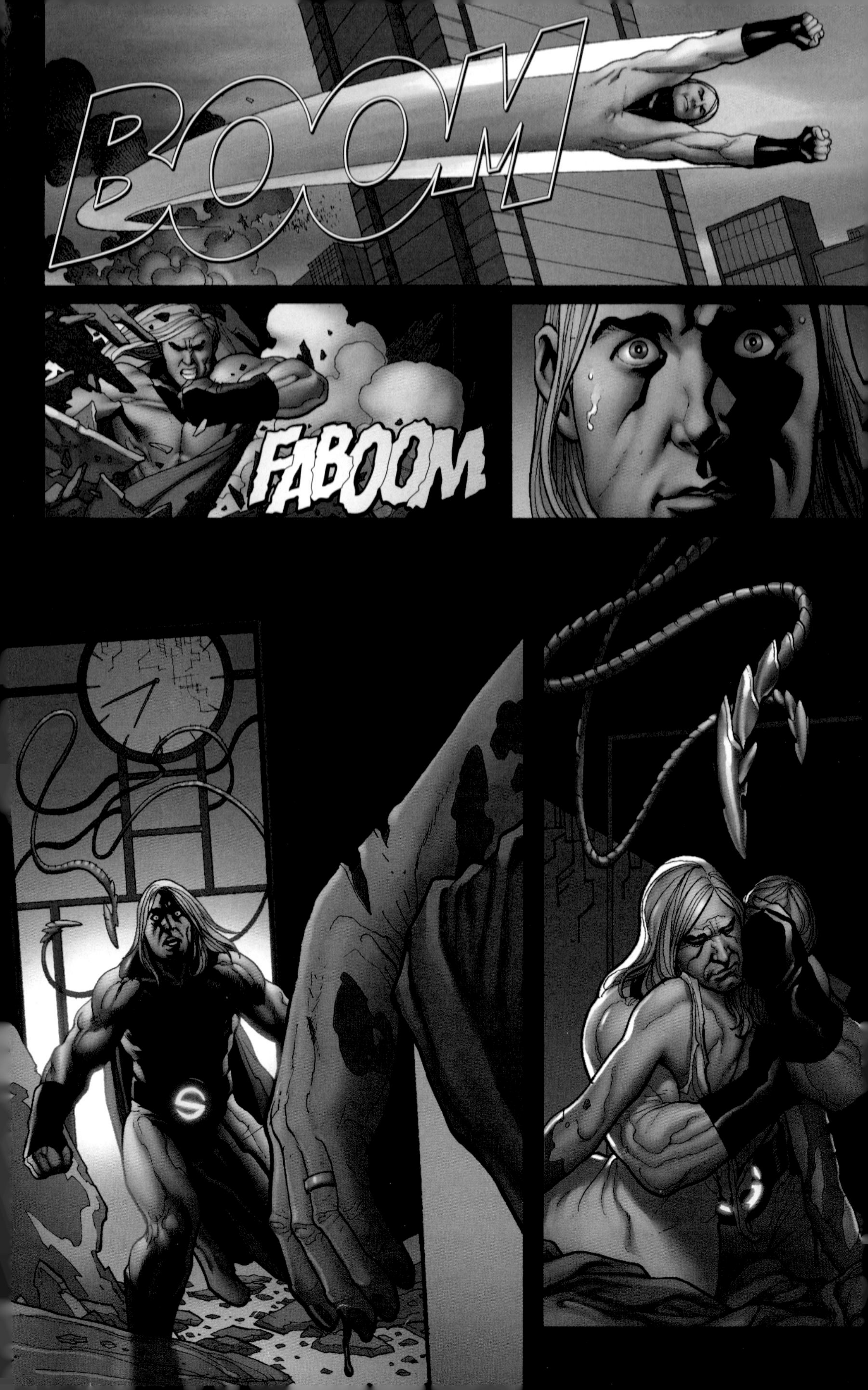
BOOM
FABOOM

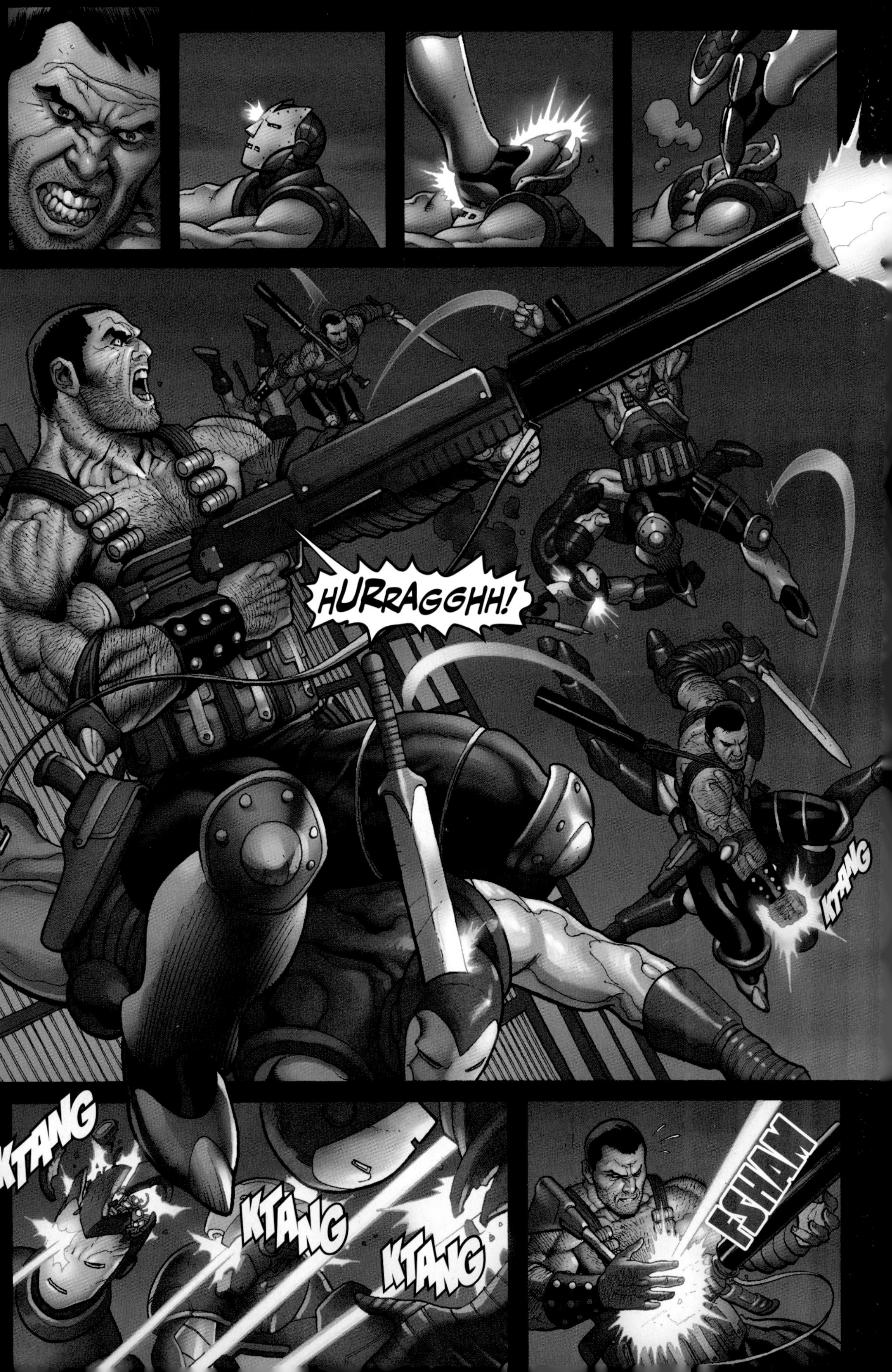
HURRAGGHH!
KTANG
KTANG
KTANG
KTANG
FSHAM

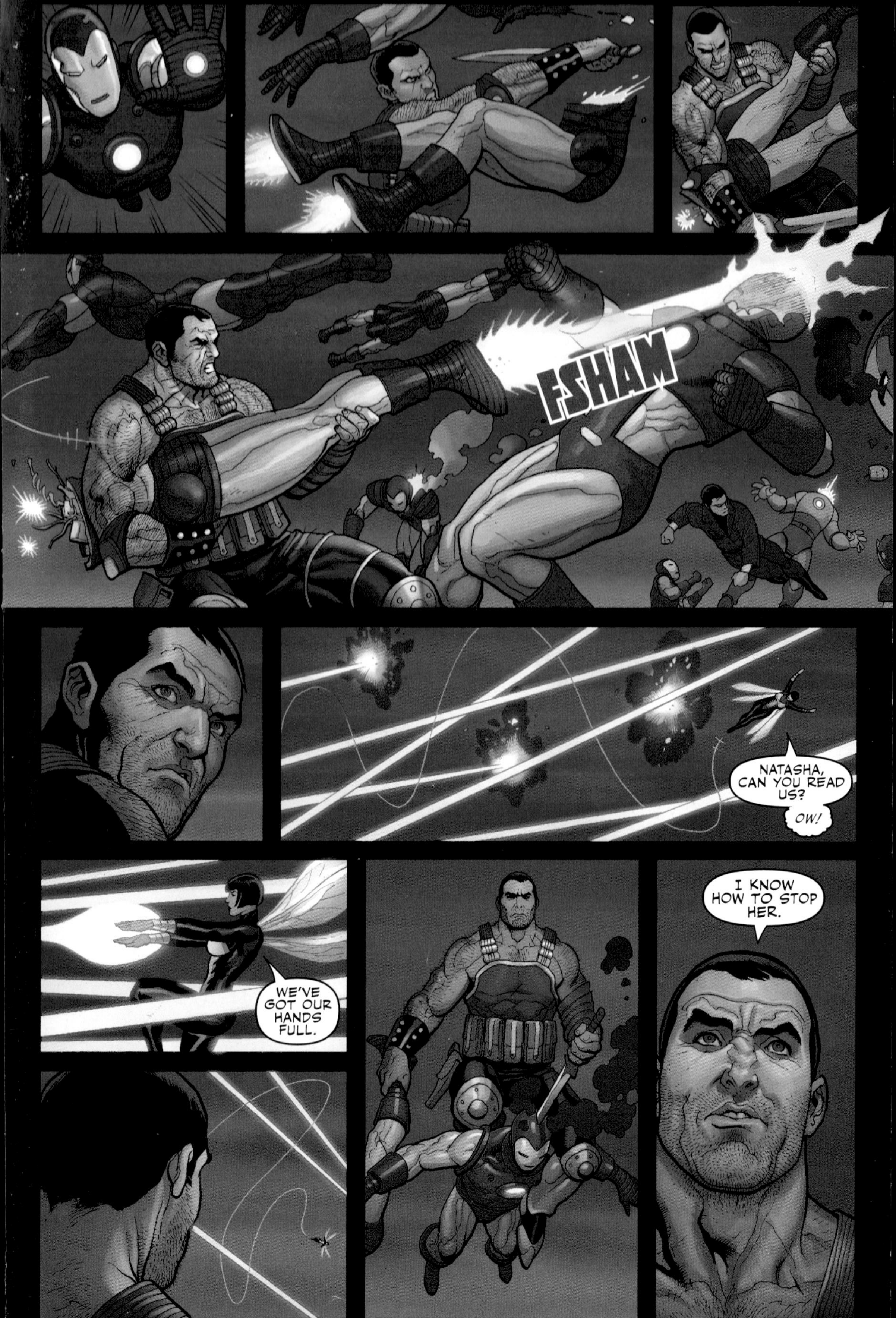
FSHAM
NATASHA, CAN YOU READ US?
OW!
WE'VE GOT OUR HANDS FULL.
I KNOW HOW TO STOP HER.

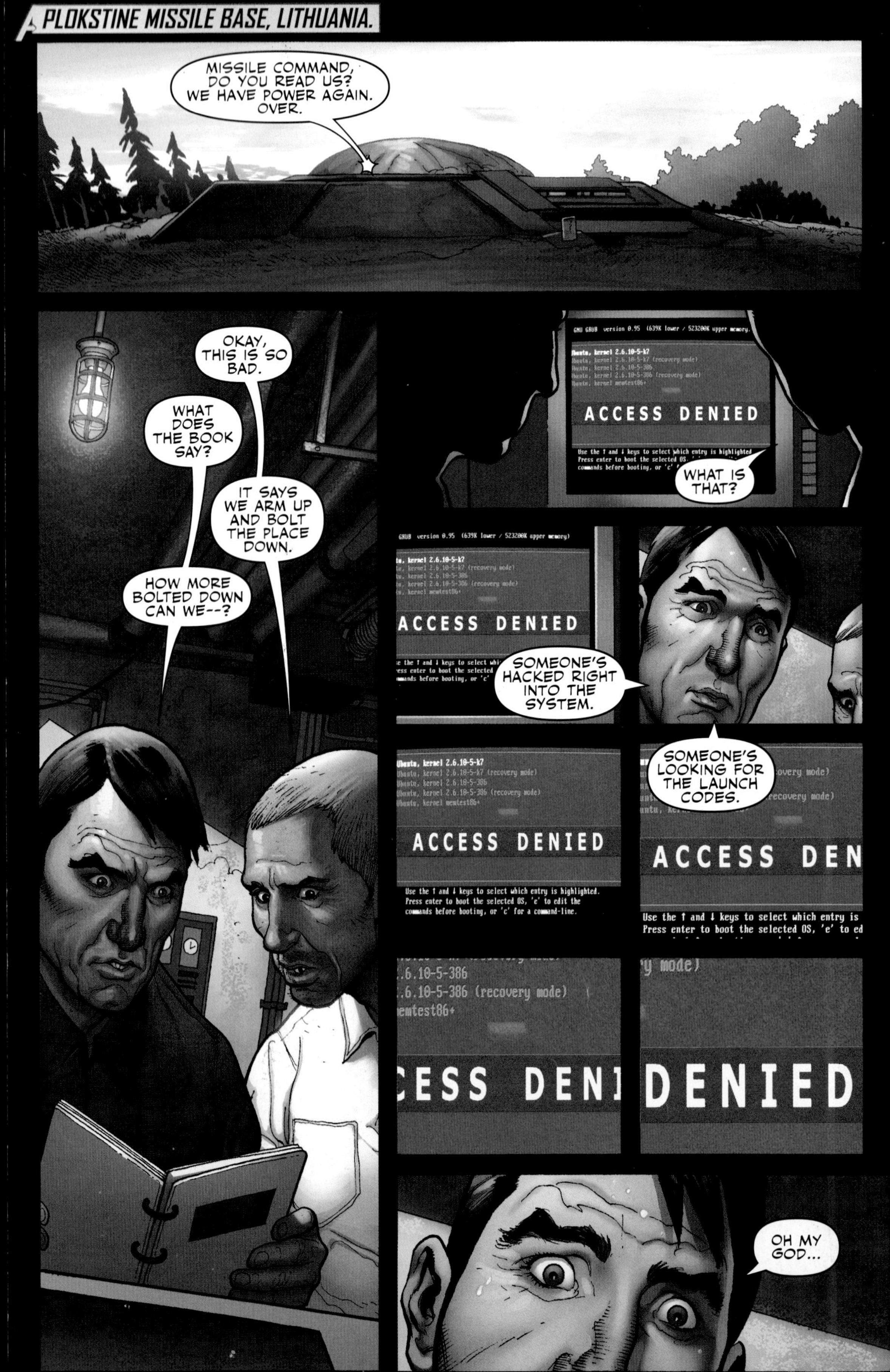
PLOKSTINE MISSILE BASE, LITHUANIA.
MISSILE COMMAND, DO YOU READ US? WE HAVE POWER AGAIN. OVER.
OKAY, THIS IS SO BAD.
WHAT DOES THE BOOK SAY?
IT SAYS WE ARM UP AND BOLT THE PLACE DOWN.
HOW MORE BOLTED DOWN CAN WE--?
GNU GRUB version 0.95 (639K lower / 523200K upper memory)
ACCESS DENIED
WHAT IS THAT?
ACCESS DENIED
SOMEONE'S HACKED RIGHT INTO THE SYSTEM.
Ubuntu, kernel 2.6.10-5-k7
Ubuntu, kernel 2.6.10-5-k7 (recovery mode)
Ubuntu, kernel 2.6.10-5-386
Ubuntu, kernel 2.6.10-5-386 (recovery mode)
Ubuntu, kernel memtest86+
ACCESS DENIED
Use the ↑ and ↓ keys to select which entry is highlighted.
Press enter to boot the selected OS, 'e' to edit the
commands before booting, or 'c' for a command-line.
SOMEONE'S LOOKING FOR THE LAUNCH CODES.
ACCESS DEN
CESS DENI
DENIED
OH MY GOD...

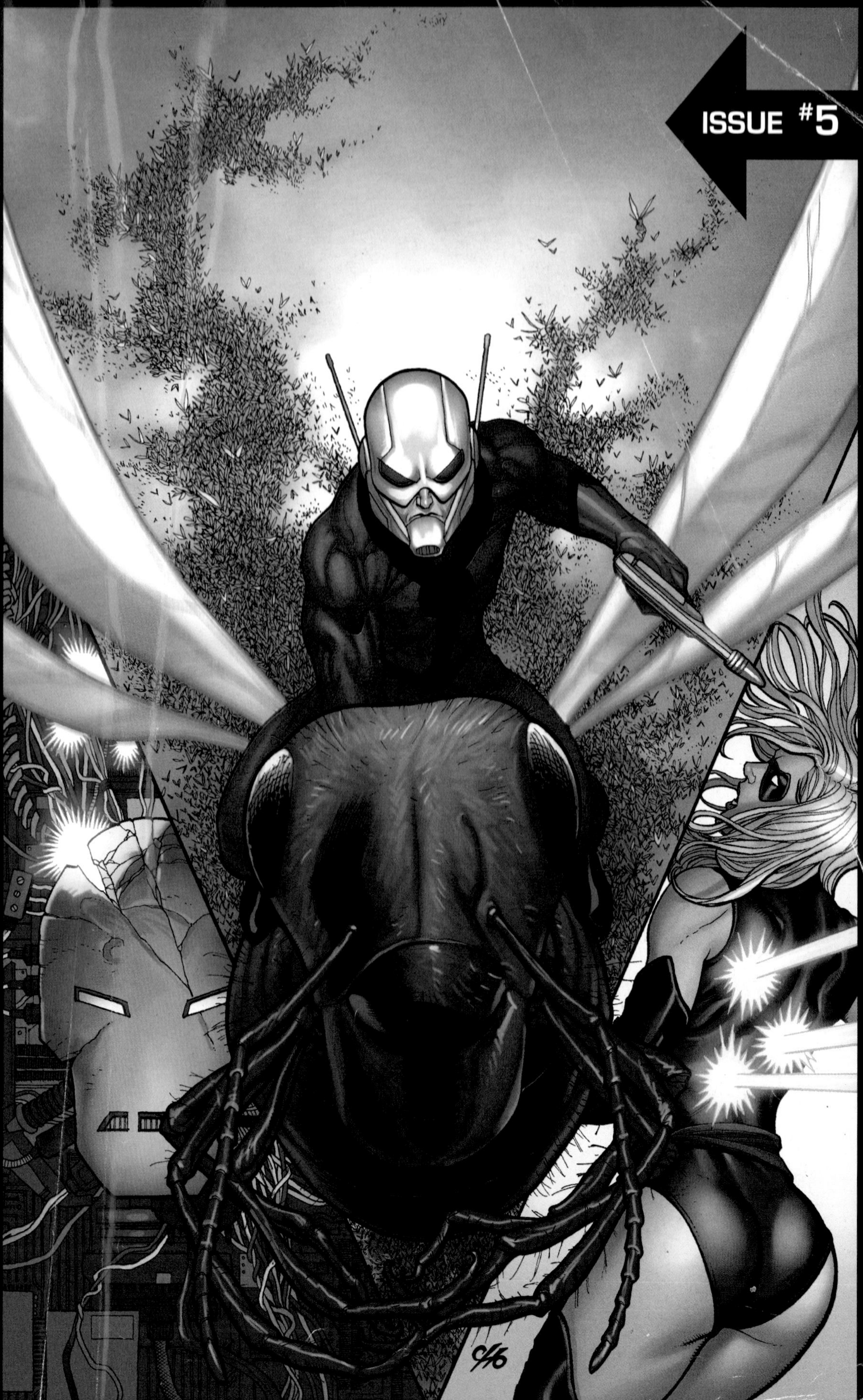
ISSUE #5

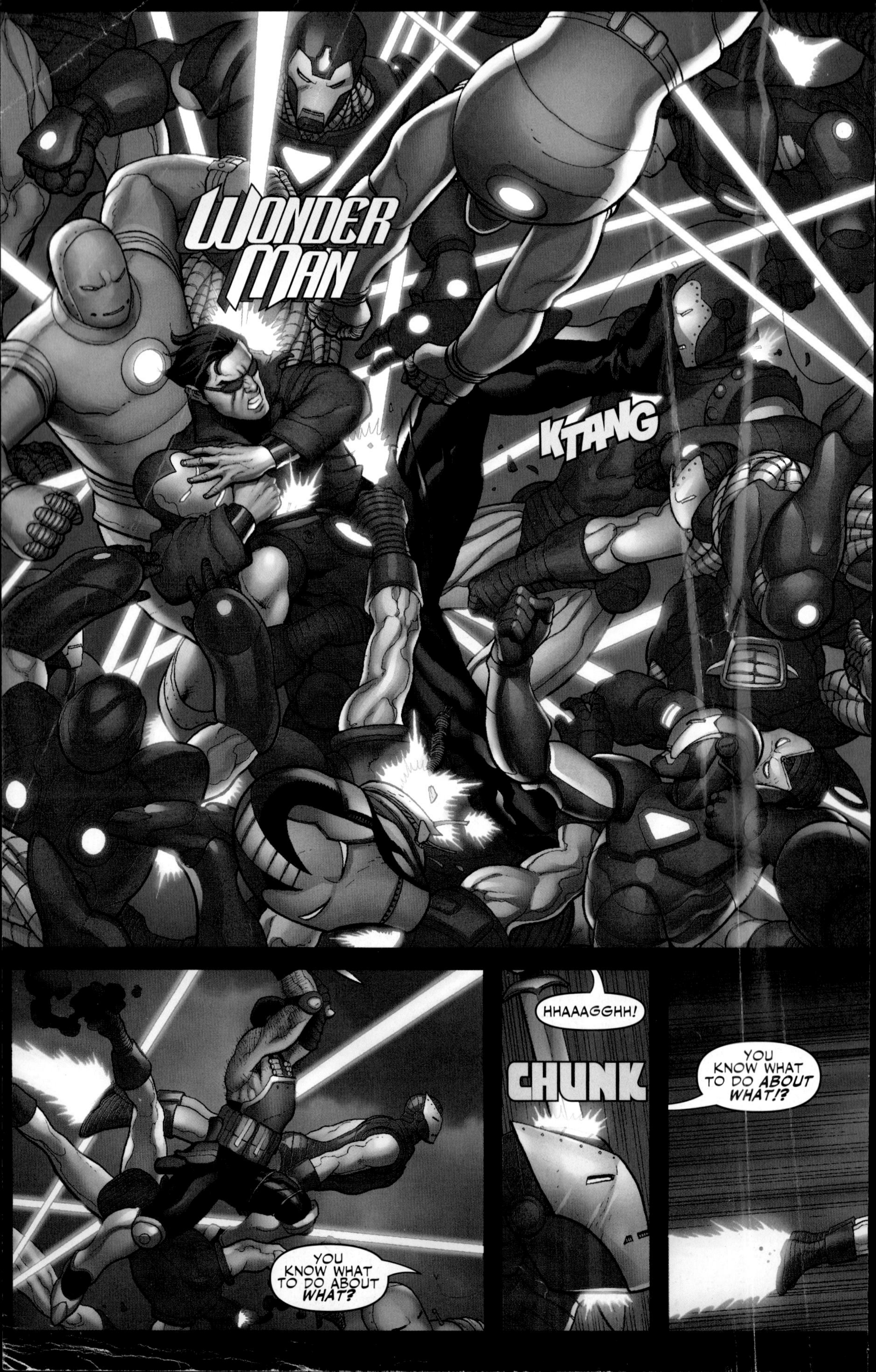
WONDER MAN
KTANG
YOU KNOW WHAT TO DO ABOUT WHAT?
HHAAAGGHH!
CHUNK
YOU KNOW WHAT TO DO ABOUT WHAT!?

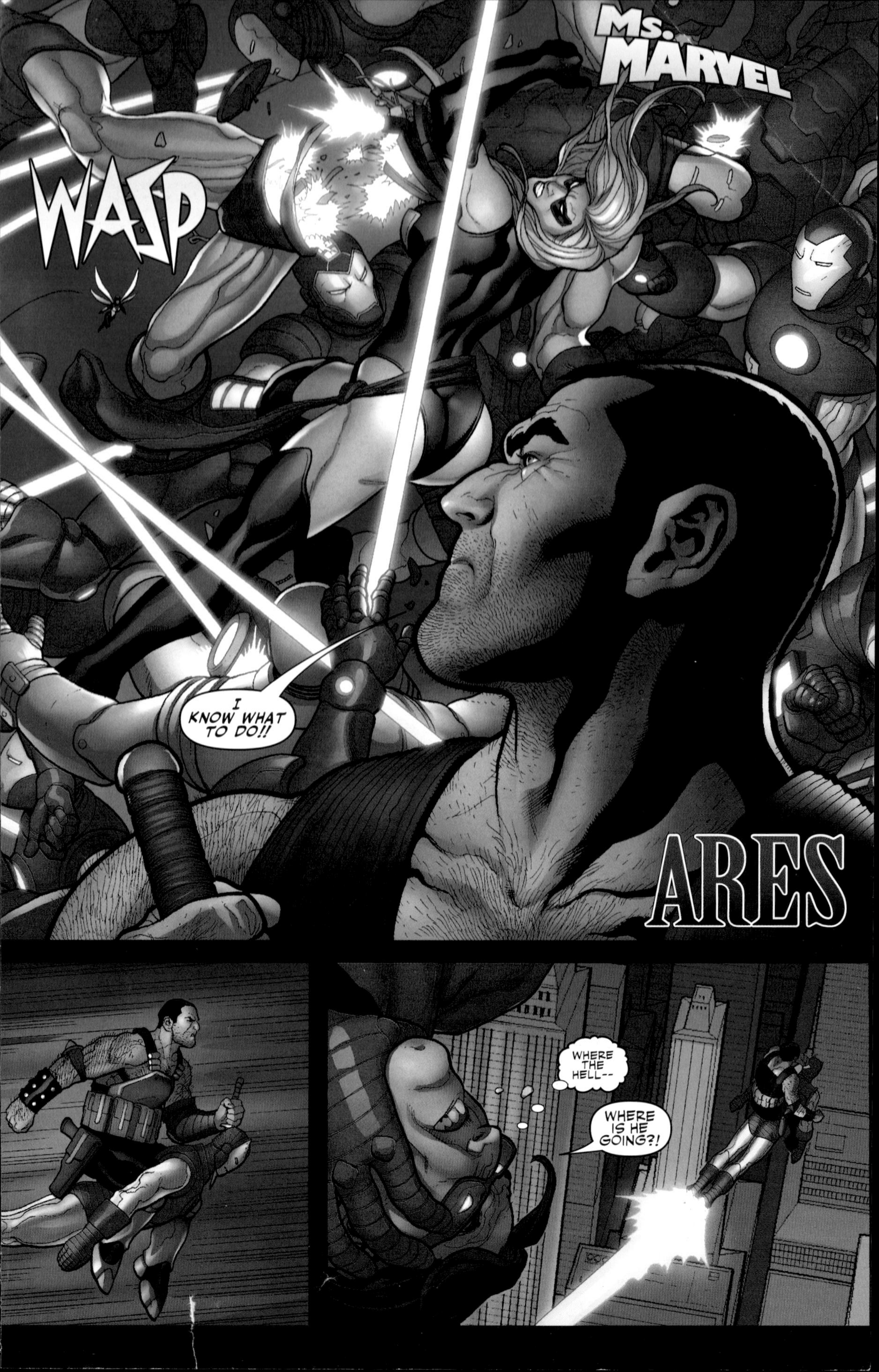
MS. MARVEL
WASP
I KNOW WHAT TO DO!!
ARES
WHERE THE HELL--
WHERE IS HE GOING?!

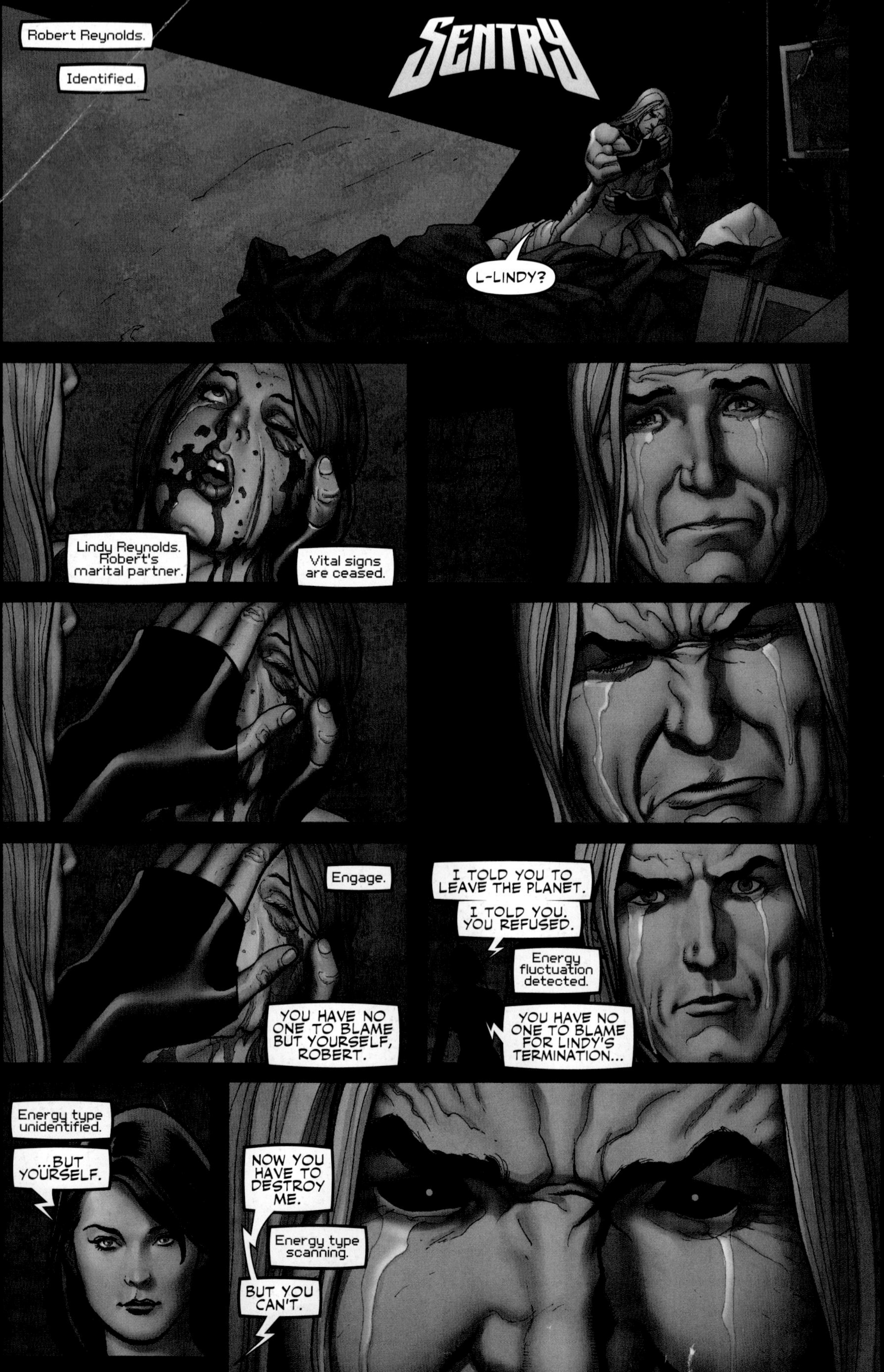
Robert Reynolds.
Identified.
SENTRY
L-LINDY?
Lindy Reynolds. Robert's marital partner.
Vital signs are ceased.
Engage.
YOU HAVE NO ONE TO BLAME BUT YOURSELF, ROBERT.
I TOLD YOU TO LEAVE THE PLANET.
I TOLD YOU. YOU REFUSED.
Energy fluctuation detected.
YOU HAVE NO ONE TO BLAME FOR LINDY'S TERMINATION...
Energy type unidentified.
...BUT YOURSELF.
NOW YOU HAVE TO DESTROY ME.
Energy type scanning.
BUT YOU CAN'T.

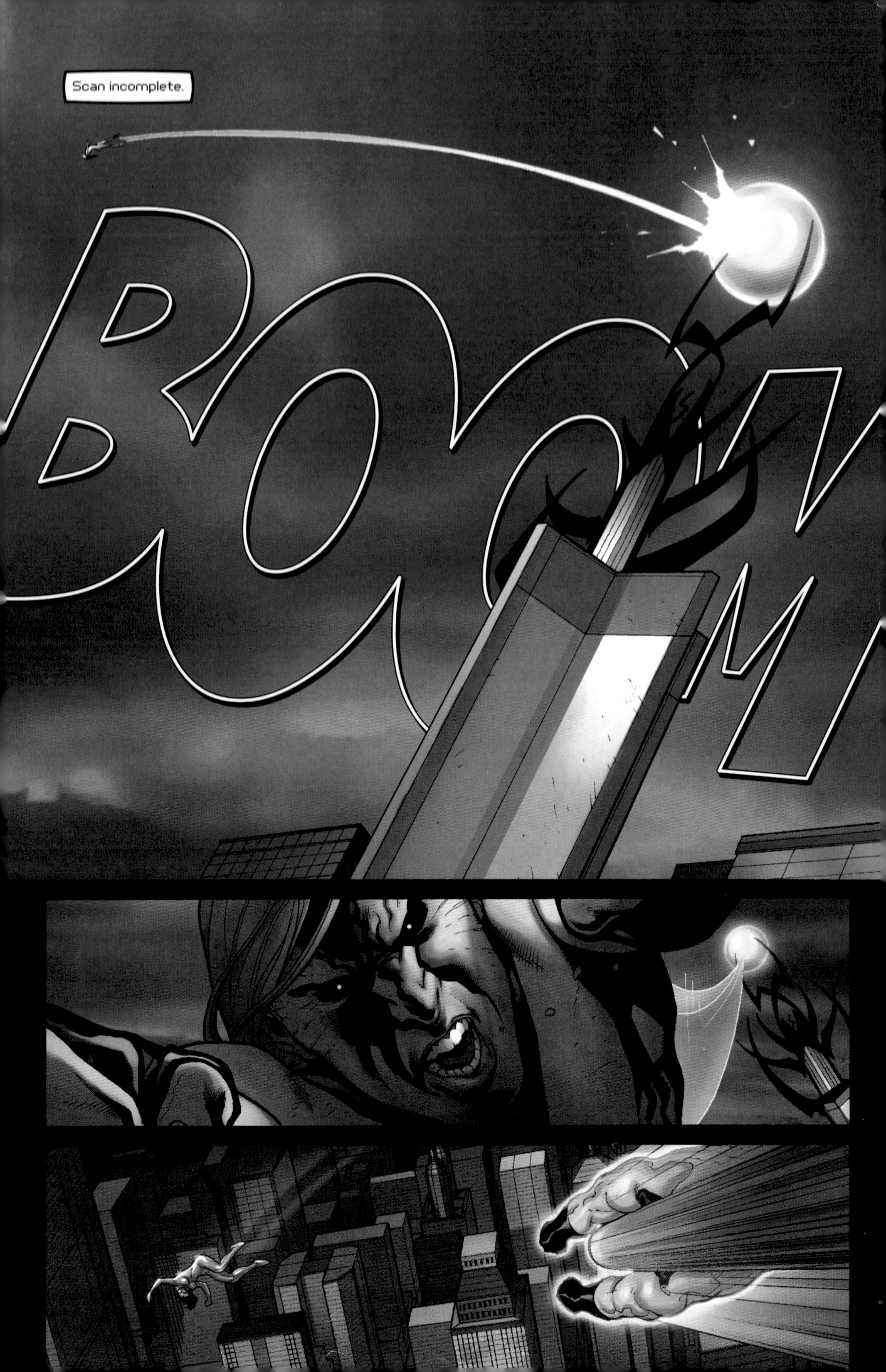
Scan incomplete.
BOOOM

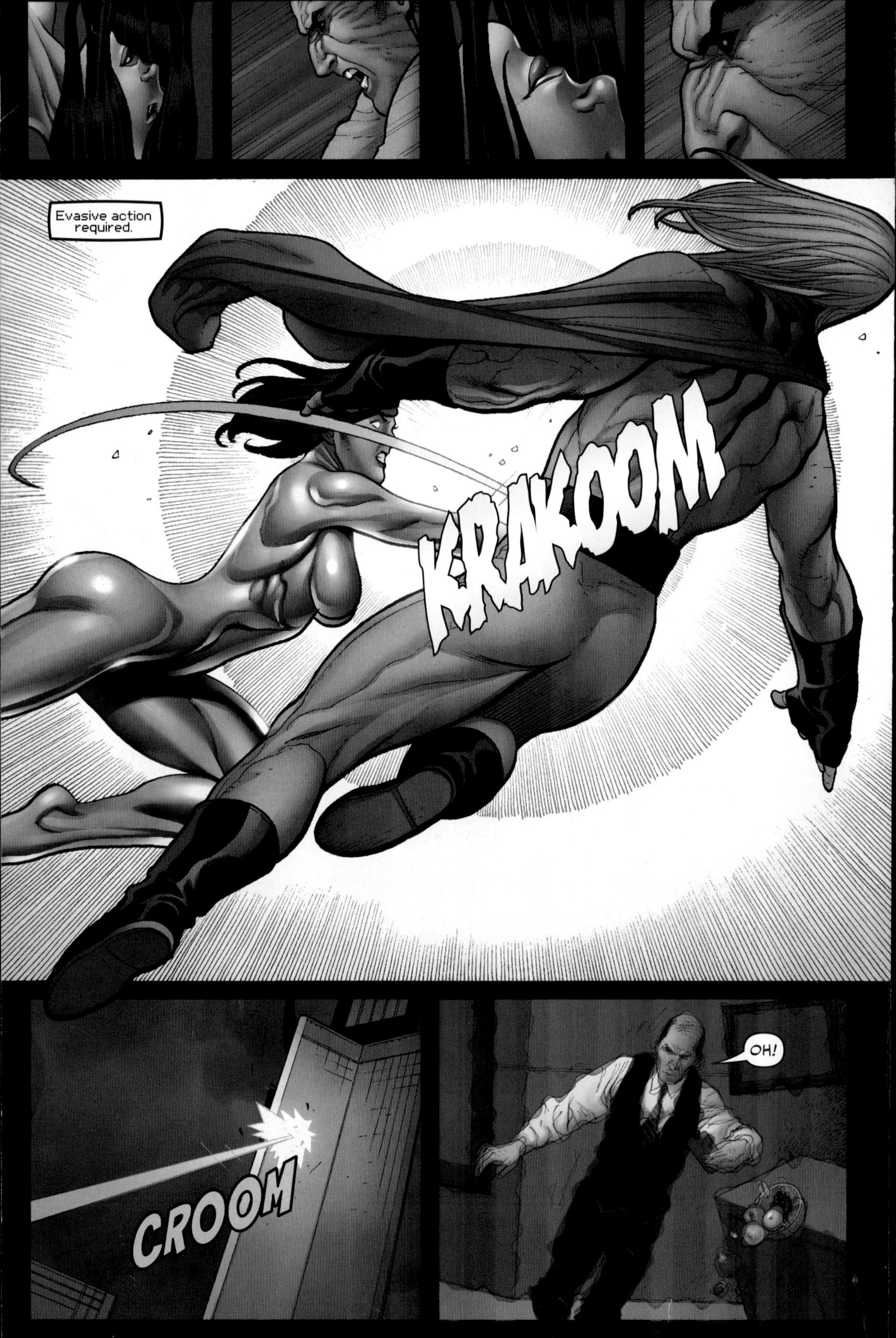
Evasive action required.
KRAKOOM
CROOM
OH!

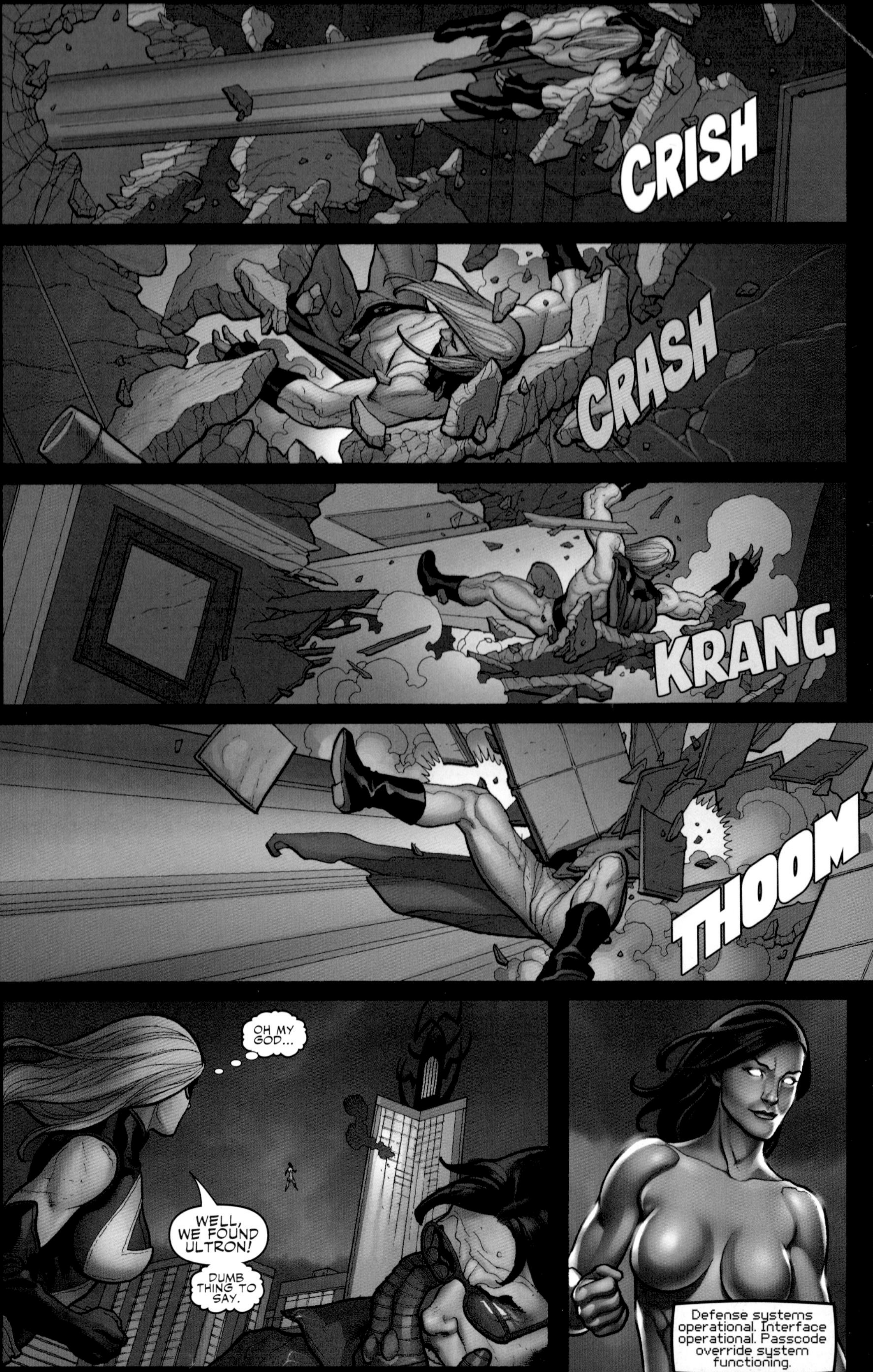

CRISH
CRASH
KRANG
THOOM
OH MY GOD...
WELL, WE FOUND ULTRON!
DUMB THING TO SAY.
Defense systems operational. Interface operational. Passcode override system functioning.

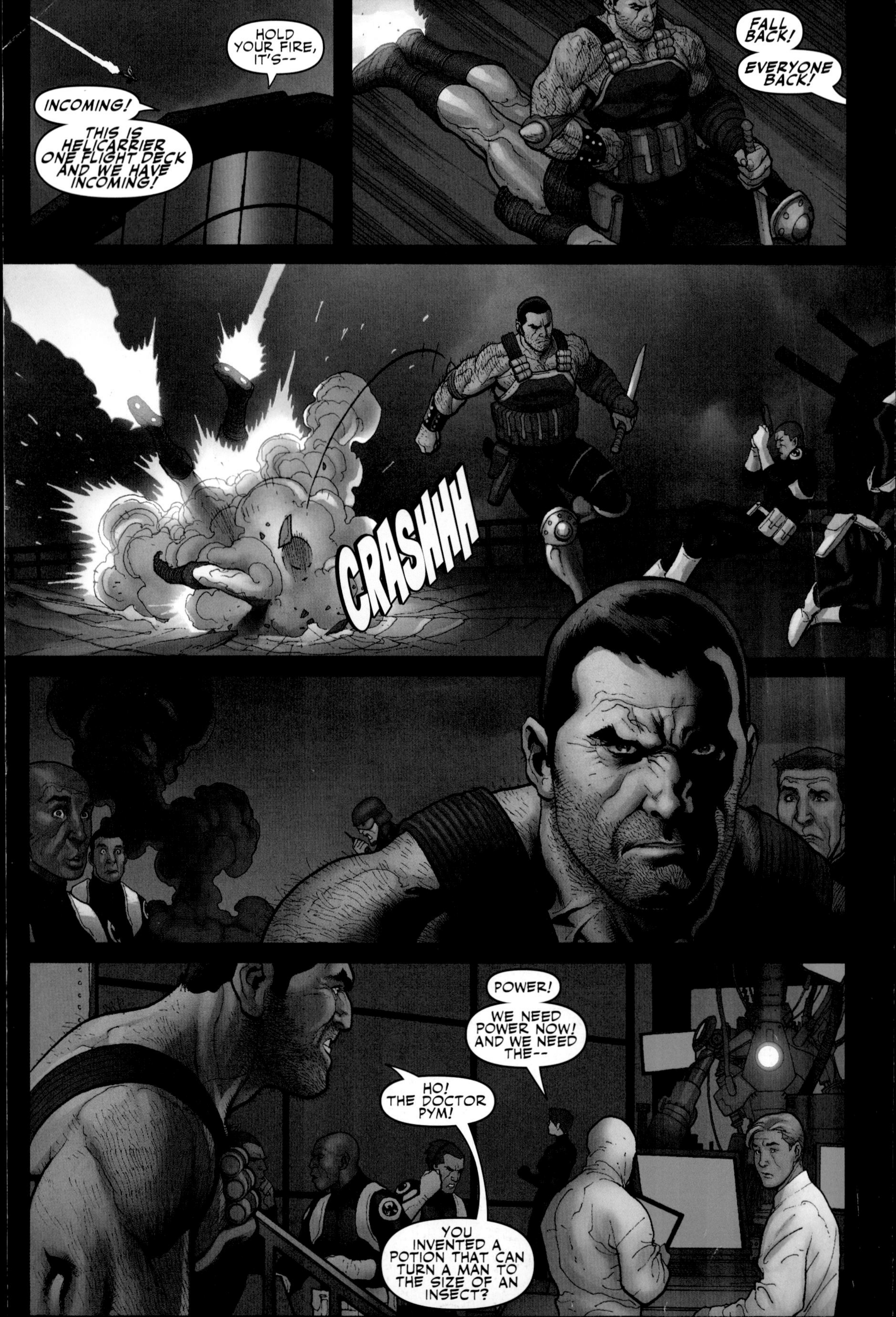
HOLD YOUR FIRE, IT'S--
INCOMING!
THIS IS HELICARRIER ONE FLIGHT DECK AND WE HAVE INCOMING!
FALL BACK!
EVERYONE BACK!
CRASHHH
POWER!
WE NEED POWER NOW! AND WE NEED THE--
HO! THE DOCTOR PYM!
YOU INVENTED A POTION THAT CAN TURN A MAN TO THE SIZE OF AN INSECT?

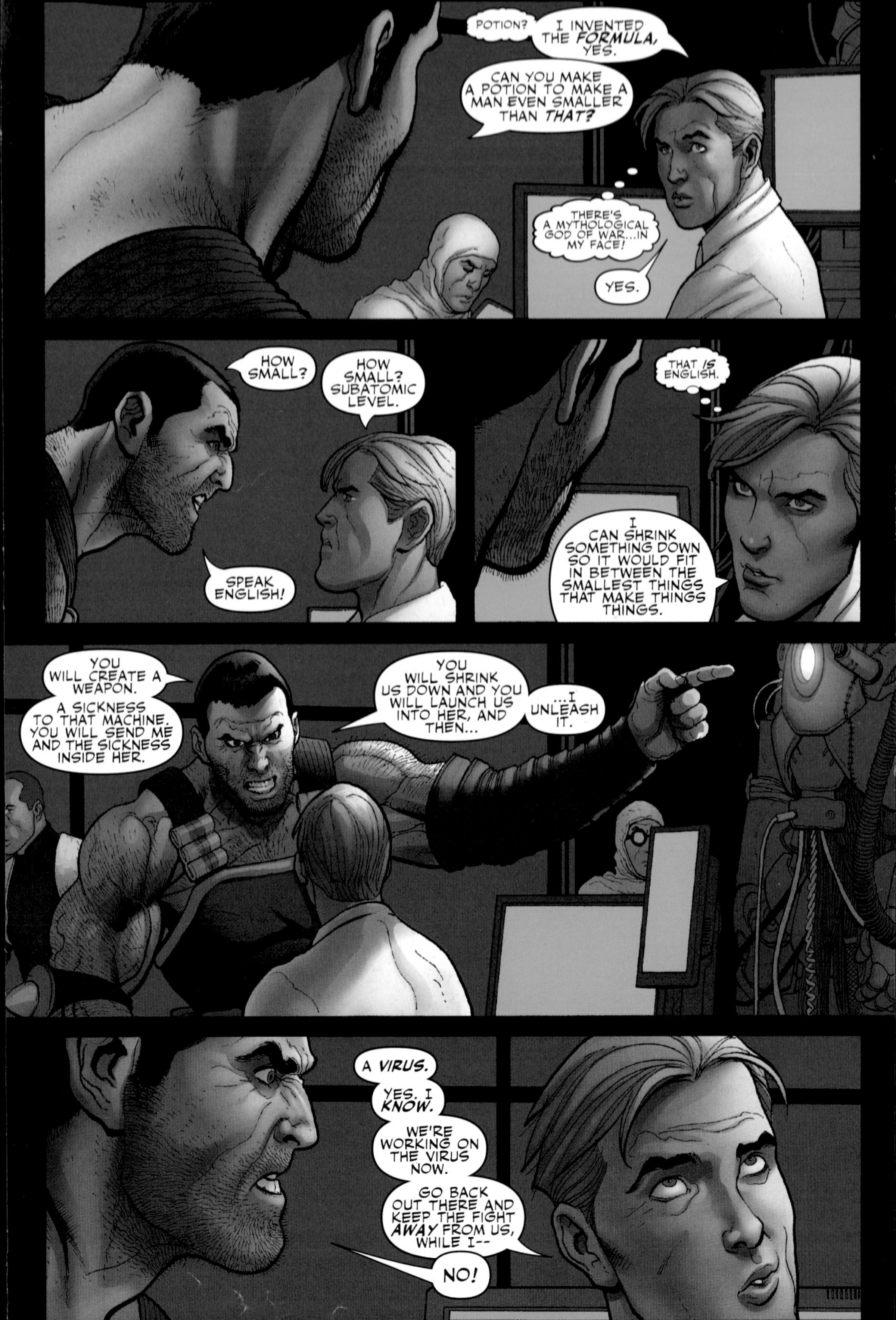

POTION?
I INVENTED THE FORMULA, YES.
CAN YOU MAKE A POTION TO MAKE A MAN EVEN SMALLER THAN THAT?
THERE'S A MYTHOLOGICAL GOD OF WAR...IN MY FACE!
YES.
HOW SMALL?
HOW SMALL? SUBATOMIC LEVEL.
SPEAK ENGLISH!
THAT IS ENGLISH.
I CAN SHRINK SOMETHING DOWN SO IT WOULD FIT IN BETWEEN THE SMALLEST THINGS THAT MAKE THINGS THINGS.
YOU WILL CREATE A WEAPON.
A SICKNESS TO THAT MACHINE. YOU WILL SEND ME AND THE SICKNESS INSIDE HER.
YOU WILL SHRINK US DOWN AND YOU WILL LAUNCH US INTO HER, AND THEN...
...I UNLEASH IT.
A VIRUS.
YES. I KNOW.
WE'RE WORKING ON THE VIRUS NOW.
GO BACK OUT THERE AND KEEP THE FIGHT AWAY FROM US, WHILE I--
NO!

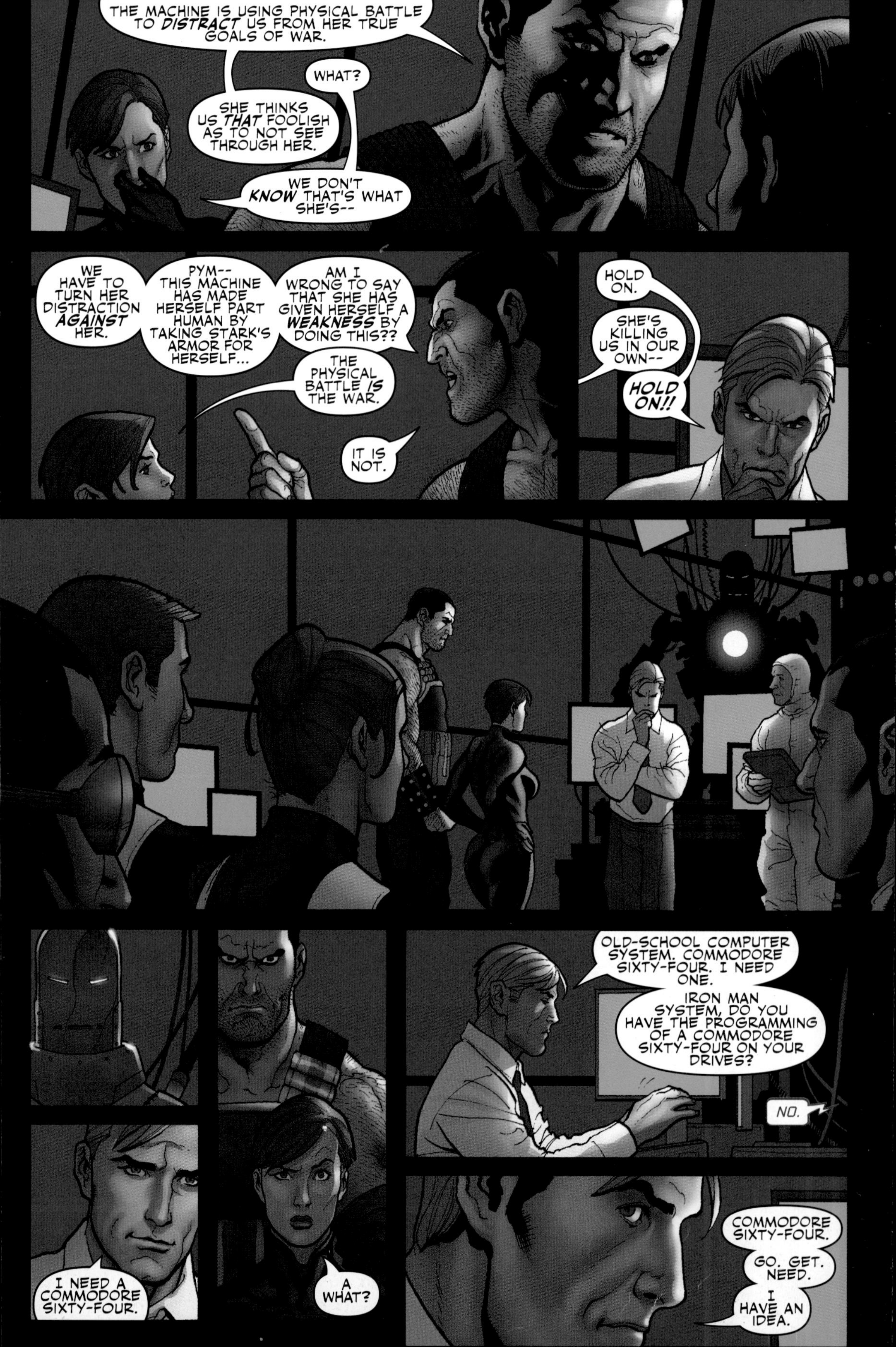
THE MACHINE IS USING PHYSICAL BATTLE TO *DISTRACT* US FROM HER TRUE GOALS OF WAR.
WHAT?
SHE THINKS US *THAT* FOOLISH AS TO NOT SEE THROUGH HER.
WE DON'T *KNOW* THAT'S WHAT SHE'S--
WE HAVE TO TURN HER DISTRACTION *AGAINST* HER.
PYM-- THIS MACHINE HAS MADE HERSELF PART HUMAN BY TAKING STARK'S ARMOR FOR HERSELF...
AM I WRONG TO SAY THAT SHE HAS GIVEN HERSELF A *WEAKNESS* BY DOING THIS??
THE PHYSICAL BATTLE *IS* THE WAR.
IT IS NOT.
HOLD ON.
SHE'S KILLING US IN OUR OWN--
*HOLD ON!!*
OLD-SCHOOL COMPUTER SYSTEM. COMMODORE SIXTY-FOUR. I NEED ONE.
IRON MAN SYSTEM, DO YOU HAVE THE PROGRAMMING OF A COMMODORE SIXTY-FOUR ON YOUR DRIVES?
NO.
I NEED A COMMODORE SIXTY-FOUR.
A WHAT?
COMMODORE SIXTY-FOUR.
GO. GET. NEED.
I HAVE AN IDEA.

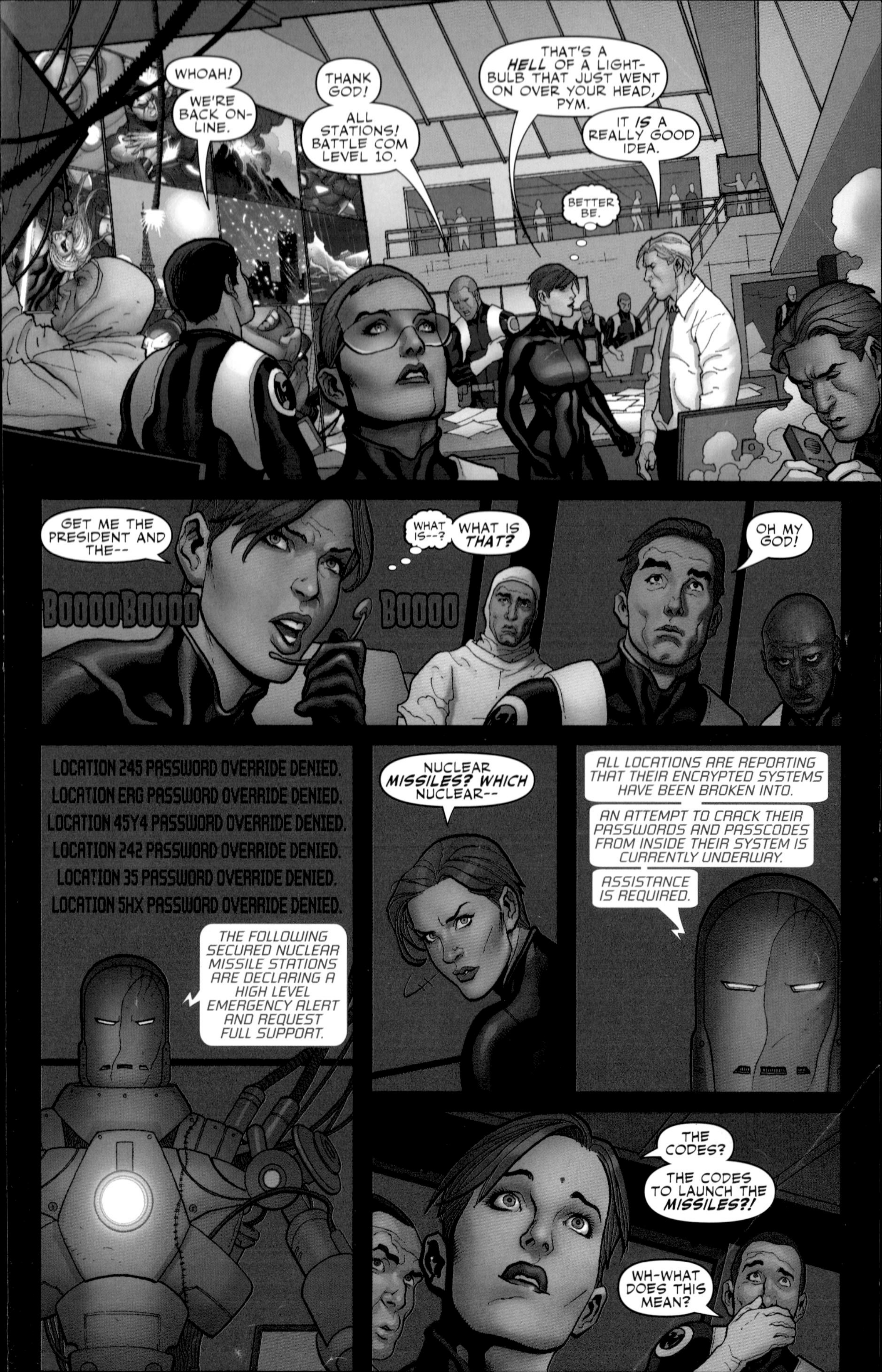
WHOAH!
WE'RE BACK ON-LINE.
THANK GOD!
ALL STATIONS! BATTLE COM LEVEL 10.
THAT'S A HELL OF A LIGHT-BULB THAT JUST WENT ON OVER YOUR HEAD, PYM.
IT IS A REALLY GOOD IDEA.
BETTER BE.
GET ME THE PRESIDENT AND THE--
BOOOOBOOOO
WHAT IS--?
WHAT IS THAT?
BOOOO
OH MY GOD!
LOCATION 245 PASSWORD OVERRIDE DENIED.
LOCATION ERG PASSWORD OVERRIDE DENIED.
LOCATION 45Y4 PASSWORD OVERRIDE DENIED.
LOCATION 242 PASSWORD OVERRIDE DENIED.
LOCATION 35 PASSWORD OVERRIDE DENIED.
LOCATION 5HX PASSWORD OVERRIDE DENIED.
THE FOLLOWING SECURED NUCLEAR MISSILE STATIONS ARE DECLARING A HIGH LEVEL EMERGENCY ALERT AND REQUEST FULL SUPPORT.
NUCLEAR MISSILES? WHICH NUCLEAR--
ALL LOCATIONS ARE REPORTING THAT THEIR ENCRYPTED SYSTEMS HAVE BEEN BROKEN INTO.
AN ATTEMPT TO CRACK THEIR PASSWORDS AND PASSCODES FROM INSIDE THEIR SYSTEM IS CURRENTLY UNDERWAY.
ASSISTANCE IS REQUIRED.
THE CODES?
THE CODES TO LAUNCH THE MISSILES?!
WH-WHAT DOES THIS MEAN?

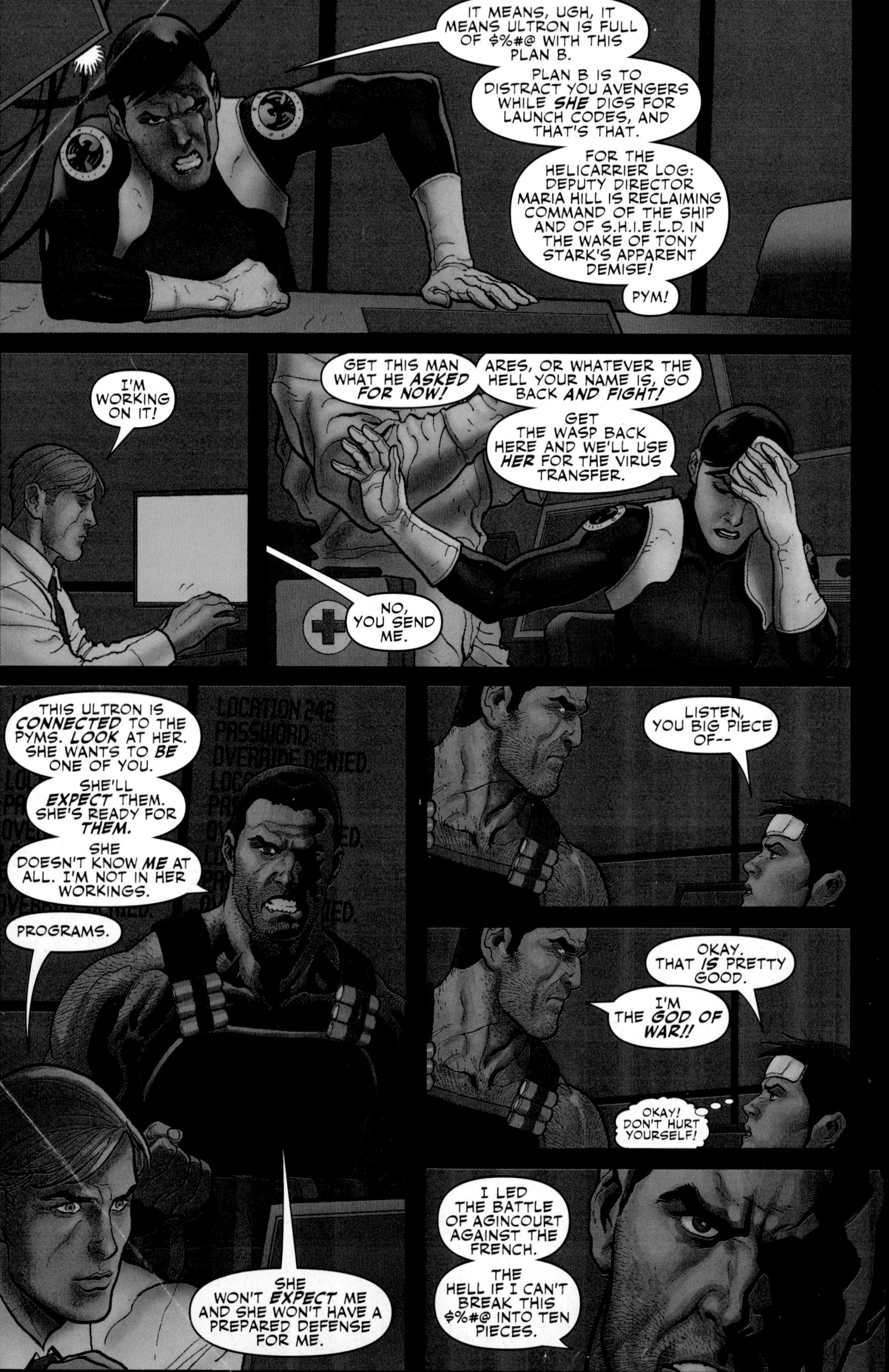

IT MEANS, UGH, IT MEANS ULTRON IS FULL OF $%#@ WITH THIS PLAN B.
PLAN B IS TO DISTRACT YOU AVENGERS WHILE *SHE* DIGS FOR LAUNCH CODES, AND THAT'S THAT.
FOR THE HELICARRIER LOG: DEPUTY DIRECTOR MARIA HILL IS RECLAIMING COMMAND OF THE SHIP AND OF S.H.I.E.L.D. IN THE WAKE OF TONY STARK'S APPARENT DEMISE!
PYM!
I'M WORKING ON IT!
GET THIS MAN WHAT HE *ASKED FOR NOW!*
ARES, OR WHATEVER THE HELL YOUR NAME IS, GO BACK *AND FIGHT!*
GET THE WASP BACK HERE AND WE'LL USE *HER* FOR THE VIRUS TRANSFER.
NO, YOU SEND ME.
LOCATION 242
PASSWORD
OVERRIDE DENIED.
THIS ULTRON IS *CONNECTED* TO THE PYMS. *LOOK* AT HER. SHE WANTS TO *BE* ONE OF YOU.
SHE'LL *EXPECT* THEM. SHE'S READY FOR *THEM.*
SHE DOESN'T KNOW *ME* AT ALL. I'M NOT IN HER WORKINGS.
PROGRAMS.
SHE WON'T *EXPECT* ME AND SHE WON'T HAVE A PREPARED DEFENSE FOR ME.
LISTEN, YOU BIG PIECE OF--
OKAY. THAT *IS* PRETTY GOOD.
I'M THE *GOD OF WAR!!*
OKAY! DON'T HURT YOURSELF!
I LED THE BATTLE OF AGINCOURT AGAINST THE FRENCH.
THE HELL IF I CAN'T BREAK THIS $%#@ INTO TEN PIECES.

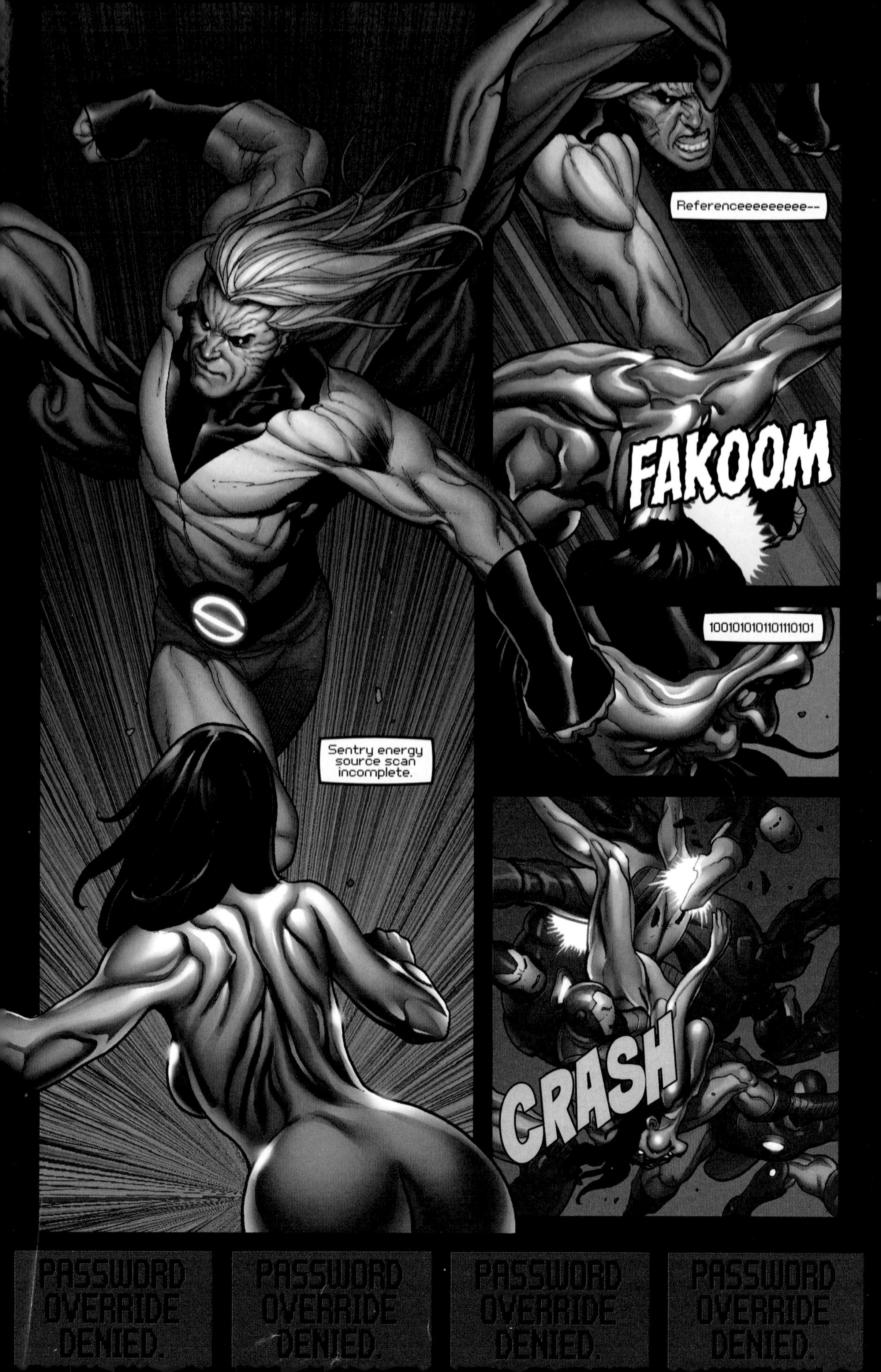

Sentry energy source scan incomplete.
Referenceeeeeeeeee--
FAKOOM
1001010101101110101
CRASH
PASSWORD OVERRIDE DENIED.
PASSWORD OVERRIDE DENIED.
PASSWORD OVERRIDE DENIED.
PASSWORD OVERRIDE DENIED.

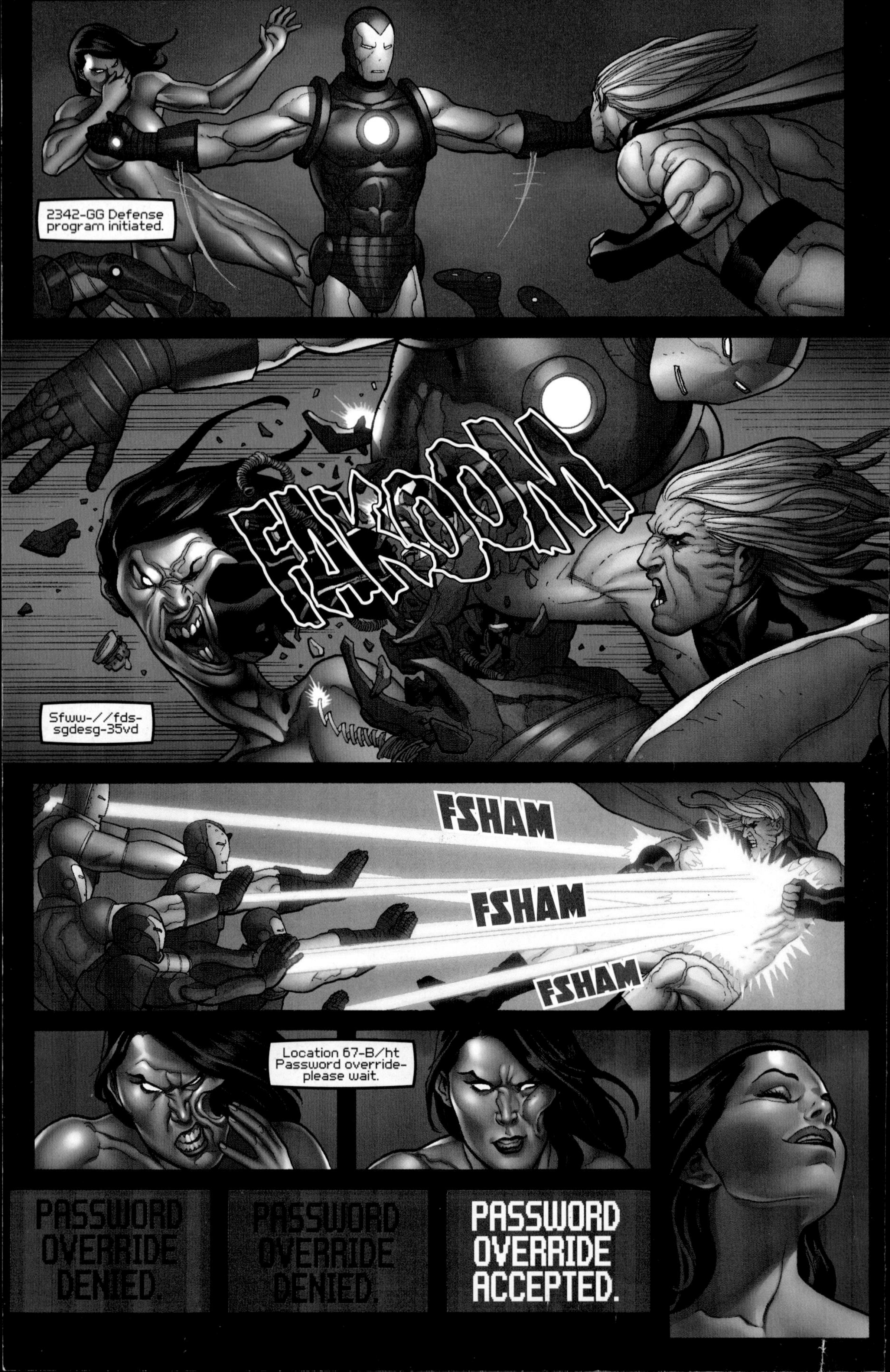
2342-GG Defense program initiated.
FAKOOM
Sfww-//fds-sgdesg-35vd
FSHAM
FSHAM
FSHAM
Location 67-B/ht Password override-please wait.
PASSWORD OVERRIDE DENIED.
PASSWORD OVERRIDE DENIED.
PASSWORD OVERRIDE ACCEPTED.

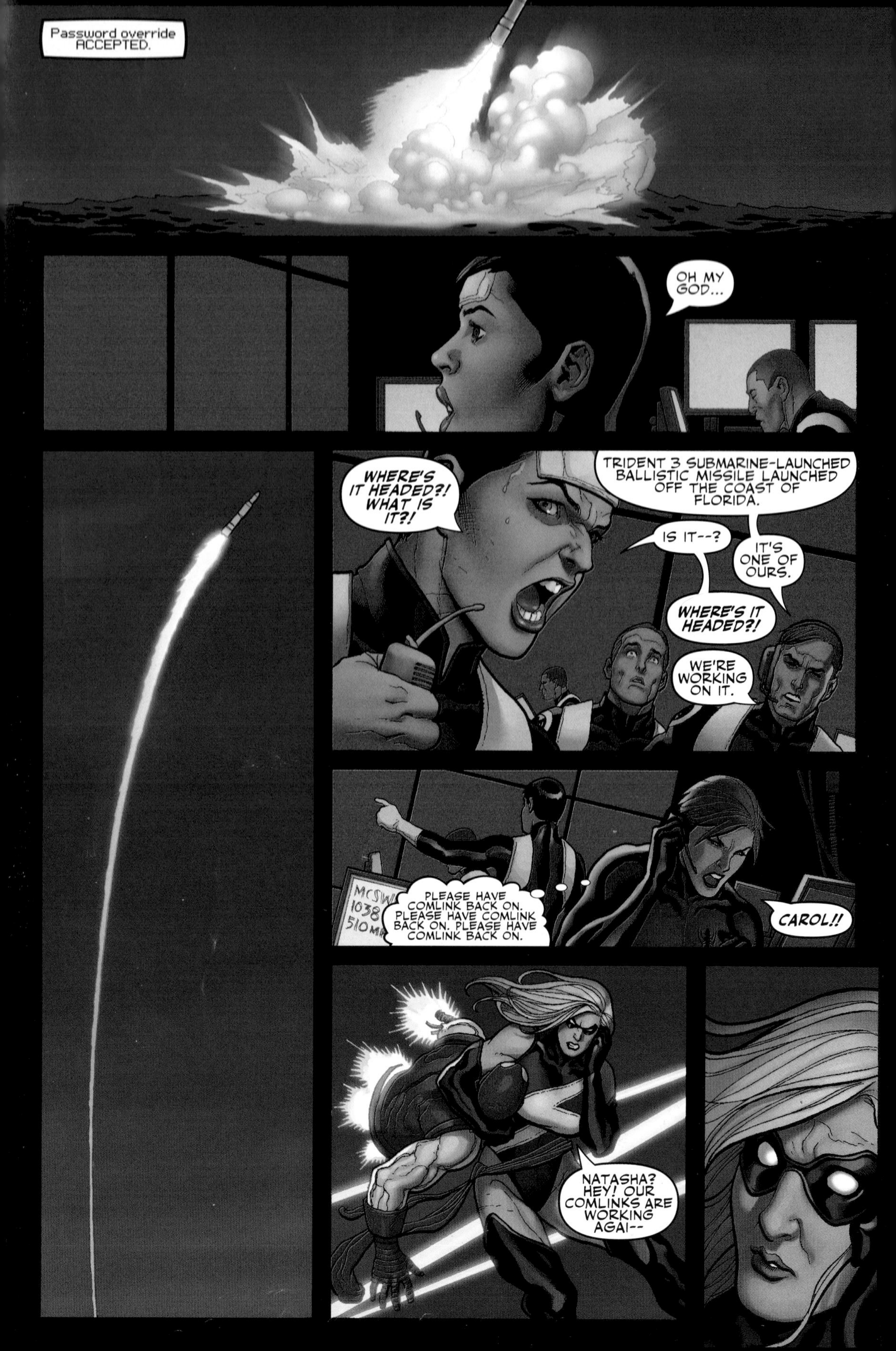
Password override ACCEPTED.
OH MY GOD...
WHERE'S IT HEADED?! WHAT IS IT?!
TRIDENT 3 SUBMARINE-LAUNCHED BALLISTIC MISSILE LAUNCHED OFF THE COAST OF FLORIDA.
IS IT--?
IT'S ONE OF OURS.
WHERE'S IT HEADED?!
WE'RE WORKING ON IT.
PLEASE HAVE COMLINK BACK ON. PLEASE HAVE COMLINK BACK ON. PLEASE HAVE COMLINK BACK ON.
CAROL!!
NATASHA? HEY! OUR COMLINKS ARE WORKING AGAI--

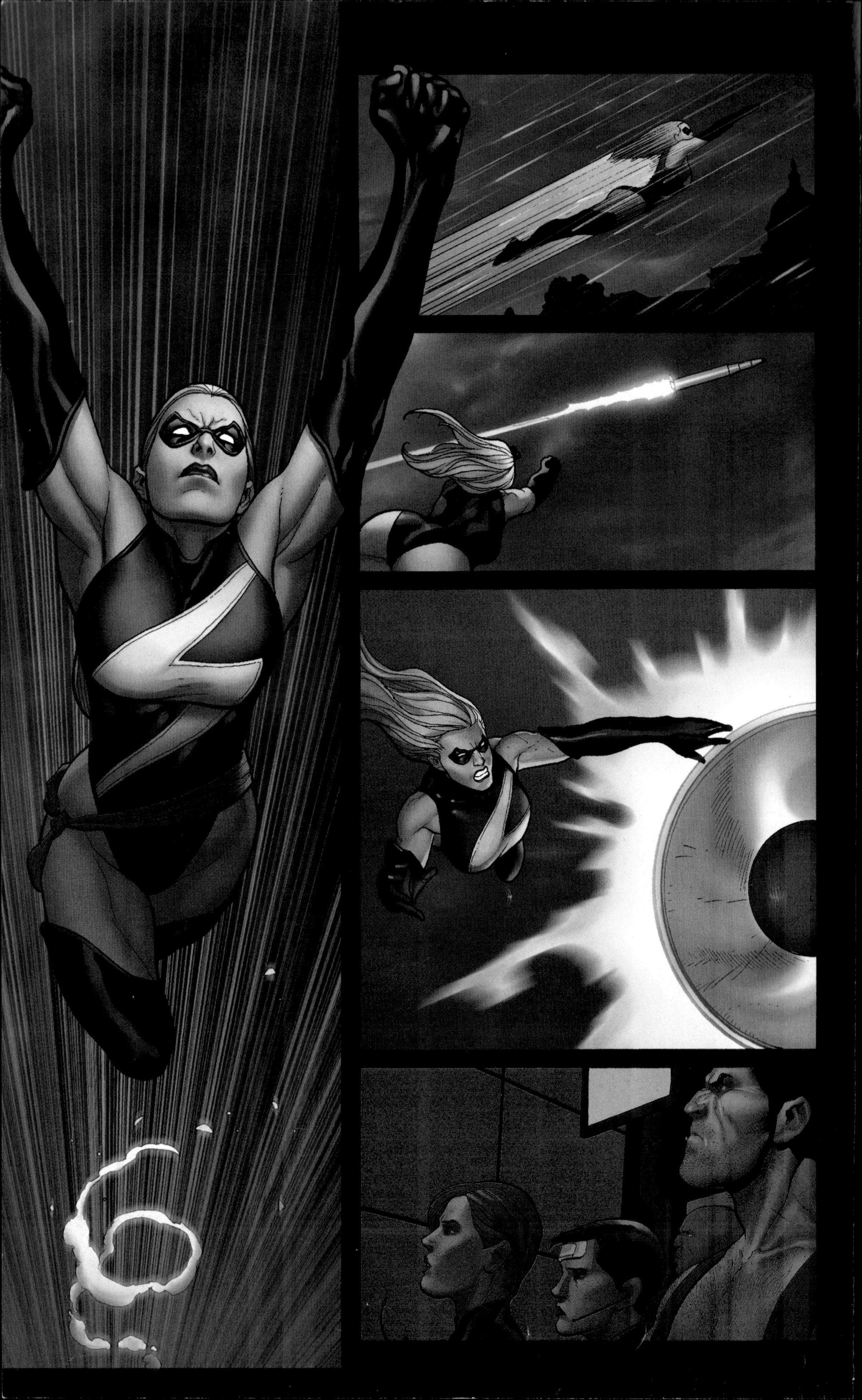

# FEED 08
## Ms MARVEL

11078 KILOMETER
23.08 N  82.22 W
HAVANA

IT'S GOING TOO FAST.

CAROL, THERE'S A CONTROL PANEL ON THE SIDE THAT HOUSES THE MISSILE TRAJECTORY COMPUTER.

HHHAA!!

CRACK

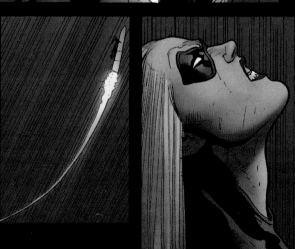

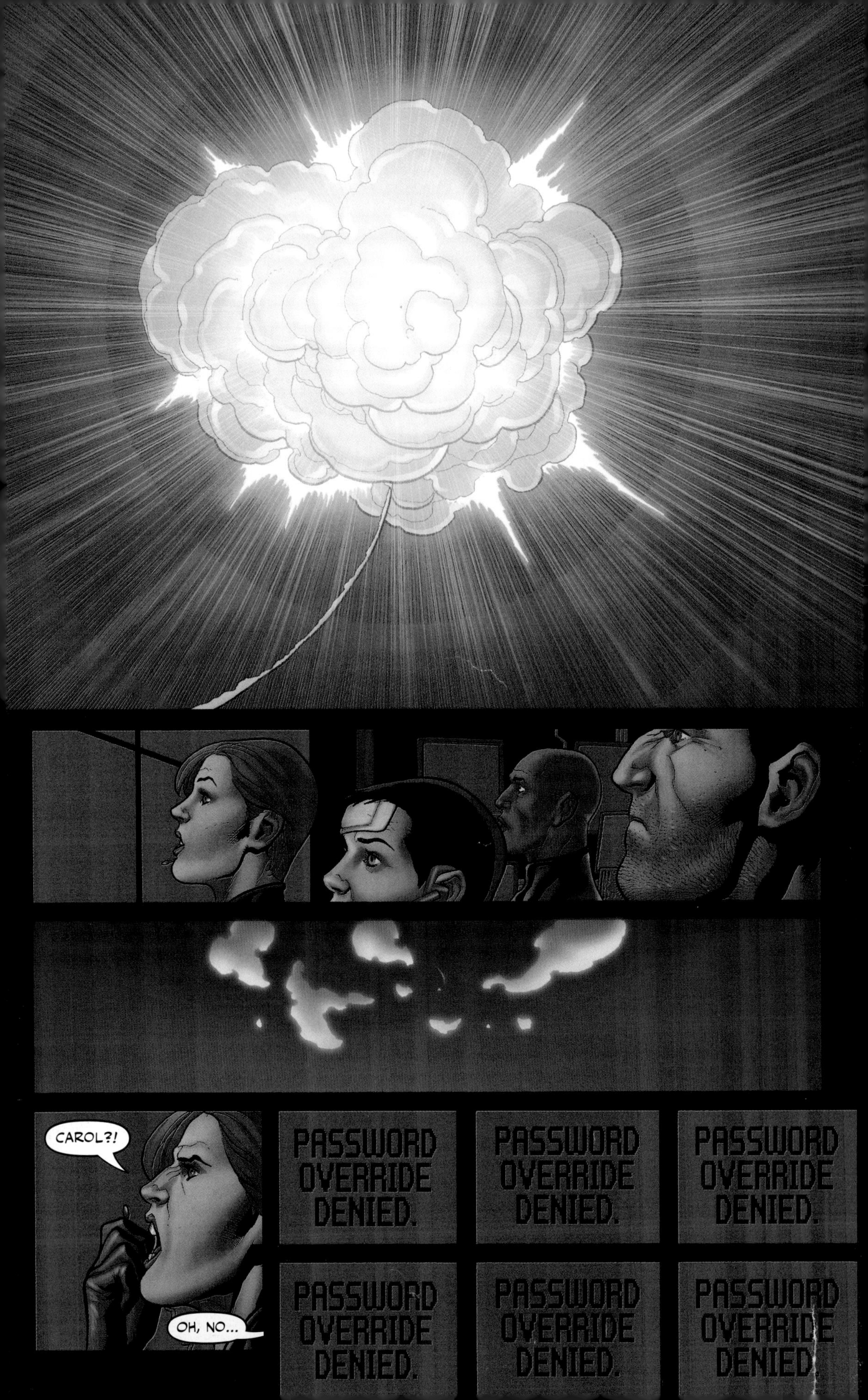
CAROL?!
OH, NO...
PASSWORD OVERRIDE DENIED.
PASSWORD OVERRIDE DENIED.
PASSWORD OVERRIDE DENIED.
PASSWORD OVERRIDE DENIED.
PASSWORD OVERRIDE DENIED.
PASSWORD OVERRIDE DENIED.

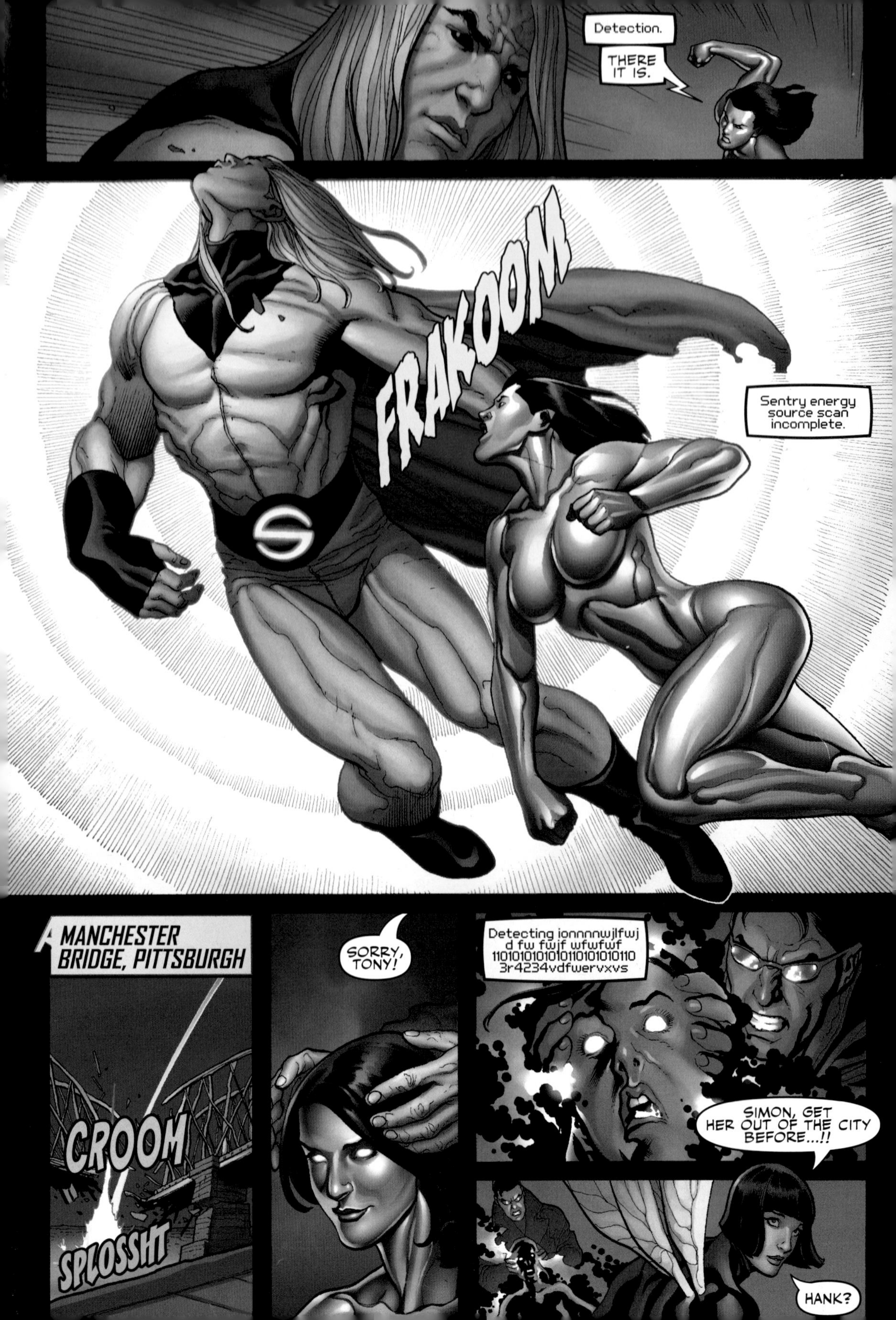

Detection.
THERE IT IS.
FRAKOOM
Sentry energy source scan incomplete.
MANCHESTER BRIDGE, PITTSBURGH
CROOM
SPLOSSHT
SORRY, TONY!
Detecting ionnnnwjlfwj d fw fwjf wfwfwf 110101010101011010101010110 3r4234vdfwervxvs
SIMON, GET HER OUT OF THE CITY BEFORE...!!
HANK?

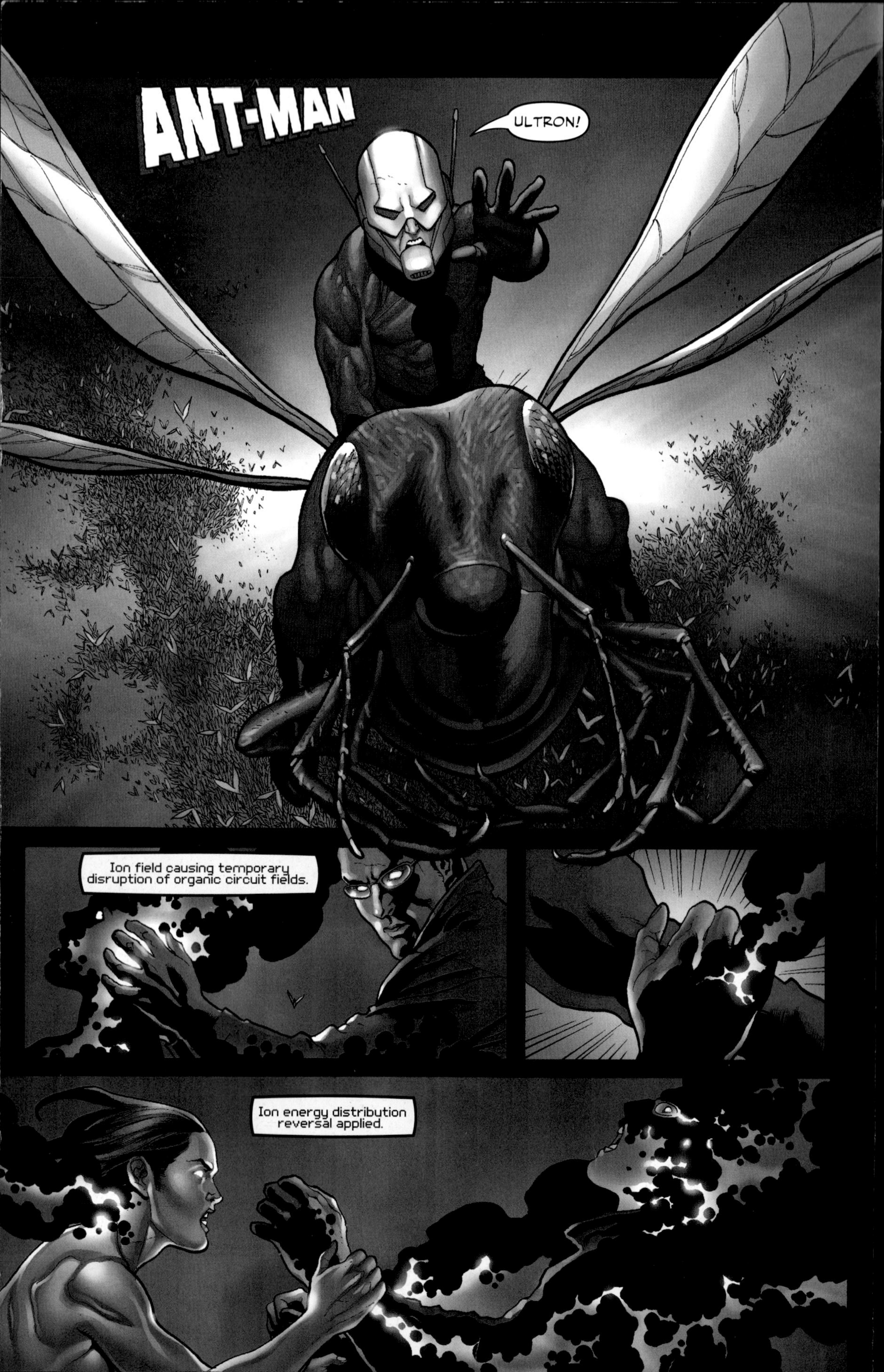
ANT-MAN
ULTRON!
Ion field causing temporary disruption of organic circuit fields.
Ion energy distribution reversal applied.

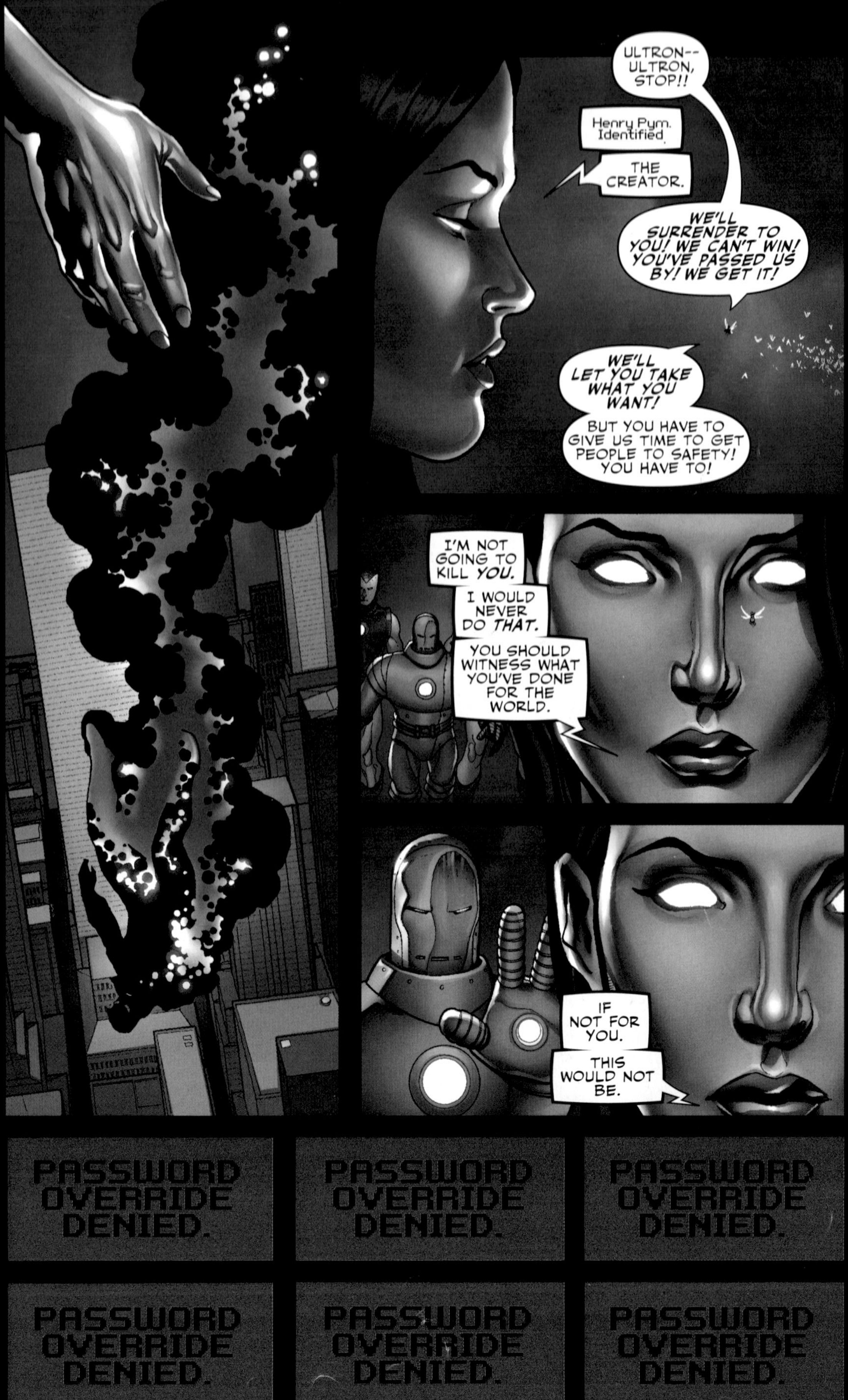
ULTRON-- ULTRON, STOP!!
Henry Pym. Identified.
THE CREATOR.
WE'LL SURRENDER TO YOU! WE CAN'T WIN! YOU'VE PASSED US BY! WE GET IT!
WE'LL LET YOU TAKE WHAT YOU WANT!
BUT YOU HAVE TO GIVE US TIME TO GET PEOPLE TO SAFETY! YOU HAVE TO!
I'M NOT GOING TO KILL YOU.
I WOULD NEVER DO THAT.
YOU SHOULD WITNESS WHAT YOU'VE DONE FOR THE WORLD.
IF NOT FOR YOU.
THIS WOULD NOT BE.
PASSWORD OVERRIDE DENIED.
PASSWORD OVERRIDE DENIED.
PASSWORD OVERRIDE DENIED.
PASSWORD OVERRIDE DENIED.
PASSWORD OVERRIDE DENIED.
PASSWORD OVERRIDE DENIED.

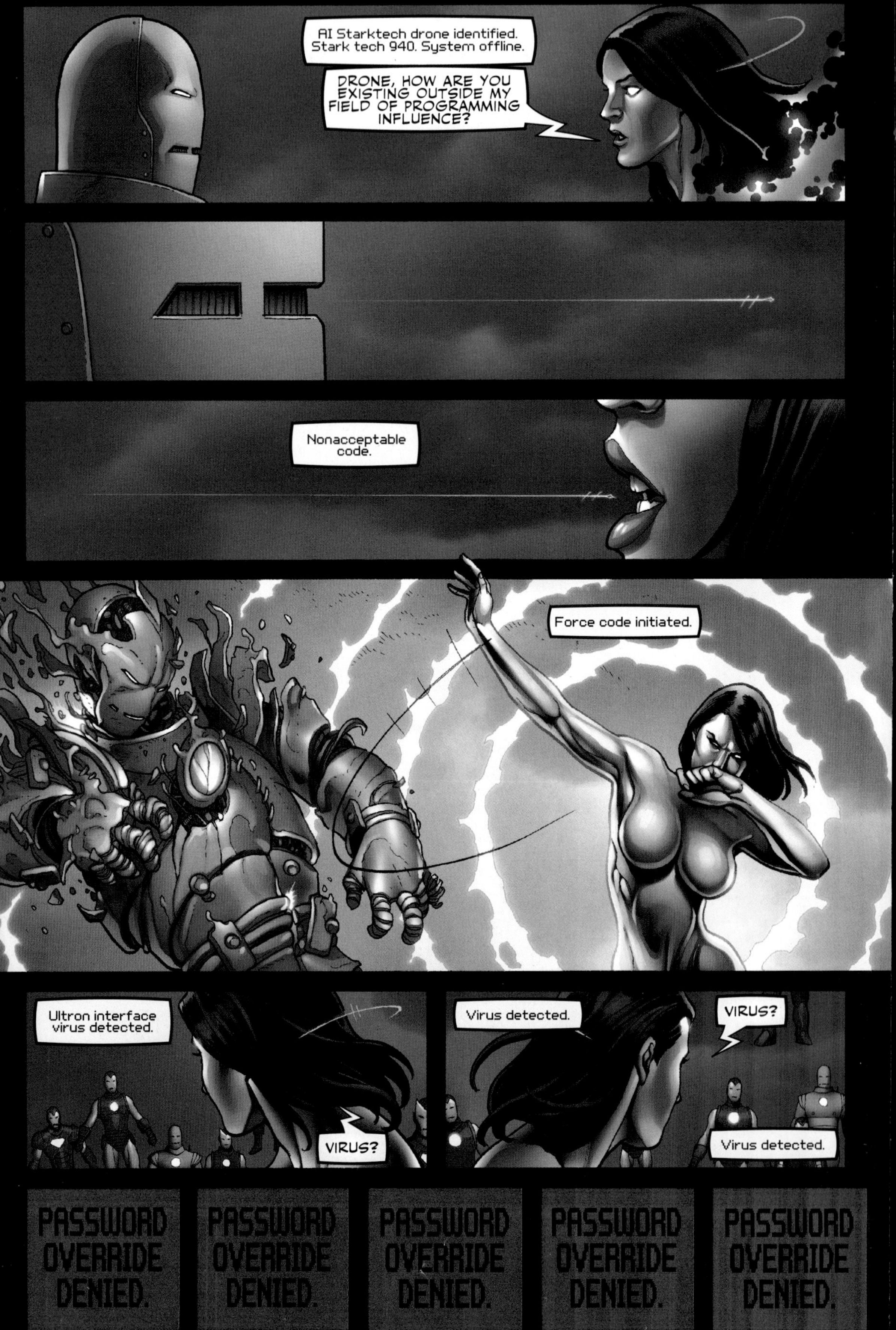
AI Starktech drone identified. Stark tech 940. System offline.
DRONE, HOW ARE YOU EXISTING OUTSIDE MY FIELD OF PROGRAMMING INFLUENCE?
Nonacceptable code.
Force code initiated.
Ultron interface virus detected.
VIRUS?
Virus detected.
VIRUS?
Virus detected.
PASSWORD OVERRIDE DENIED.
PASSWORD OVERRIDE DENIED.
PASSWORD OVERRIDE DENIED.
PASSWORD OVERRIDE DENIED.
PASSWORD OVERRIDE DENIED.

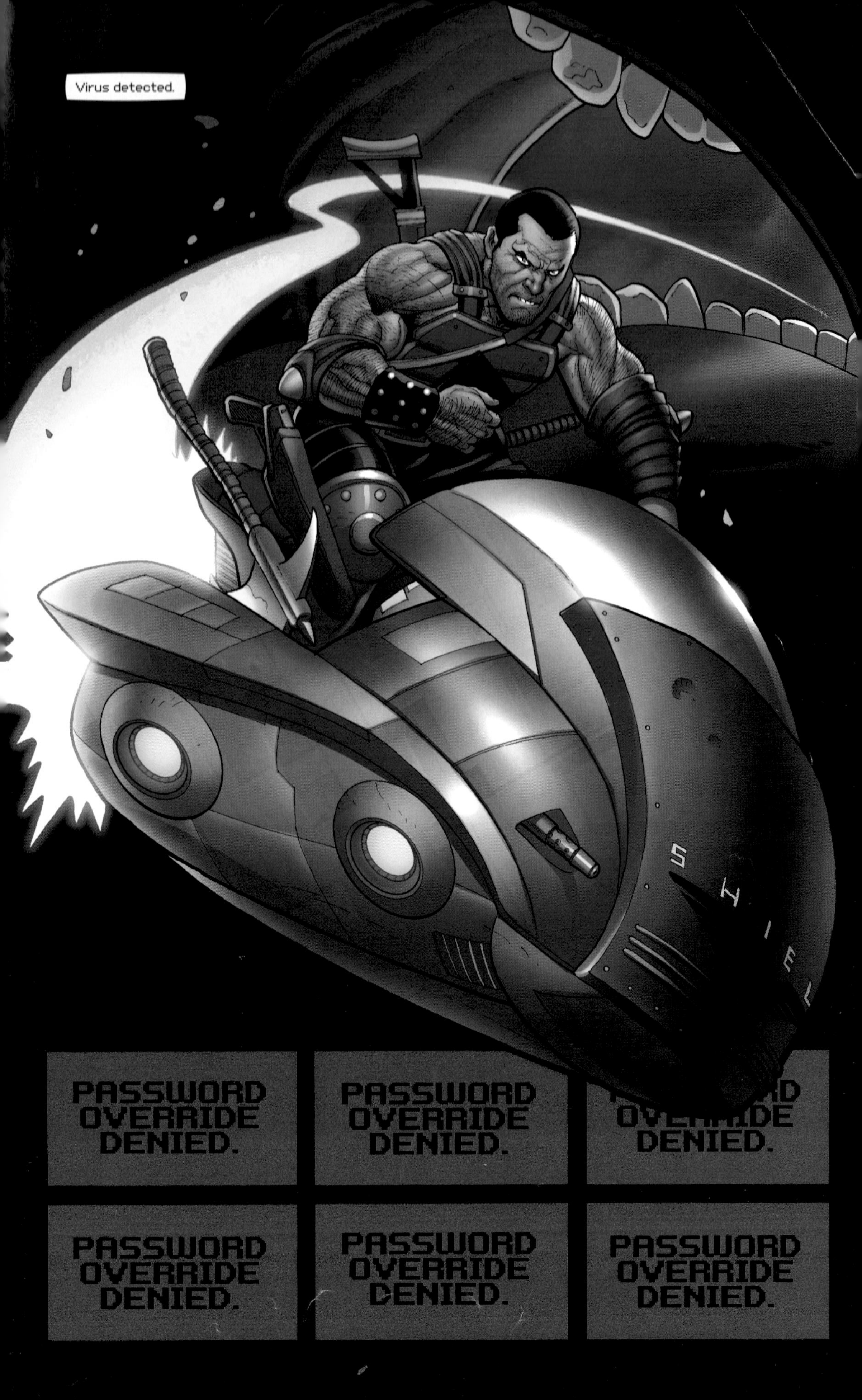
Virus detected.
S H I E L
PASSWORD OVERRIDE DENIED.
PASSWORD OVERRIDE DENIED.
DENIED.
PASSWORD OVERRIDE DENIED.
PASSWORD OVERRIDE DENIED.
PASSWORD OVERRIDE DENIED.

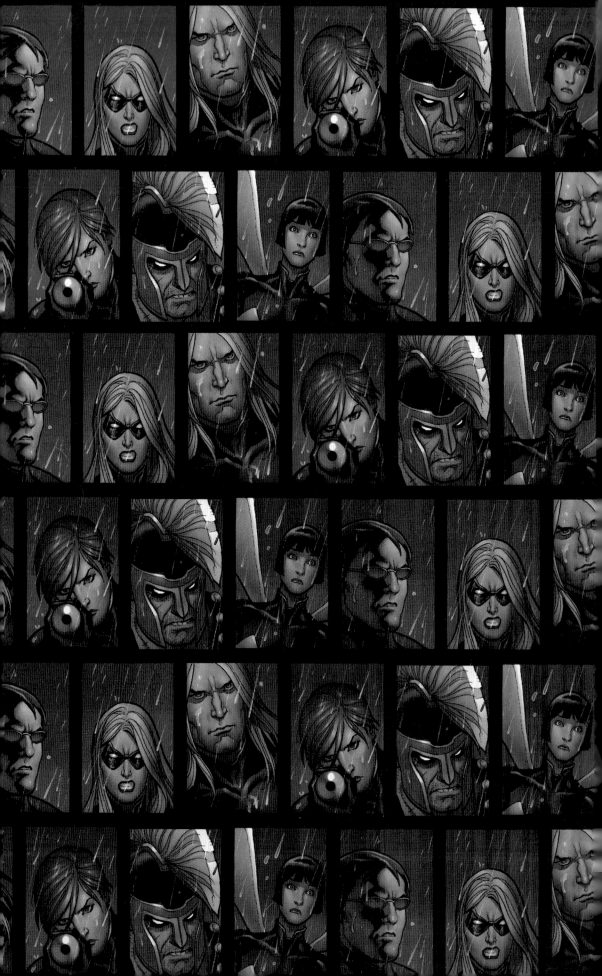

ISSUE #6

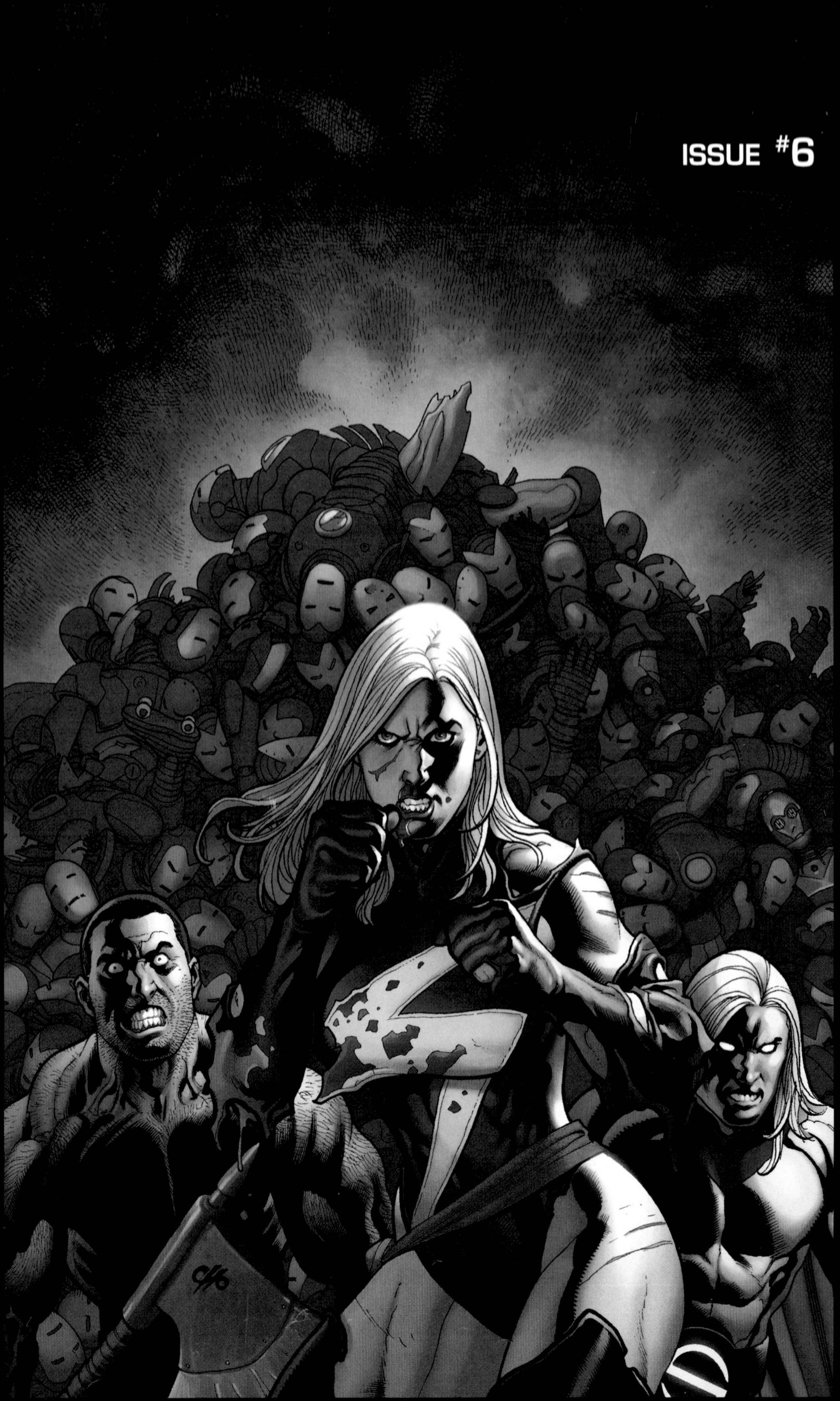

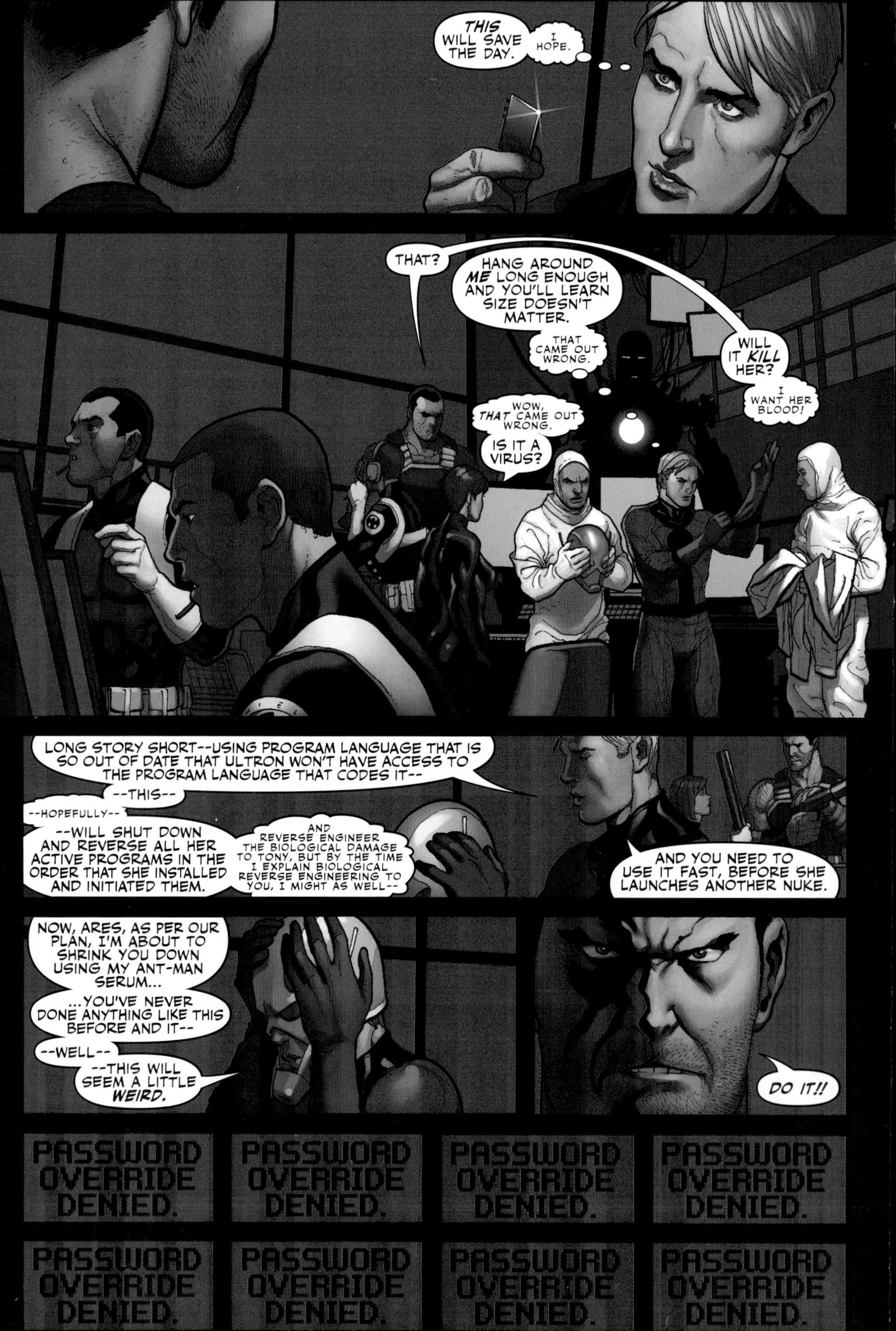
THIS WILL SAVE THE DAY.
I HOPE.
THAT?
HANG AROUND ME LONG ENOUGH AND YOU'LL LEARN SIZE DOESN'T MATTER.
THAT CAME OUT WRONG.
WILL IT KILL HER?
I WANT HER BLOOD!
WOW, THAT CAME OUT WRONG.
IS IT A VIRUS?
LONG STORY SHORT--USING PROGRAM LANGUAGE THAT IS SO OUT OF DATE THAT ULTRON WON'T HAVE ACCESS TO THE PROGRAM LANGUAGE THAT CODES IT--
--THIS--
--HOPEFULLY--
--WILL SHUT DOWN AND REVERSE ALL HER ACTIVE PROGRAMS IN THE ORDER THAT SHE INSTALLED AND INITIATED THEM.
AND REVERSE ENGINEER THE BIOLOGICAL DAMAGE TO TONY, BUT BY THE TIME I EXPLAIN BIOLOGICAL REVERSE ENGINEERING TO YOU, I MIGHT AS WELL--
AND YOU NEED TO USE IT FAST, BEFORE SHE LAUNCHES ANOTHER NUKE.
NOW, ARES, AS PER OUR PLAN, I'M ABOUT TO SHRINK YOU DOWN USING MY ANT-MAN SERUM...
...YOU'VE NEVER DONE ANYTHING LIKE THIS BEFORE AND IT--
--WELL--
--THIS WILL SEEM A LITTLE WEIRD.
DO IT!!
PASSWORD OVERRIDE DENIED.
PASSWORD OVERRIDE DENIED.
PASSWORD OVERRIDE DENIED.
PASSWORD OVERRIDE DENIED.
PASSWORD OVERRIDE DENIED.
PASSWORD OVERRIDE DENIED.
PASSWORD OVERRIDE DENIED.
PASSWORD OVERRIDE DENIED.

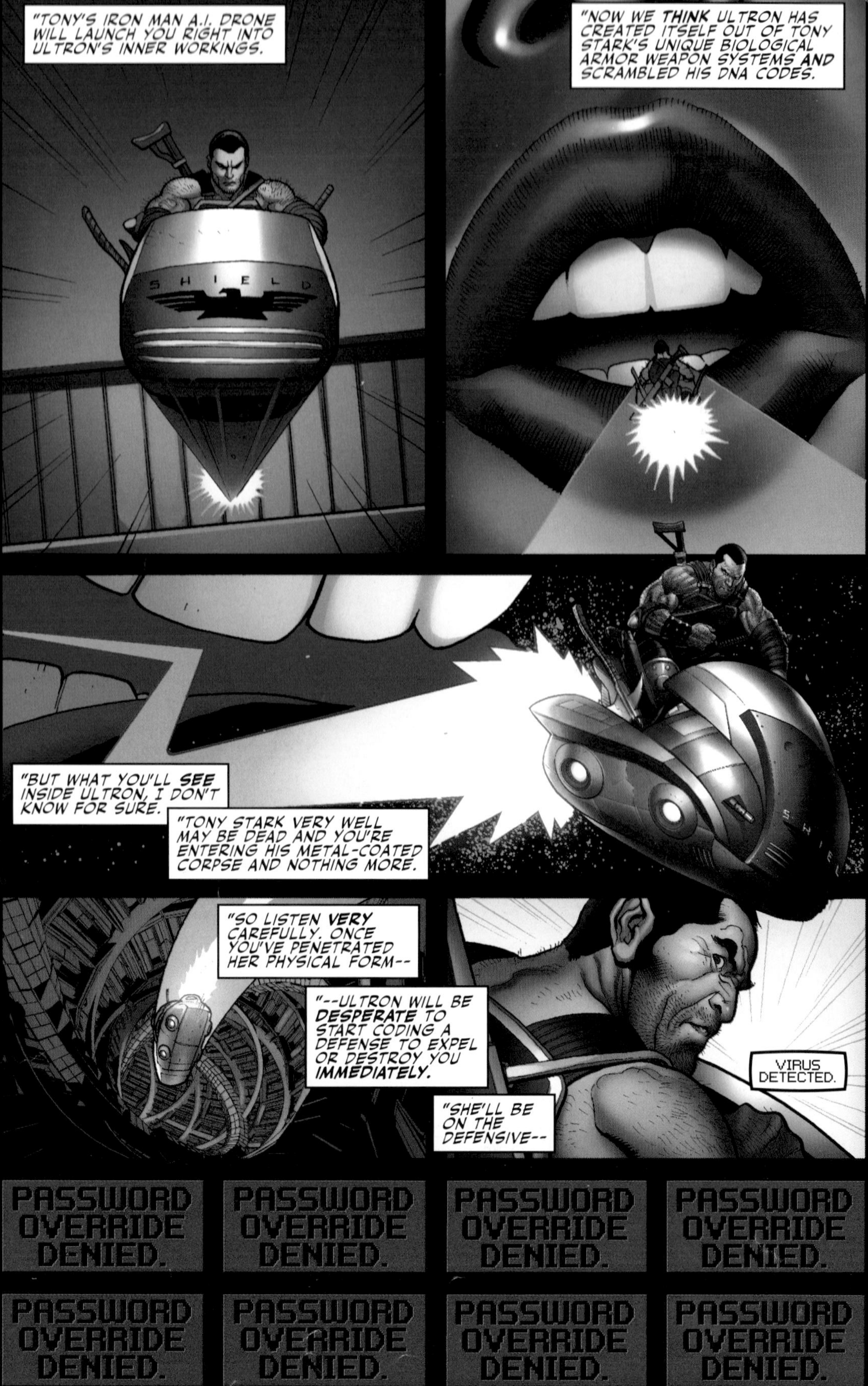
"TONY'S IRON MAN A.I. DRONE WILL LAUNCH YOU RIGHT INTO ULTRON'S INNER WORKINGS.
"NOW WE THINK ULTRON HAS CREATED ITSELF OUT OF TONY STARK'S UNIQUE BIOLOGICAL ARMOR WEAPON SYSTEMS AND SCRAMBLED HIS DNA CODES.
"BUT WHAT YOU'LL SEE INSIDE ULTRON, I DON'T KNOW FOR SURE.
"TONY STARK VERY WELL MAY BE DEAD AND YOU'RE ENTERING HIS METAL-COATED CORPSE AND NOTHING MORE.
"SO LISTEN VERY CAREFULLY. ONCE YOU'VE PENETRATED HER PHYSICAL FORM--
"--ULTRON WILL BE DESPERATE TO START CODING A DEFENSE TO EXPEL OR DESTROY YOU IMMEDIATELY.
"SHE'LL BE ON THE DEFENSIVE--
VIRUS DETECTED.
PASSWORD OVERRIDE DENIED.
PASSWORD OVERRIDE DENIED.
PASSWORD OVERRIDE DENIED.
PASSWORD OVERRIDE DENIED.
PASSWORD OVERRIDE DENIED.
PASSWORD OVERRIDE DENIED.
PASSWORD OVERRIDE DENIED.
PASSWORD OVERRIDE DENIED.

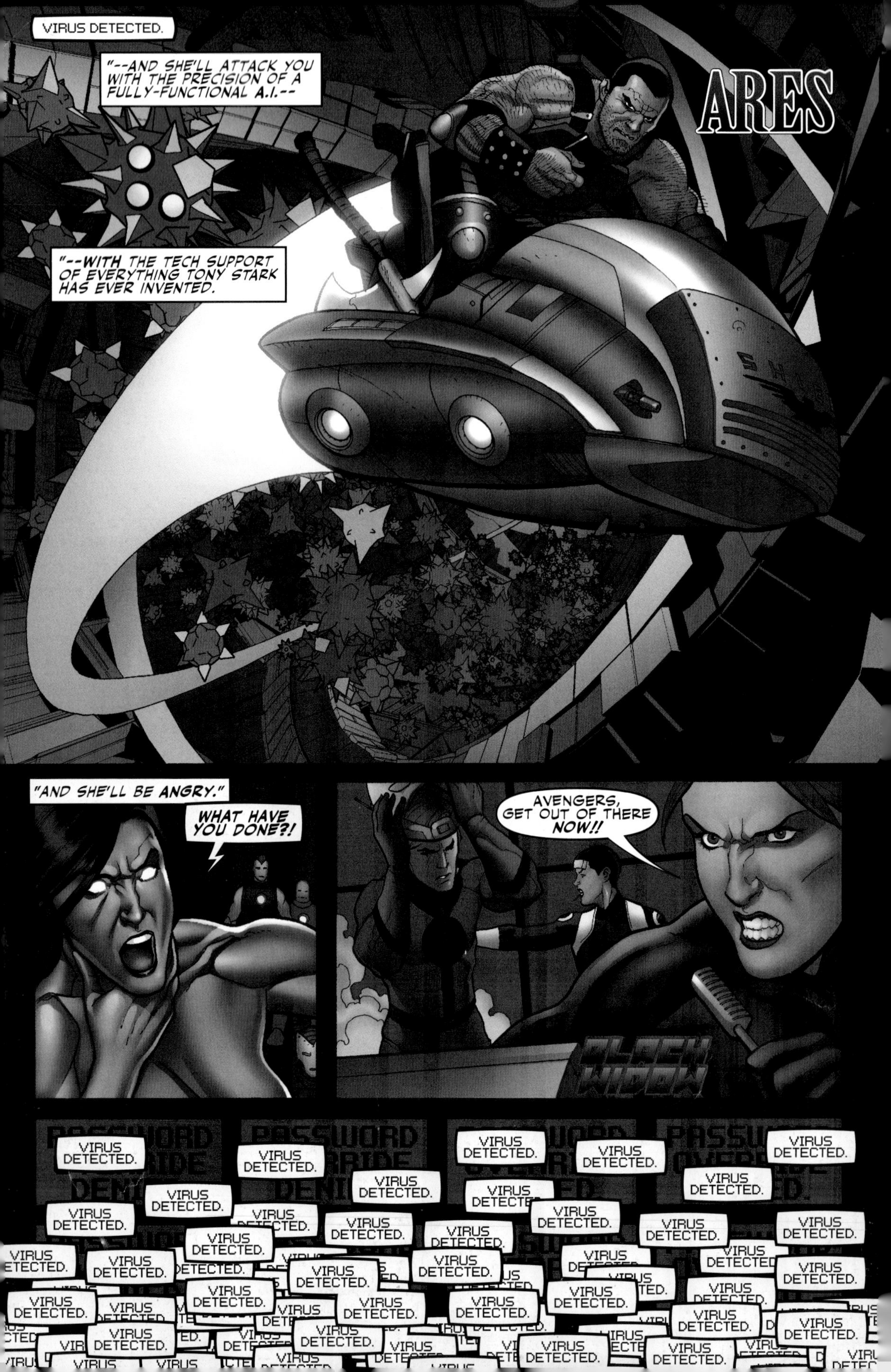
VIRUS DETECTED.
"--AND SHE'LL ATTACK YOU WITH THE PRECISION OF A FULLY-FUNCTIONAL A.I.--
ARES
"--WITH THE TECH SUPPORT OF EVERYTHING TONY STARK HAS EVER INVENTED.
"AND SHE'LL BE ANGRY."
WHAT HAVE YOU DONE?!
AVENGERS, GET OUT OF THERE NOW!!
BLACK WIDOW
VIRUS DETECTED.
VIRUS DETECTED.
VIRUS DETECTED.
VIRUS DETECTED.
VIRUS DETECTED.
VIRUS DETECTED.
VIRUS DETECTED.
VIRUS DETECTED.
VIRUS DETECTED.
VIRUS DETECTED.
VIRUS DETECTED.
VIRUS DETECTED.
VIRUS DETECTED.
VIRUS DETECTED.
VIRUS DETECTED.
VIRUS DETECTED.
VIRUS DETECTED.
VIRUS DETECTED.
VIRUS DETECTED.
VIRUS DETECTED.
VIRUS DETECTED.
VIRUS DETECTED.
VIRUS DETECTED.
VIRUS DETECTED.
VIRUS DETECTED.
VIRUS DETECTED.
VIRUS DETECTED.
VIRUS DETECTED.

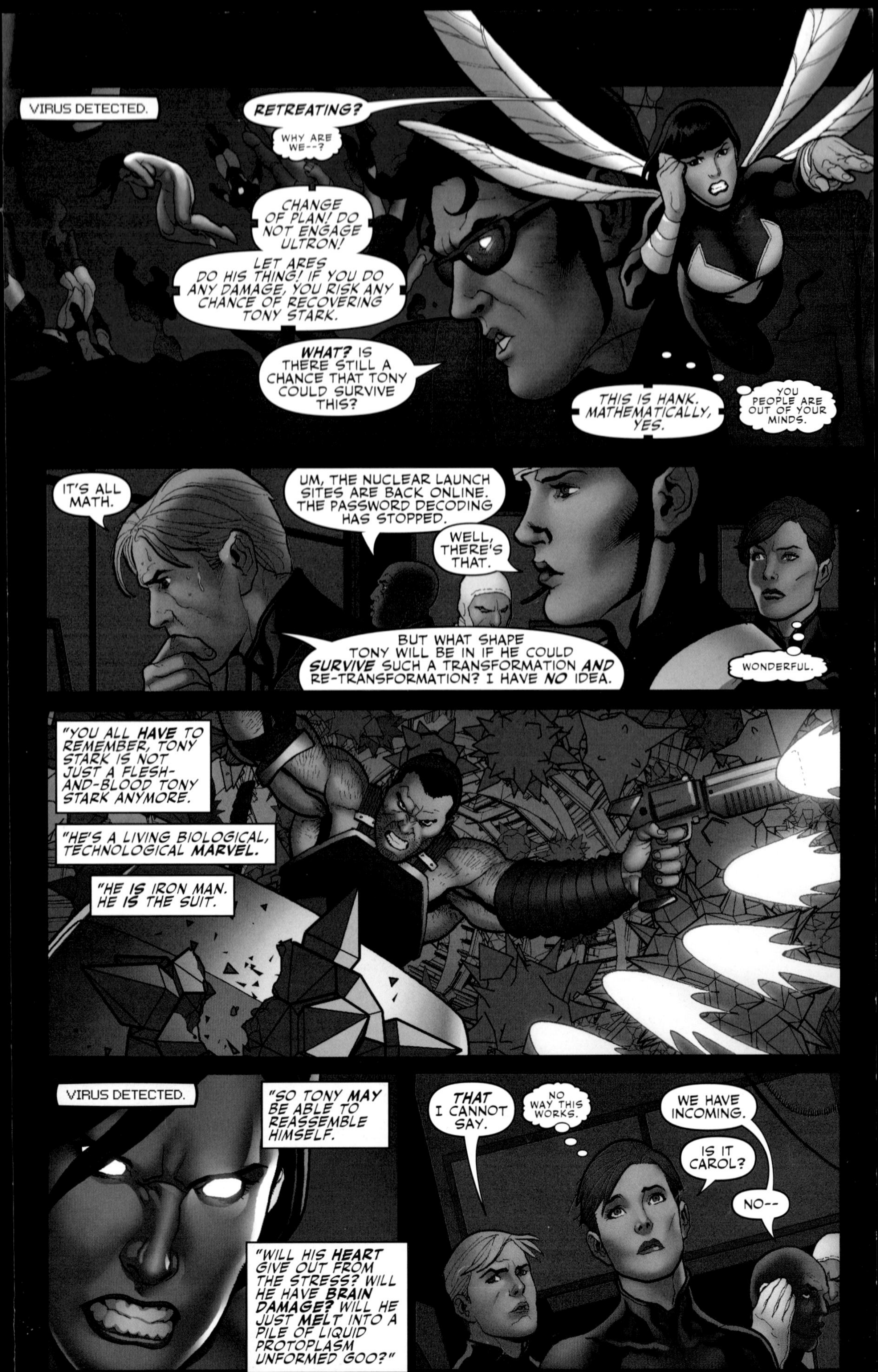
VIRUS DETECTED.
RETREATING?
WHY ARE WE--?
CHANGE OF PLAN! DO NOT ENGAGE ULTRON!
LET ARES DO HIS THING! IF YOU DO ANY DAMAGE, YOU RISK ANY CHANCE OF RECOVERING TONY STARK.
WHAT? IS THERE STILL A CHANCE THAT TONY COULD SURVIVE THIS?
THIS IS HANK. MATHEMATICALLY, YES.
YOU PEOPLE ARE OUT OF YOUR MINDS.
IT'S ALL MATH.
UM, THE NUCLEAR LAUNCH SITES ARE BACK ONLINE. THE PASSWORD DECODING HAS STOPPED.
WELL, THERE'S THAT.
BUT WHAT SHAPE TONY WILL BE IN IF HE COULD SURVIVE SUCH A TRANSFORMATION AND RE-TRANSFORMATION? I HAVE NO IDEA.
WONDERFUL.
"YOU ALL HAVE TO REMEMBER, TONY STARK IS NOT JUST A FLESH-AND-BLOOD TONY STARK ANYMORE.
"HE'S A LIVING BIOLOGICAL, TECHNOLOGICAL MARVEL.
"HE IS IRON MAN. HE IS THE SUIT.
VIRUS DETECTED.
"SO TONY MAY BE ABLE TO REASSEMBLE HIMSELF.
"WILL HIS HEART GIVE OUT FROM THE STRESS? WILL HE HAVE BRAIN DAMAGE? WILL HE JUST MELT INTO A PILE OF LIQUID PROTOPLASM UNFORMED GOO?"
THAT I CANNOT SAY.
NO WAY THIS WORKS.
WE HAVE INCOMING.
IS IT CAROL?
NO--

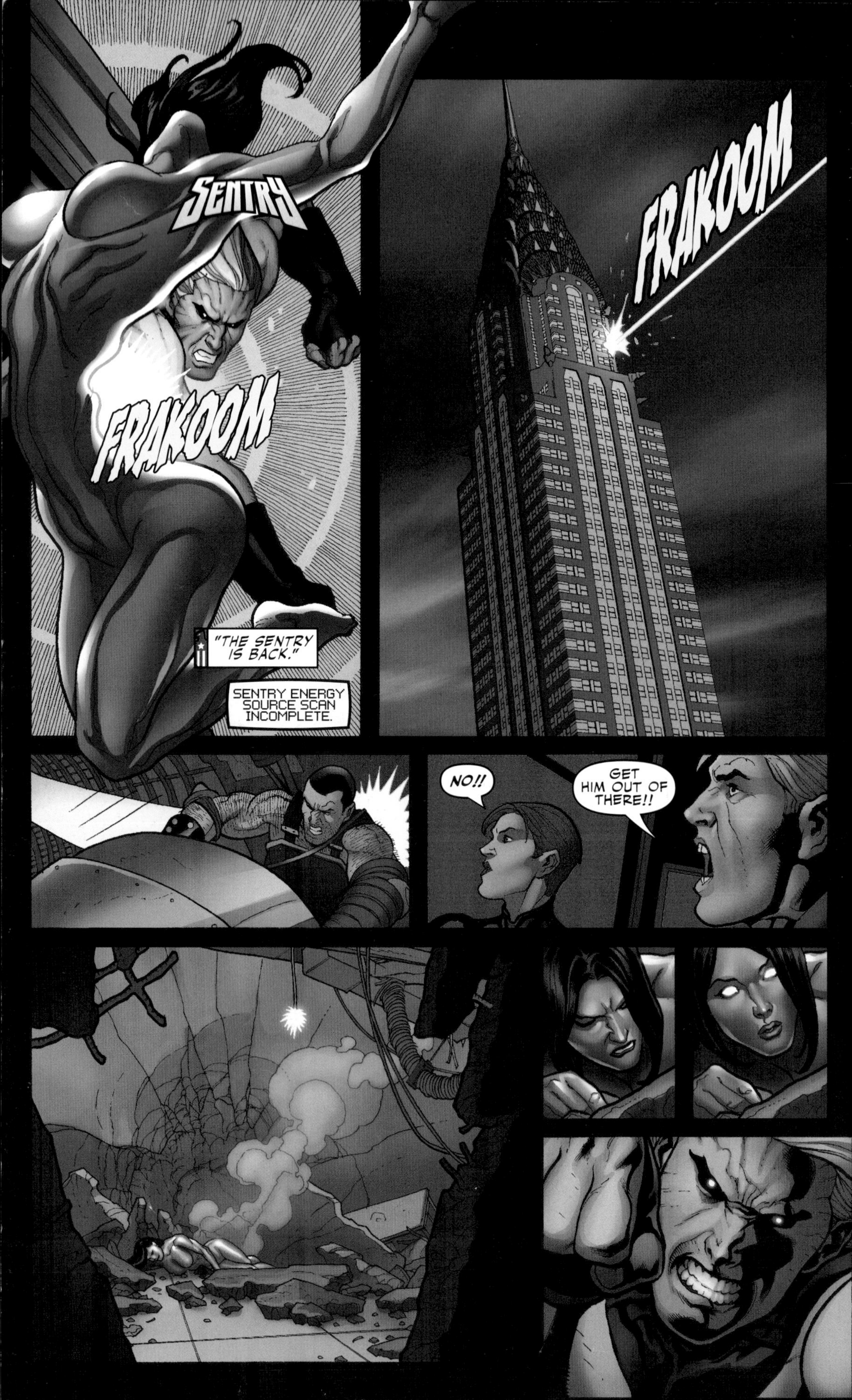
SENTRY
FRAKOOM
"THE SENTRY IS BACK."
SENTRY ENERGY SOURCE SCAN INCOMPLETE.
FRAKOOM
NO!!
GET HIM OUT OF THERE!!

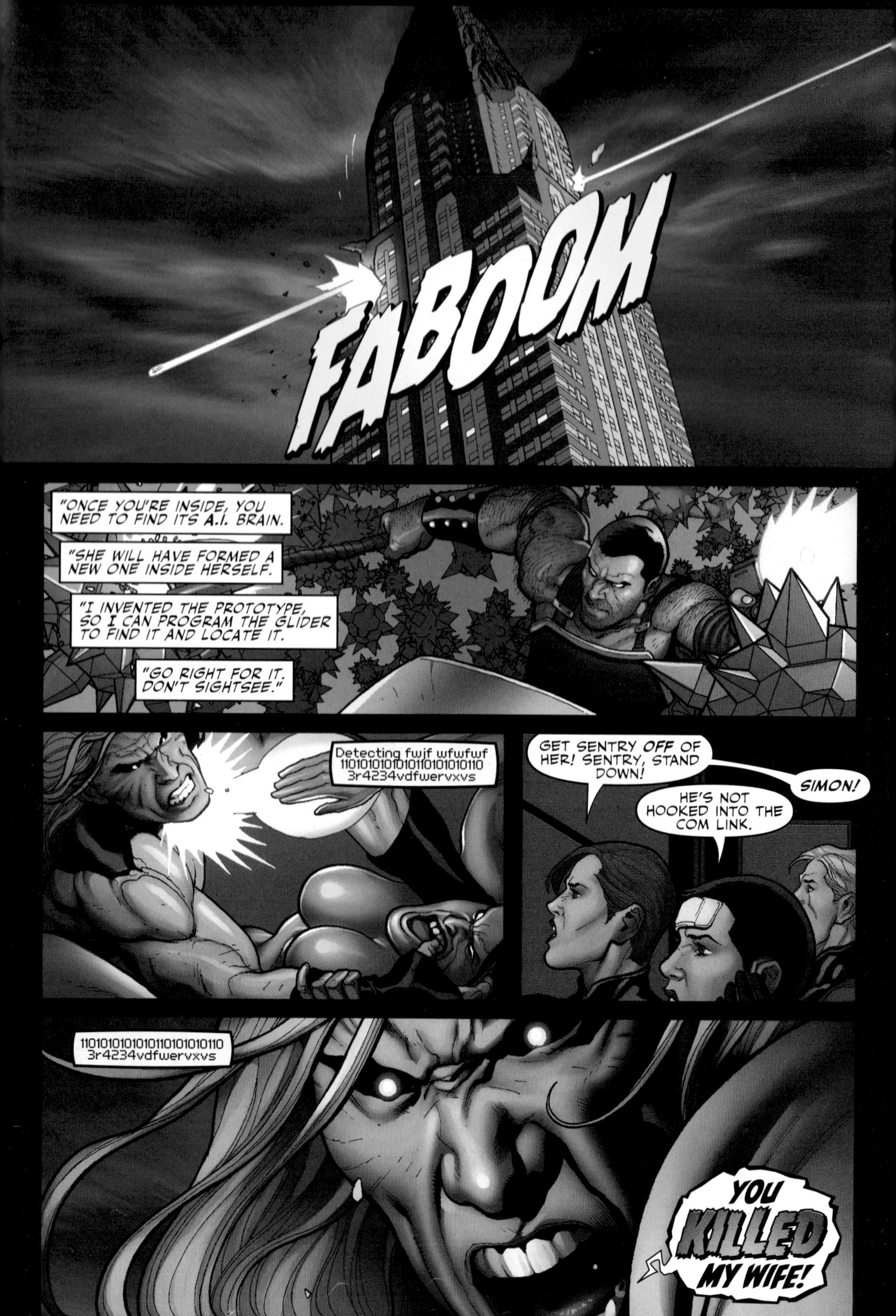
FABOOM
"ONCE YOU'RE INSIDE, YOU NEED TO FIND ITS A.I. BRAIN.
"SHE WILL HAVE FORMED A NEW ONE INSIDE HERSELF.
"I INVENTED THE PROTOTYPE, SO I CAN PROGRAM THE GLIDER TO FIND IT AND LOCATE IT.
"GO RIGHT FOR IT. DON'T SIGHTSEE."
Detecting fwjf wfwfwf 1101010101010110101010110 3r4234vdfwervxvs
GET SENTRY OFF OF HER! SENTRY, STAND DOWN!
SIMON!
HE'S NOT HOOKED INTO THE COM LINK.
1101010101010110101010110 3r4234vdfwervxvs
YOU KILLED MY WIFE!

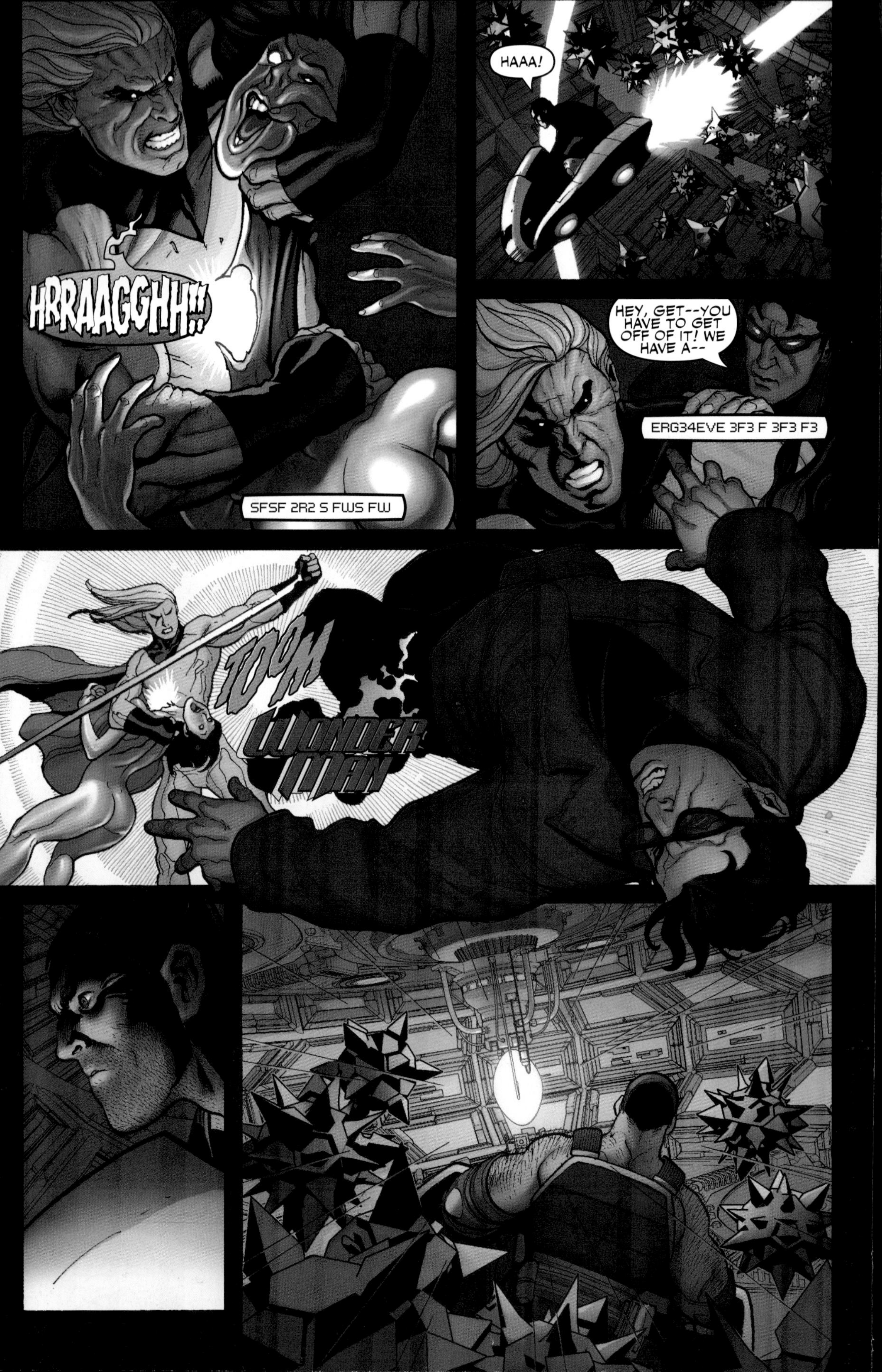
HRRAAGGHH!!
SFSF 2R2 S FWS FW
HAAA!
HEY, GET--YOU HAVE TO GET OFF OF IT! WE HAVE A--
ERG34EVE 3F3 F 3F3 F3
TOOM
WONDER MAN

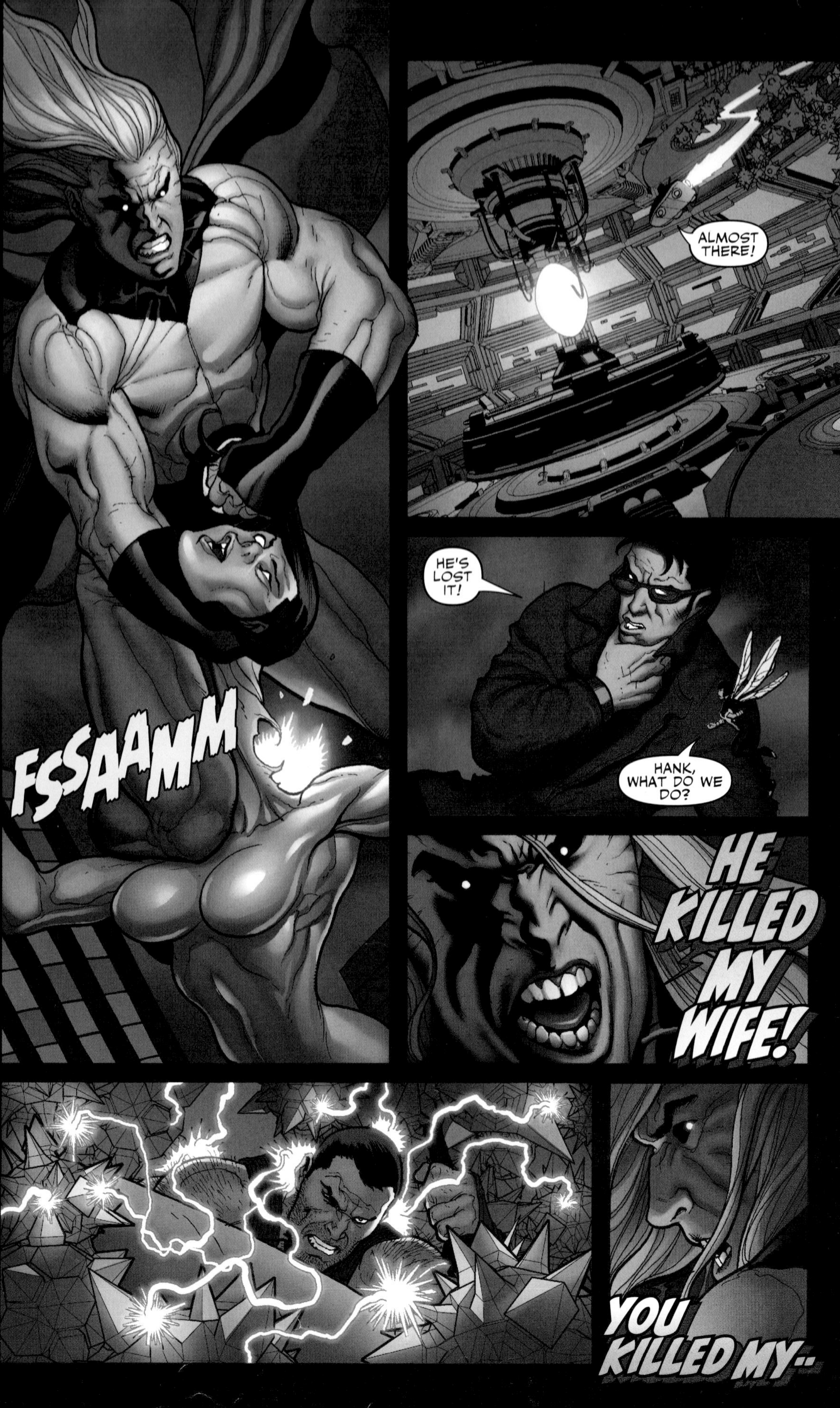
FSSAAMM
ALMOST THERE!
HE'S LOST IT!
HANK, WHAT DO WE DO?
HE KILLED MY WIFE!
YOU KILLED MY..

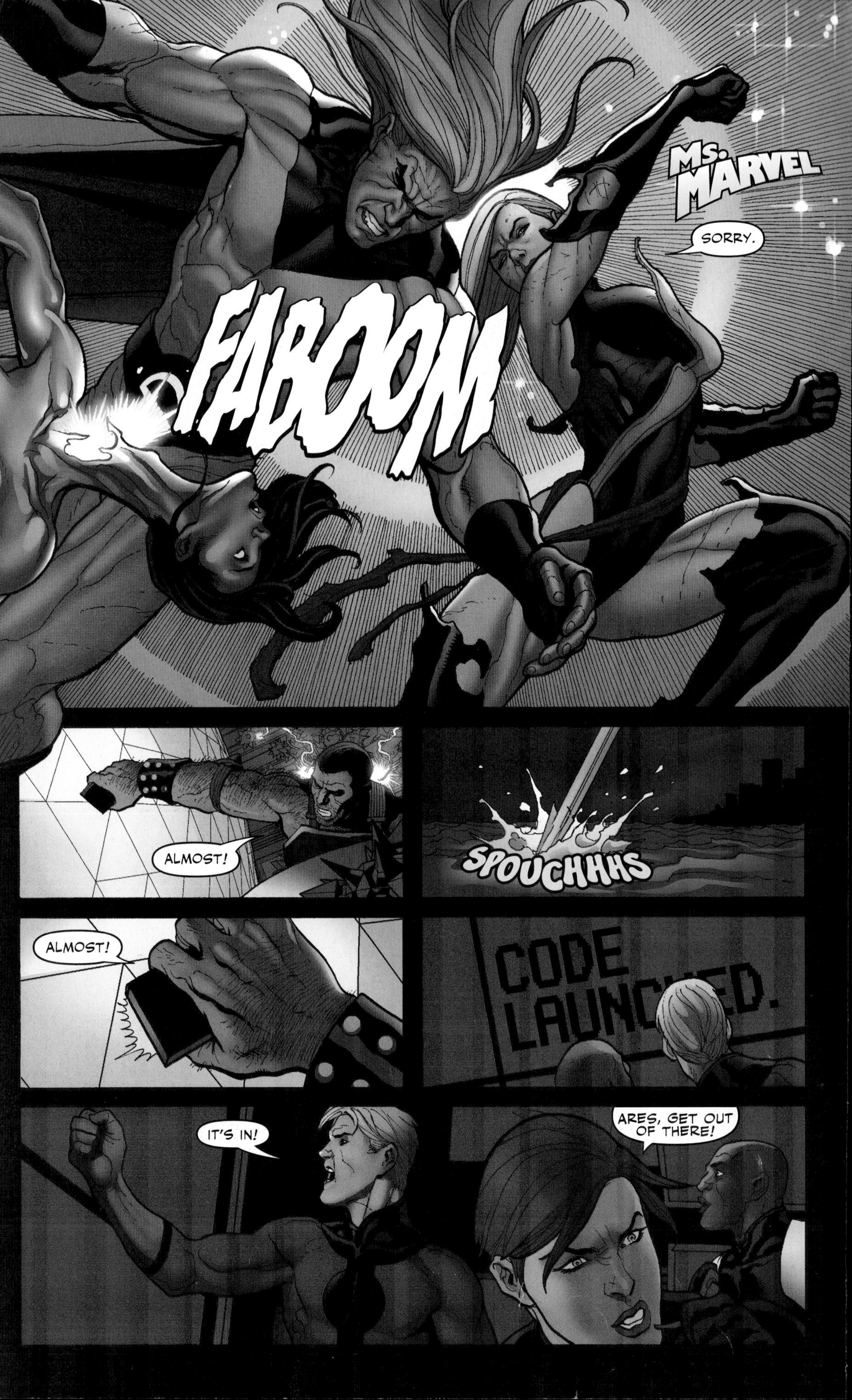
Ms. MARVEL
SORRY.
FABOOM
ALMOST!
SPOUCHHHS
ALMOST!
CODE LAUNCHED.
IT'S IN!
ARES, GET OUT OF THERE!

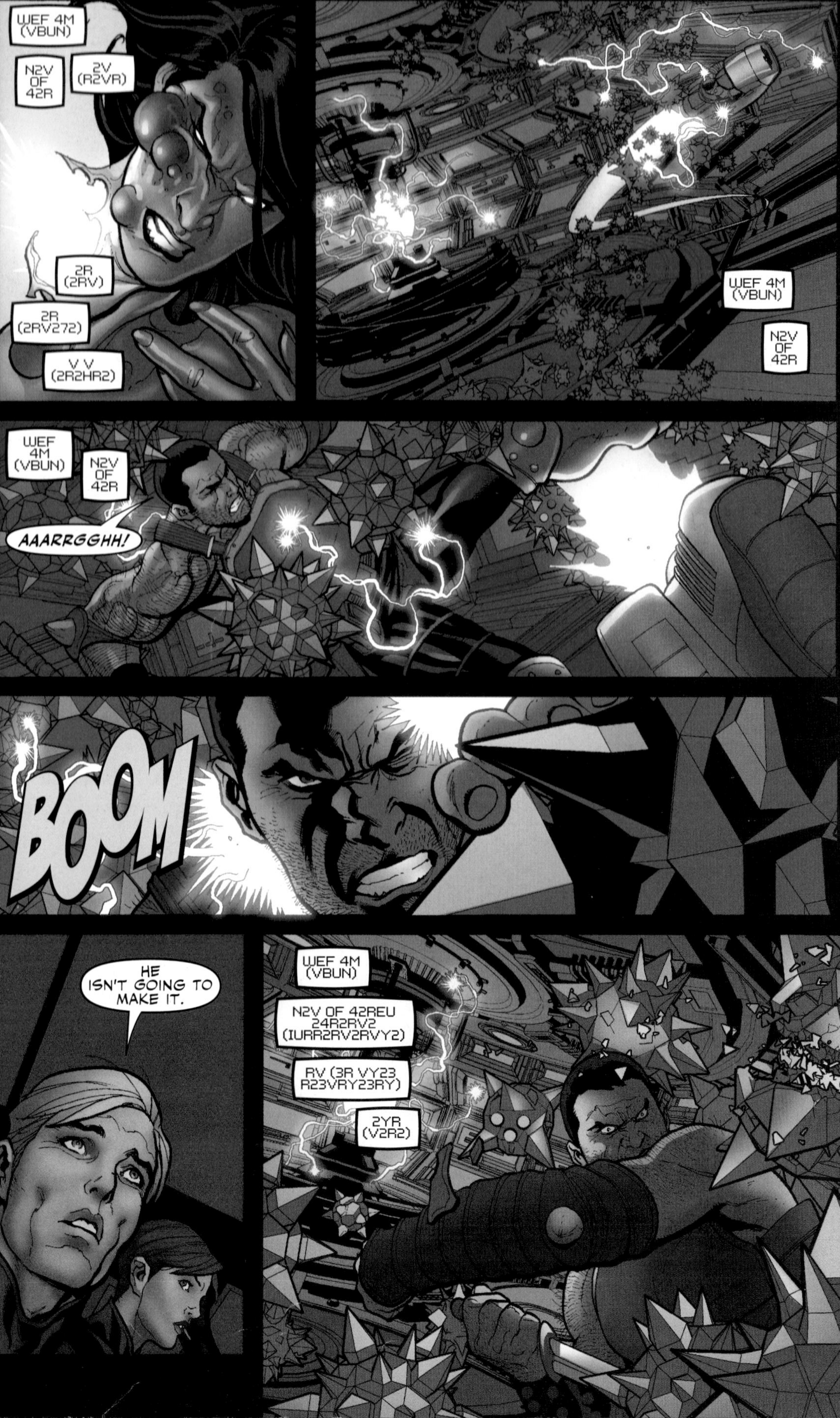
WEF 4M (VBUN)
N2V OF 42R
2V (R2VR)
2R (2RV)
2R (2RV272)
V V (2R2HR2)
WEF 4M (VBUN)
N2V OF 42R
WEF 4M (VBUN)
N2V OF 42R
AAARRGGHH!
BOOM
HE ISN'T GOING TO MAKE IT.
WEF 4M (VBUN)
N2V OF 42REU 24R2RV2 (IURR2RV2RVY2)
RV (3R VY23 R23VRY23RY)
2YR (V2R2)

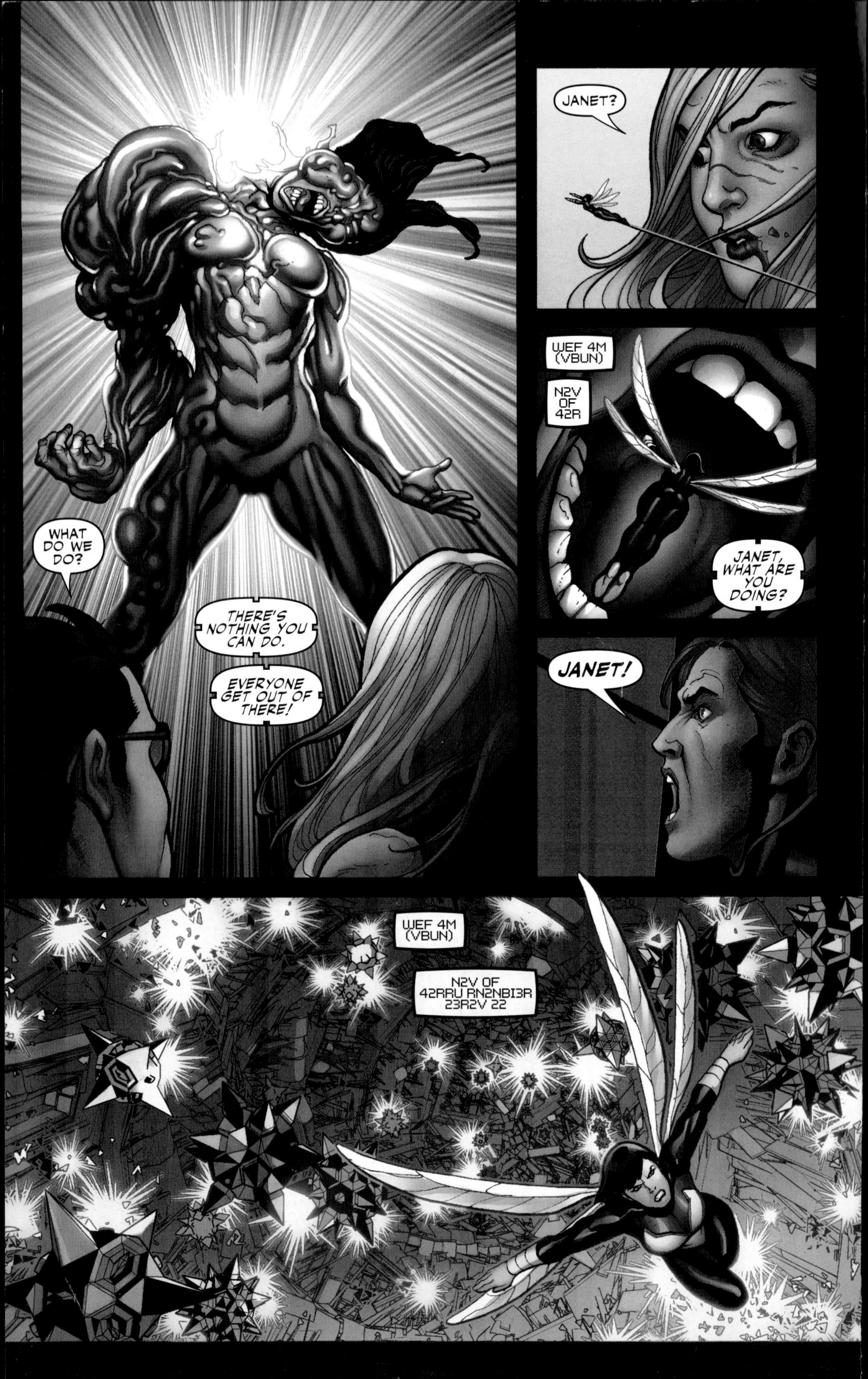
WHAT DO WE DO?
THERE'S NOTHING YOU CAN DO.
EVERYONE GET OUT OF THERE!
JANET?
WEF 4M (VBUN)
N2V OF 42R
JANET, WHAT ARE YOU DOING?
JANET!
WEF 4M (VBUN)
N2V OF 42RRU RN2NBI3R 23R2V 22

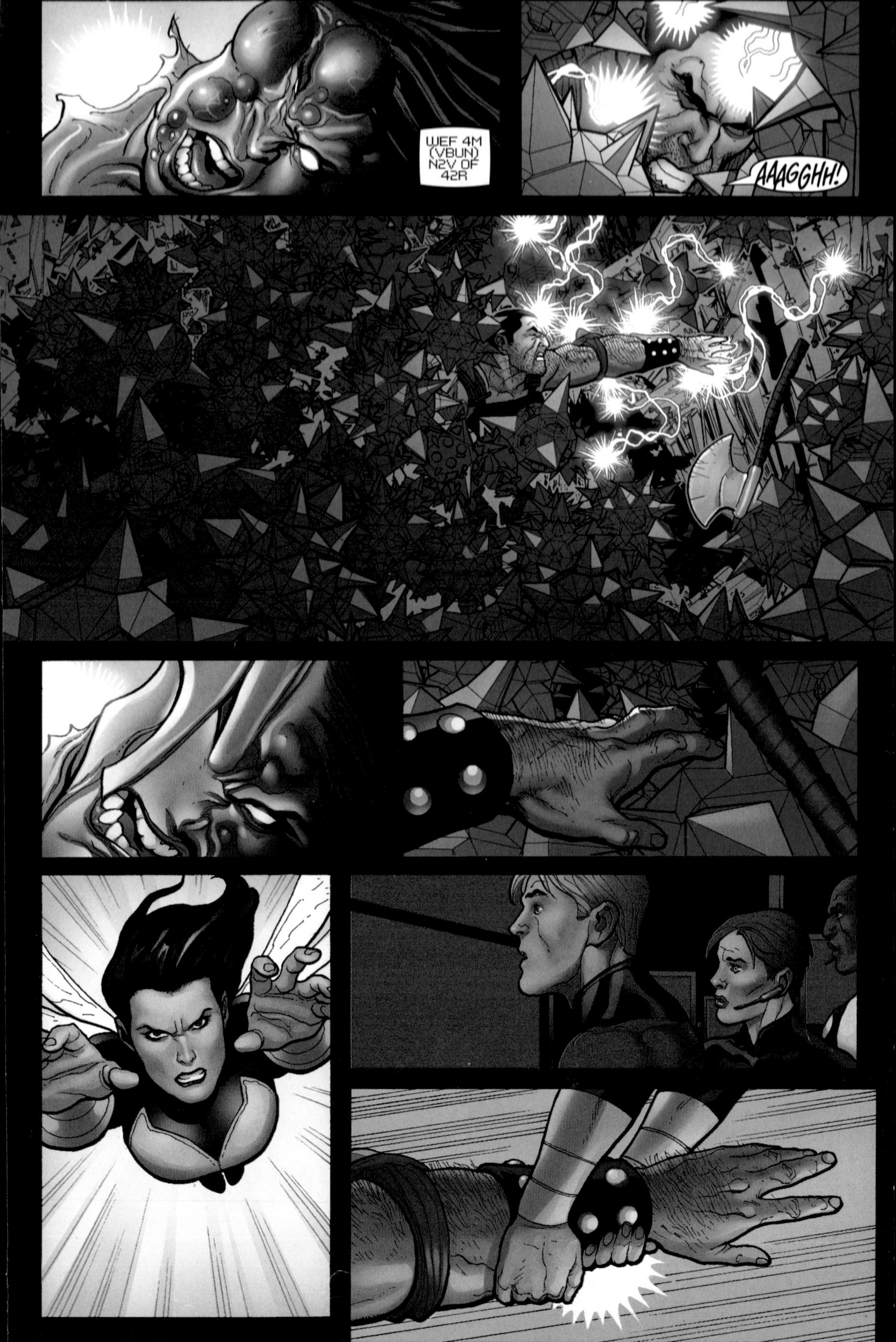
WEF 4M (VBUN) N2V OF 42R
AAAGGHH!

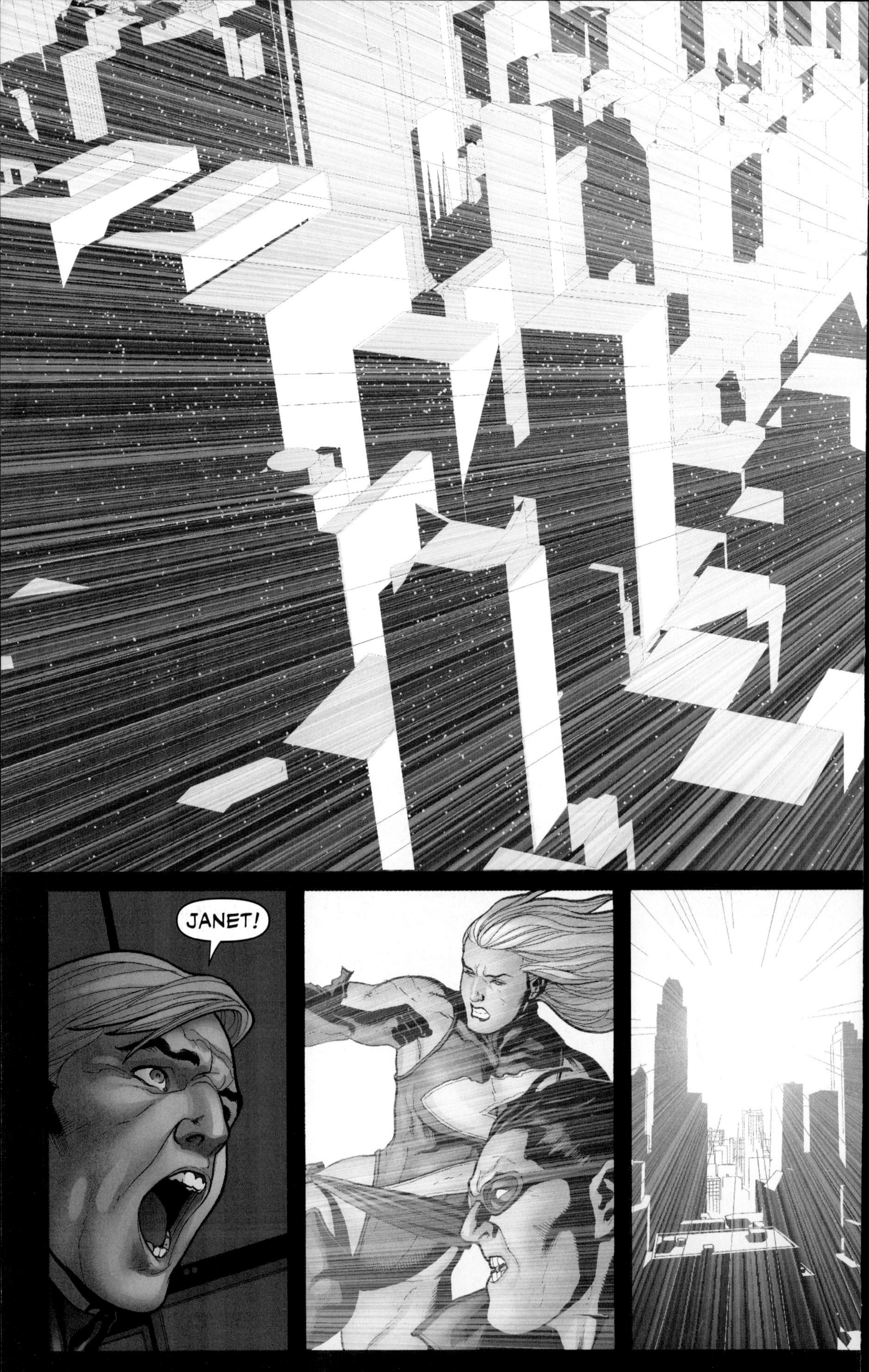
JANET!

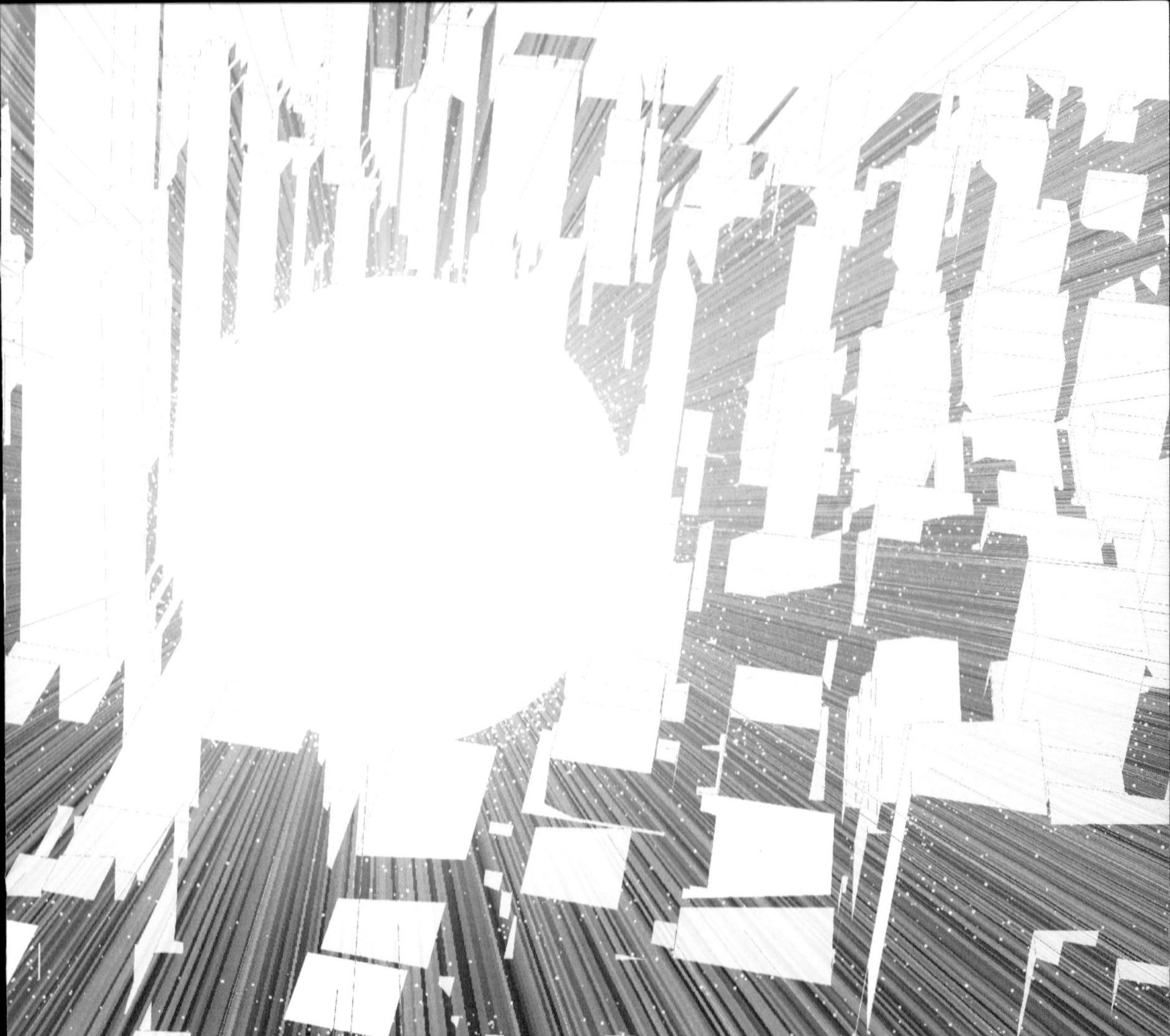

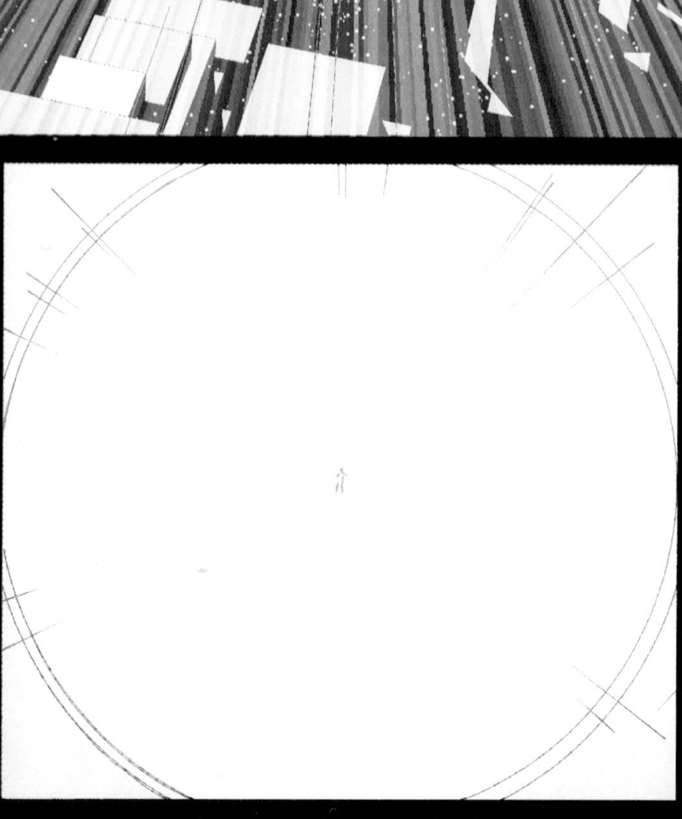

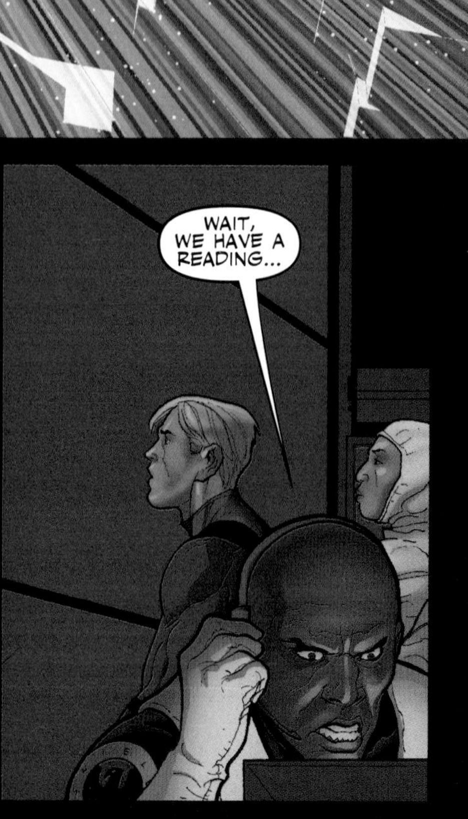
WAIT, WE HAVE A READING...

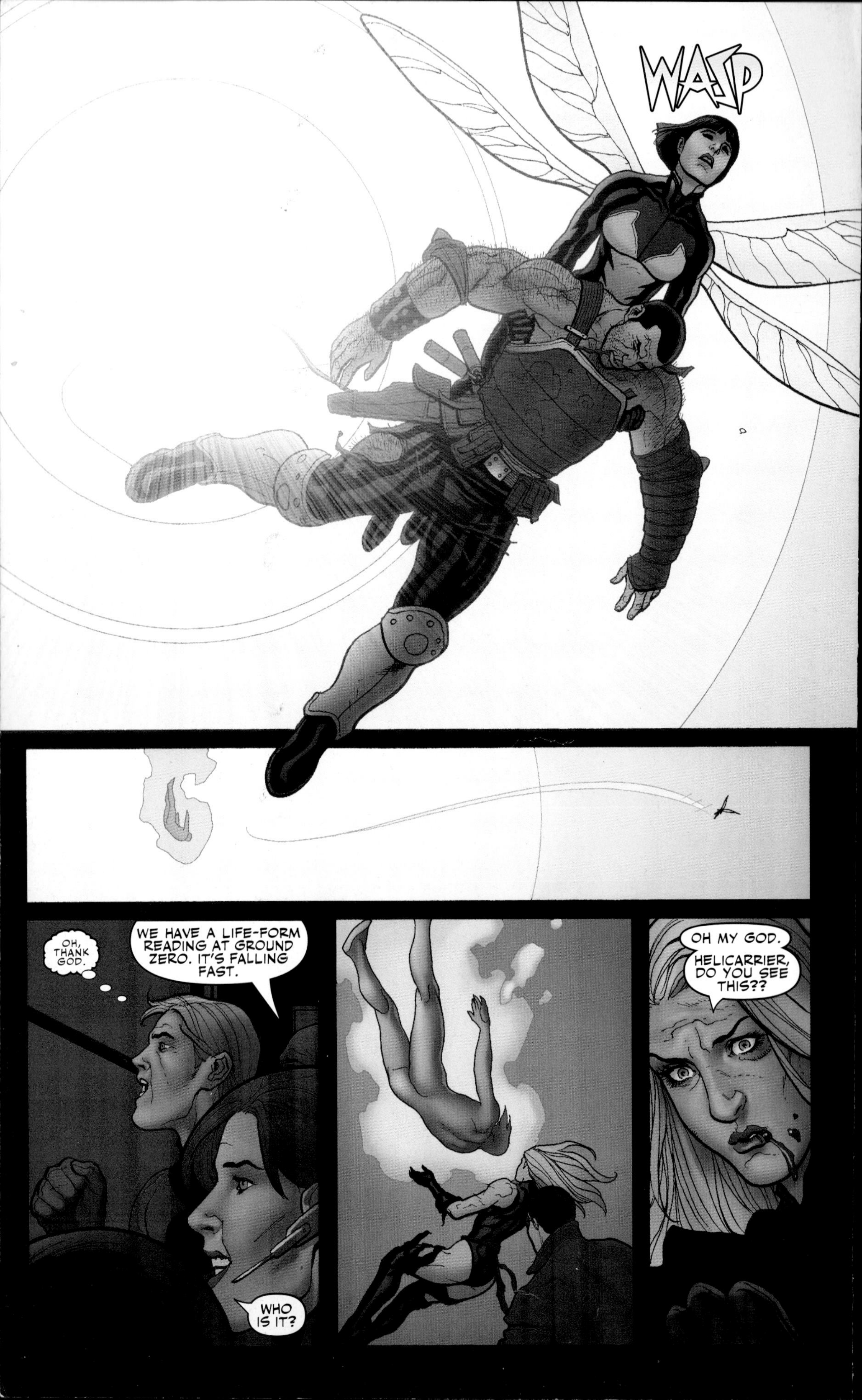
WASP
OH, THANK GOD.
WE HAVE A LIFE-FORM READING AT GROUND ZERO. IT'S FALLING FAST.
WHO IS IT?
OH MY GOD.
HELICARRIER, DO YOU SEE THIS??

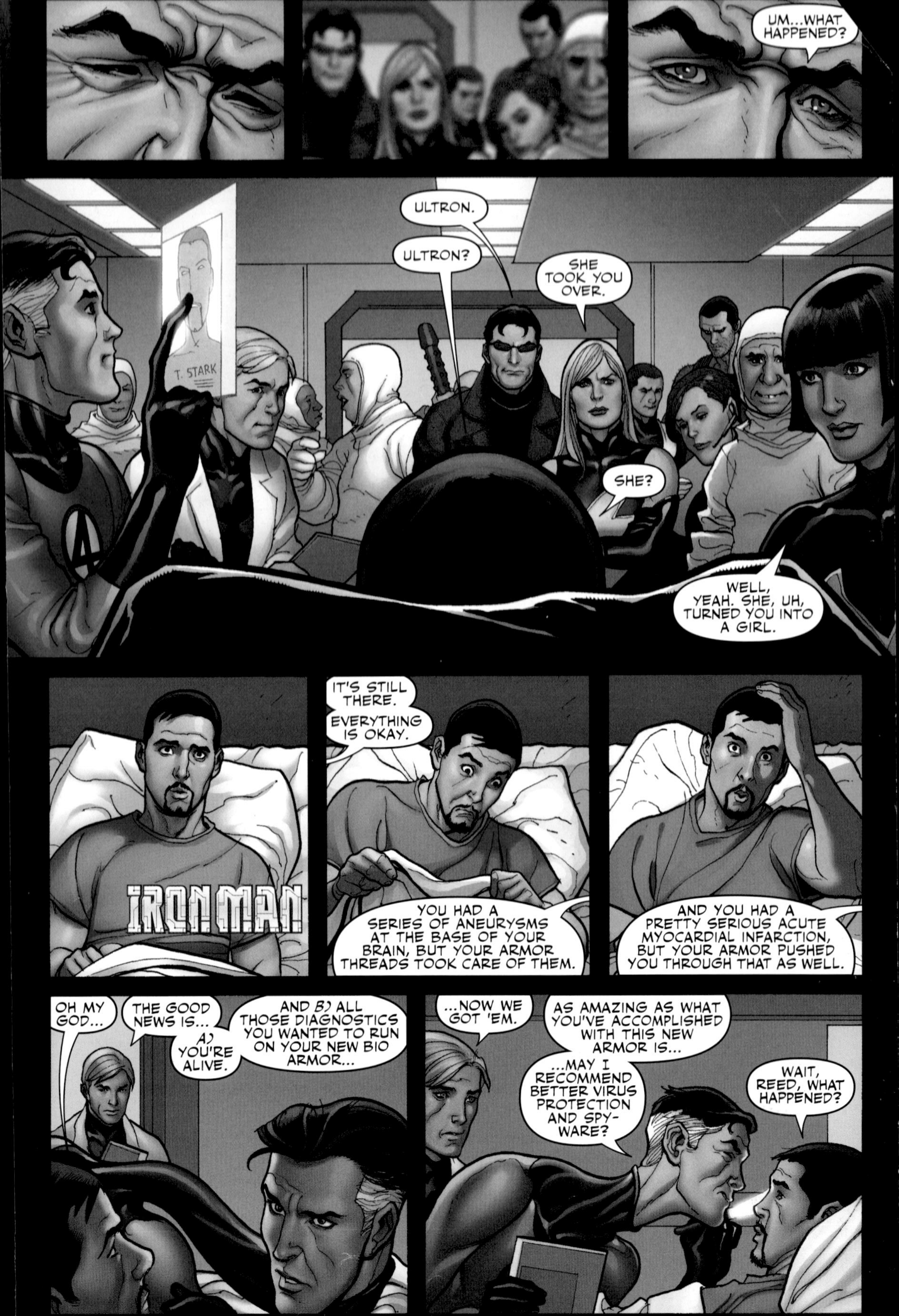
UM...WHAT HAPPENED?
ULTRON.
ULTRON?
SHE TOOK YOU OVER.
SHE?
WELL, YEAH. SHE, UH, TURNED YOU INTO A GIRL.
T. STARK
IRON MAN
IT'S STILL THERE.
EVERYTHING IS OKAY.
YOU HAD A SERIES OF ANEURYSMS AT THE BASE OF YOUR BRAIN, BUT YOUR ARMOR THREADS TOOK CARE OF THEM.
AND YOU HAD A PRETTY SERIOUS ACUTE MYOCARDIAL INFARCTION, BUT YOUR ARMOR PUSHED YOU THROUGH THAT AS WELL.
OH MY GOD...
THE GOOD NEWS IS...
A) YOU'RE ALIVE.
AND B) ALL THOSE DIAGNOSTICS YOU WANTED TO RUN ON YOUR NEW BIO ARMOR...
...NOW WE GOT 'EM.
AS AMAZING AS WHAT YOU'VE ACCOMPLISHED WITH THIS NEW ARMOR IS...
...MAY I RECOMMEND BETTER VIRUS PROTECTION AND SPY-WARE?
WAIT, REED, WHAT HAPPENED?

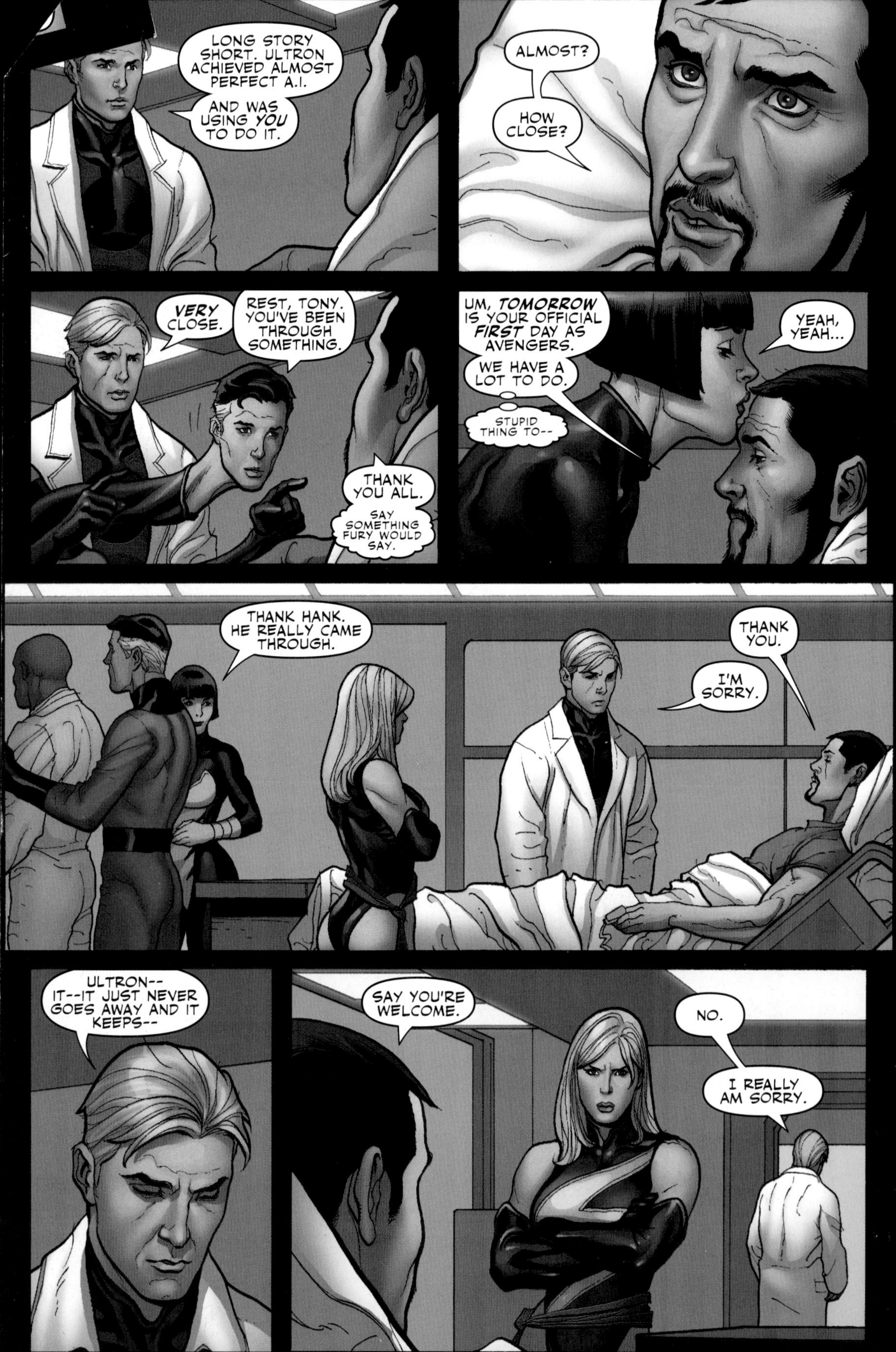
LONG STORY SHORT. ULTRON ACHIEVED ALMOST PERFECT A.I.
AND WAS USING *YOU* TO DO IT.
ALMOST?
HOW CLOSE?
*VERY* CLOSE.
REST, TONY. YOU'VE BEEN THROUGH SOMETHING.
THANK YOU ALL.
SAY SOMETHING FURY WOULD SAY.
UM, *TOMORROW* IS YOUR OFFICIAL *FIRST* DAY AS AVENGERS.
WE HAVE A LOT TO DO.
STUPID THING TO--
YEAH, YEAH...
THANK HANK. HE REALLY CAME THROUGH.
THANK YOU.
I'M SORRY.
ULTRON-- IT--IT JUST NEVER GOES AWAY AND IT KEEPS--
SAY YOU'RE WELCOME.
NO.
I REALLY AM SORRY.

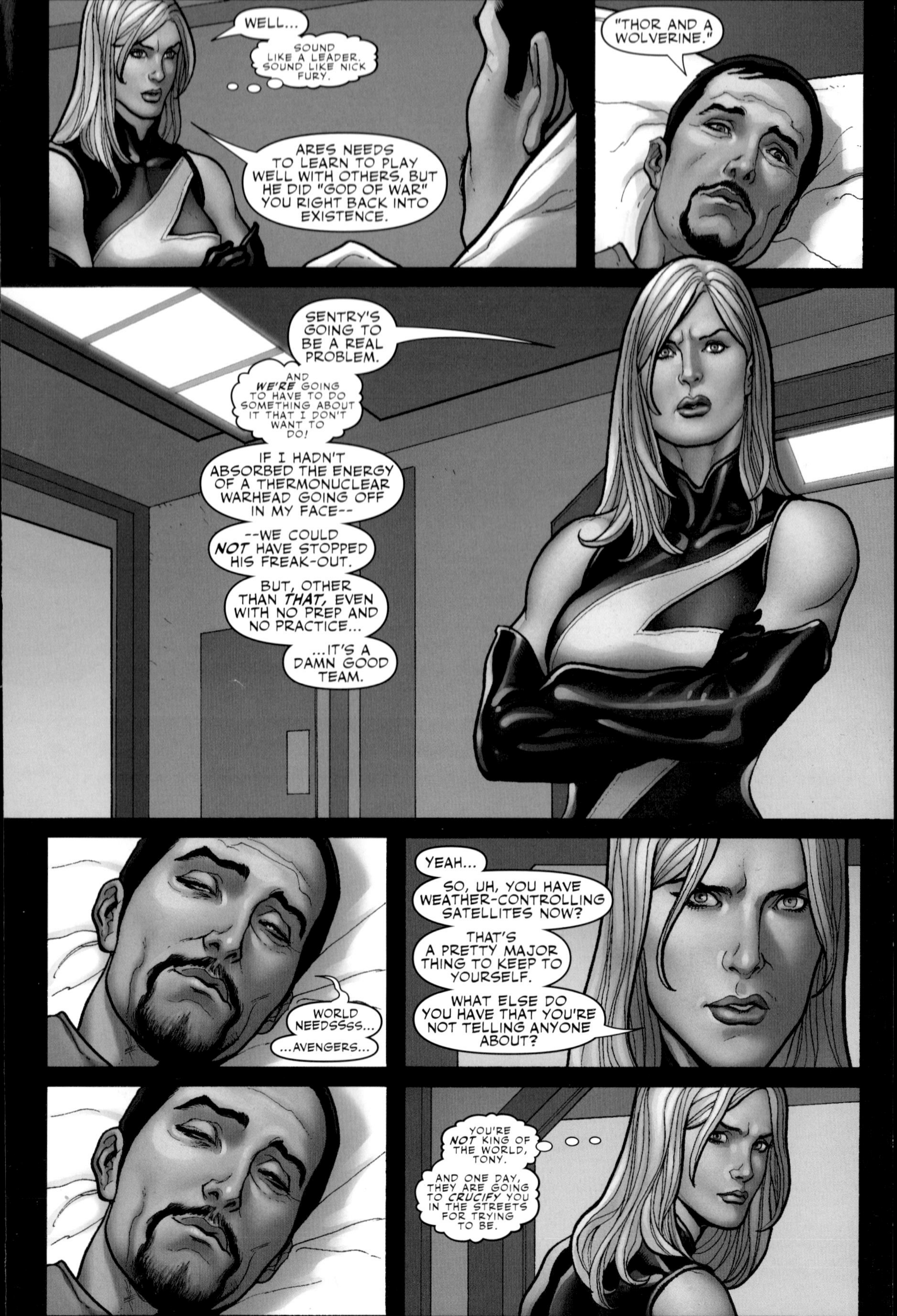

WELL...
SOUND LIKE A LEADER. SOUND LIKE NICK FURY.
ARES NEEDS TO LEARN TO PLAY WELL WITH OTHERS, BUT HE DID "GOD OF WAR" YOU RIGHT BACK INTO EXISTENCE.
"THOR AND A WOLVERINE."
SENTRY'S GOING TO BE A REAL PROBLEM.
AND *WE'RE* GOING TO HAVE TO DO SOMETHING ABOUT IT THAT I DON'T WANT TO DO!
IF I HADN'T ABSORBED THE ENERGY OF A THERMONUCLEAR WARHEAD GOING OFF IN MY FACE--
--WE COULD *NOT* HAVE STOPPED HIS FREAK-OUT.
BUT, OTHER THAN *THAT,* EVEN WITH NO PREP AND NO PRACTICE...
...IT'S A DAMN GOOD TEAM.
WORLD NEEDSSSS...
...AVENGERS...
YEAH...
SO, UH, YOU HAVE WEATHER-CONTROLLING SATELLITES NOW?
THAT'S A PRETTY MAJOR THING TO KEEP TO YOURSELF.
WHAT ELSE DO YOU HAVE THAT YOU'RE NOT TELLING ANYONE ABOUT?
YOU'RE *NOT* KING OF THE WORLD, TONY.
AND ONE DAY, THEY ARE GOING TO *CRUCIFY* YOU IN THE STREETS FOR TRYING TO BE.

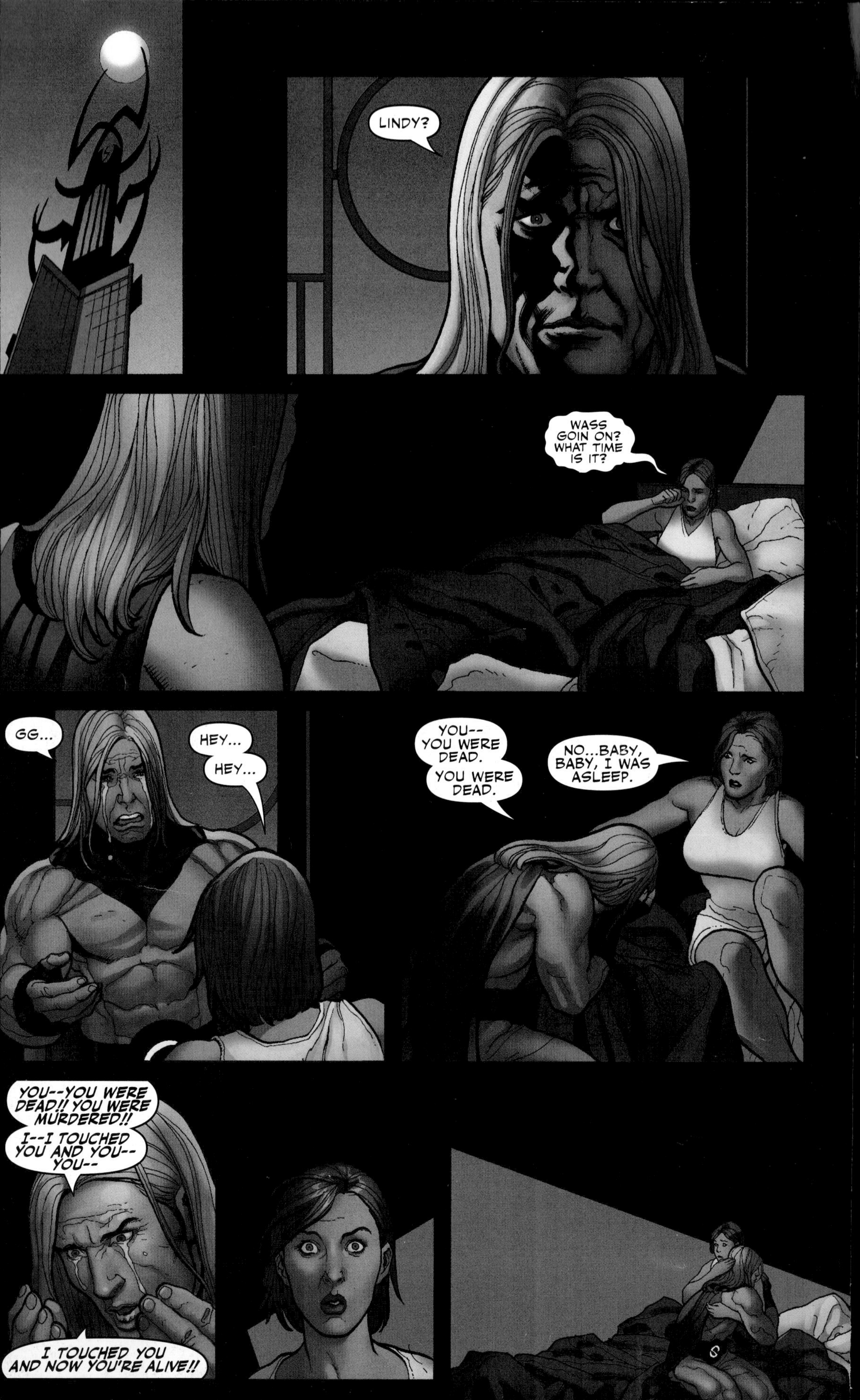

LINDY?
WASS GOIN ON? WHAT TIME IS IT?
GG...
HEY... HEY...
YOU-- YOU WERE DEAD.
YOU WERE DEAD.
NO...BABY, BABY, I WAS ASLEEP.
YOU--YOU WERE DEAD!! YOU WERE MURDERED!!
I--I TOUCHED YOU AND YOU-- YOU--
I TOUCHED YOU AND NOW YOU'RE ALIVE!!

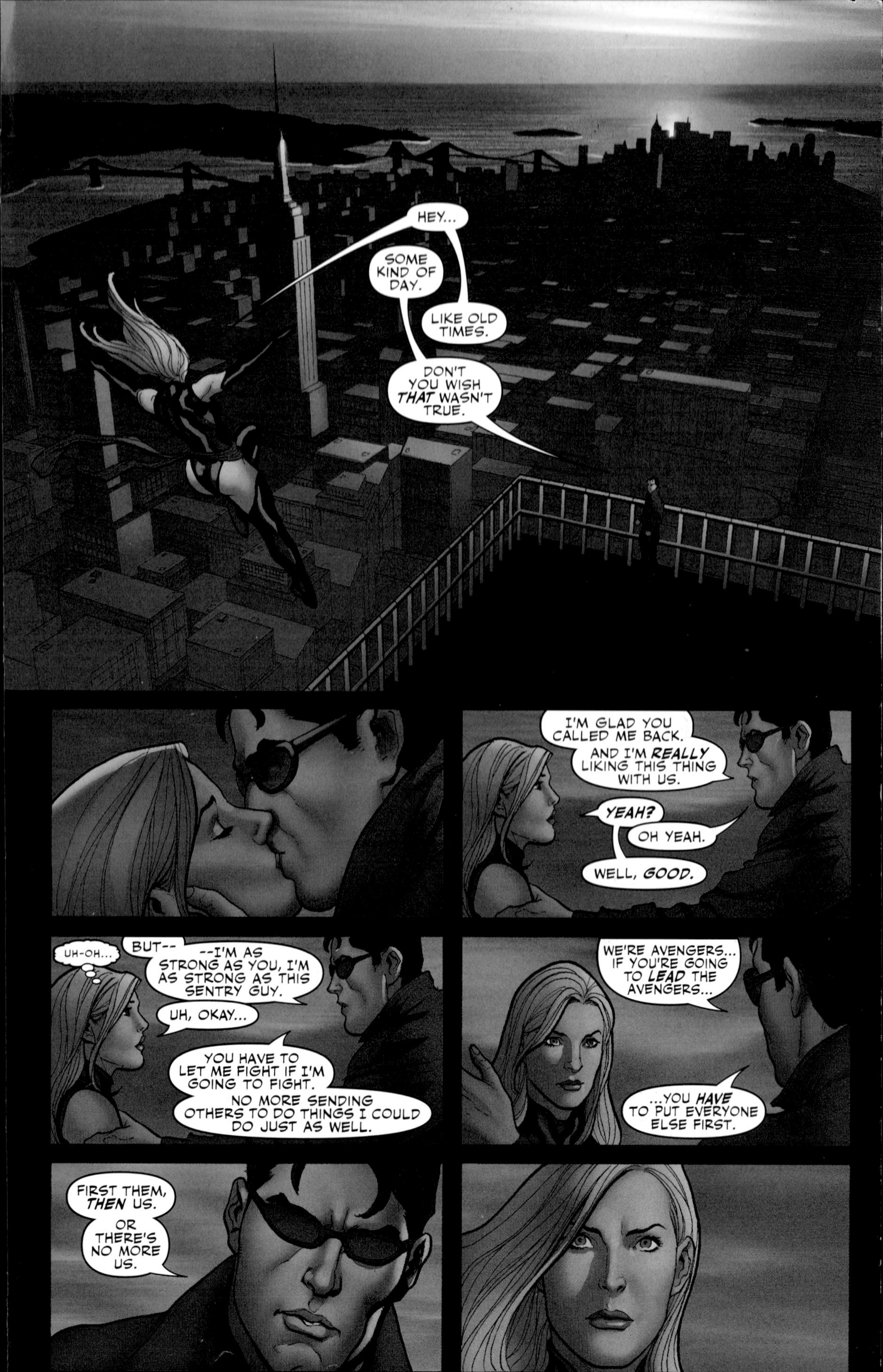
HEY...
SOME KIND OF DAY.
LIKE OLD TIMES.
DON'T YOU WISH THAT WASN'T TRUE.
I'M GLAD YOU CALLED ME BACK.
AND I'M REALLY LIKING THIS THING WITH US.
YEAH?
OH YEAH.
WELL, GOOD.
UH-OH...
BUT--
--I'M AS STRONG AS YOU, I'M AS STRONG AS THIS SENTRY GUY.
UH, OKAY...
YOU HAVE TO LET ME FIGHT IF I'M GOING TO FIGHT.
NO MORE SENDING OTHERS TO DO THINGS I COULD DO JUST AS WELL.
WE'RE AVENGERS... IF YOU'RE GOING TO LEAD THE AVENGERS...
...YOU HAVE TO PUT EVERYONE ELSE FIRST.
FIRST THEM, THEN US.
OR THERE'S NO MORE US.

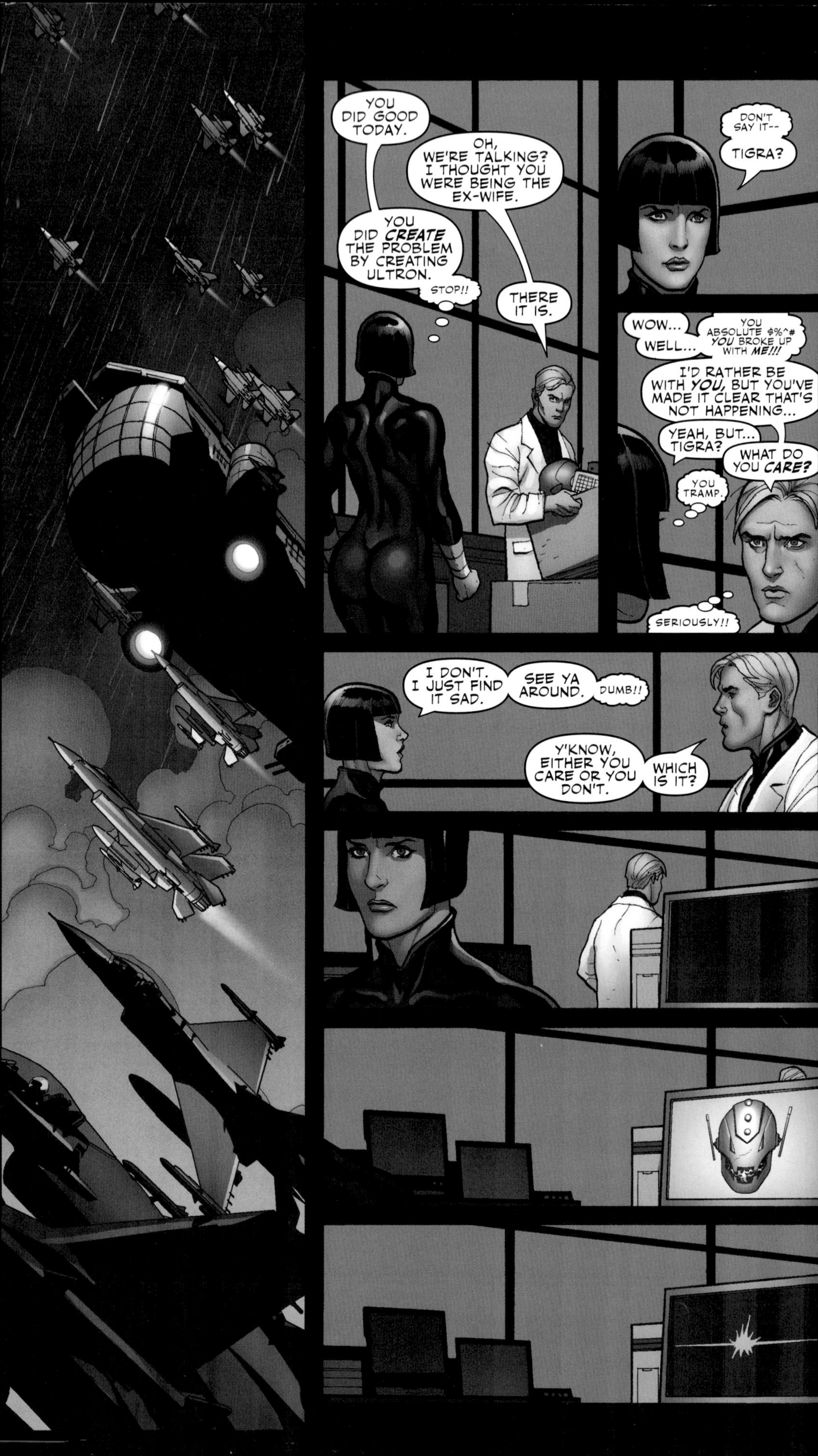
YOU DID GOOD TODAY.
OH, WE'RE TALKING? I THOUGHT YOU WERE BEING THE EX-WIFE.
YOU DID CREATE THE PROBLEM BY CREATING ULTRON.
STOP!!
THERE IT IS.
DON'T SAY IT--
TIGRA?
WOW...
WELL...
YOU ABSOLUTE $%^# YOU BROKE UP WITH ME!!!
I'D RATHER BE WITH YOU, BUT YOU'VE MADE IT CLEAR THAT'S NOT HAPPENING...
YEAH, BUT... TIGRA?
WHAT DO YOU CARE?
YOU TRAMP.
SERIOUSLY!!
I DON'T. I JUST FIND IT SAD.
SEE YA AROUND.
DUMB!!
Y'KNOW, EITHER YOU CARE OR YOU DON'T.
WHICH IS IT?

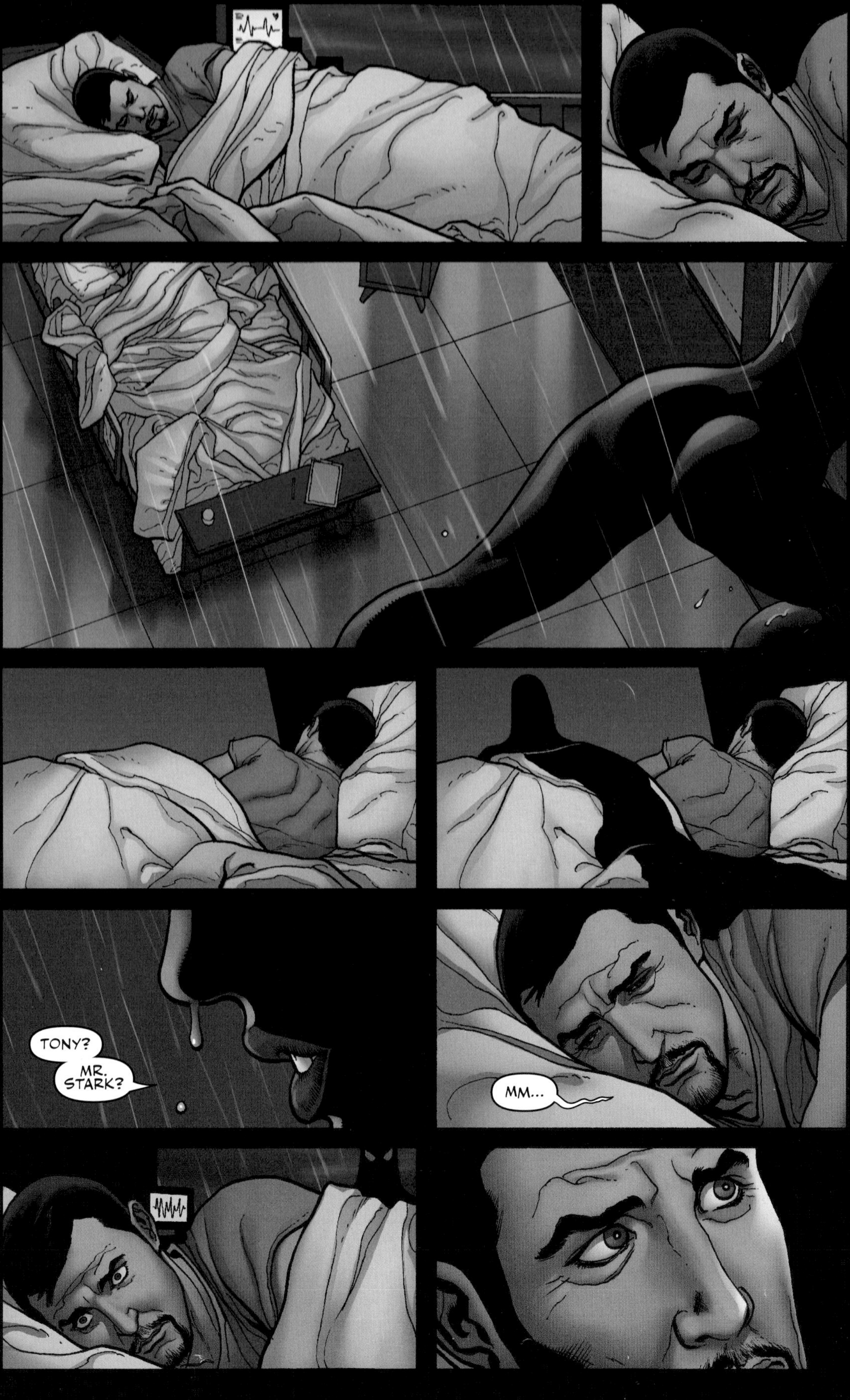
TONY?
MR. STARK?
MM...

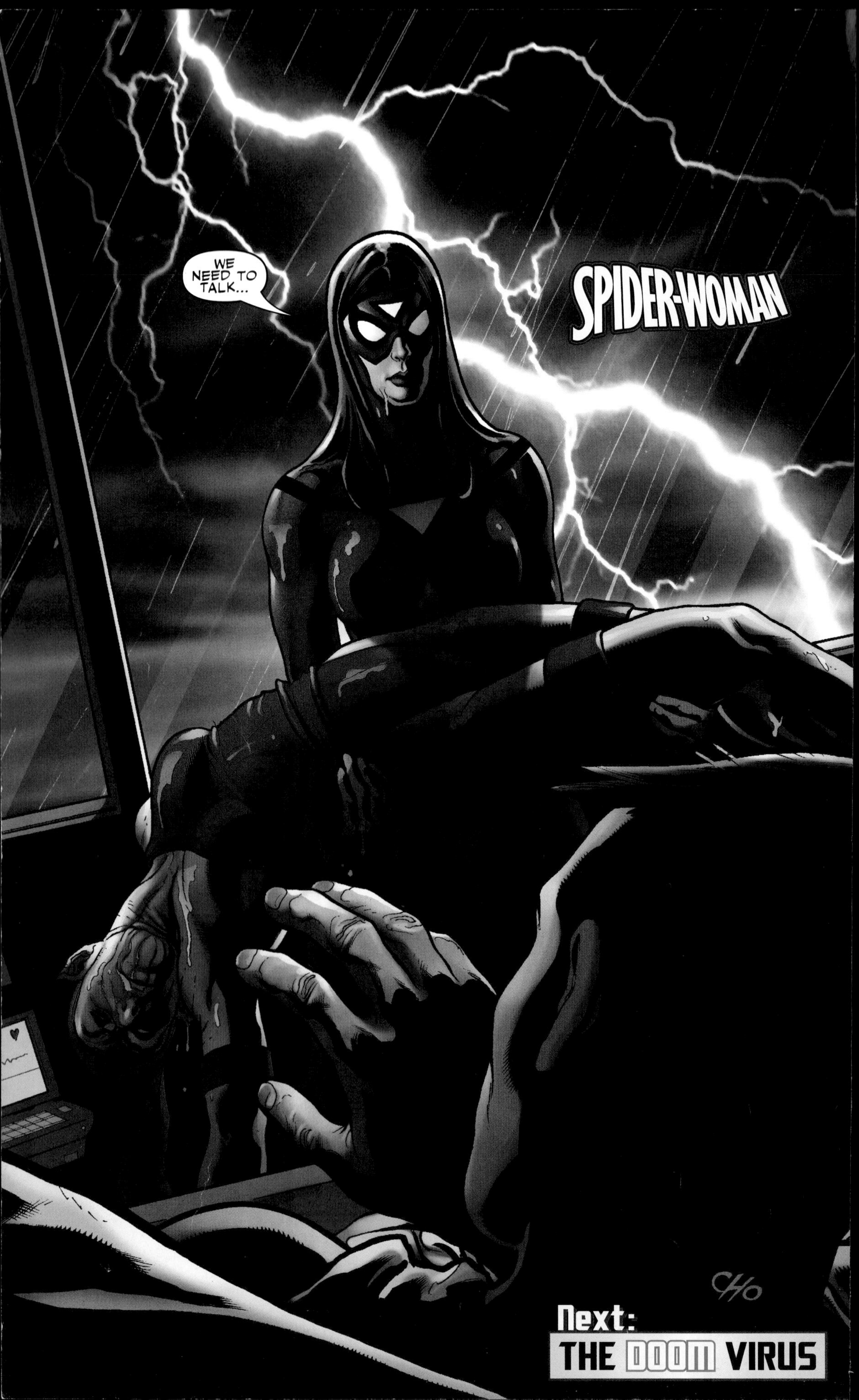
WE NEED TO TALK...
SPIDER-WOMAN
CHO
Next:
THE DOOM VIRUS

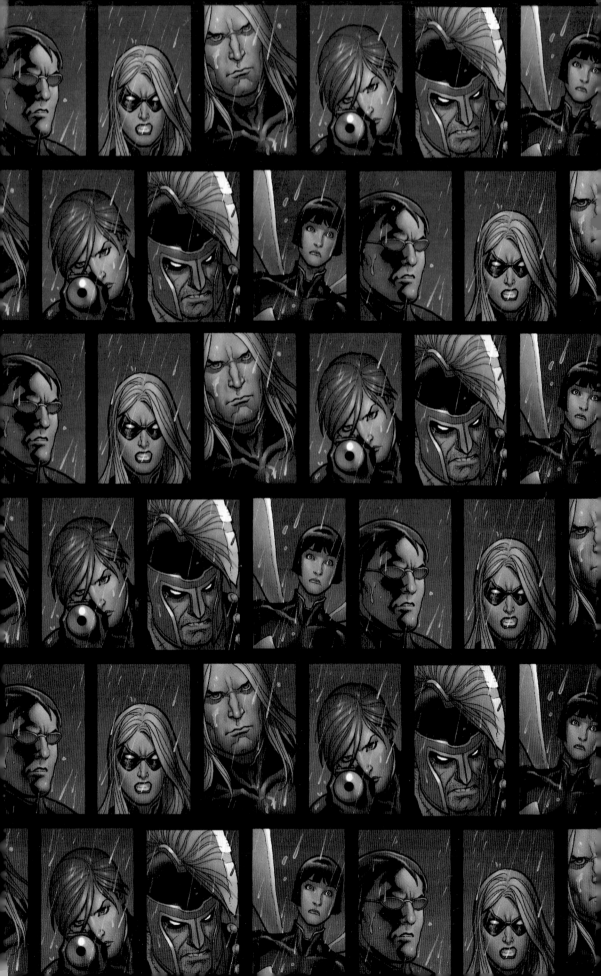

**VARIANT COVER**
Mighty Avengers #1
& New Avengers #26

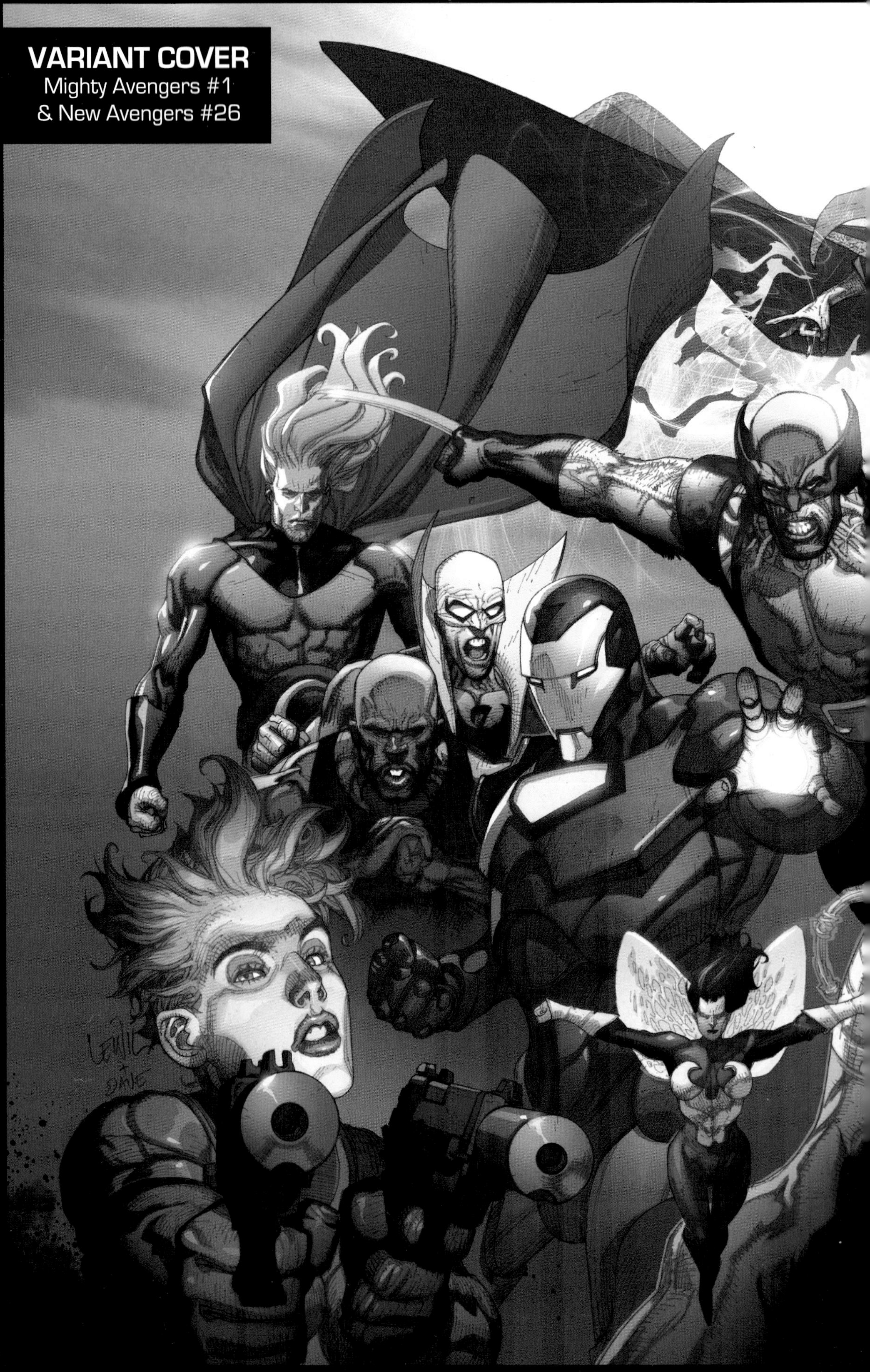

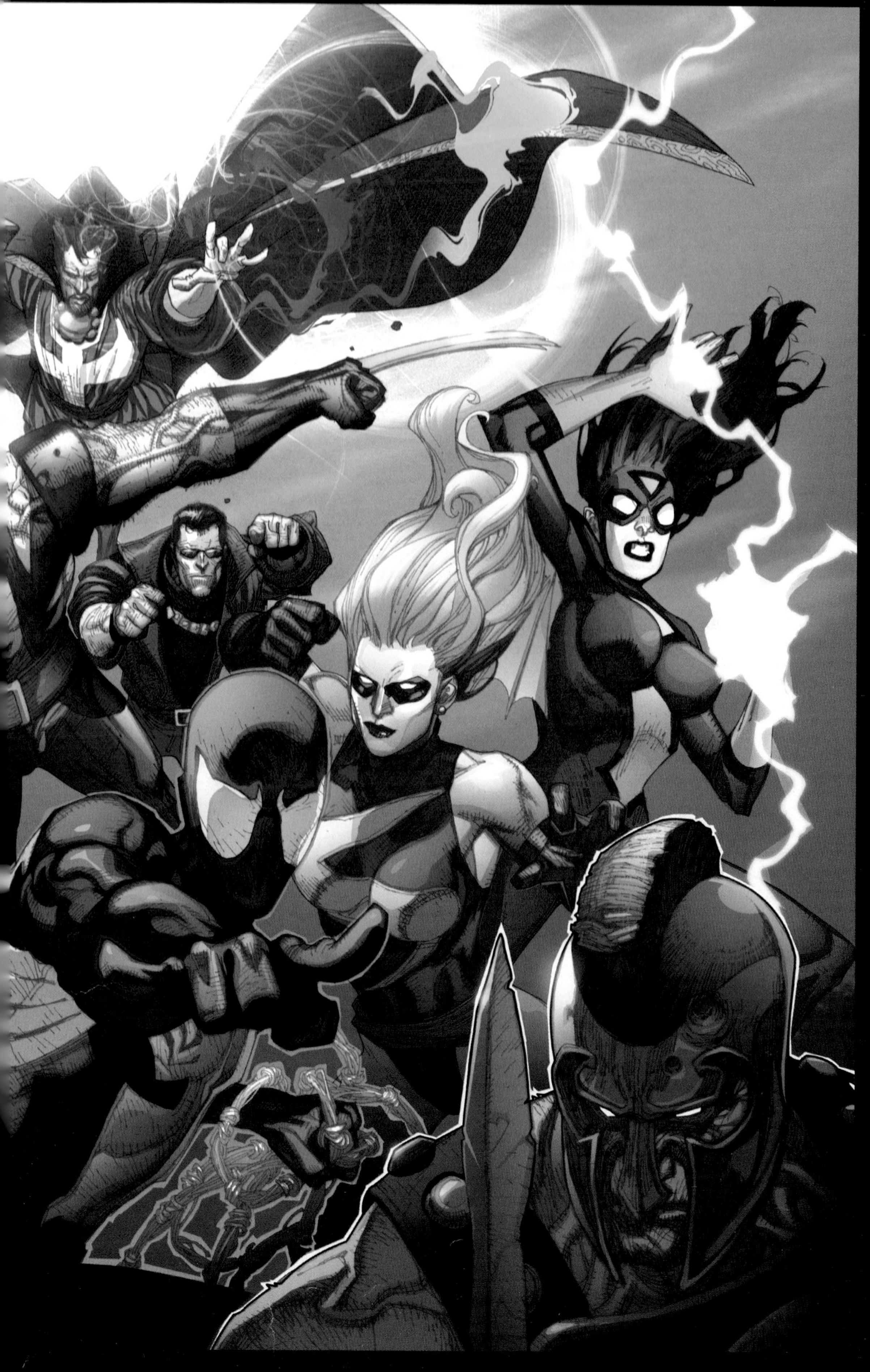

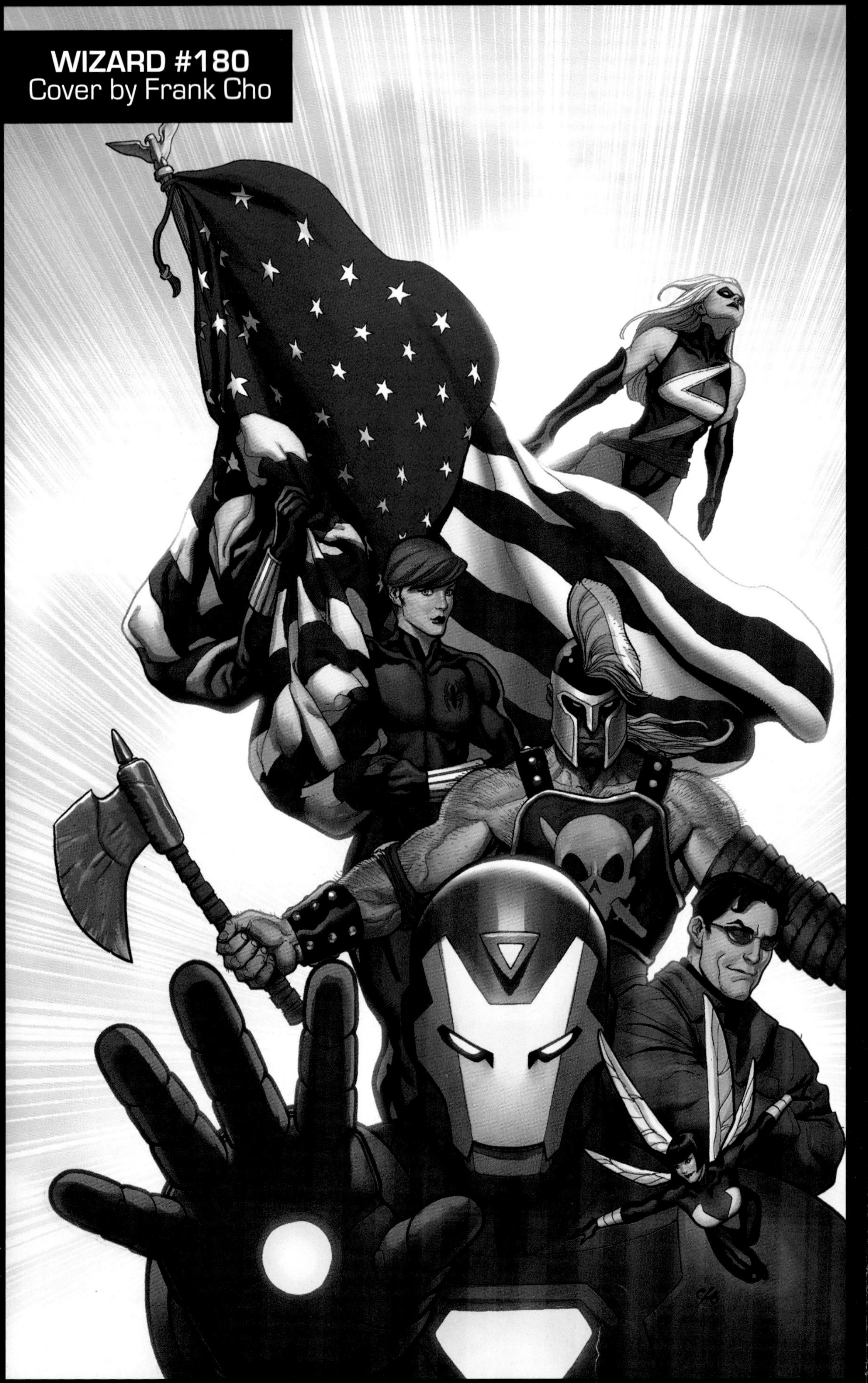

**WIZARD #180**
Cover by Frank Cho

# CHARACTER SKETCHES
by Frank Cho

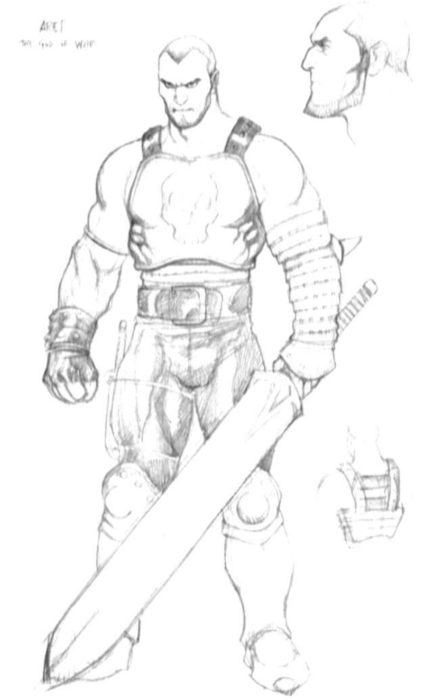
ARES

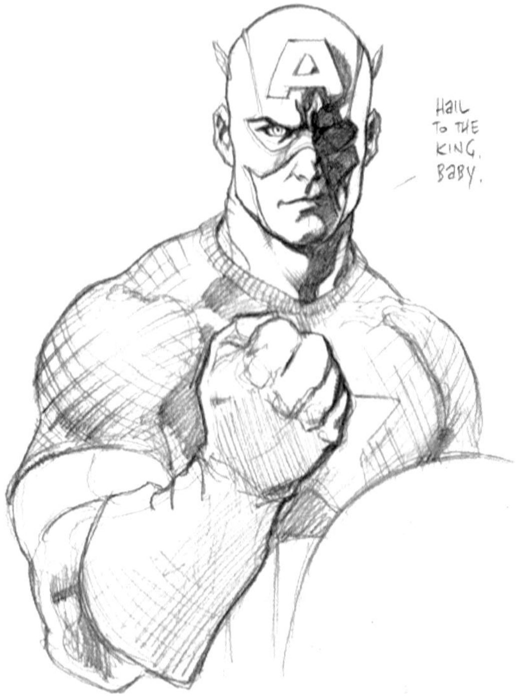
HAIL TO THE KING, BABY.

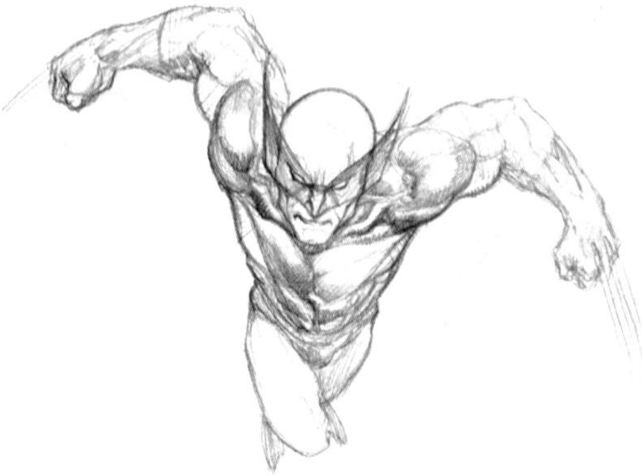

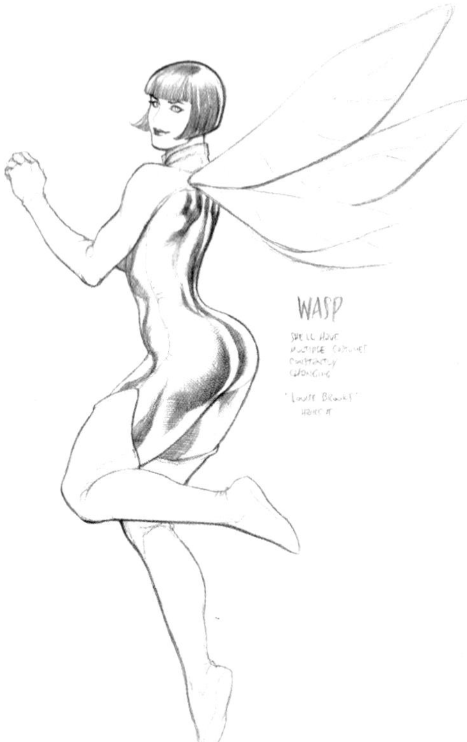
WASP

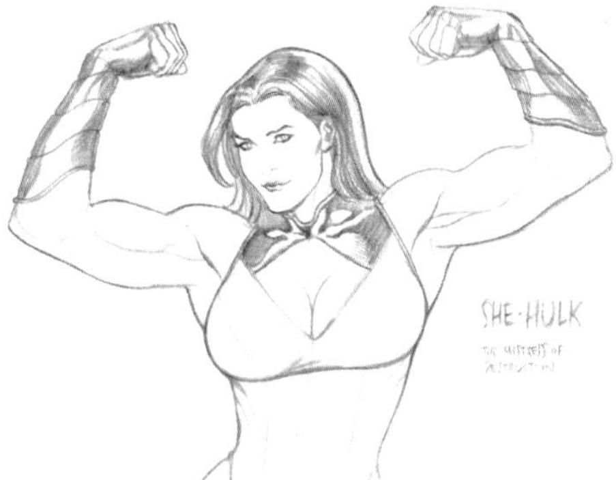
SHE-HULK

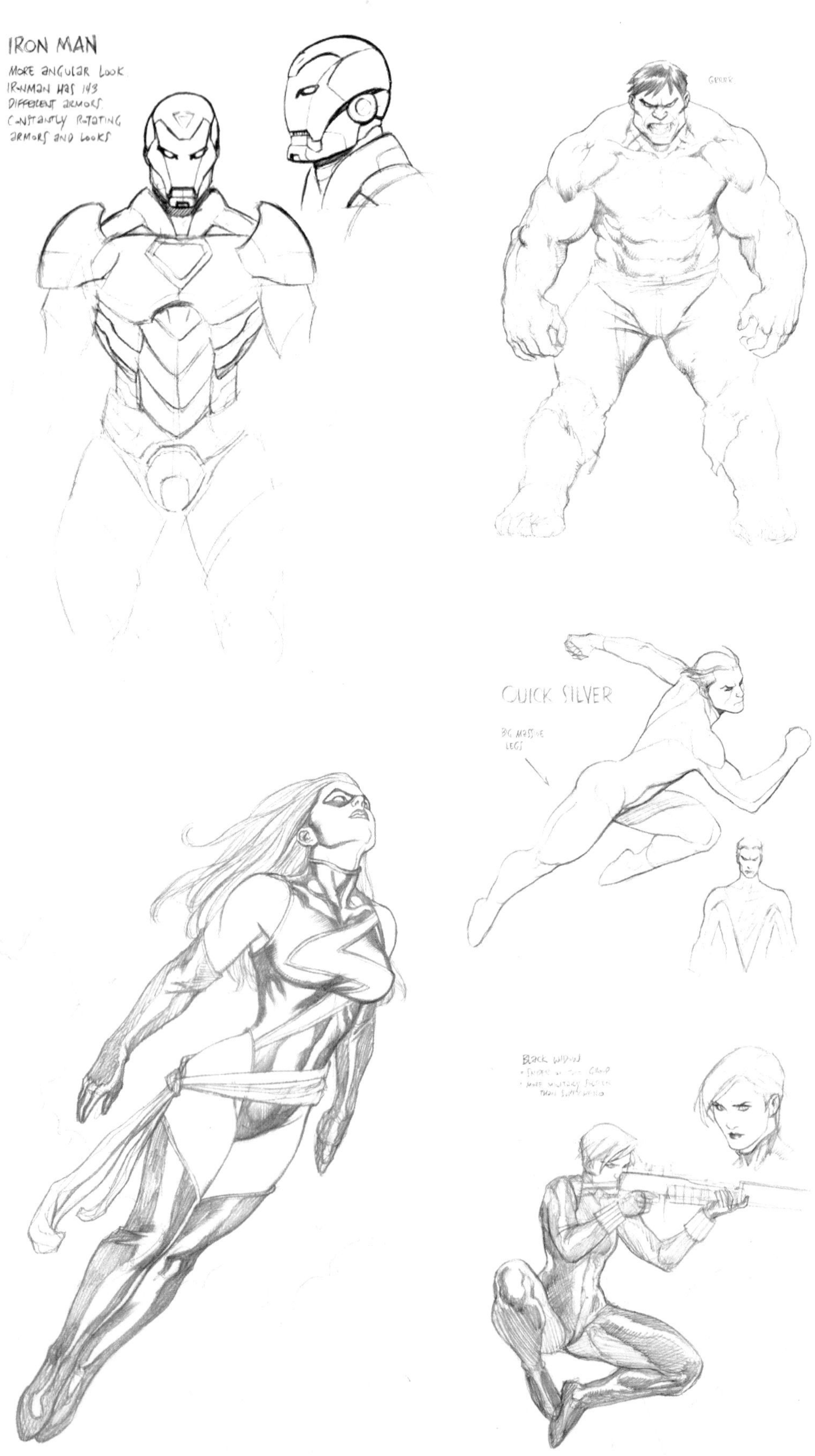
IRON MAN
MORE ANGULAR LOOK
IRONMAN HAS 143
DIFFERENT ARMORS
CONSTANTLY ROTATING
ARMORS AND LOOKS
QUICK SILVER
BIG MASSIVE
LEGS
Black Widow